# Why Do You Need the New Edition of This Book?

Here are five reasons why the fifth edition of *Public Human Resource Management: Problems and Prospects* will help you succeed in your course.

1. **New chapters covering emerging HRM topics.** This fifth edition addresses the shifting priorities in HRM with new chapters focusing on the most critical topical issues in the field including non-profit management, strategic planning, information technology, outsourcing, and "HR metrics".

2. **New contributions from distinguished HRM scholars and professionals.** More than half of the chapters in this fifth edition are newly authored by members of the expanding community of HRM scholars, providing fresh insights and perspectives on the changing nature of HRM.

century. Chapter findings from the 2007 Government Performance Project to provide the most current analysis of the growing role of Information Technology Systems in HRM practices.

4. **Updated real-world examples.** Throughout this new edition you will find concrete examples and practical information you can apply to the developing practices in the field of HRM. A new section with special emphasis on emerging personnel techniques addresses the development of traditional HRM staffing approaches.

5. **Expanded contextual information.** Gain a better appreciation for the transformation of HRM practices with contextual background information that outlines the shift in social, political, legal, and managerial trends.

# Public Human Resource Management

# Public Human Resource Management

## Problems and Prospects
### Fifth Edition

Edited by

## Steven W. Hays
*University of South Carolina*

## Richard C. Kearney
*North Carolina State University*

## Jerrell D. Coggburn
*North Carolina State University*

**Longman**

New York   San Francisco   Boston
London   Toronto   Sydney   Tokyo   Singapore   Madrid
Mexico City   Munich   Paris   Cape Town   Hong Kong   Montreal

**Editor-in-Chief:** Eric Stano
**Marketing Manager:** Lindsey Prudhomme
**Production Manager:** Kathleen Sleys
**Project Coordination, Text Design, and Electronic Page Makeup:** Chitra Ganesan/
  GGS higher education resources, A division of PreMedia Global, Inc.
**Creative Director:** Jayne Conte
**Cover Designer:** Bruce Kenselaar
**Cover Illustration/Photo:** Getty Images, Inc.
**Manufacturing Buyer:** Kathleen Sleys

**Library of Congress Cataloging-in-Publication Data**

Public human resource management: problems and prospects/edited by Steven W. Hays, Richard
  C. Kearney, Jerrell D. Coggburn. — 5th ed.
    p. cm.
  Rev. ed. of: Public personnel administration. 4th ed. c2003.
  Includes bibliographical references and index.
  ISBN-13: 978-0-13-603769-9
  ISBN-10: 0-13-603769-0
  1. Civil service—United States—Personnel management. I. Hays, Steven W. II. Kearney, Richard C.
  III. Coggburn, Jerrell D. IV. Public personnel administration.
JK765.P797 2009
352.60973—dc22

                                                                                    2008035831

Pearson Education LTD.
Pearson Education Singapore, Pte. Ltd
Pearson Education, Canada, Ltd
Pearson Education–Japan

Pearson Education Australia PTY, Limited
Pearson Education North Asia Ltd
Pearson Educación de Mexico, S.A. de C.V.
Pearson Education Malaysia, Pte. Ltd

Visit us at www.pearsonhighered.com
Printed in the United States.

Longman
is an imprint of

ISBN 13: 978-0-13-603769-9
ISBN 10:    0-13-603769-0

# Contents

# Preface

The first edition of this volume was published in 1983. When that book appeared, the Civil Service Reform Act of 1978 was just five years old, and words such as *managerialism, reinvention,* and *The New Public Management* had not yet been coined, at least in the context of public sector Human Resource Management (HRM). Subsequent editions of the anthology have attempted to keep students apprised of the massive changes that have occurred in this field over the years. As such, the tables of contents from the previous four editions mirror shifting emphases, values, techniques, and—consistent with our enduring focus—differing *problems and prospects.* In attempting to characterize the unstable ground upon which this discipline sits, we have variously used many different adjectives, including such hyperbolic expressions as *paradigm shift* (perhaps the least original of all choices) and *technical revolution.* However phrased, the central message that we have tried to convey—and which we continue to address in this version of the book—is that of rapid transformation and adjustment to diverse environmental stimuli. Today's students would not recognize the merit systems that typically existed in 1983, nor would practitioners of that era have been able to anticipate or appreciate many of the topics that are now central to this field. For that matter, the name of the field itself has been changing: from public personnel management (PPM) to public personnel administration (PPA), to HRM to strategic human resource management (SRHM) to human capital management (HCM). Such evolution (confusion?) of nomenclature reflects the field's dynamic qualities and its shifting values. Tipping our hats to this dynamism, we have adopted a new title for the fifth edition. We feel that *Public Human Resource Management: Problems and Prospects* better captures the breadth of topics contained in this edition and, arguably, earlier ones.

In contrast to previous editions, we begin this anthology with a recommendation to readers that they take a moment to contemplate just how different the field is compared to that of twenty-five years ago. As two of the editors can attest, age has few benefits. However, if graying (and thinning) hair and the other characteristics of aging are accompanied by *any* attribute, *perspective* is probably the most valuable. Age may not bring wisdom, judgment, or riches, but it does provide a historical perch from which to marvel at the accomplishments (and, perhaps, to recoil at the mistakes) that have occurred during a long and especially critical period in the evolution of Public Administration. Readers would be well served to familiarize themselves with the historical context that helped to spawn the changes documented in the twenty original chapters contained in this volume. We think you will find the differences in contemporary HRM to be both extraordinary and profound.

As has been our intent since the beginning, the basic purpose of this anthology is to provide readers with a concise overview of the challenges (problems) and adjustments (prospects) of modern public HRM. To keep pace with developments in real-world HRM, this means that major alterations have been made in the content of this volume. Past editions of the book invested perhaps inordinate amounts of space on such topics as workplace diversity, Affirmative Action and Equal Employment Opportunity (AA/EEO), merit system operation, and the like. Some of these traditional topics have become less salient, whereas new topics have emerged. We hope that we have captured the essence of these shifting priorities in the readings that follow. Although the traditional challenges and techniques retain much of their significance, no contemporary work on HRM would be complete without paying attention to such topics as nonprofit management, strategic planning, information technology, outsourcing, and the need to measure HRM's contribution to organizational performance ("HR metrics"). Not one of these topics was contained in the previous edition of this book, but all now merit a complete chapter. This is just one preliminary indication of how quickly HRM is adjusting to the unique challenges of the twenty-first century.

Consistent with past practice, this volume consists of originally authored manuscripts that represent a cross-section of the timeliest and best-informed scholarship in the area of HR administration. The book contains a mix of thought pieces, descriptive analyses, overviews of occurrences in various settings, and theoretical essays. To be true to our promise of providing a solid overview of both problems and prospects, the selections summarize the biggest challenges confronting HRM practitioners and offer substantive suggestions for improving the practice of HRM. Obviously, then, the chapters focus more on the *future* of the field than its past (which provides one more incentive to the reader to examine the precursors of contemporary HRM reform). We are more concerned with providing the reader with a firm sense of where the discipline is headed, rather than where it has been.

Each chapter was prepared specifically for inclusion in this volume. The authors are all established figures in public sector HRM; many of them practice and consult in the field as well. They were selected on the basis of their recognized competence in, and past contributions to, the topical areas that are addressed in their essays. The present volume is almost completely different from its immediate predecessor. Of the twenty chapters, twelve are authored by individuals who were not included in previous editions of the book. Only one or two of the chapters might be considered updated versions of previous writings. The number of new authors and topics provide clear evidence of the changing nature of HRM, the expanding ranks of scholars, and the inherent value found in the "new scholarship" of HRM (a promise that was made in the first edition). We confess to being quite proud of the group that has been assembled to share their perspectives, and hope that you will agree that their insights are worthy of recognition.

The contributions are organized into four broad sections: "The Setting," "The Techniques," "The Issues," and "Conclusion." Section One provides a thorough treatment of the social, political, legal, and managerial trends that serve as catalysts in the transformation of HRM. These chapters also contain sufficient contextual background to help contemporary students understand the significance of current developments across this panoramic field. Section Two summarizes developments in the practice of HRM, with special emphasis on emerging personnel techniques and the ways that traditional approaches to the staffing function are being revised. New selections within Section Two address what are perhaps the most troublesome technical challenges of the age, including strategic HRM, employee benefits, dilemmas associated with motivating public workers, workforce planning, and HR measurement practices. Section Three provides highly lucid and concise discussions of the six most critical topical "issues" in the field, including AA/EEO, gender issues, the use of information technology, ethics, labor relations, and HR outsourcing. Section Four—the Conclusion—provides both a prospective and retrospective capstone treatment of the field. In contrast to past editions, we have not made an attempt to forecast the future. Previous efforts have proven to be so humbling that we suspect any application of crystal balls should be left to those with more powerful psychic abilities than our own.

As in the case with all four previous editions, a prime consideration in the design, preparation, and organization of the book was that it be sufficiently readable for both graduate and undergraduate students. For this reason, the authors were asked to provide enough background information so that both beginning and advanced students could understand and benefit from the content. Additionally, the authors were requested to furnish concrete examples and practical information to enhance the volume's applicability to practitioners wishing to broaden their perspectives in the field. We are satisfied that these objectives have been met in every respect.

Our principal debt in assembling this anthology is to our contributing authors. They richly deserve our sincere thanks, for their efforts are obviously the heart and soul of what follows. Because there are so many luminaries and emerging scholars in the area of public sector HRM, it was very difficult to decide which ones to ask for contributions. One of our continuing objectives is to bring new perspectives to this work. In so doing, we sincerely hope that anyone not included in this particular volume is not offended. With luck, we'll be around long enough to generate a sixth edition within a few years, thereby enabling us to call upon the talents of other leading scholars. To otherwise ensure the durability of the book, a third coeditor—Jerrell D. Coggburn—has been enlisted in this endeavor. A representative member of the very best "new scholarship" in the field, Jerrell will be ready to take the baton should Steve or Rick finally decide to retire (probably to the eternal thanks of their long-suffering students and colleagues).

The contributors to the fifth edition of *Public Human Resource Management: Problems and Prospects* produced quality manuscripts on short notice (in one case, just one month!), and exhibited remarkable patience with our repeated requests for revision, clarification, and elaboration. Many endured hardships in meeting the deadlines we imposed, especially those whose chief professional responsibility is to provide HRM services, not write about them. We hope that all of the contributors are aware of the depth and sincerity of our appreciation. We are also grateful to the comments from the reviewers on this edition: Ross Alexander, North Georgia College and State University; John Aughenbaugh, Virginia Commonwealth University; and Thomas Cozzens, Cleveland State University.

Finally, we wish to thank those kind academic souls who have adopted previous editions for their courses in public personnel administration. This book has proven to have extremely "long legs" in the profession, a reality that could only be made possible by the support and thoughtfulness of our fellow HRM faculty colleagues. Should any of you wish to communicate with us about this volume, or to propose future amendments or clarifications, please do not hesitate to do so.

Steven W. Hays
Richard C. Kearney
Jerrell D. Coggburn

# Contributing Authors

JAMES S. BOWMAN is professor of public administration at the Askew School of Public Administration and Policy, Florida State University. His primary area is human resource management. Noted for his work in ethics and quality management, Dr. Bowman also has done research in environmental administration. He is author of over one hundred journal articles and book chapters, as well as editor of six anthologies. Bowman coauthored, with Berman, West, and Van Wart, *Human Resource Management: Paradoxes, Processes and Problems* (third edition, Sage) in 2009 and *The Professional Edge: Competencies in Public Service* (third edition, Sharpe) in 2009. He is editor-in-chief of the journal *Public Integrity*. A past National Association of Schools of Public Affairs and Administration Fellow as well as a Kellogg Foundation Fellow, he has experience in the military, civil service, and business.

JOSHUA CHANIN is a Ph.D. candidate in Public Administration and Justice, Law, and Society at the School of Public Affairs at American University in Washington, DC. He holds a JD-MPA from Indiana University–Bloomington, where he was a member of the Indiana Law Journal. Josh's research interests include the application of constitutional law in public administration and policy, the implementation of public law, the management of criminal justice bureaucracies, and federalism.

JERRELL D. COGGBURN is associate professor and chair of public administration in the School of Public and International Affairs at North Carolina State University.

His research interests include human resources management, public management, and public procurement. He is a past recipient (with Sandra K. Schneider and William G. Jacoby, 1997) of the William and Frederick Mosher award for the best *Public Administration Review* article written by an academician.

DENNIS M. DALEY is professor of public administration at North Carolina State University. He is the author of *Performance Appraisal in the Public Sector: Techniques and Applications* (1992) and *Strategic Human Resource Management* (2002) along with over fifty refereed articles and book chapters. He teaches classes in Human Resource/Personnel Management and in Negotiations and Mediation.

TRENTON J. DAVIS is assistant professor in the public administration program at Georgia Southern University. His research focuses on compensation systems, employee motivation and organizational change, small group behavior, and gender issues in professional city management.

GERALD T. GABRIS is distinguished teaching professor and director of the Division of Public Administration at Northern Illinois University. His primary focus of research involves organizational change, innovation management, leadership, and compensation systems at the local government level.

BETH GAZLEY is assistant professor of public and environmental affairs at Indiana University–Bloomington, where she teaches human resources management, non-profit and public management. She conducts research and publishes on volunteerism and volunteer management, government-nonprofit relations and interorganizational collaboration. Before entering academia, Professor Gazley served in public interest politics and the nonprofit sector as a fundraiser, volunteer, and management consultant.

MARY E. GUY is professor of public administration at the University of Colorado Denver. She has published widely on the subject of human resource management in public service organizations, and places special emphasis on the difference that gender makes. She is a fellow of the National Academy of Public Administration and past president of the American Society for Public Administration.

STEVEN W. HAYS is the Charles L. Jacobson Professor of Public Affairs in the Department of Political Science, University of South Carolina. He specializes in human resource management, with an emphasis on civil service reform. Together with Rick Kearney, he was a cocreator and coeditor of the *Review of Public Personnel Administration*.

WILLOW S. JACOBSON is assistant professor of public administration and government at the School of Government at the University of North Carolina at Chapel Hill. Jacobson received her Ph.D. in public administration from the Maxwell School of Citizenship and Public Affairs at Syracuse and undergraduate and master's degrees from the University of Oregon. Her teaching, research, and service activities focus on human resource management, organizational theory, and public management questions.

RICHARD C. KEARNEY is professor and director of North Carolina State University's School of Public and International Affairs. He served in faculty and administrative positions previously at East Carolina University, the University of Connecticut, and the University of South Carolina. Kearney has published extensively in the fields of human resource management, labor relations, and state and local politics. He is author of the forthcoming fourth edition of *Labor Relations in the Public Sector* (New York: Taylor and Francis).

J. EDWARD KELLOUGH is professor and department head in the Department of Public Administration and Policy at the University of Georgia (UGA). Kellough specializes in public personnel management, public administration, and program evaluation and has published widely in those fields. He has been a member of the executive council of the National Association of Schools of Public Affairs and Administration (NASPAA) and a member of the NASPAA Commission on Peer Review and Accreditation. He has served as chair of the Section on Public Administration of the American Political Science Association, and on the editorial boards of a number of academic journals. Recent books include *Understanding Affirmative Action: Politics, Discrimination, and the Search for Justice* (Georgetown University Press, 2007); *The New Public Personnel Administration*, sixth edition, with Lloyd G. Nigro and Felix A. Nigro (Thomson/Wadsworth, 2007); and *Civil Service Reform in the States: Personnel Policy and Politics at the Sub-National Level*, edited with Lloyd G. Nigro (State University of New York Press, 2006).

DONALD E. KLINGNER is an internationally recognized expert on public personnel management, public management, Latin American public HRM and public management, and international public management capacity building and technology transfer. He is president (2008–2009) of the American Society for Public Administration (ASPA) and an elected fellow (2007) of the National Academy of Public Administration (NAPA). He is coauthor of *Public Personnel Management* (sixth edition pending), also published in Spanish and Chinese. He has been a Fulbright Senior Scholar (Central America, 1994), a visiting professor at UNAM, Mexico (1999–2003), and a consultant to the United Nations, the World Bank, and the Inter-American Development Bank on public management capacity building. He coedits *Comparative Technology Transfer and Society,* published by The Johns Hopkins University Press.

ROBERT J. LAVIGNA is vice president of Research for the Partnership for Public Service, a nonpartisan nonprofit dedicated to revitalizing government. Before joining the partnership, Bob was director of Consulting Services-East for CPS Human Resource Services, a self-supporting public agency that provides HR consulting services to government. He has also served as administrator of the state of Wisconsin civil service system, and with the U.S. Government Accountability Office (GAO). Lavigna's awards and honors include selection as a Public Official of the Year by *Governing* magazine. He is also a past president of the International Public Management Association for HR and the American Society for Public Administration Section on Personnel and Labor Relations.

PATRICE M. MARESCHAL is a faculty fellow, Senator Walter Rand Institute for Public Affairs and an associate professor, Department of Public Policy and

Administration, Rutgers University. Her research and teaching interests include conflict resolution, labor unions/labor studies, and organizational behavior.

SUSAN G. MASON is assistant professor for the departments of Public Policy and Administration and Political Science as well as director of the Graduate Certificate in Community and Regional Planning at Boise State University. She coauthored the book chapter "Linear Correlation and Regression" in the *Handbook of Research Methods in Public Administration*, second edition, with Dr. Les Alm. She has also published in the *Journal of Optometric Education* and has a forthcoming article in the *Journal of Public Affairs Education*. Her current research focuses on comparative research on cities and regions in the United States and Canada as well as cooperation, urban development, community and regional planning, and their intersections with public policy.

JOAN E. PYNES is professor of public administration at the University of South Florida. She is the author of *Human Resources Management for Public and Nonprofit Organizations*, published by Jossey-Bass, Inc. Her research interests are public and nonprofit management.

GARY E. ROBERTS is associate professor at Regent University holding a joint appointment in the Robertson School of Government and the School of Global Leadership & Entrepreneurship. Dr. Roberts has worked in both the public and nonprofit sectors in the areas of human resource management and community development. His teaching areas include nonprofit administration, human resource management, and public administration. Current research interests center on workplace spiritual intelligence, servant leader human resource policy and practice, the impact of the religious-friendly workplace, and organizational policies to promote employee work-life balance. He has authored over forty journal articles and book chapters on various human resource and public management issues.

DAVID H. ROSENBLOOM is distinguished professor of public administration in the School of Public Affairs at American University in Washington, DC. His research and theory-building focus on public administration and democratic-constitutionalism. He is the 1999 recipient of the Dwight Waldo Award and the 2001 John Gaus Award for excellence in scholarship.

ROBERT SEIDNER is a Ph.D. student at the University of Illinois–Chicago's College of Urban Planning and Public Affairs. He has several years of federal human capital evaluation experience, including serving as a presidential management fellow at the U.S. Office of Personnel Management. He earned an MBA from the Heller School for Social Policy and Management at Brandeis University, as well as his undergraduate degrees from Brandeis.

SALLY COLEMAN SELDEN is a professor of management at Lynchburg College. Professor Selden's teaching and research interests include human resource management, management, and nonprofit management effectiveness. She is also a Principal Investigator for the Government Performance Project (GPP), a study of public management systems in all fifty states funded by The Pew Charitable Trusts. She was responsible for leading the academic team that graded the human resource management systems of the U.S. state governments.

JESSICA E. SOWA is assistant professor in the Maxine Goodman Levin College of Urban Affairs at Cleveland State University. She received a Ph.D. in public administration from the Maxwell School of Citizenship and Public Affairs at Syracuse University in 2003. Her major fields of research and teaching are public and nonprofit management, with a focus on human resource management, and organizational effectiveness in public and nonprofit organizations. Her work has appeared in *Public Administration Review*, the *Journal of Public Administration Research and Theory, Nonprofit and Voluntary Sector Quarterly*, and the *Review of Public Personnel Administration*.

SUSAN SPICE is a Ph.D. student in the Askew School of Public Administration and Policy at Florida State University. Her research interests include emotional labor, social capital and civil society, comparative public administration, and human rights. Recent papers include *Promoting Gender Equality and Empowering Women in Latin America; Human Rights in the Czech Republic: A Case Study;* and *Emotional Compensation: the Intangible Take-Home Pay.*

LANA STEIN is professor of political science and public policy administration at the University of Missouri–St. Louis. She specializes in urban politics and administration and is author of *Holding Bureaucrats Accountable: Politicians and Professionals in St. Louis.* She has published articles in *Public Administration Review, American Review of Public Administration*, and the *Review of Public Personnel Administration* as well as other journals. She authored a political history of St. Louis and contributed to a study of urban education reform.

JAMES R. THOMPSON is associate professor in the Graduate Program in Public Administration at the University of Illinois–Chicago where he teaches courses in public personnel management, information technology, and public management. Prior to obtaining his Ph.D. at the Maxwell School of Citizenship and Public Affairs at Syracuse University in 1996, he worked in local government in New York State at the city and county levels. At UIC, his research has focused on organizational change and bureaucratic reform in the public sector. He has also done extensive research and writing on the modernization of human resource management practices in government.

JONATHAN P. WEST is professor of political science and director of the graduate public administration program at the University of Miami. He has published eight books and over one hundred scholarly articles and book chapters. He teaches undergraduate and graduate courses in American politics, public management, and human resource management. He is managing editor of *Public Integrity* journal. He taught previously at the University of Houston and University of Arizona.

ROBERT T. WOOTERS is the lead research assistant for the People section of the 2008 Government Performance Project, an initiative of The Pew Center on the States and *Governing* magazine. He graduated Phi Beta Kappa with a BS in Mathematics from the University of California, Irvine in 2002, and is currently nearing the completion of his MBA at Lynchburg College in Lynchburg, Virginia.

# ━∿∿∿〈 **Section One** 〉∿∿∿━

# The Setting

To a great extent, public human resource management (HRM) is a mirror of the society it serves. Public jobs are public resources, and therefore subject to external political, social, economic, and legal forces that exert pressures for change. Human resource management in public and nonprofit organizations is a balancing act involving protecting employees from undue political and partisan influences, being responsive to agency and political management, serving multiple interests and stakeholders, offering flexibility while ensuring needed standardization, and many, many similar conflicting values and paradoxes. A proper understanding of contemporary public HRM must begin with an appreciation for the environmental factors shaping its practice.

In Chapter 1, Donald E. Klingner discusses the evolution of public HRM. Klingner shows how values underlying HRM can and do come into conflict. The complex web of pressures and demands that society places on the HRM function fluctuates, resulting in different human resource (HR) strategies being pursued at different points in time. The author pays particular attention to two emergent paradigms, privatization and partnerships, both of which rest on limited and decentralized government, personal accountability, and community responsibility plus, for partnerships, cooperative service delivery mechanisms.

In Chapter 2, David H. Rosenbloom and Joshua Chanin provide a thorough yet concise analysis of HRM's legal context. Given that judicial decisions affect every aspect and technique of public HRM, this chapter underscores the importance of public personnel managers possessing a sophisticated understanding of constitutional law and how to apply it to complicated issues and situations.

The remaining chapters in the section consider HRM in four separate settings: the federal government, state government, local government, and the nonprofit sector. James R. Thompson and Robert Seidner's chapter on the federal government considers some of the daunting challenges facing the federal government in the coming years, including: filling higher-level vacancies created by a massive exit of retiring baby boomers, improving employment conditions for disgruntled career employees, ensuring some degree of consistency (HR standardization) in an increasingly decentralized federal system that also affords agencies needed discretion, closing the labor-management chasm opened up by actions of the Bush administration, and successfully harnessing the promise of virtual HR to improve HR operations.

The serious nature of the federal-level HRM challenges is echoed in the chapters on state and local government. Sally Coleman Selden draws upon data from the Government Performance Project to review the characteristics of HRM in the states, how the states' HRM systems are changing to confront new challenges, and how organizational and environmental factors affect the states' adoption of various HRM strategies. Next, Susan G. Mason and Lana Stein's chapter on local government discusses the importance of Progressive Era civil service reforms at the local government level to shaping state and federal-level reforms. The authors argue that those early reforms, which focused on centralized control and standardization, set the foundation for current HRM problems being experienced across all levels of government.

In the section's final chapter, Beth Gazley examines HRM in the nonprofit setting. The nonprofit chapter is a new addition to "The Setting" section for the fifth edition. But, given the emergence of privatization and partnering (as discussed by Klingner in Chapter 1), the reliance on nonprofit providers to deliver public services, and the growing "blending" of public and nonprofit sectors, the HRM strategies followed by nonprofit organizations will go a long way in determining the quality of public services in the years to come.

—————◖◗╍╍╍╍◖◖ ▌ ◗╍╍╍╍◖◖—————

# Competing Perspectives on Public Personnel Administration
## Civil Service, Patronage, and Privatization

DONALD E. KLINGNER
University of Colorado at Colorado Springs

This chapter (1) presents a historical perspective on public human resource management; (2) examines the emergent paradigms' values and strategies; (3) evaluates their impact on traditional values and practices; and (4) explores the changing structure and role of human resource management (HRM) under alternative public personnel systems such as civil service, patronage, and privatization.

## A HISTORICAL PERSPECTIVE ON PUBLIC HUMAN RESOURCE MANAGEMENT

Public HRM in the United States can be viewed from at least four perspectives (Klingner and Nalbandian, 2003). First, it is the functions (planning, acquisition, development, and discipline) needed to manage HR in public agencies. Second, it is the processes by which public jobs, as scarce resources, are allocated.

Third, it is the interaction among fundamental societal values that often conflict. These values are responsiveness, efficiency, employee rights, and social equity. Responsiveness means a budget process that allocates positions and therefore sets priorities and an appointment process that considers political or personal loyalty along with education and experience as indicators of merit. Efficiency means staffing decisions based on ability and performance rather than political loyalty. Employee rights mean selection and promotion based on merit, as defined by objective measures of ability and performance, and employees who are free to apply their knowledge, skills, and abilities without partisan political interference. Social equity

3

means public jobs allocated proportionately based on gender, race, and other designated criteria.

And fourth, public HRM is the embodiment of human resource systems: the laws, rules, organizations, and procedures used to fulfill personnel functions in ways that express the abstract values. Historically, U.S. public HRM systems developed in evolutionary stages, analytically separate but in practice, overlapping (see Table 1.1).

In the *Patrician Era* (1789–1828), the small group of upper-class property owners who had won independence and established the national government held most public jobs. As this generation passed, an era of *Patronage* emerged (1829–1882) during which public jobs were awarded according to political loyalty or party affiliation. Next, the increased size and complexity of public activities led to an era of *Professionalism* (1883–1932) that defined public HRM as a neutral administrative function so as to emphasize modernization through efficiency and democratization by allocating public jobs, at least at the federal level, on merit (Heclo, 1977). The unprecedented demands of a global depression and World War II led to the

**TABLE 1.1   The Evolution of Public HRM Systems and Values in the United States**

| Stage of Evolution | Dominant Value(s) | Dominant System(s) | Pressures for Change |
|---|---|---|---|
| *Patrician* (1789–1828) | Responsiveness | "Government by elites" | Political parties Patronage |
| *Patronage* (1829–1882) | Responsiveness | Patronage | Modernization Democratization |
| *Professionalism* (1883–1932) | Efficiency Individual rights | Civil service | Responsiveness Effective government |
| *Performance* (1933–1964) | Responsiveness Efficiency Individual rights | Patronage Civil service | Individual rights Social equity |
| *People* (1965–1979) | Responsiveness Efficiency Individual rights Social equity | Patronage Civil service Collective bargaining Affirmative action | Dynamic equilibrium among four competing values and systems |
| *Privatization* (1980–present) | Responsiveness Efficiency Individual accountability Limited government Community responsibility | Patronage Civil service Collective bargaining Affirmative action Alternative mechanisms Flexible employment relationships | Dynamic equilibrium among four pro-governmental values and systems, and three anti-governmental values and systems |
| *Partnerships* (2002–present) | Responsiveness Efficiency Individual accountability Limited government Community responsibility Collaboration | Patronage Civil service Collective bargaining Affirmative action Alternative mechanisms Flexible employment relationships | Dynamic equilibrium among four pro-governmental values and systems, three anti-governmental values and systems |

emergence of a hybrid *Performance* model (1933–1964) that combined the political leadership of patronage systems and the merit principles of civil service systems. Next, social upheavals (1965–1979) presaged the emergence of the *People Era* in which collective bargaining emerged to represent collective employee rights (the equitable treatment of members by management through negotiated work rules for wages, benefits, and working conditions), and affirmative action emerged to represent social equity (through voluntary or court-mandated recruitment and selection practices to help ameliorate the under representation of minorities and women in the workforce). Thus, by 1980 U.S. public HRM could be described as a dynamic equilibrium among four competing values, each championed by a particular system, for allocating scarce public jobs.

## THE EMERGENT PARADIGMS: PRIVATIZATION AND PARTNERSHIPS

The *Privatization* paradigm emerged at the end of the 1970s when Jimmy Carter campaigned against public agencies and employees by running against the national government as a Washington "outsider." Following the election, he proposed the 1978 Civil Service Reform Act on grounds that included poor performance in the public service and difficulty in controlling and directing bureaucrats. Beginning in 1981, the Reagan administration, though starting from fundamentally different values and policy objectives, continued to cast government as part of the problem. Consequently, this paradigm shift was marked by increasing reliance on market-based forces, rather than program implementation by government agencies and employees, as the most efficacious tools of public policy. The emphasis on economic perspectives and administrative efficiency reflected the intense pressures on the public sector to "do more with less." This caused governments to become more accountable through such techniques as program budgeting, management by objectives (MBO), program evaluation, and management information systems. It also caused efforts to lower expenditures through tax and expenditure ceilings, deficit reduction, deferred expenditures, accelerated tax collection, service fees and user charges, and a range of legislative and judicial efforts to shift program responsibilities and costs away from each affected government.

Because most public expenditures are for employee salaries and benefits, efforts to increase accountability and cut costs focused on HR functions. The shift continued the trend set in previous eras such as the 1930s and the 1960s, emphasizing program outputs and rationally tying program inputs to outputs (e.g., program budgeting, human resource forecasting, job evaluation, MBO, objective performance appraisal, training needs assessment, cost-benefit analysis, and gain sharing/productivity bargaining). Moreover, the information systems revolution expanded access to information formerly used by management for coordination and control, resulting in organizational restructuring and the downsizing of mid-managerial positions.

The 1990s brought continued efforts to reduce government, either to increase its responsiveness and effectiveness, or to "shrink the beast" and put more resources in the hands of individuals and businesses. These were exemplified by Vice President Gore's National Performance Review (National Performance Review, 1993a,b), aimed at creating a government that "works better and costs less" through fundamental changes in organizational structure and accountability, epitomized by the terms *reinventing government* or *New Public Management* (Osborne and Gaebler, 1992). These trends decentralized most HR functions to operating agencies and a corresponding reduction in the functions and authority of the U.S. Office of Personnel Management; and reduced federal civilian employment, particularly staff positions (personnel, budget, auditing, and procurement) and middle managers with no direct relationship to productivity increases.

The Republican Party swept into control of Congress in 1994 and again in 2002 as a result of a shift toward three emergent non-governmental values: personal accountability, limited and decentralized government, and community responsibility for social services. Proponents of personal accountability expected people to make individual choices consistent with their own goals and accept responsibility for the consequences of these choices, rather than passing responsibility for their actions on to society. Proponents of limited and decentralized government believed, fundamentally, that government was to be feared for its power to arbitrarily or capriciously deprive individuals of their rights. They also believed that public policy, service delivery, and revenue generation could be controlled efficiently in a smaller unit of government in a way not possible in a larger one. And for some, a reduction in government size and scope was justified by perceived government ineffectiveness; by a high value accorded to individual freedom, responsibility, and accountability; and finally, by a desire to devote a smaller share of personal income to taxes. The values of limited and decentralized government and personal accountability were supplemented with the value of community responsibility. The most significant consequence of the emergence of this value, at least as far as public HRM is concerned, was the delivery of local governments' social services through non-governmental organizations (NGOs) funded by taxes, user fees, and charitable contributions.

Third-party social service provision became more complex with an ideologically driven emphasis that directed contracting strategies toward faith-based organizations (FBOs). With the passage of the "charitable choice" component of the 1996 Personal Responsibility and Work Opportunity Reconciliation Act, charitable choice has expanded to include a range of federal programs, such as Temporary Assistance to Needy Families (1996); Welfare to Work Formula Grants (1997); Community Services Block Grants (1998); and drug abuse treatment programs (2000). The establishment of the White House Office of Faith-Based and Community Initiatives (OFBCI) and five similar offices in the Departments of Education, Justice, Health and Human Services, Labor, and Housing and Urban Development to contract with faith-based agencies nationwide. According to a study conducted by the Rockefeller Institute of Government (2003), this also occurred at the state level. As of that date, thirty-two states had contracted with FBOs to provide some social services and eight states had enacted legislation requiring the inclusion of FBOs in contracting. More recently, state departments of labor received directives from the U.S. Department of Labor (DOL) Office of Faith-Based and Community Initiatives requiring the development of state DOL strategic plans specifically aimed at increasing the number of faith-based grantees by providing training and technical assistance to these organizations as they competed for service provision contracts.

This emerging *Partnerships* paradigm rests on the same values of personal accountability, limited and decentralized government, and community responsibility for social services that characterized the *Privatization* paradigm, with an added strategic emphasis on cooperative service delivery among governments, businesses, and NGOs. The strategic element of this paradigm is under-girded by the belief that concrete results in public service delivery can only be achieved by the skilled deployment of human assets regardless of the framework within which it occurs. This new framework's advocates also argue that the skilled deployment of human assets is best accomplished outside of the traditional civil service model. This aspect of anti-government, anti-union sentiment has resonated among state legislatures. As a result, many states are rethinking and reinventing their public personnel systems, from far-reaching efforts in Georgia and Florida to the more subtle efforts to enhance third-party service delivery options.

These two emergent paradigms of privatization and partnerships both rely upon the same basic HRM strategies: (1) using alternative organizations and mechanisms to deliver public services, and (2) increasing the flexibility of employment relationships for the remaining public employees.

## Alternative Organizations and Mechanisms

These alternatives include purchase-of-service agreements, privatization, franchise agreements, subsidy arrangements, vouchers, volunteerism, and regulatory and tax incentives (International City Management Association, 1989). These are not new. But recent examples indicate how commonplace they have become, and how much they have supplanted traditional service delivery by civil service employees hired through appropriated funding of public agencies.

Purchase-of-service agreements with other governmental agencies and NGOs have become commonplace (Mahtesian, 1994). They enable cities and counties to offer services within a given geographic area, utilizing economies of scale. They offer smaller municipalities a way of reducing or avoiding capital expenses, personnel costs, and political issues associated with collective bargaining, and legal liability risks. In addition, the use of outside consultants (individuals or businesses hired under fee-for-service arrangements on an as-needed basis) increases available expertise and managerial flexibility by reducing the range of qualified technical and professional employees that the agency must otherwise hire.

*Privatization*, as the term is generally used in the United States, means that while a public agency provides a particular service, the service is produced and delivered by a private contractor. It may result in the abolition of the agency (at times an intended ideological goal). Privatization offers all the advantages of service purchase agreements but holds down labor and construction costs on a larger scale. It has become commonplace in areas like solid waste disposal where there is an easily identifiable "benchmark" (standard cost and service comparison with the private sector), and where public agency costs tend to be higher because of higher pay and benefits (Siegel, 1999; O'Looney, 1998; and Martin, 1999).

Franchise agreements often allow businesses to monopolize a previously public function (e.g., cable TV, and jitneys as a public transit option) within a geographic area, charge competitive rates for it, and then pay the appropriate government a fee for the privilege. Cities encourage franchising because it reduces their own costs, provides some revenue in return, and results in a continuation of a desirable public service.

Subsidy arrangements enable private businesses to provide public services funded by either user fees to clients or cost reimbursement from public agencies.

Examples are emergency medical services provided by private hospitals and reimbursed by public health systems, and rent subsidies to enable low-income residents to live in private apartments as an alternative to public housing projects.

Vouchers enable individuals to purchase public goods or services from competing providers on the open market. For example, educational voucher systems allow parents to apply a voucher to defray the cost of education for their child at competing public or private institutions, as an alternative to public school monopolies.

Volunteers contribute services otherwise performed by paid employees, or not at all. These include community crime watch programs in cooperation with local police departments, classroom teachers' aides who provide tutoring and individual assistance in many public schools, community residents who volunteer services as individuals or through churches, and other nonprofit service agencies. Frequently, such contributions are required to "leverage" a federal or state grant of appropriated funds. Though they would probably not consider themselves volunteers, prison inmates are often responsible for laundry, food service, and facilities maintenance.

Regulatory and tax incentives encourage the private sector to perform functions that might otherwise be performed by public agencies with public funds. These include the zoning variances for roads, parking, and waste disposal granted to condominium associations. In return, the association provides services normally performed by local government (e.g., security, waste disposal, and maintenance of common areas).

## Flexible Employment Relationships

All the mechanisms just described provide public services without using public employees and in many cases without appropriated funds. Yet even in those cases where public services continue to be provided by public employees working in public agencies funded by appropriations, massive changes have occurred in employment practices. Chief among these are increased use of temporary, part-time, and seasonal employment, and increased hiring of exempt employees (those outside the classified civil service) through employment contracts. Increasingly, public employers reduce costs and enhance flexibility by meeting minimal staffing requirements through career civil service employees and hiring other employees "at will" into temporary or part-time positions (U.S. Merit Systems Protection Board, 1994). These "temps" usually receive lower salaries and benefits than their career counterparts, and are certainly unprotected by due process entitlements or collective bargaining agreements. Alternatively, where commitment and high skills are required on a temporary basis, employers may seek to save money or maintain flexibility by using contract or leased employees in exempt positions. While contracts may be routinely renewed with mutual approval, such "employees" may also be discharged at will in the event of a personality conflict, a change in managerial objectives, or a budget shortfall. These professional and technical contractors usually receive higher salaries and benefits than can be offered to even highly qualified civil servants, and they enable management to cut personnel costs quickly if necessary without having to resort to seniority-based layoffs and the bureaucratic chaos precipitated by the exercise of civil service "bumping rights." The impact of market mechanisms and flexible employment relationships is often accelerated by retirement "buyouts" that offer employees close to retirement age an incentive to retire early within a limited period of eligibility (a "window"). If the plan is designed strategically so that enough employees retire to save substantially but enough stay to provide for organizational continuity and skills, both employer and employee benefit. The employee gets an option to retire early at close to current salary, and the employer gets to fill the vacant position with an entry-level employee at a lower salary.

## THE EMERGENT PARADIGMS' IMPACT ON TRADITIONAL VALUES AND OUTCOMES

The effectiveness of these two emergent public HRM strategies (using alternative organizations or mechanisms for providing public services, and increasing the flexibility of employment relationships) has implications not only for the delivery of government services, but also for the values that underlie traditional public HRM.

The new strategies diminish employee rights. It is more likely that employees hired "at will" into temporary and part-time positions will receive lower pay and benefits, and will be unprotected by civil service regulations or collective bargaining agreements (Hsu, 2000). Whether or not the political neutrality of public employees suffers in this environment is unknown presently, but it seems logical to assume that as the criteria for success become more arbitrary or capricious, civil service employees— particularly those in mid-management positions—will begin to behave more like the political appointees whose jobs depend on political or personal loyalty to elected officials (Brewer and Maranto, 2000).

The new strategies also threaten social equity. Pay comparisons over the past twenty years have uniformly concluded that minorities and women in public agencies are closer to equal pay for equal work than are their private sector counterparts. Managerial consultants are overwhelmingly white and male. Many part-time and temporary positions are exempt from laws prohibiting discrimination against persons with disabilities or family medical responsibilities.

Evidence supports the conclusion that the impact of the new strategies on efficiency has been mixed. On the plus side, the change in public agency culture toward identifying customers and providing market-based services increases productivity. And the threat of privatization or layoffs has forced unions to agree to pay cuts, to reduce employer-funded benefits, and to change work rules (Cohen and Eimicke, 1994). But the personnel techniques that have become more common under these emergent systems may actually increase some personnel costs, particularly those connected with employment of independent contractors, reemployed annuitants, and temporary employees (Peters and Savoie, 1994). Downsizing may eventually lead to higher recruitment; orientation and training costs; and loss of the organizational memory and "core expertise" necessary to effectively manage contracting or privatization initiatives (Milward, 1996). Minimum staffing usually results in increased payment of overtime, and higher rates of employee accidents and injuries. As the civil service workforce shrinks, it is also aging. This means increases in pension payouts, disability retirements, workers' compensation claims and health-care costs.

Emerging then, is a human resource framework that embraces both the management of control and collaboration that is paradoxical, exposing the underlying tensions inherent in the values of monitoring (compliance) and empowerment (outcomes). The tensions are evidenced by the debates over the desire to maintain control mechanisms associated with traditional civil service systems (risk adversity) and the strategic attractiveness of responsiveness and managerial empowerment (stewardship). Yet, increasingly, research in the field calls for understandings that move beyond *either/or* thinking (Drummond, 1998; Kisfalvi, 2000). Rising levels of ambiguity and turbulence both at the national and state levels of government are demanding a more paradoxical approach to HRM—one that embraces the simultaneous need for control and collaboration.

Opposing and interwoven elements are evident throughout government as citizens and public officials struggle with the coexistence of authority and democracy, efficiency and creativity, freedom and control (Lewis, 2000). The new HR paradigm may be increasingly about the management of both control and collaboration and, more critically, about developing understandings and practices that accept, accommodate, and even encourage these tensions. As an example, increasingly state government agencies are using a model of collaborative social service provision and approaches to address social problems. These often involve overlapping partnerships with various public sector organizations, a recognition that the complexity of social issues is in part due to its residence within an inter-organizational framework and that these problems cannot be tackled by any one organization acting alone. These new and often confusing organizational relationships suggest that HR managers will not only need to manage control and collaboration simultaneously, but also become much more sophisticated in the competencies needed to work across organizational boundaries (Halley, 1997).

However, collaboration brings its own sets of problems in that contract compliance, rather than traditional supervisory practices, becomes the primary quality control mechanism. This creates a real possibility of fraud and abuse (Moe, 1987). In this regard, state and local governments' experience suggests that privatization and service contracting outcomes are most likely to be successful when governments:

- pick a service with clear objectives that can be measured and monitored;
- use in-house or external competition and avoid sole source contracting;
- develop adequate cost accounting systems to compare service alternatives and monitor contractor performance;
- consider negative externalities such as impacts on an existing work force and impacts on the local economy, other governments or functions, governmental policies, or certain societal groups (Siegel, 1999).

The impact of these contemporary HR strategies on the last traditional value (political responsiveness) is also problematic. Public-private partnerships raise fundamental accountability and performance issues for elected officials and public managers (Klingner, Nalbandian, and Romzek, 2002). The emergent values and systems alter the fundamental role of government by placing greater emphasis on individuals and by shifting the focus of governmental social service delivery from a national to a state and local level. Continual budget cuts and pressures can result in a budget-driven rather than mission-driven agency. Budget-driven agencies that address public problems with short-term solutions designed to meet short-term legislative objectives are not likely to be effective. Long-range planning, or indeed any planning beyond the current budget cycle, is likely to become less important. Agencies will not be able to prepare effective capital budgets or to adequately maintain capital assets (human or infrastructure).

Although it may be unfair to expect the values behind an embryonic paradigm to be explicit or immediately validated by reality, critics view the emergent paradigm as an abdication of political responsibility rather than as a shift in underlying values. For them, the elected and appointed officials who preside over the dismantling of social and public infrastructure for the sake of short-term political gain are abdicating their responsibility to the public welfare. Who owns the public infrastructure sold through privatization—current taxpayers or future ones? Does the emergent paradigm indeed reflect alternative values, or does it reflect simply the rationalization of covert self-interest by political and economic elites? Do these new values really represent a coherent paradigm, or are they fundamentally rhetorical sound bites and political slogans designed for emotional and symbolic appeal rather than rational clarification and compromise among competing values?

## THE CHANGING STRUCTURE AND ROLE OF PUBLIC HUMAN RESOURCE MANAGEMENT

Three main groups share responsibility for public HRM. Political leaders are responsible for authorizing personnel systems, and for establishing their objectives and funding levels. Personnel directors and specialists design and implement personnel systems, or direct and help those who do. In civil service systems, they usually work within a personnel department that functions as a staff support service for managers and supervisors. Their main responsibility is achieving agency goals within a prescribed budget and a limited number of positions. HR directors and specialists both help line managers to use human resources effectively and to constrain their personnel actions within the limits imposed by political leaders, laws, and regulations. Managers and supervisors are responsible for implementing the rules, policies, and procedures that constitute personnel systems, as they work with employees on a day-to-day basis.

While the basic HRM functions remain the same, the relative emphasis among functions and how they are performed differs depending on the system. HR under a patronage system heavily emphasizes recruitment and selection of applicants based on personal or political loyalty. Once hired, political appointees are subject to the whims of the elected official. Few rules govern their job duties, pay or rights, and they are usually fired at will. Nor is development a priority.

In a civil service system, HR is a department or office that functions as an administrative support service to the city manager, school superintendent, hospital director, or other agency administrator. Because civil service is a complete system, HR has a balanced emphasis on each of the four major personnel functions— planning, acquisition, development, and sanction. HR is responsible for maintaining the classification system of positions that have been categorized according to type of work and level of responsibility. The pay system is usually tied to the classification system, with jobs involving similar degrees of difficulty being compensated equally. HR is also responsible for developing and updating the agency's retirement and benefits programs. It also handles eligibility and processing of personnel action requests (retirements and other related changes in job status). HR is responsible for advertising vacant or new positions, reviewing job applications, administering written tests, and providing a ranked list of eligible applicants to managers in units where vacancies exist. After the manager conducts interviews and selects one applicant, HR processes the paperwork required to employ and pay the person. HR is responsible for orienting new employees to the organization, its work rules, and the benefits it provides. It may conduct training itself, or contract for it. HR implements an employee grievance and appeals procedure; advises supervisors throughout the organization of appropriate codes of conduct for employees; establishes the steps necessary to discipline an employee for violation of these rules, and the procedures to follow in the event the employee appeals this disciplinary action or files a grievance. If employees are covered by a collective bargaining agreement, the personnel department is usually responsible for negotiating the agreement (or hiring an outside negotiator who performs this function), bringing pay and benefit provisions into accord with contract provisions, orienting supervisors on how to comply with the contract, and representing the agency in internal grievance resolution or outside arbitration procedures.

HR is responsible primarily for implementing human resource acquisition rules emphasizing social equity for minorities, women, and persons with disabilities. Thus, it most heavily affects recruitment, selection, and promotion policies and procedures. The affirmative action director shares responsibility with the personnel director in this area. Once members of these protected classes are hired, other personnel systems (civil service or collective bargaining) influence the ways planning, development, and discipline occur.

In general, reliance on NGOs reduces the absolute number of public employees, thereby reducing the HR department's functions. But it also increases the importance of planning and oversight because these functions are necessary to estimate the type and number of contract employees needed to provide a desired level of service. HR must develop requests for proposals to outside contractors, evaluate responses to proposals by comparing costs and services, and oversee contract administration. HR directors, staff, and managers work increasingly with citizen volunteers and community-based organizations to supplement paid staff. In these cases, public managers need to become more skilled in recruiting, selecting, training, and motivating volunteer workers (Pynes, 1997).

Flexibility in employment relationships is achieved primarily by the increased use of temporary, part-time, and seasonal employment; and by increased hiring of exempt employees (those outside the classified civil service) through employment contracts. Employee development is largely irrelevant: most contingent workers are hired with the skills needed to perform the job immediately. Objective performance evaluation may still be required to maintain effectiveness, but not to maintain equity or discipline. Because at-will employees have no job retention rights, it's easy for employers to control the terms of the relationship. If employees do their jobs adequately, they get paid; if not, they are simply released at the end of their contract and not called back when workload once again increases.

The evolution of public personnel management in the United States adds emergent systems without replacing their predecessors. Instead, new and emergent systems interact and conflict in ways that reflect the dynamic interaction of laws, conditions, and policies. But regardless of the particular system or combination of systems that control HR policy and practice within a particular agency, the organizational structure and relationships within which public HR functions are carried out are established and regulated by law. Usually, the organization of public HRM follows a pattern that is tied closely to the evolution of personnel systems themselves. In the United States nationally, this process was represented by passage of the Pendleton Act (1883) and creation of the U.S. Civil Service Commission. This in some cases followed and in other cases encouraged the establishment of similar state and local civil service agencies. As public personnel management tried to unify the opposing roles of civil service protection and management effectiveness, the organizational location and mission of the central personnel agency became increasingly significant. In some cases it remained an independent commission. In others, it split into two agencies like the U.S. Merit Systems Protection Board and the U.S. Office of Personnel Management, one responsible for protecting employees against political interference under civil service rules, and the other for administering and enforcing the chief executive's HRM policies and practices in other executive branch agencies. As collective bargaining and affirmative action emerged as separate personnel systems, separate agencies were often created at all levels of government to focus on these responsibilities. Other agencies like a department of labor (federal, state, or local) may have additional personnel responsibilities for regulating public employee pay, benefits, and working conditions. Often, these agencies have conflicting or overlapping roles in particular HRM functions.

Over time, the role of HR in public agencies has evolved with changes in the political and administrative context. The primary roles have been watchdogs against the spoils systems, collaboration with legislative restrictions, cooperation with management, and compliance with legislative mandates. During the *Professionalism Era* (1883–1932), HR professionals championed merit system principles because public HRM was generally viewed as a conflict between two systems, one evil and the other good. Public HR managers were considered responsible for guarding employees, applicants, and the public from the spoils system. This required knowledge of civil service policies and procedures, and the courage to apply them in the face of political pressure.

During the *Performance Era* (1933–1964), HR sought to maintain efficiency and accountability, and legislators and chief executives sought to maintain bureaucratic compliance through budgetary controls and position management. Through such devices as personnel ceilings and average grade-level restrictions, it became the role of public personnel management to control the behavior of public managers and to help assure compliance with legislative authority. In effect, it was the responsibility of HR to synthesize two distinct values (bureaucratic compliance as the operational definition of organizational efficiency and civil service protection as the embodiment of employee rights). There was tension between them because they were both symbiotic and conflicting. And together with the value of bureaucratic neutrality, they supported the concept of political responsiveness.

During the *People Era* (1965–1979) the focus of public HRM shifted to consultation as HR managers demanded flexibility and equitable reward allocation through such alterations to classification and pay systems as rank-in-person personnel systems, broad pay banding, and group performance evaluation and reward systems. This trend coincided with employee needs for utilization, development, and recognition.

In the *Privatization Era* (1980–present), public HR still works consultatively with agency managers and employees, and with compliance agencies. But its role and objectives are more contradictory. First, HR is required, more than ever, to manage government employees and programs in compliance with legislative and public mandates for cost control. Given the common public and legislative presumption that the public bureaucracy is an enemy to be controlled rather than a tool to be used to accomplish public policy objectives, its authority may be diminished by legislative micromanagement, or the value of cost control may be so dominant as to preclude concern for employee rights, organizational efficiency, or social equity. Second, HR may work increasingly with volunteers and NGOs (particularly FBOs). Because many public employees (particularly school teachers and administrators, police, and firefighters) are still covered by union contracts and collective bargaining agreements,

**TABLE 1.2   The Role of Public HR Management in the United States**

| Stage of Evolution | Dominant Value(s) | Dominant System(s) | HRM Role |
|---|---|---|---|
| *Patrician* (1789–1828) | Responsiveness | "Government by elites" | None |
| *Patronage* (1829–1882) | Responsiveness | Patronage | Recruitment and political clearance |
| *Professionalism* (1883–1932) | Efficiency Individual rights | Civil service | "Watchdog" over agency managers and elected officials to ensure merit system compliance |
| *Performance* (1933–1964) | Responsiveness Efficiency Individual rights | Patronage Civil service | Collaboration with legislative limits |
| *People* (1965–1979) | Responsiveness Efficiency Individual rights Social equity | Patronage Civil service Collective bargaining Affirmative action | Compliance Policy implementation Consultation |
| *Privatization* (1980–present) | Responsiveness Efficiency Individual accountability Limited government Community responsibility | Patronage Civil service Collective bargaining Affirmative action Alternative mechanisms Flexible employment relationships | Compliance Policy implementation Consultation Contract compliance Strategic thinking about HRM |
| *Partnerships* (2002–present) | Responsiveness Efficiency Individual accountability Limited government Community responsibility Collaboration | Patronage Civil service Collective bargaining Affirmative action Alternative mechanisms Flexible employment relationships | Compliance Policy implementation Consultation Contract compliance Strategic thinking about HRM Tension management Boundary spanning |

civil service and collective bargaining are still important. But as risk management, cost control, and management of other types of employment contracts become more important, a calculating perspective of the joint possibilities for organizational productivity and individual growth tends to supplant a uniform and idealistic view of public service motivations. This represents a narrowing of the public HR perspective.

Third, and somewhat paradoxically, even as this minimalist view of personnel management emerges, there are countervailing pressures to develop an employment relationship characterized by commitment, teamwork, and innovation. Productivity is prized, risk taking is espoused, and variable pay systems that reward individual and group performance are touted. Perhaps the key to the paradox is the emerging distinction between "core employees" (those regarded as essential assets) and "contingent workers" (those regarded as replaceable costs). It is likely that public HR success will continue to require the ability to develop two divergent personnel systems, one for each type of worker within a dual labor market system, and to maintain both at the same time despite their conflicting objectives and assumptions.

With the emergence of the *Partnership Era* (2002–present) public HR is increasingly expected to operate within a framework of structures, processes, and people that are to a large extent outside of immediate control yet are part of the collective enterprise. The ability to manage tensions will be the defining characteristic in shaping and managing collaborative agendas that will be made even more difficult as frequent changes in government policy and in the organizations involved in partnership will impact the roles of and job changes for public sector employees. Recognizing the effects of emerging structures and processes on employment systems, mobilizing, and capacity building will be the benchmarks of collaborative success.

The impact of changing values and systems can be seen in Table 1.2.

## CONCLUSION

Public HRM can be viewed from several perspectives. First, it is the planning, acquisition, development, and discipline functions needed to manage human resources in public agencies. Second, it is the process by which public jobs are allocated as scarce resources. Third, it reflects the influence of seven symbiotic and competing values (political responsiveness, efficiency, individual rights, and social equity under the traditional pro-governmental paradigm; and individual accountability, downsizing and decentralization, and community responsibility under the emergent privatization and partnership paradigms) over how public jobs should be allocated. Fourth, it is the personnel systems (i.e., laws, rules, and procedures) used to express these abstract values—political appointments, civil service, collective bargaining, and affirmative action under the traditional model; and alternative mechanisms and flexible employment relationships under the emergent paradigms of privatization and partnerships.

Conceptually, U.S. public HRM can be understood as a historical process through which new systems emerge to champion emergent values, integrate with the mix, and in turn supplement—neither supplant nor replace—their own successors. From a practical perspective, this means that the field of public HRM is laden with contradictions in policy and practice resulting from often unwieldy and unstable combinations of values and systems, and fraught with the inherent difficulties of utilizing competitive and collaborative systems to achieve diverse goals. Civil service is the predominant public HRM system because it has articulated rules and procedures for performing the whole range of HRM functions. Other systems, though incomplete, are nonetheless legitimate and effective influences over one or more HRM functions. While HR functions remain the same across different systems, their organizational location and method of performance differ depending upon the system and on the values that underlie it.

## REFERENCES

Brewer, G., and R. Maranto. 2000. Comparing the Roles of Political Appointees and Career Executives in the U.S. Federal Executive Branch. *American Review of Public Administration* 30 (1):69–86.

Cohen, S., and W. Eimicke. 1994. The Overregulated Civil Service. *Review of Public Personnel Administration* 15 (2):11–27.

Drummond, H. 1998. Is Escalation Always Irrational? *Organization Studies* 19:911–929.

Halley, A. 1997. Applications of Boundary Theory to the Concept of Service Integration in the Human Services. *Administration in Social Work* 21 (3/4):145–168.

Heclo, H. 1977. *A Government of Strangers.* Washington, D.C.: Brookings Institution.

Hsu, S. 2000. Death of "Big Government" Alters Region: Less-Skilled DC Workers Lose Out as Area Prospers. *Washington Post:* September 4, p. A1+.

International City Management Association. 1989. *Service Delivery in the '90s: Alternative Approaches for Local Governments.* Washington, DC: ICMA.

Kisfalvi, V. 2000. The Threat of Failure, the Perils of Success and CEO Character: Sources of Strategic Persistence. *Organization Studies* 21:611–639.

Klingner, D., and J. Nalbandian. 2003. *Public Personnel Management: Contexts and Strategies,* 5th ed. Upper Saddle River, NJ: Prentice Hall.

Klingner, D., J. Nalbandian, and B. Romzek, 2002. Politics, Administration and Markets: Competing Expectations and Accountability. *American Review of Public Administration* 32 (2):117–144.

Lewis, M. 2000. Exploring Paradox: Toward a More Comprehensive Guide. *Academy of Management Review* 25:760–776.

Mahtesian, C. 1994. Taking Chicago Private. *Governing:* April, pp. 26–31.

Martin, L. 1999. *Contracting for Service Delivery: Local Government Choices.* Washington, DC: International City/County Management Association.

Milward, H. B. 1996. Introduction: Symposium on the Hollow State: Capacity, Control, and Performance in Interorganizational Settings. *Journal of Public Administration Research and Theory* 6 (4): 193–197.

Moe, R. 1987. Exploring the Limits of Privatization. *Public Administration Review* 47 (6):453–460.

National Performance Review (1993a). *From Red Tape to Results: Creating a Government That Works Better and Costs Less. Executive Summary.* Washington, DC: U.S. GPO.

———. 1993b. *Reinventing Human Resource Management: Accompanying Report of the National Performance Review.* Washington, DC: U.S. GPO.

O'Looney, J. 1998. *Outsourcing State and Local Government Services: Decision Making Strategies and Management Methods.* Westport, CT: Greenwood.

Osborne, D., and T. Gaebler. 1992. *Reinventing Government: How the Entrepreneurial Spirit Is Transforming the Public Sector.* Reading, MA: Addison Wesley Longman.

Peters, B., and D. Savoie. 1994. Civil Service Reform: Misdiagnosing the Patient. *Public Administration Review* 54 (6):418–425.

Pynes, J. 1997. *Personnel Administration in Non-Profit Agencies.* San Francisco: Jossey-Bass.

Rockefeller Institute of Government. 2003. *The Public Benefit of Private Faith: Religious Organizations and the Delivery of Social Services:* Albany, NY: Rockefeller IOG.

Siegel, G. 1999. Where Are We on Local Government Service Contracting? *Public Productivity and Management Review* 22 (3):365–388.

U.S. Merit Systems Protection Board. 1994. *Temporary Federal Employment: In Search of Flexibility and Fairness.* Washington, DC: U.S. MSPB.

# What Every Public Personnel Manager Should Know About the Constitution

DAVID H. ROSENBLOOM
JOSHUA CHANIN
American University

Constitutional law is central to public personnel management (PPM) at all levels of American government. Judicial branch interpretation of constitutional law regulates in one way or another merit examinations, recruitment, selection, training, promotions, drug testing, and disciplinary procedures. These court decisions are not just another concern to be balanced among the many competing pressures that public managers face; they form the basis of our public administration and are central to its operation. Should individual administrators or local governmental agencies violate the constitutional rights of applicants or employees, they are subject to legal action and may be held liable for monetary damages. Consequently, public personnel administrators are expected to maintain a sophisticated knowledge of constitutional law. This chapter explains the basic structure underlying current constitutional doctrine and reviews the leading cases in the areas of greatest concern to today's public personnel administration. The following eight sections will rely on an up-to-date survey of relevant case law to familiarize those interested in public personnel with the First, Fourth, Fifth, and Fourteenth Amendments to the U.S. Constitution. The chapter concludes with a brief summary of these constitutional concepts and a few examples of the critical role constitutional law plays in maintaining the integrity of our public administration.

## CONSTITUTIONAL DOCTRINE

Constitutional law has not always been central to the operation of our public administrative agencies. As surprising as it may seem to the modern public personnel manager, prior to the 1950s public employees in the United States had very few federally protected constitutional rights, and even less of an ability to effectively assert these rights within the framework of their employment. These public positions were governed by the "doctrine of privilege," a constitutional reasoning which held that because public employment was a privilege rather than a right, it could be offered on almost any terms the governmental employer saw fit, no matter how arbitrary. Not having a right to a position in the public service, the employee, upon dismissal, lost nothing to which he or she was entitled. As Justice Oliver Wendell Holmes made clear in an early case establishing the constitutionality of disciplining public employees for the content of their speech, "The petitioner may have a constitutional right to talk politics, but he has no constitutional right to be a policeman" (*McAuliffe v. New Bedford*, 1892:220). Under this approach, the Constitution failed to provide public employees and applicants with the very basic protections enjoyed by private citizens.

Although the doctrine of privilege had a certain logic, it also ignored the realities of citizens' interactions with government in the modern administrative state. If the Constitution did not protect public employees and applicants fired or denied jobs for virtually any reason, would not the same principle apply to other kinds of privileges, such as welfare benefits, government contracts, passports, public housing, drivers' licenses, and so forth? Could those be denied, as public employment sometimes was, partly because the individual favored racial integration, read Tom Paine or The *New York Times,* failed to attend church services, or engaged in a host of nonconformist and unconventional activities (Rosenbloom, 1971:160–168)? To the extent that big government creates a dependency of the people on government services, which were considered privileges, strict adherence to the doctrine of privilege could easily lead to circumvention of the fundamental protections found in the Constitution's Bill of Rights.

Notwithstanding a variety of twists and turns in the development of case law since the 1970s, the courts eventually developed an alternative method for analyzing the constitutional rights of public employees. The contemporary approach, termed the "public service model," calls on judges to balance three often competing concerns: (1) public employee or applicant's interests as a member of the political community in exercising constitutional rights and enjoying constitutional protection from arbitrary or repressive treatment by the governmental employer; (2) the government's interest as an employer in having an efficient and effective workforce; and (3) the public's interest in the operation of public administration and government more generally (*Harvard Law Review*, 1984). Importantly, the public's interest can coincide with either that of the employee or the government, depending on the specific circumstances. For instance, the public shares a strong interest in robust First Amendment protection of whistle-blowers who alert the media to gross governmental mismanagement or government created or abetted dangers to the community's health or safety. On the other hand, the government and the public share an interest in having very limited constitutional constraints on the dismissal of inefficient, dishonest, or unreliable civil servants.

Despite its imperfections, the public service model is certainly an advance over less complicated approaches such as the doctrine of privilege. However, because this approach requires a subjective and often elaborate balancing of the interest of employees, government, and the public, reasonable judges and personnel managers will often disagree on what the Constitution requires in specific circumstances. Judicial decision-making under the public service model not only has the potential to cause disagreement, but can also generate results that are difficult to follow and defy application to specific personnel decisions. As then Supreme Court Justice, and later Chief Justice, William Rehnquist noted:

> This customary "balancing" inquiry conducted by the court . . . reaches a result that is quite unobjectionable, but it seems to me that it is devoid of any principles which will either instruct or endure. The balance is simply an ad hoc weighing which depends to a great extent upon how the Court subjectively views the underlying interests at stake. (*Cleveland Board of Education v. Loudermill*, 1985:562)

Rehnquist was specifically addressing procedural due process issues involved in the dismissal of a municipal employee. Much the same can be said of judicial decision-making regarding free speech and other areas under the public service model, as is demonstrated by the following review of the contemporary constitutional law of public personnel.

## FREEDOM OF SPEECH

*Rankin v. McPherson* (1987) outlines the current approach for analyzing public employees' constitutional rights to nonpartisan free speech. Ardith McPherson was a nineteen-year-old probationary clerk in the office of Constable Rankin in Texas. While talking with a coworker shortly after an assassination attempt on President Ronald Reagan, she remarked, "Shoot, if they go for him again, I hope they get him" (322). Another office employee overheard her remark and reported it to Constable Rankin, who fired McPherson after hearing her admit to making the comment. Believing that the dismissal violated her right to free speech under the First and Fourteenth Amendments,[1] McPherson sued for reinstatement, back pay, and other relief. In analyzing the case, the Supreme Court's majority noted that "even though McPherson was merely a probationary employee, and even if she could have been discharged for any reason or for no reason at all, she may nonetheless be entitled to reinstatement if she was discharged for exercising her constitutional right to freedom of expression" (324).

The Court went on to explain the logical structure of public employees' right to free speech, beginning with whether the employee's remark touched on a matter of public concern (that is, of potential interest to the public). If a remark relates to a matter of public concern, it is considered of value to the public's informed discussion of government and public policy. Such comments are part of the free marketplace of ideas that is vital to the operation of our constitutional democracy. By contrast, statements of purely private concern, such as what one employee thinks of another's personality, intelligence, or clothes, are afforded minimal (if any) protection when they interfere with the proper functioning of government offices.

In *Rankin*, a 5–4 majority concluded that McPherson's remark touched upon a matter of public concern. It had been made in the context of a discussion of

Reagan's policies, and McPherson, an African American, apparently offered it as a way of punctuating her disdain for the administration's approach to minorities.[2] Next, upon determining that McPherson's comment touched on a matter of public concern, the Court proceeded with the balancing required by the public service model. When weighing the government's interest in discharging an employee for statements that somehow undermine the mission of the public employer, courts must consider the responsibilities of the employee within the agency. An employee's burden of caution and responsibility for the words they speak will vary with the extent of authority and public accountability that employee's role entails. Where, as was the case with McPherson, "an employee serves no confidential, policymaking, or public contact role," the potential harm to the public office as a result of that employee's private speech is minimal and is outweighed by the employee's First Amendment rights (328).

Public employees' free speech protections include a right to "whistle-blow," which generally involves alerting the public to gross waste, fraud, mismanagement, abuse, or specific government-created or abetted dangers to the health or safety of the community. The Supreme Court has reasoned that due to their positions inside government, public employees are sometimes uniquely able to contribute to the "free and open debate, which is vital to informed decision-making by the electorate" and "accordingly it is essential that they be able to speak out freely without fear of retaliatory dismissal" (*Pickering v. Board of Education*, 1968:571–572). A public employee's First Amendment protection for whistle-blowing is much narrower following the Court's decision in *Garcetti v. Ceballos* (2006). In *Garcetti*, the Court held that the First Amendment does not protect public employee speech made pursuant to one's professional duties, regardless of whether the content of the remarks is deemed a matter of public concern. In the 5—4 *Garcetti* holding, the Court's conservative majority conjured up the doctrine of privilege in determining that "Restricting speech that owes its existence to a public employee's professional responsibilities does not infringe any liberties the employee might have enjoyed as a private citizen. It simply reflects the exercise of employer control over what the employer itself has commissioned or created" (*Garcetti v. Ceballos*, 2006:421–422). In short, a public employee's expression as part of his or her work product does not enjoy First Amendment protection.

Though the true impact of *Garcetti* is not yet known, Justice Kennedy's opinion for the majority seems to suggest that whistle-blowers have more constitutional protection in their role as private citizens than they do as public employees. In other words, an employee garners more First Amendment protection if he or she raises a concern through external channels such as the media rather than through the professional chain of command or other internal channels established to protect whistle-blowers. Furthermore, rather than relying on the First Amendment to shield them from retaliatory action, the Court urges public employees who whistle-blow to familiarize themselves with and rely on protective statutes, such as the federal Civil Service Reform Act of 1978, as well as relevant state and local statutory protections. If a statement is covered by the terms of such statutes, it is automatically considered a matter of public concern and the government is prohibited from retaliating, regardless of how disruptive the comments may be.

Public employees' constitutional right to free speech does not extend to partisan management or campaigning. In the Supreme Court's view, the governmental interests in workplace efficiency and the appearance of partisan neutrality out-weigh the damage that governmental restrictions on political activity do to public employees' rights. Such measures also protect civil servants from being coerced by elected and politically appointed officials to support parties and candidates (*United Public Workers v. Mitchell*, 1947; *Civil Service Commission v. National Association of Letter Carriers*, 1973). The Court has given wide berth to govern-mental employers in this policy area by allowing considerable flexibility in the drafting of restrictions (*Broadrick v. Oklahoma*, 1973). Of course, the fact that political neutrality regulations are apt to be constitutional does not mean that governments will choose to impose them. The trend has been away from com-prehensive restrictions on public employees' participation in partisan activities. For example, the 1993 Federal Hatch Act reform modified a variety of restric-tions, some of which reached back to the early 1900s (see Rosenbloom, 1971:94–110). The Hatch Act reforms allow most federal employees to distribute partisan campaign literature, solicit votes (though not funds), work for partisan campaigns, and hold office in political parties. The amended law does not extend to members of the Senior Executive Service, however, and does not un-Hatch some agencies, including the Merit Systems Protection Board, and positions, such as Administrative Law Judge, on grounds that overt partisanship would undermine their missions or functions.

Can whistle-blowing and related political speech always be distinguished from partisan expression? The answer is clearly no, but the Supreme Court has yet to be confronted with the need to create a legal distinction between them. In terms of public personnel management, therefore, some uncertainty remains in this area, especially during electoral campaign periods. Applying the public service model to employees' speech can sometimes be further complicated by disputes over the exact content of the remarks at issue. In cases where the interpretations of speakers and bystanders differ, the public employer is permitted to act on what it reasonably believes was said, even in the absence of substantial evidence. The Supreme Court case law requires merely that the employer take reasonable steps to find out what the employee may actually have said. However, the Court's guidance in this area has been exceptionally vague: "only procedures outside the range of what a rea-sonable manager would use may be condemned as unreasonable" (*Waters v. Churchill*, 1994).

It is clear that the Supreme Court has given public personnel administrators much to think about regarding the scope of public employees' constitutionally pro-tected speech. In sum, the following must be considered: whether the remarks at issue were on a matter of public concern; whether they were made pursuant to an employee's official duties; the specific context in which they were uttered; the nature of the employee's position with reference to confidentiality, policymaking, and pub-lic contact; the relative value of the remarks' to the public discourse; and the remark's potential for disruption. To these factors must be added others from earlier case law, including, whether the speech involves prohibited political partisanship, suggests disloyalty to the United States, or is so without foundation that the employee's basic competence is called into question. Under the circumstances, it is not surprising the Supreme Court admits that "competent decision-makers may rea-sonably disagree about the merits of a public employee's First Amendment claim" (*Bush v. Lucas*, 1983:note 7).

## FREEDOM OF ASSOCIATION

The contemporary constitutional law regarding public employees' First Amendment right of freedom of association is also central to some aspects of public personnel management. In general, public employees' right to join organizations voluntarily (including political parties, labor unions, and even extremist racist and other anti-social groups) is well established, as is their right to refrain from associating with or supporting organizations (*AFSCME v. Woodward*, 1969; *Elfbrandt v. Russell*, 1966; *Shelton v. Tucker*, 1960; *Elrod v. Burns*, 1976; *Abood v. Detroit Board of Education*, 1977). However, two areas of public personnel management that have been specifically "constitutionalized" in this context should be noted.

First, it is possible for union security agreements to violate public employees' constitutionally protected freedom not to associate; no public employee can be required to join a union as a condition of holding his or her job. However, an agency shop is permitted: This arrangement requires nonunion members to pay a "counterpart" or "fair share" fee to the union that represents their collective bargaining unit. In *Abood v. Detroit Board of Education* (1977) the Supreme Court "rejected the claim that it was unconstitutional for a public employer to designate a union as the exclusive collective-bargaining representative of its employees, and to require nonunion employees . . . to pay a fair share of the union's cost of negotiating and administering a collective bargaining agreement" (*Chicago Teachers Union v. Hudson*, 1986:243–244). But the Court also held that "nonunion employees do have a constitutional right to 'prevent the Union's spending a part of their required service fees to contribute to political candidates and to express political views unrelated to its duties as an exclusive bargaining representative' " (*Chicago Teachers Union v. Hudson*, 1986:244).

Certain procedural safeguards accompany a public employee's First Amendment protection against being compelled to underwrite a union's political agenda. In the Supreme Court's words, ". . . the constitutional requirements for the Union's collection of agency fees include an adequate explanation of the basis for the fee, a reasonably prompt opportunity to challenge the amount of the fee before an impartial decision maker, and an escrow account for the amounts reasonably in dispute while such challenges are pending" (*Chicago Teachers Union v. Hudson*, 1986:249).

Beginning with its holding in *Elrod v. Burns* (1976), the Court establish substantial constitutional barriers to the use of political partisanship in public personnel decisions. *Elrod* was triggered when the newly elected sheriff of Cook County, Illinois, fired or threatened to dismiss Sheriff's Office employees who were not members of or sponsored by the Democratic Party. The employees bringing the suit were all Republicans holding non-civil service positions and had no statutory or administrative protection against arbitrary discharge. The Court held for the first time that patronage dismissals could violate public employees' freedom of association and belief. But it was divided and unable to form a majority opinion on the standard that the government must meet when dismissing someone based on partisan affiliation. Four years later, in *Branti v. Finkel* (1980), the Court revisited the issue of patronage dismissals. Two employees of the Rockland County, New York, Public Defenders Office were dismissed solely due to their affiliation with the Republican Party. The Court's majority now agreed that "the ultimate inquiry is not whether the label 'policy maker' or 'confidential' fits a particular position; rather, the question is whether hiring authority can demonstrate that party affiliation is an appropriate requirement for the effective performance of the public office involved" (518). This standard places a heavy burden of persuasion on elected officials and political appointees who would dismiss employees based on their partisan affiliation.

The next patronage case to reach the Supreme Court was *Rutan v. Republican Party of Illinois* (1990). The governor of Illinois ordered a hiring freeze prohibiting state officials from filling vacancies, creating new positions, or recalling furloughed employees without his "express permission." About 5,000 positions became open annually and several employees who were denied promotions, transfers, or recalls charged that the governor was "operating a political patronage system" by granting permission to fill openings only with employees having "Republican credentials" (62, 67). The Court held that "the rule of *Elrod* and *Branti* extends to promotion, transfer, recall, and hiring decisions based on party affiliation and support" (79). Accordingly, for most intents and purposes, partisanship is an unconstitutional justification for taking public personnel actions.

In reaching these decisions regarding public employees' freedom of association, the Supreme Court considered the various claims that union security arrangements strengthen labor-management relations and that patronage promotes democracy and loyalty to elected officials, as well as governmental efficiency. However, using the public service model, the Court concluded that these interests could be secured by means that were less invasive of public employees' First Amendment rights. The patronage cases illustrate that constitutional law is forever changing and that even "a practice as old as the Republic" may eventually succumb to new constitutional thinking (*Elrod v. Burns*, 1976:376).

## PRIVACY

The Fourth Amendment affords protection to private individuals against "unreasonable" government searches and seizures. Traditionally, courts have addressed Fourth Amendment issues in the criminal justice context. During the 1980s, however, as drug testing became common practice, the scope of the amendment's application to public employees emerged as an important issue in public personnel management. In law enforcement cases, the amendment requires that searches and seizures be pursuant to warrants, or, where these are impracticable, probable cause (reasonable suspicion that an individual is engaged in criminal wrong doing). In applying the public service model, courts have construed the Fourth Amendment to require that government employers meet a much lower standard to justify administrative (non-law enforcement) searches. Consistent with the public service model, this lower threshold both manifests and facilitates the government's significant interest in the performance of its employees and the efficiency of its agencies.

In *O'Connor v. Ortega* (1987), a divided Supreme Court held that "individuals do not lose Fourth Amendment rights merely because they work for the government instead of a private employer" (723). The justices also agreed that the relevant threshold question is whether the employee has a reasonable expectation of privacy in the workplace. Such an expectation is defined as one that, according to the courts, society is prepared to share. If there is no reasonable expectation of privacy, then the search will not violate the Fourth Amendment. If there is such an expectation, then the search must be reasonable in its inception and scope. In practice, this approach often requires that judges analyze cases individually on their own merits rather than according to broad principles. *O'Connor* requires that workplace searches of offices, desks, files, and so forth be based on a reasonable suspicion that an employee may have engaged in behavior for which discipline would be appropriate. Although the Supreme Court has yet to explicitly extend these protections to public employees' digital property, such as computer files or internet search records, public personnel managers may reasonably assume that the same legal framework applies in such cases. In *United States v. Simons* (2000), the Fourth Circuit held that the existence of an internal Central Intelligence Agency (CIA) policy outlining the Agency's intention to " 'audit, inspect, and/or monitor' employees' use of the Internet, including all file transfers, all websites visited, and all e-mail messages, 'as deemed appropriate,' . . . placed employees on notice that they could not reasonably expect that their Internet activity would be private" (398). With that said, this area of Fourth Amendment jurisprudence is changing rapidly, and a prudent public manager should keep a close eye on future developments.

The Supreme Court has held that in certain cases where the "special needs" of the government outweigh the privacy rights of individuals, public employers may conduct warrantless searches, even in the absence of a reasonable suspicion that an employee has engaged in wrongdoing. In most of these situations, the government's interests (as well as the public's) are asserted through suspicionless drug-testing programs, which randomly test certain public employees, regardless of whether there is a reasonable basis for believing that any of these employees use illegal drugs. For example, in *Skinner v. Railway Labor Executives Association* (1989), the Court held that the Federal Railroad Administration (FRA) may subject certain railroad employees, although working for private corporations, to random, suspicionless blood and urine tests for the presence of drugs or alcohol. The Court reasoned that the government's legitimate interest in protecting its citizens from railroad employees under the influence of alcohol or drugs significantly outweighed the Fourth Amendment privacy interests of the employees. In *National Treasury Employees Union v. Von Raab* (1989), the Court extended this rationale to those public employees who carry firearms or are engaged in drug interdiction. Accordingly, the Court noted that such employees have a reduced expectation of privacy "by virtue of the special, and obvious, physical and ethical demands of those positions" (711).

HIV and other health-related testing programs present similar legal issues. In this context, blood- and urine-testing regimes must be reasonable in terms of purpose and procedure. However, as such practices become more common it is increasingly difficult for employees and applicants to claim that they violate a reasonable expectation of privacy (see, e.g., *Fowler v. New York*, 1989).

Further, anyone engaged in law enforcement, public safety, and national security positions can be subjected to a reasonably designed suspicionless drug-testing program. Public personnelists should remember that such testing programs are for administrative objectives only, and evidence generated by them may not be used as the basis for criminal prosecution.

## LIBERTY

The broad issue of public employees' constitutional liberty has also been the subject of significant litigation. This area of jurisprudence, called *substantive due process*, focuses on the meaning of the word *liberty* in the Fifth and Fourteenth Amendments, which respectively prohibit the federal government and states (and their political subunits) from depriving anyone within their jurisdictions of life, liberty, or property without due process of law. Courts have interpreted the due process clause to include those fundamental rights that are "implicit in ordered liberty" and are "deeply rooted" in our society's history and traditions. Many of these rights, including, for example, the right to use contraception or the right to travel, are not mentioned explicitly in the text of the Constitution.

It is common, even natural, for government employers to exercise control over public employees, particularly where matters of public policy, workplace efficiency, and employee morale are concerned. To this end, Senator Sam Ervin found that in the 1960s public employees were requested "to lobby in local city councils for fair housing ordinances, to go out and make speeches on any number of subjects, to supply flower and grass seed for beautification projects, and to paint other people's houses" (United States Senate, 1967:9). Today, it is more common for federal employers to pressure employees to participate in blood drives, charitable campaigns, or other similar programs. A court will deem such conditions unconstitutional only if they are found to violate an employee's fundamental rights, or if the court determines the conditions to be nothing more than tenuously connected to the interests of the government (see *United States v. National Treasury Employees Union,* 1995). The liberty interests of public employees have the potential to affect government employment practices, but to date have not done so significantly. Public employees' reproductive decisions are an exception; their grooming preferences and residency requirements illustrate the general tendency.

*Cleveland Board of Education v. LaFleur* (1974) focused on the constitutionality of a policy requiring mandatory, unpaid maternity leave for public school teachers. The Court found the mandatory leave policy unconstitutionally restrictive, but used language broad enough to provide protection for public employees' reproductive choices. The Court stated that it ". . . has long recognized that freedom of personal choice in matters of marriage and family life is one of the liberties protected by the Due Process Clause of the Fourteenth Amendment" and that "there is a right 'to be free from unwarranted governmental intrusion into matters so fundamentally affecting a person as the decision whether to bear or beget a child' " (639).

In the Court's view, the liberty to bear children must remain free of undue or purposeless governmental interference. Choices with regard to grooming and residence have been given lesser protection. In *Kelley v. Johnson* (1976) the Court found no constitutional barrier to grooming regulations applying to male police officers. Although a lower court held that "choice of personal appearance is an ingredient of an individual's personal liberty" (241), the Supreme Court placed the burden of persuasion on the employee challenging the regulation to "demonstrate that there is no rational connection between the regulation . . . and the promotion of safety of persons and property" (247). The challengers were unable to do this despite the government's questionable rationale: The government claimed that the grooming standards would make the police more readily identifiable to the public (ignoring apparently, that police officers wear uniforms) and that they would promote esprit de corps, despite the police union's vehement opposition to them.

Finally, in *McCarthy v. Philadelphia Civil Service Commission* (1976), the Court upheld the constitutionality of residency requirements for firefighters. It did so without much discussion and in the face of petitioner McCarthy's rather compelling concern for the well-being of his family. The decision remains good law and, consequently, public employees can be required to live within the jurisdictions in which they work. Though these issues are not frequently litigated, and are no longer capturing headlines, the principles are still very much alive in current constitutional jurisprudence; public personnel managers should understand and follow the law established in this line of cases.

## EQUAL PROTECTION

Contemporary equal protection analysis under the Fourteenth and Fifth Amendments is of critical importance to public personnel management. Equal protection doctrine regulates government affirmative action policies and those government procedures that have a disparate impact on different social groups, as well as prevents overt discrimination against individuals based on race, ethnicity, citizenship, gender, age, and other factors. The threshold question in an equal protection inquiry is whether a law, policy, decision, or practice, classifies individuals according to some characteristic such as race, gender, wealth, residency, or education. Such categorizations—either overt or implicit—must be present in order to justify an equal protection challenge.

What distinguishes an actual classification, such as one created by law, from practices that are ostensibly neutral but have a disparate impact on different categories of people, such as racial groups or males and females? The Court addressed that difference in *Washington v. Davis* (1976), a case in which unsuccessful candidates to the Washington D.C. police academy sued on grounds that the department's use of an exam testing verbal skills, which African Americans failed disproportionally, amounted to a racially discriminatory hiring practice. In finding for the police department, the Supreme Court made clear that public personnel practices that appear neutral on their face but bear more harshly on one racial group than another, as has often been the case with merit examinations, will not be unconstitutional simply because of their disparate impact. To violate the equal protection clause, public practices must manifest a discriminatory purpose of some kind. The Court emphasized that such a purpose need not be "express or appear on the face of the statute" and made clear that it could be "inferred from the totality of the relevant facts" (*Washington v. Davis*, 1976:241–242). Such implicit classifications are treated identically to explicit ones.

Once they have determined that a classification exists, courts rely on a three-tiered structure to determine its constitutionality. What follows is a brief description of this framework, with a particular focus on the application of each tier in the context of public personnel management.

### Suspect Classifications

Courts consider classifications based on race or ethnicity as "suspect," or highly likely to violate equal protection principles. These suspect classifications, historically employed to disadvantage members of minority groups, are very difficult for governments to justify. Reviewing courts subject laws that create suspect classifications to "strict scrutiny," the most intense and exacting form of judicial review. In these cases, the government will bear a heavy burden of persuasion and receive little if any deference. Courts deem suspect classifications constitutional only if they are found to serve a compelling governmental interest and are "narrowly tailored" to achieve that purpose. To date, workforce diversity has not been considered a compelling governmental interest by the Supreme Court.[3] Affirmative action for members of minority groups may be viable if its purpose is to remedy past, proven discrimination against racial or ethnic groups. The leading case in this area is *United States v. Paradise* (1987), in which a federal judge imposed hiring and promotion quotas for African Americans in the Alabama Department of Public Safety. The case so divided the Supreme Court that it was unable to form a majority opinion. Nevertheless, most of the justices agreed that the remedy was a constitutional means to overcoming decades of discrimination and resistance to equal protection in the Alabama state patrol. A majority also agreed that the relief was adequately narrowly tailored.

In the public personnel context, narrow tailoring requires that five conditions be met:

1. Less drastic and equally efficacious remedies, such as fines, are impractical or unavailable.
2. There must be a fixed stopping point at which use of the classification ends. This may be based on time, for example, 3–5 years, or successful remediation of the previous violation of equal protection, such as minorities having gained 25 percent of the positions the governmental workforce involved.
3. The quotas, goals, or targets must be proportionate to the racial and/or ethnic composition of the relevant population base. For example, a 25 percent quota for African Americans would be disproportionate in Vermont, but not in Alabama.
4. Waivers must be available so that if the agency is unable to find qualified candidates then it will not be forced to hire or promote incompetents, on the one hand, or remain understaffed, on the other.
5. The approach cannot place a harsh burden on "innocent third parties." Firing or furloughing nonminorities to free up positions for minorities would be such a burden (see *Wygant v. Jackson Board of Education*, 1986).

In *Grutter v. Bollinger* (2003), dealing with affirmative action in the University of Michigan Law School, the Court added a sixth condition that logically applies in the public personnel context as well: That each candidate be afforded an individualized assessment of his or her qualifications.

It is important to note that racial and ethnic classifications will be considered suspect even if their purpose is to enhance minority employment opportunities. At various times since the 1970s, when the Supreme Court began hearing affirmative action cases, efforts have been made to distinguish between classifications based on "invidious discrimination" and those that are deemed "benign," or intended to promote the employment interests of minorities and women. In *Adarand Constructors v. Pena* (1995), a 5–4 majority of the Supreme Court deviated from previous Court jurisprudence and defied considerable academic commentary suggesting that benign racial or ethnic classifications pose little threat to equal protection because they lack a discriminatory purpose. The Court held that ". . . all racial classifications, imposed by whatever federal, state, or local governmental actor, must be analyzed by a reviewing court under strict scrutiny" (227). In the majority's view, requiring such scrutiny is the only way to ensure that there is no intent to discriminate, or if there is one, it is somehow justified by a compelling governmental interest and is narrowly tailored. In a concurring opinion, Justice Clarence Thomas took pains to explain that, in his view, the entire distinction between invidious and benign was untenable and irrelevant: ". . . government-sponsored racial discrimination based on benign prejudice is just as noxious as discrimination inspired by malicious prejudice. In each instance, it is racial discrimination, plain and simple" (241). In *Johnson v. California* (2005), a case involving prison administration, the Supreme Court held that racial classifications purported to be neutral rather than invidious or benign are also subject to strict scrutiny.

## Quasi-Suspect Classifications

Classifications based on gender are "quasi-suspect" and subject to an intermediate level of scrutiny. In these cases, the burden of proof is on the government to show that the classification is substantially related to the achievement of important governmental objectives. Originally, courts considered gender-based classifications nonsuspect, and evaluated them using a much less rigorous standard of review. As society and the judiciary became more conscious of the discriminatory effects of efforts to "protect" women from long working hours, physically demanding jobs, and so on, these classifications were raised to an intermediate level. In practice, courts evaluate gender-based classifications using a standard comparable to that of a strict scrutiny review, requiring governments to provide an "exceedingly persuasive justification" for their use (*United States v. Virginia*, 1996:533). Intermediate scrutiny poses a challenge to government employment practices based on traditional thinking about "male" and "female" jobs, workplace behavior, physical strength, and other capacities. Practices based on outdated perceptions of gender roles may be vulnerable to constitutional challenge. Although it is currently easier in a technical sense to justify affirmative action for women than for racial or ethnic minorities, public personnel managers should be alert to the likelihood that such programs will be unconstitutional in the absence of a very strong governmental interest.

## Nonsuspect Classifications

Courts consider classifications based on residency, wealth, age, and other similar factors to be nonsuspect. Public policies use such classifications frequently and for a variety of reasons—eligibility for benefits of some kind, voting, granting drivers' licenses, and so forth. Judges subject these classifications to a lower level of scrutiny through what has become known as the "rational basis" test. The burden of persuasion is generally on the challenger to show that such classifications are not rationally related to the achievement of a legitimate governmental purpose. Courts typically grant a large amount of deference to the judgment of lawmakers and governmental employers in such cases. For instance, the Supreme Court found a rational connection between the state's interest in public safety and its policy requiring police officers to retire at age 50. No equal protection violation was found, despite the fact that many officers would be physically and mentally fit to continue in their jobs well beyond age 50 (*Massachusetts Board of Retirement v. Murgia*, 1976).

## PROCEDURAL DUE PROCESS

In addition to its substantive aspects, the due process clauses of the Fifth and Fourteenth Amendments guarantee certain procedural rights to individuals being deprived of life, liberty, or property by a federal, state, or local government. In determining the extent of procedural due process to be afforded in administrative matters, courts balance three factors: (1) the individual's interests at stake; (2) the risk that the procedures used, if any, will result in an erroneous decision, and the probable value of additional procedures in reducing the likelihood of error; and (3) the government's interests, including administrative burdens and financial costs, in using the procedures in place. The underlying assumption in this formula is that although additional procedures will generally reduce mistakes, they also add costs. For example, the high cost of guaranteeing a full-fledged adjudicatory hearing, which includes the right to witness confrontation, cross-examination, and legal representation, might be considered necessary in cases where the interest at stake is substantial enough to require a very low error rate. On the other hand, where an individual's interest is minimal, the government may be required to provide nothing more than notice of the decision-maker's rationale and an opportunity to challenge the decision in writing. Cases involving the rights of public employees illustrate that procedural due process balancing takes place within the framework of the public service model.

In *Board of Regents v. Roth* (1972), the Supreme Court identified four individual interests which would give public employees a right to a full hearing in dismissal actions: (1) where the dismissal was in retaliation for the exercise of constitutionally protected rights, such as freedom of speech; (2) "where a person's good name, reputation, honor or integrity is at stake because of what the government is doing to him . . ." (573); (3) where the dismissal diminishes a public employee's future employability; and (4) where the employee has a property right or property interest in the position, such as tenure or a contract. The public service model is important in determining both the timing and the nature of the hearing. In *Cleveland Board of Education v. Loudermill* (1985), the Supreme Court held that a security guard who allegedly lied on his application was entitled to notice of the allegations, an explanation of the employer's evidence, and an opportunity to respond—all prior to being terminated. The Court noted that Loudermill had a property right in his job by virtue of being a "classified civil servant." The pretermination requirement is an "initial check against mistaken decisions—essentially, a determination of whether there are reasonable grounds to believe that the charges against the employee are true and support the proposed action" (545–546). This serves the interests of the employee, as well as those of the public and the government. In cases involving employment terminations, such as those at issue in *Roth* and *Loudermill*, a pretermination hearing frequently helps the state avoid additional personnel costs caused by unnecessary turnover and complex post-termination litigation.

A court's procedural due process balancing changes when employee suspensions are at issue. In *Gilbert v. Homar* (1997), the Supreme Court reasoned that no due process was required prior to suspending a law enforcement officer who had been charged with a felony. In this case, the governmental and public interests in an effective workforce outweighed those of the employee. As the Court explained, "So long as a suspended employee receives a sufficiently prompt post-suspension hearing, the lost income is relatively insubstantial, and fringe benefits such as health and life insurance are often not affected at all" (932). The Court also noted that the government has reasonable grounds for suspending an employee who has been formally charged with criminal behavior.

An adverse action triggering procedural due process protections may be based on a mix of factors, some of which involve constitutional rights and others that do not. For instance, an employer may also consider an employee who has engaged in controversial speech to be incompetent or disruptive for reasons unrelated to his or her speech. In such a case, the employer will have the opportunity to demonstrate "by a preponderance of the evidence that it would have reached the same decision . . . even in the absence of the protected conduct" (*Mount Healthy School District Board of Education v. Doyle*, 1977:287).

Because procedural due process analysis considers the probability that the government is acting in error, the public employer will often investigate an employee before taking disciplinary action. In *LaChance v. Erickson* (1998), the Supreme Court held that employees suspected of lying to or attempting to mislead investigators in an effort to defend themselves may be disciplined for their falsehoods without any violation of their due process rights. Courts have determined that the due process "right to be heard" does not protect an employee from sanctions resulting from lying. However, where an investigation may lead to criminal charges, the public employee does maintain the right to remain silent under the Fifth Amendment. As in other areas, the public service model's balancing approach in procedural due process cases provides public personnelists with a rough set of guidelines, but may not prove sufficient to inform particular administrative decisions. Individual facts and circumstances may ultimately determine close legal questions. For example, it is difficult in the abstract to know how quickly after suspending an employee must an employer provide a hearing in order to meet the current "prompt post-termination hearing" requirement. As always, the best way to keep track of answers to such questions is to follow the case law in one's jurisdiction, including rulings by the federal district courts and courts of appeals in one's judicial circuit.

## LIABILITY

It is important to emphasize that a public personnel manager's need for knowledge and understanding of relevant constitutional doctrine is much more than academic. As a result of several Supreme Court decisions over the past three decades, such knowledge has become a positive job requirement (Rosenbloom, 1992). Today, a public personnel manager occupying a position at any level of government may well be personally liable for compensatory and even punitive damages, if found to have violated "clearly established . . . constitutional rights of which a reasonable person would have known" (*Harlow v. Fitzgerald*, 1982:818; see also *Smith v. Wade*, 1983; *Hafer v. Melo*, 1991). *Clearly established* in this context does not require a judicial precedent in a case with materially similar facts; only that the public employee has "fair warning" from constitutional law and values that his or her behavior will violate someone's rights (*Hope v. Peltzer*, 2002).[4]

An exception to personal liability exists for federal personnelists in some cases where the individual whose rights have been violated is able to obtain a remedy in another way, such as through appeal to the Merit Systems Protection Board (*Bush v. Lucas*, 1983). Moreover, public employees have absolute immunity from civil suits for damages for violations of individuals' constitutional rights when the are performing adjudicatory functions, such as hearing examiners or "prosecuting" adverse actions (*Forrester v. White*, 1988; *Burns v. Reed*, 1991). Nevertheless, it is important to emphasize that absolute immunity attaches to the specific function rather than the job title. Thus, a hearing examiner has absolute immunity when engaged in adjudication, but not when hiring or firing his or her secretary.

It should be noted in this context that in addition to the federal constitutional principles outlined in this chapter, public personnelists must be aware of state constitutional law, which may also affect public personnel matters. Where a state's protection of public employees' rights such as privacy or substantive due process exceeds that of the federal Constitution, state and local personnelists must meet the higher state standard. Personnelists at all levels of government may avoid liability by exercising their constitutional "right to disobey" any order requesting implementation of an unconstitutional law or policy so as to prevent any infringement of others' protected rights (*Harley v. Schuylkill County*, 1979). This ability, of course, is premised on an understanding of the constitutional rights at issue and a comfort with the public service model for balancing all the interests at stake. Gaining reasonable knowledge of the constitutional law—both state and federal—that governs one's actions is the best way to avoid violating rights. Public personnelists need not be lawyers, but must develop the ability to recognize if and when decisions, actions, procedures, or policies run afoul of the law.

## CONCLUSION

The push to "reinvent" the public sector in order to improve program results generally serves two components of the public service model—the governmental and public interests. However, the interests and rights of employees may receive limited attention. The tools of reinvention—downsizing, reengineering, information technology, outsourcing, and competitive sourcing—can increase the immediacy of the Constitution to public administration. For instance, downsizing and reengineering can bump up against procedural due process and equal protection rights. Where civil service status or other property interests in employment are involved, dismissals cannot constitutionally be arbitrary, capricious, or discriminatory. If individual employees are picked as targets for reductions in force, they will almost certainly have substantial due process rights. Depending on the circumstances, and especially in cases where agencies have been under court order to increase diversity (as in *United States v. Paradise*), downsizing that has a harmful impact on the employment interests of minorities or women will be subject to challenge under the equal protection clause. Information technology, such as e-mail, voice mail, and database systems, pose obvious threats to employees' Fourth Amendment privacy rights.

Outsourcing presents a special set of constitutional issues when it involves a public function (such as incarceration) or so entwines the government and a private organization that it is impossible to tell where one begins and the other ends (e.g., public-private partnerships). In those circumstances, the private organization and its employees may well become liable for violating individuals' constitutional rights.

A private prison guard has the same constitutional obligations to the prisoners as does one who is publicly employed. However, the private guard faces a tougher standard of liability. Unlike a public employee, he or she will be liable for the violation of constitutional rights regardless of whether they were clearly established or a reasonable person would have known of them (*Richardson v. McKnight*, 1997). A public personnelist aware of constitutional principles and current doctrine could bring this constitutional dimension to bear on organizational decisions concerning outsourcing. Are the private organizations likely to be involved able to protect constitutional rights? Could their employees withstand liability suits?[5] Would it be better public policy to keep the function within the government agency in order to make sure that the employees are properly trained with respect to their constitutional responsibilities?

By taking a proactive role in alerting decision-makers to constitutional issues, particularly those presented in First, Fourth, Fifth, and Fourteenth Amendment jurisprudence, public personnelists will not only protect individual rights, but also reduce susceptibility to lawsuits. Incorporating a constitutional dimension into public administration will give managers better and more consistent information and skills to protect employees' rights as well as to achieve organizational goals within the framework of our democratic-constitutional government.

## NOTES

1. The first ten amendments to the Constitution, known as the Bill of Rights, apply directly to the federal government. The Fourteenth Amendment, which was ratified in 1868, prohibits the states (and their political subunits) from violating many of these rights as well. The due process clause of the Fourteenth Amendment protects individuals from the deprivation of life, liberty, or property by subnational governments. Over the years, the term *liberty* has been read by the Supreme Court to "incorporate" much of the Bill of Rights, including the First and Fourth Amendments, which are of particular importance to public personnel administration. This is why McPherson can argue that her First Amendment rights, which are incorporated into the Fourteenth Amendment, have been violated. Because the Fourteenth Amendment is what applies the First Amendment to state and local governments, she argues that it has been violated as well. As is discussed later in the chapter, the Fourteenth Amendment also prohibits the states and their subunits from depriving any person within their jurisdiction "equal protection of the laws." Known as the equal protection clause, this provision is interpreted to apply to the federal government through the word *liberty* in the Fifth Amendment, a process called "reverse incorporation."

2. *Connick v. Myers,* 461 U.S. 138 (1983), establishes that courts must consider a public employee's comment in its original context when evaluating whether the comment touches on a matter of public concern.

3. In *Grutter v. Bollinger* (2003), the Supreme Court held that diversity in higher education can constitute a compelling governmental interest. The Court's reasoning would seem to apply to diversity in public personnel administration as well: "In order to cultivate a set of leaders with legitimacy in the eyes of the citizenry, it is necessary that the path to leadership be visibly open to talented and qualified individuals of every race and ethnicity" (332).

4. As an interesting and relevant aside, courts may also hold local governments and agencies liable for monetary damages when their policies are closely connected to violations of individuals' constitutional rights, regardless of whether those rights can be said to be clearly established or should be reasonably known (Monell v. *New York City Department of Social Services, 1978; Pembaur v. Cincinnati, 1986*).

5. When considered governmental actors for constitutional purposes, private organizations contracting with state or local governments can be sued for violations of individuals' constitutional rights. Such organizations are not subject to suit for actions taken pursuant to a contract with the federal government (see *Correctional Services Corporation v. Malesko, 2001*).

# REFERENCES

*Abood v. Detroit Board of Education*, 431 U.S. 209 (1977).
*Adarand Constructors v. Pena*, 515 U.S. 200 (1995).
*AFSCME v. Woodward*, 406 F.2d 137 (8th Cir. 1969).
*Board of Regents v. Roth*, 408 U.S. 564 (1972).
*Branti v. Finkel*, 445 U.S. 507 (1980).
*Broadrick v. Oklahoma*, 413 U.S. 601 (1973).
*Burns v. Reed*, 500 U.S. 478 (1991).
*Bush v. Lucas*, 462 U.S. 367 (1983).
*Chicago Teachers Union v. Hudson*, 475 U.S. 292 (1986).
*Civil Service Commission v. National Association of Letter Carriers*, 413 U.S. 548 (1973).
*Cleveland Board of Education v. LaFleur*, 414 U.S. 632 (1974).
*Cleveland Board of Education v. Loudermill*, 470 U.S. 532 (1985).
*Connick v. Myers*, 461 U.S. 138 (1983).
*Correctional Services Corporation v. Malesko*, 534 U.S. 61 (2001).
*Elfbrandt v. Russell*, 384 U.S. 11 (1966).
*Elrod v. Burns*, 427 U.S. 347 (1976).
*Forrester v. White*, 484 U.S. 219 (1988).
*Fowler v. New York*, 704 F. Supp. 1264 (S.D.N.Y. 1989).
*Garcetti v. Ceballos*, 547 U.S. 410 (2006).
*Gilbert v. Homar*, 520 U.S. 924 (1997).
*Grutter v. Bollinger*, 539 U.S. 306 (2003).
*Hafer v. Melo*, 502 U.S. 21 (1991).
*Harley v. Schulykill County*, 476 F. Supp. 191 (E.D. Penn 1979).
*Harlow v. Fitzgerald*, 457 U.S. 800 (1982).
*Harvard Law Review*, "Developments in the Law-Public Employment," Vol. 97, pp. 1611–1800 (1984).
*Hope v. Peltzer*, 536 U.S. 730 (2002).
*Johnson v. California*, 543 U.S. 499 (2005).
*Kelley v. Johnson*, 425 U.S. 238 (1976).
*LaChance v. Erickson*, 522 U.S. 262 (1998).
*Massachusetts Board of Retirement v. Murgia*, 427 U.S. 304 (1976).
*McAuliffe v. New Bedford*, 155 Mass. 216 (1892).
*McCarthy v. Philadelphia Civil Service Commission*, 424 U.S. 645 (1976).
*Monell v. New York City Department of Social Services*, 436 U.S. 658 (1978).
*Mount Healthy School District Board of Education v. Doyle*, 429 U.S. 274 (1977).
*National Treasury Employees Union v. Von Raab*, 489 U.S. 656 (1989).
*O'Connor v. Ortega*, 480 U.S. 709 (1987).
*Pembaur v. Cincinnati*, 475 U.S. 469 (1986).
*Pickering v. Board of Education*, 391 U.S. 563 (1968).
*Rankin v. McPherson*, 483 U.S. 378 (1987).
*Richardson v. McKnight*, 521 U.S. 399 (1997).
Rosenbloom, David H. 1971. *Federal Service and the Constitution*. Ithaca, N.Y.: Cornell University Press.
———. 1992. Public Administrative Liability for Constitutional Torts, the Rehnquist Court, and Public Administration. *Administration and Society* 24, 2 (August):115–131.
*Rutan v. Republican Party of Illinois*, 497 U.S. 62 (1990).
*Shelton v. Tucker*, 364 U.S. 479 (1960).
*Skinner v. Railway Labor Executives Association*, 489 U.S. 602 (1989).
*Smith v. Wade*, 461 U.S. 30 (1983).
*United Public Workers v. Mitchell*, 330 U.S. 75 (1947).
*United States Senate*, "Protecting Privacy and the Rights of Federal Employees" S. Rept. 519. 90th Cong., 1st Sess. August 21, 1967.
*United States v. National Treasury Employees Union*, 513 U.S. 454 (1995).
*United States v. Paradise*, 480 U.S. 149 (1987).
*United States v. Simons*, 206 F.3d 392 (4th Cir. 2000).
*United States v. Virginia*, 518 U.S. 515 (1996).
*Washington v. Davis*, 426 U.S. 229 (1976).
*Waters v. Churchill*, 511 U.S. 661 (1994).
*Wygant v. Jackson Board of Education*, 476 U.S. 267 (1986).

# Human Resource Management in the Federal Government During a Time of Change

JAMES R. THOMPSON
ROBERT SEIDNER
University of Illinois–Chicago

The fifteen-year period from 1993 through 2007 was one of significant change in HRM policies and practices in the federal government. The most obvious manifestation of that change is the proliferation of agency-specific personnel systems. These systems represent a sharp departure from the long-standing practice whereby the vast majority of federal employees worked under the same set of rules. Associated with the new personnel systems has been an expanded use of paybanding in which pay is tied more closely to employee performance than is the case under the traditional General Schedule. Both paybanding and category rating, in which job candidates are ranked by category instead of by numerical score, represent ways in which line managers have been given greater authority over personnel matters.

The HRM changes have been driven by a host of demographic, political, and technological developments. For example, the impending retirement of large numbers of baby boomers from the federal workforce has precipitated what some have called a "human capital crisis." It is crisis in part because of the prospective loss by agencies of the knowledge, skills, and experience of this cohort of workers. There is further a concern about difficulties the federal government has had in recruiting replacements for departing workers. This is particularly the case for positions that require high levels of skill and expertise, such as scientists, engineers, and information technology specialists.

## THE FEDERAL PERSONNEL SYSTEM

The HR challenges facing the federal government are made more difficult by the large size and extreme complexity of the federal personnel system. With approximately

1.8 million civilian employees, the federal government is the largest employer in the country.[1] The federal workforce is spread across fourteen major departments and hundreds of independent agencies. These departments and agencies are engaged a broad range of functions from defense and national security to criminal justice, education, food safety, and tax collection. Each agency has a specialized mission and, as a result, special HRM needs and requirements. The workforce is also widely dispersed geographically with only about 12 percent located in the Washington DC metropolitan area (OPM, 2006b). A major challenge for policy makers is to create a single system that can accommodate the extreme diversity of the federal workforce.

## THE HUMAN CAPITAL "CRISIS"

Adding to that challenge are demographic trends that have raised questions about agency preparedness. In 2000, the Senate Subcommittee on Oversight of Government Management issued the *Report to the President: The Crisis in Human Capital* (U.S. Senate, 2000) based on a series of hearings on a range of HR-related topics including training, employee empowerment, workforce planning, employee retirements, and recruitment. The subcommittee found government practices in these and other areas to be deficient, concluding that, "these results constitute a stinging indictment of federal management" (14). The report contained multiple recommendations, some of which agencies could resolve within their existing structure (e.g., workforce planning, transforming HR specialists from support staff to strategic partners, making expanded use of technology) and some of which required legislative action (e.g., improving hiring, providing more training opportunities, linking pay more closely to performance).

The Government Accountability Office (GAO) has taken a similar position in labeling human capital management a "high risk area" along with other intractable issues such as procurement, financial accounting, entitlement programs, and information security.* Stating that human capital, "is the critical missing link in reforming and modernizing the federal government's management practices," the GAO commented in 2001 that, "the combined effect of these challenges serves to place at risk the ability of agencies to efficiently, economically, and effectively accomplish their missions, manage critical programs, and adequately serve the American people both now and in the future" (GAO, 2001:8). Human capital remained on the 2007 "high risk" list because GAO analysts believe agencies still often lack the right people in many jobs and because the loss of institutional knowledge from retirements has precipitated a "war for talent." The GAO identified a need for agencies to engage in strategic planning, to better manage employee performance, adding that, "to successfully transform themselves they must often fundamentally change their cultures so that they are more results-oriented, customer-focused, and collaborative in nature" (GAO, 2007d:9).

Two other high profile reports that focused on public service issues and the federal human crisis were issued by the National Commission on the Public Service (1989, 2003). The bipartisan committees urged policy makers to improve recruiting, limit the number of political appointments, increase the pay of federal workers, and reorganize inefficient operations. The 2003 report explicitly declares, "the organization

---

*The terms *human resources* and *human capital* are used interchangeably in this chapter.

of the federal government and the operation of public programs are not good enough: Not good enough for the American people, not good enough to meet the extraordinary challenges of the century just beginning, and not good enough for the hundreds of thousands of talented federal workers who hate the constraints that keep them from serving their country with the full measure of their talents and energy" (3).

The primary theme that emerges from these various reviews is the inadequacy of traditional approaches to HRM in the federal government. Of particular concern are (1) the long-standing philosophy that all agencies should abide by the same set of rules and (2) the lack of flexibility in the application of those rules by agencies and managers. These same two issues are at the heart of a set of HRM prescriptions that have been labeled *strategic human resource management* (SHRM). Prior to reviewing SHRM tenets in greater detail, we provide some background on the two most critical elements of the human capital crisis, the impending "retirement tsunami," and challenges relating to the recruitment of members of Generation Y to public service.

## The Retirement Tsunami

As of May 2006, the Office of Personnel Management (OPM) estimated that 60 percent of all federal employees would be eligible to retire within the following ten years and that 40 percent would actually retire (OPM, 2006a). More than 90 percent of the Senior Executive Service (SES), which includes the highest-ranking civil servants, will be eligible to retire within that span (GAO, 2007c). Turnover will be even higher in some categories of positions including Federal Aviation Administration (FAA) flight controllers at major airports (Rosenberg, 2007) and mine safety inspectors (GAO, 2007a).

Policy makers are concerned not just with the impending retirements, but with the approximate ten-year gap in hiring during the 1990s. As a result of large cutbacks in the size in the workforce during that period, only a thin pool of talent from which these positions can be filled is available. With the federal workforce increasingly dominated by oversight, regulatory, and contracting functions instead of the more traditional clerical and blue-collar functions, most new hires require years of experience and training before they are fully capable of performing their duties.

## The Recruitment Challenge

Complicating the challenge of replacing retiring workers are the negative attitudes toward public service exhibited by the members of "Generation Y."[2] The Partnership for Public Service (PPS) (2005) reported in 2005 that less than 10 percent of college seniors consider serving their country as the top reason to work in government. Less than 25 percent of the seniors believed that their parents would be proud of them for accepting government jobs.

Two of the major reasons the federal government has trouble attracting top college graduates are the slow pace of hiring and a lack of understanding of government employment. As recently as 2004, it was common for agencies to take more than a year to hire a new employee (Partnership for Public Service, 2006b). Another PPS survey (2006a) found that only 13 percent of college students felt knowledgeable about federal positions. The OPM has been leading efforts to reduce the amount of time it takes to hire and conduct background checks, but the reality of upholding merit principles adds levels of review not found in the private sector.

One way to expedite the hiring process is to make greater use of "excepted" appointments that allow agencies to make hires without going through lengthy competitive hiring procedures. The most prestigious such appointment is the Presidential Management Fellow (PMF), created by President Carter in 1978. The program is designed to lure holders of advanced degrees and develop them into future leaders.

The Federal Career Intern Program (FCIP) also offers a convenient alternative to traditional hiring methods. With FCIP, recruits are hired for an initial two-year period during which they receive extensive training in an effort to get them to the journeyman level. The employee is on probation for the entire two years and can be converted to permanent status at the end of that period at the agency's discretion. Agencies hired more than 11,000 FCIPs in 2005.

## STRATEGIC HUMAN RESOURCE MANAGEMENT

Both the GAO and the Senate Subcommittee on Government Oversight have urged the federal government to be more strategic in the development and application of HR policies. The key ideas associated with SHRM are that (1) HRM policies and practices should be tailored to agency mission and strategy and (2) that line managers should be allowed substantial discretion in making decisions regarding matters of hiring, pay, and promotion.

Traditionally, HRM was considered to be the province of the technicians. The assumption was that there was "one best way" to select, hire, pay, and promote employees and that the function should therefore be administered by those with expertise in the field. With SHRM, there is a recognition that there are a range of acceptable HR practices and further that the set of practices appropriate for an organization are those that best fit the organization's strategy.

Several important conclusions derive from these assumptions. One is that rather than have a single set of rules for everyone, agencies should be permitted to customize the rules to their own needs. A second conclusion is that, with a recognition that HRM practices are consequential for the achievement of agency goals and objectives, hiring, pay, and promotion authorities should be shifted from the personnel technicians to line managers. At the same time, the status of the HRM function generally is elevated within the organization. If HRM practices are critical to mission accomplishment, then HR officials need to be "at the table" when strategic decisions are made. This was the intent of the Chief Human Capital Officers Act of 2002 which directed that each of the larger federal agencies designates a chief human capital officer with status equivalent to that of the chief financial officer and the chief information officer.

### Paybanding

Compensation policies and procedures provide a good example of how strategic HRM differs from traditional HRM. In the federal government, the pay of most employees has long been set according to the provisions of the General Schedule.

Under the General Schedule each position is assigned to one of fifteen grades. Each grade is divided into ten "steps" such that a new hire would begin at step one and then move up a step every one, two, or three years depending on where he or she is in the range. Steps have become virtually automatic for the vast majority of federal employees with the result that longevity is a more important factor than performance in determining the relative pay of employees holding the same position.

The relative neglect of employee performance in the pay-setting process is one of the criticisms that has been levied against the General Schedule. Another is that the rules are simply too constraining; that managers have too little discretion on how the rules are applied. A third is that the system gives too much authority to the technicians, for example in deciding what grade a position is assigned.

Paybanding has emerged as the primary alternative to the General Schedule. To date, every agency that has been authorized to establish a separate personnel system has incorporated paybanding as part of that system. With paybanding, broad bands replace narrow grades with the salary range in some bands as high as 150 percent compared to only 30 percent in the General Schedule (Thompson, 2007b). Under this approach, there is less need for classification experts in the personnel office to make fine distinctions between the relative responsibilities of positions at different grade levels. Instead, a supervisor or manager equipped with some technical support can decide the band to which a position is assigned.

Paybands generally lack the steps that characterize the General Schedule. Within each band, pay increases are determined not by longevity but by the relative performance of each employee. The manager or supervisor of the unit makes the assessment. An advantage, especially in light of the increased emphasis on organizational performance that has ensued from passage of the Governmental Performance and Results Act of 1993, is that the individual who is held accountable for the performance of a unit has greater authority over compensation matters.

Paybanding also offers recruitment advantages. The salaries of new recruits can be set anywhere within the range to which their position is assigned, rather than, as with the General Schedule, only at the bottom of the range. This enhances the ability of agencies to compete with outside employers for scarce talent.

## Category Rating

Just as paybanding systems give line managers more authority over pay, so category rating gives line managers more authority over hiring. With the "rule of three," which traditionally guided federal hiring practices, job candidates were ranked according to test results. The hiring official was limited to selecting one of the top three individuals on the list even if other candidates scored nearly as well and even if, in the opinion of the hiring official, another candidate would be better suited to the job. With category rating, all candidates are grouped into categories, for example, "highly qualified," "qualified," and "not qualified." The appointing official can then select anyone from the top category for an open position, or once the top category is exhausted, from the second category. The effect is to allow managers more discretion in hiring individual(s) who, in their opinion, can best meet the needs of the unit. Category rating was first tested as part of a personnel demonstration project at the Department of Agriculture.[3] Congress extended category rating authority to all federal agencies in 2002.[4]

## Linking HR to Mission

One of the ideas associated with SHRM is that personnel systems should be tailored to organizational mission and strategy. This idea stands in sharp contrast to the federal tradition of a "one-size-fits-all" personnel system. In recent years, a number of agencies have asked Congress to be freed from some of the constraints of the Civil Service Law. Congress has responded by granting personnel flexibilities, particularly with regard to hiring and pay, to a number of agencies. Among the agencies authorized to create alternative personnel systems have been the Federal Aviation Administration (1995), the Internal Revenue Service (1998), the Department of Homeland Security (2002), and the Department of Defense (2003).

## The IRS and Strategic Human Resource Management

The Internal Revenue Service (IRS) provides a useful example of how one agency has employed the HR flexibilities it was granted to accommodate its mission and strategy. In 1998, Congress passed the IRS Restructuring and Reform Act (RRA 98), which was intended to address various management shortcomings that surfaced in the context of a failed attempt at modernizing the agency's data systems. The law directed the agency to improve the quality of services provided to taxpayers. A new commissioner, Charles Rossotti, was appointed to carry out that mandate. Rossotti led the agency through a massive restructuring, the centerpiece of which was a change from a geographically based organization structure to one centered on four divisions, each serving a different group of taxpayers. Accompanying this change was a reduction in the number of organizational layers and the implementation of a new set of "balanced" performance measures to include measures of employee and customer satisfaction as well as of "business results" (Rainey and Thompson, 2006).

In executing his strategy, Rossotti took advantage of a number of the personnel flexibilities incorporated into RRA 98. For example, the law included a provision for forty "critical pay" positions, the salary for which could be as high as that of the vice president (Rainey, 2001). The intent was to free the agency from the salary and hiring constraints associated with the General Schedule and the SES. Rossotti used the critical pay positions to bring in experts to help with the data systems modernization and also to hire individuals from the private sector who could drive his service-oriented change agenda within the new customer-oriented operating divisions.

RRA 98 also authorized the IRS to implement paybanding that was of value to the agency as it proceeded to reduce the number of hierarchical layers. With this authority, all GS-14 and GS-15 level positions were consolidated into a single "senior manager" payband and thereby eliminated any hierarchical distinction between the two. The IRS also created two additional payband systems, one for department managers and one for frontline managers.[5]

Workforce planning was another element of Rossotti's strategic approach to HRM. Historically, the agency had engaged in "binge hiring" whereby large numbers of employees were hired when budget conditions were favorable and very few when budget conditions were adverse. The problem facing the IRS was that large numbers of employees in mission-critical occupations like revenue officer and revenue agent would be retiring simultaneously, leaving the workforce denuded of mid- and senior-level managers. As a result of its analysis, the agency determined that the recruitment of new employees would be made a high priority and further that hiring would be kept at a constant level from year to year to ensure a continuous flow of new blood into the organization and to eliminate the binge hiring phenomenon (Thompson and Rainey, 2003).

RRA 98 also provided the IRS with workforce "shaping" tools, including early retirement, buy-outs, and retention bonuses. As the agency went through its restructuring, some employees were left without positions. To accommodate these "transition" employees, the agency made carefully targeted early retirement and buy-out offers.

## The President's Management Agenda

The Bush administration jumped on the SHRM bandwagon by including the "strategic management of human capital" as one of five government-wide initiatives included in the President's Management Agenda (PMA).[6] Of particular concern to the president were (1) the lack of workforce planning in the context of the retirement tsunami, (2) a lack of performance incentives within the General Schedule, (3) the "one size fits all" nature of the General Schedule, and (4) poor recruitment practices (OMB, 2002).

As a means of inducing agencies to address these problems the OPM created the "Human Capital Assessment and Accountability Framework" (HCAAF), which consists of "strategic alignment," "leadership and knowledge management," "results-oriented performance culture," "talent management," and "accountability" (OPM, 2007a). Within each of these five elements, OPM sets out quarterly goals and holds agencies responsible for meeting these goals. As of the June 30, 2008 "scorecard," only one agency (the National Science Foundation) was not either green or yellow, compared to the 2001 baseline results when only three agencies were yellow and the rest red. Once attaining green status, agencies still need to continue progressing or they can be downgraded.

One of the most significant operational changes to occur during this period was to embed accountability for human capital management within each agency. During the early years of the PMA, OPM engaged in oversight through compliance reviews. Starting in 2006, agencies with green ratings were required to conduct compliance reviews of their own in each of the HCAAF elements. Agencies are also required to submit annual reports to OPM that detail the results of their actions, not just list programs and activities. For example, agencies that identify a need to increase workforce diversity need to track how their outreach programs have resulted in new diversity hires. The intent is to institutionalize human capital planning practices and to embed proper human capital operations in the organizational culture.

## HUMAN RESOURCE MANAGEMENT CHALLENGES IN THE FEDERAL GOVERNMENT

In this section we review the HR challenges facing the federal government at the end of the first decade of the twenty-first century.

### Improving Employment Conditions

One such challenge is to improve workplace conditions as part of an effort to become the "employer of choice" for workforce entrants. Toward this end, OPM conducts the Federal Human Capital Survey (FHCS) in even-numbered years to gauge employees' impressions of how the government is managing its workforce. More than 220,000 employees completed the 2006 survey (OPM, 2007b). More than 90 percent of respondents agreed with the statement, "my work is important," more than 83 percent like the work they do, and a similar proportion believe their colleagues do high quality work. The lowest levels of satisfaction were with the management of poor performers, the lack of a link between pay and performance, and a lack of childcare subsidies.

Based on the results of the FHCS, the PPS issues a "Best Places to Work in Government" report that compares employee attitudes across agencies. The goal is to create a metric that inspires agencies to improve human capital management practices. Agencies are rated in six categories: employee skills/mission match, strategic management, effective leadership, work/life balance, pay and benefits, and teamwork. Two overall rankings are compiled, one for large agencies, and one for small agencies. In 2007, the Nuclear Regulatory Commission, the GAO, and the Security and Exchange Commission were rated best among the large agencies (Partnership for Public Service, 2007).

## Creating One System from Many

A second major challenge results from the "disaggregation" phenomenon: As a result of the successful attempts by a number of agencies to secure exemptions from various portions of the Civil Service Law, the federal sector is now characterized by diverse sets of employment rules across agencies. Among the most prominent agencies in this regard are the departments of Defense and Homeland Security, which collectively employ approximately 45 percent of the federal workforce. Other agencies that have been granted special personnel authorities include the FAA and the IRS.

The challenge that arises is to devise a framework that identifies common personnel rules to which all agencies must adhere, but to simultaneously allow some degree of customization of HR practices at the agency level. Although there has been a broad consensus that the traditional civil service model was too inflexible in this regard, there has not been agreement on the shape of a new system.

Although the decentralized model has enabled individual agencies to meet specific HR needs, there are a number of disadvantages with this approach from a governance standpoint. One is that as departments create their own personnel rules, there is a danger that employees will identify with their agency rather than with the government as a whole and the collective sense of identity that characterizes the civil service will be eroded as a result. The notion of acting on behalf of the public interest is displaced by a focus on agency-specific goals and objectives (Thompson, 2001).

Another issue is that while some agencies have been freed from the constraints of the Civil Service Law, others remain subject to its provisions. The danger is in creating separate "have" and "have not" groups. For example, agencies with paybanding systems gain a recruitment advantage over those that must continue to adhere to the General Schedule. There is the potential that talent will migrate from the "have not" agencies to the "have" agencies.

The central question that arises as a result of the disaggregation phenomenon is the identification of the elements that will remain common across the entire government. In 2004, the GAO convened a forum of HR experts to address the issue of fragmentation and to identify a government-wide framework for human resources reform (GAO, 2004). The principles that were identified, such as that, "merit principles that balance organizational mission, goals and performance objectives with individual rights and responsibilities," were so broad as to provide little guidance as to reformers. More discussion on this subject is likely at the policy level when a new president takes office in 2009.

## Accommodating Diverse Work Arrangements

An issue that has generated a lot of interest in federal HR circles partly as a result of pressures to privatize government work and partly because of changing workforce demographics is what has come to be called the *blended workforce*. This term refers to the use of part-time, seasonal, and contract workers as well as full-time, permanent employees to accomplish the government's work.

Discussions of the blended workforce highlight several interrelated issues. One is that in light of the recruitment challenges facing the government it makes sense for agencies to explore the use of alternative work arrangements that can serve to expand the pool of potential workers. For example, some categories of workers such as individuals with responsibility for caring for a family member may prefer part-time work. It would therefore be in an agency's interest to have part-time slots available to accommodate individuals in these categories.

Part-time work is particularly appealing to students and some agencies, accordingly, make extensive use of interns. Internship slots not only help the agency accomplish its mission but can serve as a vehicle to recruit for full-time, permanent positions. Once an intern's studies are complete, if he or she has performed in a satisfactory manner, he or she can be converted to a full-time position.

The blended workforce concept also highlights the issue of workforce flexibility. Some agencies need to be able to respond to surges in workload. For example, the park service needs to staff up during the warm weather months to accommodate visitors to the national parks. Similarly, the IRS has to bring in additional employees during tax season. Both agencies make extensive use of seasonal positions to accommodate their needs. The seasonal work pool in turn serves as a good source of recruits when full-time jobs open up.

Contract workers also offer flexibility advantages. The Naval Research Laboratory (NRL) enters into contracts with staffing firms whereby individuals with specialized skills are brought in on a temporary basis to work alongside regular employees on a research project (Thompson and Mastracci, 2005). Once the project is complete, the contract worker can be reassigned or simply released. From the agency perspective, the use of contract workers in place of permanent employees offers significant advantages. First, staffing firms are not bound by federal hiring and pay restrictions and thus have recruitment advantages over the agency. Second, permanent employees cannot be let go at the end of a project without going through lengthy reduction-in-force procedures. According to NRL officials, the costs associated with contract workers are higher than for permanent workers but not dramatically so.

With the increasing volume of retirements, some agencies have turned to retired workers to help them with their employment needs. The agency gets the advantage of an individual who has needed skills and experience while the annuitant is provided with a source of additional income. In most cases, the work is on a part-time or temporary basis. One obstacle to this arrangement is a policy that was designed to deter "double dipping" by reducing the annuitant's pension by the amount of any federal earnings. However, in recognition of the potential value of such workers to the government, OPM has changed its policy to allow agencies to bring back retired workers on a limited basis without financial penalties (Barr, 2007a). The challenge facing agencies is how to integrate a diverse array of possible work arrangements in a way that is most conducive to mission accomplishment.

## Technology and HRM

Similar to other employers, the federal government is seeking to take advantage of new information technologies to expedite and enhance HR practices. The biggest change has been the adoption of automated hiring software. The three major systems, OPM's USAStaffing, Monster's QuickHire, and Resumix all operate with the same principles. Position descriptions, job announcements, and question libraries are all saved. When a selecting official wants to recruit for a new position, the announcement can be created using online tools. Once the announcement is created, it is posted on OPM's USAJobs. gov web site. Applicants apply online thereby eliminating the delays associated with paper. Selecting officials determine how much weight they want to give each question, while the HR office creates "screen-outs" that automatically reject candidates who do not have the minimum qualifications. The systems then score and rank the applicants. The only manual process is to validate the qualifications of the top candidates to ensure they are indeed eligible and have submitted required documents.

USAJobs.gov is rapidly changing the nature of how agencies hire. Applicants are able to save five different versions of their resume and create ten "search agents" who e-mail them when the types of positions they are looking for are open. OPM has invested significant resources in the web site to include functions that include how to choose a federal position based on previous interests and experience, how to apply for a position, and how to understand federal service. Approximately 20,000 jobs are posted daily.

Technology is changing other HR functions as well. The majority of HR forms are now electronic, eliminating much of the paper-intensive work. Electronic Official Personnel Files (eOPFs) are replacing the hard copy folders that formerly required constant upkeep as an employee progressed through his or her career. OPM is also in the midst of major technology upgrades to digitize retirement processing, which previously relied on 144,000 file cabinets and to enhance background investigations, which used to take more than a year to complete because of the paper-intensive processes.

## Labor-Management Relations

Relations between the administration and the federal employee unions were extremely contentious during the second Bush presidency. Shortly after taking office, Bush revoked an executive order that had been issued by President Bill Clinton mandating the creation of partnership councils within which management could discuss workplace issues with their unions. And in 2003, the head of the newly created Transportation Security Agency directed, over union protests, that agency employees would not be allowed to bargain collectively.

The labor-management issue that garnered the most attention was the Bush administration's proposal to limit the collective bargaining rights of employees in the departments of Homeland Security and Defense. The Bush administration proposed that management at the two agencies be granted exclusive authority over matters that, in the rest of government, agencies were permitted to bargain with unions over (Thompson, 2007a). The proposals for the two systems would further have denied employees the right to appeal labor-management matters to the Federal Labor Relations Authority. The only appeal rights would have been to internally constituted boards in the two agencies.

A coalition of federal employee unions took the administration to court over provisions that would have allowed the secretaries of both Defense and Homeland Security to unilaterally abrogate contracts with the unions. In the case of Homeland Security, the courts ruled in favor of the unions and directed the proposed HR regulations be revised. Although the decision related only to labor-management matters, the department put implementation of the entire system, including the paybanding and pay-for-performance elements, on hold. Further action is not likely until a new administration takes office in 2009.

The Defense Department's new personnel system, called the National Security Personnel System (NSPS), was upheld by the courts. However, the labor-management provisions of that system have generated opposition in Congress and the department has refrained from implementing them. The paybanding/pay-for-performance elements of NSPS have gone forward.

## CONCLUSION

The next president will face a host of HR challenges. Foremost among them is that of devising a new framework to replace the traditional one-size-fits-all approach embodied in the Civil Service Law. A key issue will be to determine what features of the system should be common across agencies and on which agencies can be given flexibility. There is widespread consensus in favor of giving agencies more discretion on matters such as pay and hiring but there has not been an agreement on specifics. Another challenge is how to make government employment more appealing to younger workforce entrants, This is closely related to quality of work issues: what can agencies do to develop a work environment in which employees feel challenged and engaged? Yet another challenge is to help each agency develop the optimal mix of full-time, part-time, seasonal, temporary and contract workers that enables the accomplishment of the agency's mission in as efficient and effective manner as possible. A common theme is change and a key question is whether policy makers can be proactive in addressing these challenges.

## NOTES

1. U.S. Office of Personnel Management, "Trend of Federal Civilian On-Board Employment for Executive Branch (U.S. Postal Service Excluded) Agencies," 2007. http://www.opm.gov/feddata/html/ExecBranch.asp (accessed October 9, 2007).
2. Defined as those born between the years of 1978 and 2000. See http://en.wikipedia.org/wiki/Generation_Y.
3. As part of the Civil Service Act of 1978, agencies can apply to be a personnel demonstration project for purposes of experimenting with a new HRM technique.
4. As part of the National Defense Authorization Act of 2002.
5. Under the provisions of RRA 98, paybanding for bargaining unit personnel can only be instituted upon agreement with the union. As of 2007, no such agreement has been forthcoming.
6. The others were competitive sourcing, improved financial performance, expanded electronic government, and budget and performance integration.

# REFERENCES

Barr, Stephen. 2007a. OPM Suggests Retirement Reforms. *Washington Post.*
———. 2007b. Union Suit Against Intern Program May Revive Debate on Fairness in Hiring. *Washington Post.*
GAO. 2001. *High Risk Series: An Update.* Washington, DC: Government Printing Office.
———. (2004). Forum: Human Capital: Principles, Criteria and Processes for Governmentwide Federal Human Capital Reform.
———. 2007a. *MSHA's Mine Inspector Recruiting and Workforce Planning.* Washington, DC: Government Printing Office.
———. 2007b. *High Risk Series: An Update.* Washington, DC: Government Printing Office.
———. 2007c. *Human Capital: Diversity in the Federal SES and in the Senior Levels of the U.S. Postal Service.* Washington, DC: Government Printing Office.
———. 2007d. *Human Capital: Federal Workforce Challenges in the 21st Century Issues.* Washington, DC: Government Printing Office.
National Commission on the Public Service. 1989. *Leadership for America: Rebuilding the Public Service.* Washington, DC: National Commission on the Public Service.
———. 2003. *Urgent Business for America: Revitalizing the Federal Government for the 21st Century.* Washington, DC: National Commission on the Public Service.
GAO. (2007b). High Risk Series: An Update. Washington, DC, Government Printing Office.
OMB. 2002. *The President's Management Agenda.* Washington, DC: U.S. Office of Management and Budget.
OPM. 2006a. *OPM Director Springer Launches Major Media Campaign During Newsmaker Event at the National Press Club.* Press Release May 1, 2006.
———. 2006b. *Federal Civilian Workforce Statistics.* Washington, DC: U.S. Office of Personnel Management.
———. 2007a. Human Capital Accountability and Assessment Framework Resource Center. https://www.opm.gov/hcaaf_resource_center/. Accessed on October 20, 2007.
———. 2007b. Federal Human Capital Survey 2007. http://www.fhcs2006.opm.gov/What/#What. Accessed on October 20, 2007.
Partnership for Public Service. 2005. *The Class of 9/11: Bringing a New Generation of Practical Patriots into Public Service.* Washington, DC: Partnership for Public Service.
———. 2006a. *Back to School: Rethinking Federal Recruiting on College Campuses.* Washington, DC: Partnership for Public Service.
———. 2006b. *Hire Education: U.S. Department of Education.* Washington, DC: Partnership for Public Service.
———. 2007. *Best Places to Work in the Federal Government 2007 Rankings.* Washington, DC: Partnership for Public Service.
Rainey, H. G. 2001. *A Weapon in the War for Talent: Using Special Authorities to Recruit Crucial Personnel.* Washington: IBM Center for the Business of Government.
Rainey, H. G., and J. R. Thompson. 2006. Leadership and the Transformation of a Major Institution: Charles Rossotti and the Internal Revenue Service. *Public Administration Review* 66:596–604.
Rosenberg, Allysa. 2007. Empty Towers. *Government Executive* 39:28–34.
Thompson, J. R. 2001. The Civil Service Under Clinton: The Institutional Consequences of Disaggregation. *Review of Public Personnel Administration* 21:87–113.
———. 2007a. Federal Labor–Management Relations Reforms Under Bush: Enlightened Management or Quest for Control? *Review of Public Personnel Administration* 27:105–124.
———. 2007b. *Designing and Implementing Performance-Oriented Payband Systems.* Washington, DC: IBM Center for the Business of Government.
Thompson, J. R., and H. G. Rainey. 2003. *Modernizing Human Resource Management in the Federal Government: The IRS Model.* Washington: IBM Center for the Business of Government.
Thompson, J. R., and S. Mastracci. 2005. *The Blended Workforce: Maximizing Agility Through Nonstandard Work Arrangements.* Washington: IBM Center for the Business of Government.
U.S. Senate, 2000. *Report to the President: The Crisis in Human Capital.* Washington, DC: Government Printing Office.

# Personnel and Human Resource Management in the States

SALLY COLEMAN SELDEN
Lynchburg College

*Produced by Sally Selden in partnership with the Government Performance Project of the Pew Center on the States. The views expressed are those of the author and do necessarily reflect the views of the Government Performance Project, the Pew Center on the States or The Pew Charitable Trusts.*

## INTRODUCTION

Much has been written in recent years regarding changes that are taking place within the field of public personnel or HRM (Kellough and Nigro, 2006). Increasingly, personnel or HR professionals are assuming more of a strategic partner role within state government organizations (Effron, Grandossy, and Goldsmith, 2003; Selden, 2006). Specifically, in the better managed states, HR professionals are taking a much more active role in helping their agencies achieve their objectives by designing HR systems and practices that emphasize the goals and values of their agencies, as well as improving efficiency and flexibility. The state of the art for HRM in states is evolving rapidly, largely due to constant technology changes, but also because of ever increasing long-term fiscal pressures (which require savvier management), and massive shifts in the state workforce. These changes are particularly important in an increasingly knowledge-based economy, where the value of a state government is often based upon intangible assets within the minds of employees themselves. The ability of state governments to hire and retain talented individuals, who leverage knowledge to deliver value to citizens, is indispensable to achieving and maintaining high-quality public services.

The challenges of a knowledge-based environment are exacerbated by the graying state government workforces. Many state governments could have more than 25 percent of their workforces retire by 2012. This will be beneficial to the younger generation, who will have numerous career opportunities ahead, but will be detrimental to state government agencies that will face increasing competition to find and hire qualified individuals.

This chapter draws upon the experience of state governments as documented by the Government Performance Project (GPP), which analyzed states' HR systems in 1998, 2000, 2003, and 2007.[1] Over the past ten years, the GPP has witnessed many changes in state HR (civil and non-civil service) systems. At the same time, the legacies of traditional civil service systems and collective bargaining are deeply entrenched in some states where changes have been more challenging to implement, although states, such as Wisconsin, have been successful in doing so (Fox and Lavigna, 2006). First, this chapter discusses the concept of civil service in state governments. Second, it explores characteristics of state HR systems, highlighting the complexity and differences that exist across states. Third, it describes broad HR change strategies witnessed in states between 2004 and 2007 and examines factors associated with those changes. Finally, it discusses the most important predictors of employee retention within state governments—compensation and benefits.

## CIVIL SERVICE IN STATE GOVERNMENTS

The origins of state merit systems are inextricably linked to the depoliticization of the civil service (Aronson, 1974; Conover, 1925). Over 125 years ago, the Pendleton Act provided the blueprint for a modern, unified, and politically impartial civil service. The hallmarks of a "merit" system include relative security of tenure in office, the use of written, competitive examinations, and neutral administration (Sylvia and Meyer, 2001). New York enacted the first civil service system in 1883—the same year Congress passed the Pendleton Act (Conover, 1925). The following year, Massachusetts implemented its civil service (Conover, 1925). It took more than twenty years before another state, Wisconsin, established a merit system for its state government (Aronson, 1974; Conover, 1925). In the 1920s and 1930s, technical developments in the field of personnel, including testing and classification, laid the groundwork for a more scientific approach to HRM. Despite the advances, many states did not adopt civil service legislation until the passage of the Social Security Act in 1935, which included a provision for grants to states. The act stipulated that states must be "federally approved," which meant that states needed to guarantee proper and efficient administration to receive funding. Leonard White, proclaimed in a 1945 article in the *Public Personnel Review*, "the importance of this amendment to the steady improvement of personnel standards in the State and county government cannot be exaggerated" (Aronson, 1974:136). The legacy of the type of civil service system established by the Pendleton Act is evident. Today, some states have a civil service system characterized by an elaborate, and sometimes fragmented, web of laws, rules, regulations, and techniques embracing the merit principle. For example, New York's structure governing its civil service system is, according to Riccucci (2006:305), "fragmented and overlapping. This is statutorily driven. For managers and human resources specialists, it engenders a good deal of frustration and tension." States, however, vary in terms of the percentage of employees covered by their classified civil service system.

Employees covered by civil service systems are often referred to as *classified* or *merit* employees. In Table 4.1, the GPP data show that the percent of classified employees across states did not change between 1999 and 2007. In the mid-to-late

**TABLE 4.1    State Government Workforce Characteristics (as of June 30, 1999 and June 30, 2007)**

| State Workforce Characteristic | 1999 (percentage) | 2007 (percentage) |
| --- | --- | --- |
| Classified | 87 | 87 |
| Political appointee* | | 3.8 |
| Covered by labor agreements | 46.30 | 47.30 |
| Temporary | 6.33 | 7.11 |

* GPP did not collect this data in 1999.

1990s, a few states, such as Florida and Georgia, shifted a significant amount of their workforce from the classified service to the non-classified service or an employment-at-will system.[2] Most civil service systems provide employees certain administrative and legal due process rights before discharging them for cause, although the rights vary across classified merit systems (Lindquist and Condrey, 2006). The rationale for providing such protections was to protect public sector employees from partisan pressure and removal. "Employment at will" typically connotes an employer's right to terminate an employee without a reason and an employee's right to leave when she or he elects. Both federal legislation and state laws provide exceptions to the doctrine of employment at will, including, but not limited to, participation in union activities, whistleblowing, public policy, employer motivation, race, ethnicity, religion, national origin, sex, and disabilities. Montana, for example, is the only state that has passed legislation that prohibits employers from discharging employees without "good cause."

Today, more than 80 percent of Georgia's workforce is in the non-classified service—a number likely to rise as members of the classified service retire. Other states have allowed employees to voluntarily shift from the classified to non-classified system. In 2006, Utah consolidated its Department of Technology Services, and 92 percent of its employees converted voluntarily to the non-classified service and became at-will employees. Kansas has increased its use of non-classified service because the non-classified service provides the state greater flexibility with respect to compensation. Louisiana's Civil Service Commission established a new category of non-classified positions for hospitals to augment their regular staff but the use of these positions is limited to 10 percent of a hospital's staffing needs. According to the state, the newly created non-classified "pool" of employees prefer to work under short-term contracts with higher salaries instead of benefits. Despite changes within states, the percentage of classified positions in states has not changed (see Table 4.1).

States take different approaches to managing their non-classified employees. Employees in the non-classified service in some states, such as Alabama and Connecticut, are subject to the same rules and regulations of employment that apply to employees in the classified service except regarding appointment and dismissal. In other states, such as Nebraska and New Hampshire, the central HR department does not have any authority over non-classified employees and therefore they do not maintain records in the central HR department on those employees. In Virginia, state

TABLE 4.2   Correlation of Percentage of Workforce Classified and Termination Metrics

| Termination Metric | Pearson Correlation |
| --- | --- |
| Involuntary turnover FY 06—classified employees | 0.16 |
| Involuntary turnover FY 05—classified employees | 0.13 |
| Involuntary turnover FY 04—classified employees | 0.25 |
| Involuntary turnover FY 06—non-classified employees | 0.04 |
| Involuntary turnover FY 05—non-classified employees | −0.03 |
| Involuntary turnover FY 04—non-classified employees | −0.06 |
| Average days to terminate classified employee for performance | 0.15 |
| Average days to terminate classified employee for behavior | −0.01 |
| Average days to terminate non-classified employee for performance | −0.00 |
| Average days to terminate non-classified employee for behavior | −0.06 |

agencies with non-classified employees are responsible for establishing their own set of HR policies for those employees.

One of the key assumptions underlying the argument to move from a classified to non-classified or at-will employment personnel system in the public sector according to Lindquist and Condrey (2006:102) is that civil service "procedures impede discipline and termination of unsatisfactory employees." Thus, we might expect more terminations in states with a larger share of employees in non-classified service. As shown in Table 4.2, the GPP did not find significant relationships between the percentage of a state's classified workforce and different termination metrics. For example, the percentage of a state's workforce that was classified is not correlated significantly with the percentage of classified or non-classified state employees fired in FY 2004, FY 2005, or FY 2006.

## CHARACTERISTICS OF STATE HUMAN RESOURCE SYSTEMS

Historically, in a traditional classified civil service system, the authority to administer HR activities belonged to a central personnel or HR department. The purported benefits of this approach included equitable treatment of employees, consistency in the delivery of services, efficiency gains through economies of scale, and clearly delineated roles between central HR department and state agencies. In the 1990s, many scholars and practitioners pushed for state central HR departments to decentralize their authority over some HR practices and provide more flexibility to public agencies and their managers (for a discussion, see Kellough and Nigro, 2006). Today, as shown in Table 4.3, the development of HR policies, classification, and compensation are the operations most likely to be centralized, whereas responsibility for workforce planning and recruitment are significantly more likely to be shared between the central HR department and operating agencies.

**TABLE 4.3   Division Responsibilities for Selected HR Operations**

| HR Operation | Mean* |
|---|---|
| HR policy development | 1.39 |
| Compensation | 1.53 |
| Classification | 1.63 |
| Administration of employee benefits | 1.69 |
| Labor relations | 2.00 |
| Testing | 2.15 |
| Training and development | 2.18 |
| Workforce planning | 2.22 |
| Recruitment | 2.29 |

* Scale: 1: Completely or mostly centralized; 2: Responsibilities
are split evenly among central and operating agencies;
3: Completely or mostly decentralized to operating agencies.

As shown in Table 4.4, states on average employ approximately 1.2 HR staff (both operating agency and central HR) per 100 state employees. The majority of HR employees are housed in state operating agencies, but some states, such as Iowa, Indiana, Michigan, South Dakota, and Utah have over 30 percent of their HR staff located centrally. After centralizing all of its HR services in July of 2006, Utah's Department of HRM grew from 38 to 182 staff members. On the other end of the spectrum of centralization is Texas, which is the only state without a central HR office. Each Texas state agency is responsible for implementing and managing its own administrative and HR functions (Coggburn, 2006). A report released in January 2007 by the Texas Legislative Budget Board Staff (2007:53) indicates some concerns about Texas' decentralized HR model. In light of a number of weaknesses identified in its decentralized HR structure, the Texas Legislative Budget Board Staff (2007:53) recommended amending the Texas Labor Code as follows:

- create a statewide Office of HRM;
- create a uniform state employee handbook that allows necessary flexibility while ensuring that all state employees are treated fairly and consistently;

**TABLE 4.4   Characteristics of States' Central HR Department (as of June 30, 2007)**

| Characteristic | |
|---|---|
| Total HR staff per 100 state employees | 1.2 |
| Central HR staff per 100 state employees | 0.25 |
| HR staff working in central HR office | 23.19% |
| Central HR staff certified by SHRM | 7.43% |
| Central HR staff certified by IPMA-HR | 2.16% |
| Average HR costs per employee | $228 |

- require the Office of HRM to study opportunities to strategically consolidate HR administration; and
- repeal the cap on HR staff at state agencies (currently there is one HR employee for every eighty-five agency employees).

While many people may assume that the central state HR department has authority over executive branch employees only, this is true in about half of the states. Some states, such as South Carolina and Nevada, oversee higher education—colleges, universities, and polytechnics—employees; while other states, such as Minnesota and Georgia, are responsible for employees in the legislative and judicial branches. Local employees in North Carolina, New Jersey, and New York are served by the state's central HR system. The New York State Department of Civil Service works with approximately one hundred state agencies, authorities, boards, councils, commissions, development corporations, and foundations. The Department of Civil Service's Municipal Service Division also provides technical assistance and examination services to improve the administration of the state's 101 municipal civil service agencies (excluding New York City), which cover approximately 387, 921 local government employees. The Department of Civil Service focuses attention on providing state and local government managers with HR services that anticipate the changing nature of work and the increasing diversity of the workforce.

## CHANGES TO STATE HUMAN RESOURCE SYSTEMS

Selden, Ingraham, and Jacobson (2001) found that there was no single approach to contemporary merit system reform; this remains true. Between 2004 and 2007, only 20 percent of states indicated that they had implemented civil service reforms. Colorado indicated that it had tried to implement reforms to its civil service but voters defeated it; New Jersey responded that it hoped to implement civil service reforms in the future. Washington implemented the most significant state civil service reform during this period. On July 1, 2005, following three years of intense work and unprecedented collaboration across state government, Washington implemented the Personnel System Reform Act of 2002. Washington's personnel reform touched every state general government employee and more than one hundred agencies, boards, and commissions. The reform represents the most sweeping changes to the state's civil service system in more than forty years and was accomplished by "balancing the demands of many constituencies served by government, including elected political leaders and their appointees, legislators, line managers, rank-and-file employees, labor unions, veterans, minority groups, women's groups, personnel appeals commissions and boards, courts, job applicants, the public" (Fox and Lavigna, 2006:281–282). Washington's reforms include the following provisions:

- new rules covering virtually all aspects of human resource management, such as hiring, compensation, performance management, training, corrective action, and layoff;
- a streamlined and consolidated classification system;
- representation of state employees by labor unions, allowing collective bargaining with the Governor for wages and benefits;
- reduced restrictions on contracting for work traditionally done by state employees;

TABLE 4.5   Percentage of States Implementing HR Changes or Initiatives

| | Implemented in Past Two Fiscal Years (percentage) | Planning to Implement in the Next Two Fiscal Years (percentage) | No Plans to Implement (percentage) |
|---|---|---|---|
| Process improvement | 65.9 | 34.1 | 0.0 |
| Shared services | 39.0 | 26.8 | 34.1 |
| Decentralization | 24.4 | 12.2 | 63.4 |
| Outsourcing | 19.5 | 9.8 | 70.7 |

- new HR information management system capable of supporting personnel reform, including e-recruiting;
- "just cause" discipline system; and
- flextime.

Moreover, Washington's new personnel system integrates competencies (knowledge, skills, abilities, and behaviors) across HR processes, including recruitment, assessment, selection, development, performance management, and succession planning.

As shown in Table 4.5, the GPP found that states implemented an array of different HR restructuring or change initiatives which is consistent with Hal Rainey's observation that (2006:36) "the continuing complaints about the rigidity of the civil service personnel systems have motivated governments to pursue flexibility using many different paths." A review of state efforts show that some are targeted toward improving HR processes, such as the hiring and classification examples discussed next, and others introduce more sweeping changes to a state's civil service or HR system, such as the Michigan example, which will be discussed later.

## HR Process Improvements

Arizona, for example, deployed four automated HR applications, including its Hiring Gateway, an automated recruitment system. It provides a paperless Internet-based process that eliminates time-consuming paper tasks and reduces the calendar time to complete the process. Interested job seekers can locate all state job opportunities on one web site. Moreover, all participants in the hiring process (hiring supervisors, personnel liaisons, recruiters, agency approvers, agency executives, and applicants) use Hiring Gateway in an integrated symphony of actions to complete the process rapidly. Hiring Gateway replaced the state's previous paper-driven process where a typical recruitment action took seventy days, and required paper to be moved between eleven different agency staff members multiple times. Job applicants had to search out 130 individual agency web sites if they hoped to find statewide job opportunities. According to the state, Hiring Gateway has reduced the calendar time to hire by eighteen days or 30 percent.

In 2007, Georgia developed a new job classification system that consolidated more than 3,400 job descriptions, many of which were developed at the agency level, into approximately 650 jobs across 17 occupational areas. According to the state, the changes were driven by the state's inability to compete in the labor market because of the gap between salaries in the state government and in the competitive labor market.

## System-Wide Changes

Michigan adopted more sweeping changes when it created its HR Service Center in 2004. The HR Service Center provides employees with a single point of contact for HR questions, routine HR transactions, and enrollment in group insurance programs. Michigan was the first state to implement a service center of this type, and its process is being used as a model. According to the state's response to the 2007 GPP survey, it is on target to achieve savings of over $28 million projected over five years based on initial position reductions and attrition. The state indicated that the centralization of HR transactions is providing more efficient processing of step increases, automated processing of pre-authorized position reallocations, and reduced administrative errors and rework. In May 2007, Michigan's Executive Directive 2007-30 called for consolidation of HR services from their locations in principal state operating departments to the Civil Service Commission which will be an autonomous entity housed within the Department of Management and Budget. According to the state, the transfer of functions relating to management of state employees and related programs will result in enhanced accountability, more effective control and coordination of personnel management functions, and enhanced service both to state agencies and state employees, while eliminating unnecessary duplication.

As noted earlier, the nature of HR reforms varies considerably among states. Although many states have implemented reforms, a few states, such as Alabama, Colorado, Missouri and West Virginia, indicated that they had not and were not planning to implement any significant HR change initiatives. The following section explores the impact of two sets of factors, organizational and environmental, on a state's ability to implement HR change initiatives.

## DRIVERS OF CHANGES TO STATE HUMAN RESOURCE SYSTEMS

Building upon the work of Kellough and Selden (2003) and Selden (2006), this chapter explores the impact of organizational and environmental factors on state implementation of HR change initiatives presented in Table 4.5. The study developed a reform index by summing the number of changes *implemented* across the four categories, as reported by each state, between 2004 and 2007, in its survey response to the GPP in 2007.[3] The model presented in this chapter moves beyond the earlier two studies by incorporating both characteristics of the central HR department and the state workforce (see Table 4.1 and 4.4). The rationale for including these variables is discussed next.

## Organizational Context

According to Nigro and Kellough (2006), one of the three primary reasons for implementing reforms to state civil service systems is technical. By altering HR operations, reformers expect to improve government performance. "These interventions, while they may serve as vehicles for the ideological and political agendas of other interest, are the 'bread and butter' of human resource professionals and specialists" (Nigro and Kellough, 2006:317). Because HR professional staff are likely to focus on technically driven changes to a state's civil service, this study considers the professional certifications of a state's central HR staff. Specifically, it examines the percentage of staff with the Society of Human Resource Management (SHRM) and International Public Management Association for Human Resources (IPMA-HR) certifications. Certification by both organizations requires mastery and currency of knowledge, including leading trends, in HRM. Moreover, employees seeking out such certification are likely to be actively engaged in the HR professional communities sponsoring those certifications. States with more HR professions holding either SHRM or IPMA-HR certification are likely to implement more changes to their personnel system. This study also examines whether the central HR structure, as measured by the percentage of state government HR professionals working in the central personnel office and the number of HR staff per one hundred state employees, and the size of state government influences the implementation of HR change initiatives.

Like Selden (2006), this study will include the 2005 GPP people grade as a proxy measure of the performance of a state's HR system. Selden (2006) found that higher performing states were more likely to implement and to experiment with new personnel strategies, policies, and practices. Similarly, this study anticipates that HRM performance, as measured by the 2005 GPP, will be linked to the adoption of different HR reforms. There is no overlap between the 2005 GPP people grade and the initiatives examined in this study because the changes explored as dependent variables were implemented after the data collection period covered by the 2005 GPP.

## Environmental Context

This study examines the effects of politicization, unionization, economic conditions, and region on the adoption of civil service reform. According to Nigro and Kellough (2006), a second force driving state civil service changes is political. Reforms serve as a means for elected officials to demonstrate to their constituents that they are improving the efficiency and effectiveness of their state civil service systems (Nigro and Kellough, 2006). States with a greater percentage of political appointees serving in the executive branch are more likely to implement reform agendas of governors and other elected state officials.

Both practitioners and scholars often mention that reforms are more difficult to implement in states with more unionization or collective bargaining (e.g., Selden, 2006). States that allow collective bargaining need union support to implement many types of HR reforms. Moreover, states that allow collective bargaining often operate "dual, and sometimes, conflicting personnel systems," which create a more complex environment to navigate change (Kearney, 2006:82). Collective bargaining personnel systems often face criticisms, such as being rigid, slow, and protective of their employees, similar to complaints made about civil service systems (Kearney, 2006). This study posits that the percentage of state government employees covered by collective bargaining agreements will be negatively associated with the implementation of HR changes.

A state's economic environment may influence the pressures placed on a state from its citizenry. States with less unemployment may be performing better financially and therefore government officials may have access to resources needed to implement new changes (Kellough and Selden, 2003). On the other hand, tight labor markets may drive states to implement reforms in order to compete more effectively for labor (Leonard, 1998; Selden, 2006). Selden (2006) found that states with higher unemployment were more likely to make changes to personnel authority and hiring policies.

Region is also likely to influence efforts to implement changes to a state's civil service system because cultural and regional traditions influence political and management decisions, including HR decisions (Elazar, 1984; Selden, 2006). For example, Selden (2006) found that region was an important predictor of adoption of formal workforce planning in state government.

## Results

As illustrated in Table 4.6, the independent variables included in the multivariate analysis explain a substantial degree of the observed variations in HR reforms ($R^2 = 0.75$). Three of the organizational variables included in this analysis significantly influenced state implementation of HR changes. States with a larger core of HR professionals and

**TABLE 4.6   Results Explaining States Implementing HR Changes or Initiatives**

|  | Unstandardized Coefficient | Standard Error |
|---|---|---|
| Constant | −4.7** | 1.6 |
| Percentage of HR staff certified by SHRM | 0.04*** | 0.01 |
| Percentage of HR staff certified by IPMA-HR | 0.01 | 0.06 |
| Percentage of HR staff working in central HR office | 0.01 | 0.01 |
| Total HR staff per 100 state employees | 0.10** | 0.04 |
| Total number of state employees | 0.00 | 0.00 |
| 2005 GPP people grade | 0.81** | 0.31 |
| Percentage of state workforce that are political appointees | 0.16** | 0.08 |
| Percentage of state workforce that is covered by labor agreements | 0.00 | 0.01 |
| Unemployment 2006 | 0.48* | 0.25 |
| Region |  |  |
| Midwest | −0.85* | 0.44 |
| Northeast | −1.31** | 0.56 |
| South | 0.13 | 0.42 |
|  | $R^2 = 0.75$ | Adjusted $R^2 = 0.59$ |
|  | $F$ value = 4.7*** |  |

*** Significant at .01, ** Significant at .05, * Significant at .10.

those with more HR professionals with SHRM certifications are much more likely to implement HR changes. This finding supports Nigro and Kellough's (2006) view that many reforms may be driven by technical motives. That is, having a professional staff that is large enough and fully knowledgeable about the most current practices in the field may enable a state to usher through efforts to improve the performance of its civil service system.

This is further supported by the finding that higher performing states are more likely to implement new practices and innovations as demonstrated by the statistically significant relationship between the HR performance, as measured by the 2005 GPP people grade, and the dependent variable, implementation of HR reforms. Since this finding is consistent with Selden's (2006) earlier study of innovations adopted in state civil service systems, it suggests that the ability to navigate changes (and resist changes) within a state's civil service system may be inculcated into the culture of state government. Likely, it reflects strong leadership within the state's professional HR ranks. Chief HR officials in some states, such as Virginia, Oklahoma, South Carolina, and Michigan, have held their position for a number of years, are extremely active in their larger HR professional communities, are focused on improving the professional certification of their state HR staff, and have developed relationships over the years with administrative and political stakeholders that may enable them to more easily broker changes within their state civil service systems.

In terms of the environmental factors considered in this study, two factors are statistically significant: percent of political appointees in the Executive Branch and northeastern states. States with more political appointees are significantly more likely to implement changes to their civil service systems. These changes may be aligned with the agendas of the chief elected official. In interviews with state political and administrative officials in 2007, the GPP found that a number of governors were particularly attuned to state government management and were personally involved in improving management of their state's agencies.

Finally, compared to western states, northeastern states are significantly less likely to implement changes to their HR systems. Civil service in this region is deeply entrenched in rules and collective bargaining agreements. The structural and political complexity of such systems may create significant barriers to change. Moreover, states in the Northeast may face additional challenges when trying to implement and fund civil service reforms due to their tax structures and general economic conditions.

As shown previously, this study supports Nigro and Kellough's (2006) observation that both technical and political motives are key drivers of state civil service changes. The findings indicate that the size and professional credentials of a state's HR professions are important indicators of a state's ability to implement changes to its HR system. Moreover, the study also demonstrates that political leadership within the executive branch influences implementation of HR reforms.

As noted earlier, the nature of the HR reforms varies considerably among states. Although states have specific goals tied to these reforms, ultimately all states seek to create systems that will contribute to their ability to attract and retain high quality state government employees. The next section examines the ability of state governments to retain their classified workforces.

## THE NEED TO RETAIN STATE GOVERNMENT EMPLOYEES

Nearly all state administrators worry about their workforces: States are anticipating a large wave of retirements in the next five years (see Table 4.7). States are concerned about retention rates, especially amongst new hires. On average, about 7 percent of state governments' workforces left voluntarily in FY 2006 and about 22 percent of new hires quit or were fired in FY 2006. Over 30 percent of new hires in Arizona, Delaware, Louisiana, Mississippi, New Mexico, South Carolina, Utah, Virginia, and West Virginia either quit or were fired in FY 2006. Of the hundreds of data points collected in its 2007 survey about state governments' HR systems, the GPP found that compensation and benefits were the most important predictors of employee retention. Increasingly, state employees expect a mix of base pay and incentives. In all sectors, the emerging workforce seeks even more balance between life and work. At the same time, they want high performance recognized. The GPP found that state governments are responding rapidly to these changing expectations by increasing benefits spending, implementing work flexibilities, and adopting incentive-based pay programs.

As part of its 2004 and 2007 survey, the GPP asked state governments about various features of their compensation strategies. It asked about benefits such as health insurance and working arrangements; deferred compensation, such as retirement programs; and monetary incentives, such as salary increases and bonuses. The GPP also asked states what percentage of state employees had access to various benefit options or were eligible for certain types of compensation.

The GPP learned that, like other employers, states are finding it increasingly difficult to maximize benefit dollars (discussed later). Many factors contribute to the increasing cost of employee benefits, including an aging workforce, more retirees, increased technology costs in health care services, and union resistance to renegotiating current benefit levels. For example, Kaiser Family Foundation's Annual Employer Health Benefits Survey in 2005 indicated that since 2000, health insurance premiums have grown 73 percent, compared to cumulative inflation of 14 percent and cumulative wage growth of 5 percent over the five-year period. Yet despite increasing costs, the GPP found, states continue to provide their employees a rich array of benefits. Most states offer retirees health insurance coverage. Vacation and sick leave offerings are generous.

However, the GPP noted that state HR executives are concerned about the lack of competitive salaries in their states and the escalating costs of health insurance for

**TABLE 4.7  Percent of State Workforce Eligible to Retire (as of June 2007)**

| Years to Eligible Retirement | Classified Workforce (percentage) | Non-Classified Workforce (percentage) |
|---|---|---|
| One | 13.39 | 12.73 |
| Three | 19.25 | 17.11 |
| Five | 25.90 | 22.34 |

**TABLE 4.8    Average Cost of Total Compensation for Classified State Employees\* (as of June 30, 2003 and 2007)**

|      | 25th Percentile (dollars) | Mean (dollars) | Median (dollars) | 75th Percentile (dollars) |
|------|---------------------------|----------------|------------------|---------------------------|
| 2003 | 42,631                    | 49,471         | 47,405           | 53,493                    |
| 2007 | 48,843                    | 57,042         | 56,611           | 64,252                    |

\**n* = 42.

state employees and their families. In some states, such as Michigan and Minnesota (78 and 48 percent at top of salary range, respectively), a substantial portion of employees are at the top of the salary grade, which may limit states' abilities to offer performance-based rewards. Also, with about 25 percent of state employees eligible to retire within five years, along with funding benefits for current employees, states must address changing demographics and offer competitive market compensation packages to attract high-quality employees in a shrinking workforce.

One trend stood out in the GPP findings: an increased use of total compensation. Moreover, the GPP found that total compensation was the most important predictor of voluntary turnover, predicting over 54 percent of the variance. A strategy used in the private sector as well, total compensation integrates both salary and benefits and is presented to the employees as a package. A commonly used model of total compensation includes benefits, base pay, and incentive pay.

Base pay and benefits contribute to a state's ability to attract and retain employees, while performance-based pay increases employee productivity. Several states, such as Delaware, Idaho, and Virginia, have embraced this approach. Indeed, to better communicate its strategy, Delaware provides its employees with a total compensation statement.

Table 4.8 presents the average cost of total compensation, which includes salary and benefits, as of June 30, 2003 and June 30, 2007. On average, in 2007, states spent $57,042 on salary and benefits per classified state employee, an increase of 15 percent since 2004. At the top, Connecticut spent, on average, over $90,000 per classified employee, and Ohio spent over $82,000. Arkansas, Kansas, Mississippi, North Dakota, and West Virginia spent the least on salary and benefits—on average less than $43,000 per classified employee. As of June 30, 2007, on average, salary comprises 64 percent of total compensation. Expenditures on benefits account for the remaining 36 percent of total compensation. Just three years earlier (June 30, 2003), expenditures on benefits accounted for 26 percent of total compensation.

## Compensation: Base Salary and Incentive Pay

As shown in Table 4.9, the average base salary of classified state government employees increased from $37,547 in 2003 to $42,219, or approximately 12 percent. New Mexico's average salary increased by approximately 27 percent, the highest increase in the nation. This increase is likely due to the implementation of 236 alternative pay band assignments. Here, the state uses an alternative pay band when the internal worth of a job classification has not changed, but external forces of supply and

TABLE 4.9   Classified Employees Average Base Salary (as of June 30, 2003 and 2007)

| | 2007 Salary (dollars) | 2003 Salary (dollars) | Change (percentage) |
|---|---|---|---|
| Alabama | 39,511.00 | 35,018.00 | 12.83 |
| Alaska | | 47,124.00 | |
| Arizona | 37,151.00 | 31,824.00 | 16.74 |
| Arkansas | 32,267.62 | 31,197.00 | 3.43 |
| California | 61,383.00 | 50,615.00 | 21.27 |
| Colorado | 53,088.00 | | |
| Connecticut | 58,479.00 | 51,005.00 | 14.65 |
| Delaware | 40,453.00 | 35,731.00 | 13.22 |
| Georgia | 38,589.86 | 35,670.85 | 8.18 |
| Hawaii | | 32,094.80 | |
| Idaho | 40,365.00 | 35,212.00 | 14.63 |
| Illinois | 52,614.36 | 55,735.00 | −5.60 |
| Indiana | 34,775.00 | 28,760.06 | 20.91 |
| Iowa | 47,596.69 | 41,450.83 | 14.83 |
| Kansas | 36,398.00 | 33,295.00 | 9.32 |
| Kentucky | | 36,185.00 | |
| Louisiana | 38,180.00 | 32,789.00 | 16.44 |
| Maine | 37,334.00 | 34,336.00 | 8.73 |
| Maryland | 43,974.00 | | |
| Michigan | 51,667.00 | 44,844.00 | 15.21 |
| Minnesota | 46,700.00 | 45,800.00 | 1.97 |
| Mississippi | 30,736.00 | 28,075.00 | 9.48 |
| Missouri | 30,716.25 | 27,807.00 | 10.46 |
| Montana | 38,234.00 | 34,512.00 | 10.78 |
| Nebraska | 36,760.00 | 33,534.00 | 9.62 |
| Nevada | 49,954.00 | | |
| New Hampshire | 39,530.00 | 33,603.00 | 17.64 |
| New Jersey | 56,353.60 | 47,511.09 | 18.61 |
| New Mexico | 38,692.00 | 30,535.00 | 26.71 |
| New York | | 46,841.00 | |
| North Carolina | 39,220.00 | 33,988.00 | 15.39 |
| North Dakota | 35,772.00 | | |
| Ohio | 63,502.40 | | |
| Oklahoma | 34,356.00 | 29,946.00 | 14.73 |
| Oregon | 54,578.00 | 46,302.00 | 17.87 |
| Pennsylvania | 45,779.00 | 43,717.00 | 4.72 |
| Rhode Island | | 46,986.00 | |
| South Carolina | 34,585.00 | 35,131.00 | −1.55 |
| Tennessee | 33,219.00 | 28,492.00 | 16.59 |
| Utah | 37,909.00 | 35,466.00 | 6.89 |
| Vermont | 43,882.00 | 40,144.00 | 9.31 |

(continued)

TABLE 4.9   Classified Employees Average Base Salary (as of June 30, 2003 and 2007)—continued

|  | 2007 Salary (dollars) | 2003 Salary (dollars) | Change (percentage) |
|---|---|---|---|
| Virginia | 41,290.59 | 35,519.00 | 16.25 |
| Washington | 39,158.00 | 42,267.00 | −7.36 |
| West Virginia | 29,981.98 | 29,126.00 | 2.94 |
| Wisconsin | 46,282.00 | 38,001.00 | 21.79 |
| Wyoming | 39,952.00 | 33,238.00 | 20.20 |
| Mean | 42,218.76 | 37,547.02 | 11.88 |

demand require a higher pay band to recruit and retain employees. According to the state, the use of a higher pay band allows the state to recruit and retain employees in these positions by using a higher pay band minimum, midpoint, and maximum value.

Indiana's average classified state salary also increased by over 20 percent. The state implemented a three-fold pay-for-performance program for its employees. First, the state authorized annual performance-based increases to base salary based upon accomplishment of measurable performance objectives or results as documented on written performance appraisals. Salary increases are 4 percent for employees rated as *Meets Expectations* and 10 percent for employees rated *Exceeds Expectation*. Employees rated *Does Not Meet Expectations* do not receive a salary increase. According to the state, the average pay increase exceeded 4 percent, which was more than double what Indiana state employees had received annually (on average) in recent years. Second, state agency heads offered spot bonuses consisting of cash awards ranging from $100 to $1,000. In 2006, agency heads recognized 3,070 employees, who have demonstrated extraordinary performance, with spot awards (expending over $865,000). Third, the state implemented the Governor's Public Service Achievement Award program to recognize and reward with individual employees ($1,000 bonus) and teams ($5,000 bonus), who made significant measurable accomplishments to improving government efficiency, providing better customer service or stretching tax dollars. Eighty-eight employees received this recognition in 2006.

As illustrated by the Indiana example, incentive pay is a mechanism to financially reward employees for their organizational contributions. The GPP collected data about the percentage of state employees eligible to receive different types of incentive pay: PFP salary increase, individual bonus, group bonus, and gainsharing. Eligibility does not guarantee a reward will be given; it only indicates whether state employees have any chance of receiving one.

As shown in Figure 4.1, the use of incentive pay is increasing. After Cost of Living Adjustments (COLA), PFP salary increases are the second most available compensation strategy. The availability of both COLA and PFP increased between 2003 and 2007. Individual and group bonuses were offered more frequently in 2007 as well. Few states, however, are using gainsharing as an incentive. Louisiana uses the "Exceptional Performance and Efficiency Incentive Program" to reward state employees with up to 20 percent of their annual salary for activities that result in cost savings

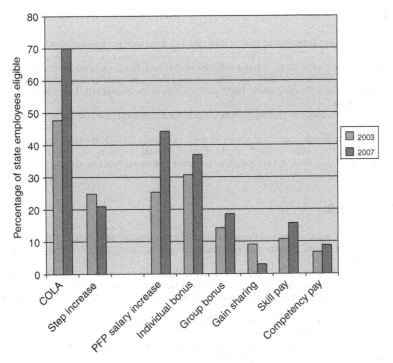

**FIGURE 4.1    Percentage of State Employees Eligible for Different Compensation Programs—2003 and 2007**

or increased efficiencies. The trend in the private sector is to rely heavily on monetary incentives to differentiate outstanding performers from average performers (White, 2006). It appears that this approach is receiving more traction in state governments.

## WHAT THE FUTURE HOLDS

With at least one of every four state employees eligible to retire within five years, states have both opportunities and challenges ahead. As baby boomers exit state work forces, the overall labor participation rate is projected to go down (Toossi, 2005). Not only must states address the declining number of applicants, they must also deal with the changing expectations of a new generation of workers. States must engage in succession planning and position themselves—in terms of total compensation—to recruit and retain the types of workers they seek. To do this, many states will need to implement changes to their HR systems. The extent to which states are able to implement such changes may be hindered by the nature of their organizational and environment contexts. As suggested by the analysis presented in this chapter, states that are interested in modernizing their civil service systems should focus on strengthening and capitalizing upon the expertise of their HR professional staff and garnering the support of political stakeholders, especially within the ranks of the Executive Branch.

## NOTES

1. The Government Performance Project collected data from state government human resource management professionals between the months of June and December in 1998, 2000, 2003, and 2007. The GPP administered a survey and collected over twenty-five documents from the central HRM departments. In 2003 and 2007, the GPP surveyed two state agencies about their HR practices. In addition, the GPP interviewed HRM professionals in the central HR department and selected state agencies.
2. As for June 30, 2007, 29 percent of Florida's workforce was part of the non-career or non-classified workforce.
3. The GPP administered an online survey to states in summer 2007. Forty-two states completed the survey as of December 31, 2007. Alaska, Florida, Hawaii, Kentucky, New York, South Dakota, Rhode Island, and Texas did not complete the survey and are excluded from this analysis.

## REFERENCES

Aronson, Albert H. 1974. State and Local Personnel Administration. In *Classics of Public Personnel Policy,* 2nd ed., Frank J. Thompson ed. Pacific Grove, CA: Brooks/Cole Publishing Company, pp. 133–142.

Coggburn, Jerrell D. 2006. The Decentralized and Deregulated Approach to State Human Resource Management in Texas. In *Civil Service Reform in the States: Personnel Policy and Politics at the Subnational Level,* J. Edward Kellough and Lloyd Nigro, eds. Albany, NY: State University of New York, pp. 203–237.

Conover, Milton. 1925. Merit Systems of Civil Service in the States. *The American Political Science Review* 19 (3): 544–560.

Effron, Marc, Robert Grandossy, and Marshall Goldsmith, eds. 2003. *Human Resources in the 21st Century.* Hoboken, NJ: John Wiley & Sons.

Elazar, Daniel J. 1984. *American Federalism: A View from States,* 3rd ed. New York, NY: Harper and Row.

Fox, Peter D. and Robert J. Lavigna. 2006. Wisconsin State Government: Reforming Human Resource Management While Retaining Merit Principles and Cooperative Labor Relations. In *Civil Service Reform in the States: Personnel Policy and Politics at the Subnational Level,* J. Edward Kellough and Lloyd Nigro, eds. Albany, NY: State University of New York, pp. 279–302.

Kaiser Family Foundation and Health Research and Educational Trust. 2005. Annual Employer Health Benefits Survey. http://www.kff.org/insurance/7315/upload/7315.pdf. Accessed on January 14, 2008.

Kearney, Richard. 2006. The Labor Perspective on Civil Service Reform in the States. In *Civil Service Reform in the States: Personnel Policy and Politics at the Subnational Level,* J. Edward Kellough and Lloyd Nigro, eds. Albany, NY: State University of New York, pp. 77–93.

Kellough, Edward J., and Lloyd Nigro, eds. 2006. *Civil Service Reform in the States: Personnel Policy and Politics at the Subnational Level.* Albany, NY: State University of New York.

Kellough, Edward J., and Sally Selden. 2003. The Reinvention of Public Personnel Administration: An Analysis of the Diffusion of Personnel Management Reform in the States. *Public Administration Review* 63 (2):165–176.

Leonard, Bill. 1998. What Do HR Executives Want from CEOS? *HR Magazine* 43 (13):92–98.

Lindquist, Stefanie A., and Stephen E. Condrey. 2006. Public Employment Reforms and Constitutional Due Process. In *Civil Service Reform in the States: Personnel Policy and Politics at the Subnational Level,* J. Edward Kellough and Lloyd Nigro, eds. Albany, NY: State University of New York, pp. 95–114.

Nigro, Lloyd, and Kellough, J. Edward. 2006. The States and Civil Service Reform: Lessons Learned and Future Prospects. In *Civil Service Reform in the States: Personnel Policy and Politics at the Subnational Level,* J. Edward Kellough and Lloyd Nigro, eds. Albany, NY: State University of New York, pp. 315–324.

Rainey, Hal G. 2006. Reform Trends at the Federal Level with Implications for the States: The Pursuit of Flexibility and the Human Capital Movement. In *Civil Service Reform in the States: Personnel Policy and Politics at the Subnational Level,* J. Edward Kellough and Lloyd Nigro, eds. Albany, NY: State University of New York, pp. 95–114.

Riccucci, Norma M. 2006. Civil Service Reform in New York State: A Quiet Revolution. In *Civil Service Reform in the States: Personnel Policy and Politics at the Subnational Level,* J. Edward Kellough and Lloyd Nigro, eds. Albany, NY: State University of New York, pp. 303–313.

Selden, Sally. 2006. Classifying and Exploring Reforms in State Personnel System. In *Civil Service Reform in the States: Personnel Policy and Politics at the Subnational Level,* J. Edward Kellough and Lloyd Nigro, eds. Albany, NY: State University of New York, pp. 59–76.

Selden, Sally, Patricia W. Ingraham, and Willow Jacobson. 2001. Human Resource Practices: Findings from a National Survey. *Public Administration Review* 61 (5):598–607.

Sylvia, Ronald, and C. Kenneth Meyer. 2001. *Public Personnel Administration,* 2nd ed. New York, NY: Wadsworth Publishing.

Texas Legislative Budget Board Staff. 2007. Texas State Government Effectiveness and Efficiency: Select Issues and Recommendations. (January 2007). http://www.lbb.state.tx.us/Performance%20Reporting/ TX_Govt_Effective_Efficiency_Report_80th_0107.pdf. Accessed on January 14, 2008.

Toossi, Mitra. 2005. Labor Force Projections to 2014: Retiring Boomers. *Monthly Labor Review.* November. http://www.bls.gov/opub/mlr/2005/11/art3full.pdf. Accessed on January 13, 2008.

White, Erin. 2006. The Best vs. the Rest. *The Wall Street Journal,* January 31, 2006. http://www.careerjournal. com/hrcenter/articles/20060131-white.html. Accessed on January 13, 2008.

# Local Government Personnel Administration
## Heritage, Contemporary Practice, and Portents

SUSAN G. MASON
Boise State University

LANA STEIN
University of Missouri–St. Louis

Roughly a century ago, American cities were the fulcrum of development of professional public personnel administration. Although the federal government had enacted the Pendleton Act in 1883, the principal components of the merit system—job testing, selection rules, classification, and pay—were forged in municipal research bureaus in many large cities (Finegold, 1995). These bureaus provided the intellectual organization for Progressive reformers, who battled political machines and machine politics in countless locales. The reforms they devised dominated the principal personnel functions in most cities for well over six decades. During the past thirty-five years, cities have found it necessary to modernize their personnel systems and to augment the functions of HRM. Civil rights laws and the impetus to create a representative workforce as well as the government reinvention movement and the growth of information systems technology have all stimulated a reexamination of and recreation of basic practices. This chapter will examine the history and the present state of traditional personnel functions, as well as new functions caused by workforce diversity, technology, and the rise of e-government. Since there are so many local governments that can range in size from a few thousand to 8 million, certain elements will pertain to all while some will not be as widely shared.

## THE PROGRESSIVE LEGACY

Progressive reform was by and large based in the nation's cities. Members of the upper class (Hays, 1984) and most often native-born white Protestants, the Progressives revolted against machine politics excesses and attempted to install men like themselves in the seats of government (Schiesl, 1977). In terms of personnel administration, Progressives fought the rampant patronage then extant throughout government. Under machine rule, municipal jobs were payments for election work and often required a monetary emolument from the job seeker as well. In many cities, those hired by the machine were frequently immigrants or the children of immigrants. In the less complicated world of 1900, governmental tasks were often simple and frequently required physical strength rather than intellectual capacity. But, the United States was changing markedly by the turn of the century. The nation became an industrial power and the economy expanded significantly after the Civil War. Growing businesses and burgeoning corporations needed infrastructure and reliable governmental service. Progressives and their allies saw a greater need for workers with education and technical training in the municipal workforce, and replaced those with political ties.

Progressive reform touched every local jurisdiction in the United States, but not to the same degree. Some cities adopted a very stringent civil service system, governed by an appointed commission. In other locales, most often the growing number of council-manager cities, a personnel department handled hiring, classification, and related functions utilizing the merit system. In addition, a number of northeastern and midwestern cities—New York City, Albany, Chicago, Cleveland, Pittsburgh, Philadelphia, St. Louis—retained a machine politics structure at some point alongside a civil service.

The diversity of American cities in terms of governance and the sheer number of cities makes generalizability difficult. Regarding personnel functions, there is no either/or set of practices; rather, there is a continuum ranging from strict adherence to "merit principles" to a highly politicized personnel operation.

In recent years, the personnel function in local government has faced new challenges. The old *bête noire* of patronage has been supplanted by opportunities created from information systems technology, new specializations needed by the changing work of local government and, perhaps especially, the need to be more flexible in rapidly changing times. Too often, practices developed a century before had calcified and prevented greater managerial discretion and making the best hires.

Further, unionization of employees in many cities also affected personnel prerogatives. The emphasis on the group contrasted with the traditional focus on an individual or on a particular classification. State legislatures determine whether their municipal governments may allow public employees to organize. According to Tobias (2005:358), twenty-five states have comprehensive laws providing for bargaining. Sixteen states provide collective bargaining or *meet and confer* for a limited category of employee (e.g., police and fire). Only nine states do not confer collective bargaining or *meet and confer* rights to any public employee. Although some cities are not affected by the union movement, unions play a significant role in the majority of the larger cities in the United States.

The civil rights movement highlighted significant biases within merit-based systems throughout the country. Although merit was supposed to be race and gender neutral, the mores of the time, shared by personnel staffs in many cities, did not exhibit such neutrality. In addition, for the cities of the industrial heartland, loss of industry and population since 1950 adversely affected public workforce size and compensation. Declining resources put new pressure on personnel systems in affected cities. Further, the desire to reinvent government created pressure for decentralization in personnel administration. The need for training in many areas as well as the need to discern ways of motivating staff adds to the responsibilities of human resources staff. Hays and Kearney (2001:594) feel that HRM will change significantly in the near future. Traditional personnel practices such as "position classification, paper and pencil exams, the rule of three, [and] conventional performance appraisal techniques are expected to decline substantively." Local government is in flux and the variation is likely to grow in the near future.

## CORE FUNCTIONS

We will now look at local personnel administration in terms of its traditional core functions: recruitment, selection, classification, evaluation, and discipline and termination. These sections will illustrate how unionization, the drive for equality, and the movement for effective government have affected and reshaped traditional merit system practices forged by Progressives at the turn of the twentieth century.

### Recruitment

Recruitment generally played a small role in Progressive reform strategy. Reformers wanted to recruit men like themselves for government positions and dislodge the growing number of immigrant workers from Ireland and southern and eastern Europe. Progressives used selection techniques, especially testing, to accomplish their goal and were originally fairly successful in their displacement of immigrant workers (Shiesl, 1977). That success was short-lived, however. The heirs of the foreign-born eventually recaptured their places in local workforces.

Many cities followed a passive recruitment strategy until the second half of the twentieth century. They merely posted vacancies and often relied on word of mouth to draw applicants. Municipal workforces frequently were not representative in terms of minorities or women. According to Rodgers and Bullock (1972:123), "Local governments practice many of the discriminatory acts found in private industry. They (1) discriminate in hiring and promoting minority group members; (2) make no special effort to recruit minority group members; (3) use methods of hiring and promoting which place minorities at a serious disadvantage." The U.S. Commission on Civil Rights (1969) found discrimination particularly evident in the protective services, police, and fire. Similar to the skilled crafts, referrals from existing employees and familial ties frequently played strong roles in recruiting members of the protective services in many cities (Thompson, 1975; Stein, 1991). Civil rights laws and affirmative action forced many changes.

In 1972, the Equal Employment Opportunity (EEO) Act brought local government under the jurisdiction of the 1964 Civil Rights Act and presidential affirmative action orders. As recipients of federal funds, cities had to report on a yearly basis (using an EEO-4 form) their workforce composition and prepare goals and timetables aimed at creating a municipal staff reflective of local population and workforce population. Federal officials examined the plans when awarding funds to cities. In certain instances, cities were taken to court and had to enter into consent decrees regarding their hiring practices and formulas for selection.

Regarding recruitment, the push for diversity in municipal employment led to a much wider advertising for positions. Job postings were sent to colleges and universities, minority newspapers, and community and neighborhood organizations. In the case of minority recruitment, it was often necessary to demonstrate that nonwhites could be welcome in a department previously considered hostile. For example, in the late 1960s, the Atlanta Police Department began a large recruitment of black officers (Stein and Condrey, 1987). Recruitment vans visited many locales around Atlanta and toured other southern cities. A widely circulated recruitment poster featured an African American officer with sergeant's stripes in order to assure African Americans that these were not dead-end positions.

More intense recruiting at post-secondary schools became more common in recent years because of the increasing skill levels needed in local government. The Internet and World Wide Web have also altered the way cities conduct recruitment. In 2004, 91 percent of cities responding to an International City Management Association (ICMA) survey indicated they had a web site up and running (Coursey, 2005:14). A number of jurisdictions post job listings on the Web and often require applicants to apply online as well. This may appear to enhance outreach but has its downside as well. As Mossberger, Tolbert, and Gilbert (2006) note, computers are not present in every household. Many, in particular those of low income, do not have their own personal computers and cannot readily access the technology. Although public libraries in a number of cities provide Web access for their patrons, e-government in recruitment can conflict with the goal of workforce diversity. It may particularly affect applicants for more labor intensive jobs in parks, sanitation, or the protective services. To that end, the Web might better serve as augmentation rather than the only means of entry. Hays and Sowa (2005:111–112) note that using electronic interactions in the application process can allow managers to peruse resumes on their own computers. Further, a resume database allows skills to be matched with new job openings. Previous applicants can receive e-mails, asking if they wish to be considered for new openings. This is a genuine growth area but personnel staff must ensure that privacy concerns are addressed throughout the process (Coursey and McCreary, 2005:194).

Another factor complicating recruitment in some large cities is a residency requirement. Some cities require applicants to be city residents while others give successful job candidates a set period in which to move to the city after they are hired. The residency requirement may adversely influence prospective job candidates with families because of the troubled public school systems in many cities. Most cities do not have residency requirements however, and some cities with them have modified their terms in recent years.

## Selection

Progressives and their descendents placed enormous faith in standardized tests as selection instruments. They considered them to be the most scientific and efficient means of assessing applicants. Early personnelists placed such value on these tests that they often debated whether merit would be better served by scores carried to the second or to the third decimal place. In the early twentieth century, tests were related sometimes to particular positions but, frequently, the tests covered general knowledge. The same intelligence test was given to those seeking clerical positions as well as those wishing to become police officers.

From the 1960s onward, court decisions mandated changes to selection methods in the public and private sectors. Because standardized test scores frequently showed evidence of racial disparity, the U.S. Supreme Court in *Griggs v. Duke Power* ruled that testing had to be job-related or indicative of future performance. Further, multiple means of assessment of job capability were deemed desirable. The assessment center was developed as an alternative or supplement to standardized tests although it was costly to utilize when the number of applicants for a position was quite large. The Civil Rights Act of 1991 reestablished consideration of disparity and the validation of testing instruments after the Supreme Court had previously struck down key provisions of *Griggs*.

In cities with municipal craft unions, often larger cities, the union hiring hall remained the selection mechanism for carpenters, painters, electricians, laborers, and others. This could militate against affirmative action; craft unions were highly segregated and integrated very slowly.

For administrative positions today, oral interviews are quite common. Federal EEOC guidelines can alert the interviewers to questions that are now considered illegal, many of which relate to the job seeker's personal life. The interviews are coupled with reviews of experience and skills.

From the Progressive heyday came the rule of three: One of the top three scorers had to be hired for an open position. In some locations, the rule of one was followed: Only the top scorer could be hired. An eligibility list of all those passing an exam would be created, perhaps to last two years, and the top or one of the top three scorers would be selected. The rule of three has limited hiring discretion by administrators, and a number of cities have altered this requirement to provide greater flexibility, particularly when scores are bunched closely together. This flexibility is certainly desired by government reinventers. As Osborne and Gaebler (1992:125), the fathers of reinvention, note:

> Managers in civil service systems cannot hire like normal managers: advertise a position, take resumes, interview people, and talk to the references. They have to hire most employees from lists of those who have taken written civil service exams. Often they have to take the top scorer, or one of the top three scorers—regardless of whether that person is motivated or otherwise qualified. . . . The hiring process usually takes forever. When E.S. Savas studied New York City's system during the 1970s, he found that the higher people scored on the civil service exams, the less likely they were to be hired, because they had the savvy to find other jobs in the seven months that normally passed between testing and hiring.

The scientific methods designed to select the most meritorious new employee clearly showed signs of wear as the twentieth century came to a close.

Ironically, some cities with formal civil services and all the incumbent rules also have maintained a strong degree of politicization in hiring. Philadelphia (Shafritz, 1973) and St. Louis (Stein, 1991) are good examples. Both cities have never lost their machine politics approach to governance. St. Louis voters enacted civil service in 1941 and Philadelphia in 1952. In St. Louis, top scorers seek recommendations from elected officials and the applicant with the strongest reference wins out. Philadelphia has an informal selection network embedded among its civil service rules. Loosening the rule of three to the rule of six, which St. Louis voters did in 2006, could allow even more politicization of merit, along with the enhanced managerial flexibility (Stein, 1994).

## Classification

A cardinal canon of twentieth century personnel reform was that jobs were classified, not individual job holders. No less a figure than Robert Moses devised a very detailed classification scheme for New York City (Caro, 1975). These meticulous interrelationships used duties, level of difficulty, and the degree of supervision given to place positions in a hierarchy and link them to pay ranges. The methodology was thought to be scientific and purely merit-driven.

These methods have met with challenges on a variety of fronts. Changing governmental roles and technology have affected job duties significantly while classifications have not adapted nearly so quickly. Some employees may have transferred or resigned because their classification could not be modified to reflect their enhanced responsibilities.

Another problem is that classification structures frequently encoded the gender stereotypes of earlier eras, undervaluing positions dominated by women. Although the campaign for comparable worth (see Aaron and Lougy, 1986) may have sputtered, gender stereotyping is yet another reason for an overhaul of—in some cases—century old classifications.

Greater flexibility, particularly decentralization to the departments, could address some of the shortcomings found in classification. However, the lessening of centralized control might create greater disparities in compensation among workers with similar attributes and tasks who are located in different units. Given the litigious nature of American society, that is not a small consideration.

## Evaluation

Many local personnel departments prepare evaluation forms to be used during an employee's probationary period and then on a yearly basis. Many of these forms have measured traits (such as an employee's ability to work well with others) as opposed to assessing actual fulfillment of job components. When the same evaluations are used throughout a municipality, the fallback to traits is more likely.

Evaluation tied to specific positions and tasks could be more useful in securing improvements on the job. The process would have to be taken seriously and could be linked to raises based on performance or "merit pay." However, the straitened finances of many cities make merit pay unlikely and even raises greater than cost of living can be rare these days.

In many locations, evaluation still remains pro forma and often an unenlightening process. Although not a traditional merit system component, evaluation frequently has not been utilized to its potential. However, it could become a critical element in government reinvention and in the modernization of human resources in local government.

## Discipline and Termination

Disciplinary action may be undertaken against employees for reasons such as unbecoming conduct, alcohol and drug use, acceptance of bribes, abuse of authority, or lack of care of or maintenance of equipment (Coplin and Dwyer, 2000:30). Many might consider discipline and termination in local government to be oxymorons because they rarely occur. It has been extremely difficult for local governments to rid themselves of nonproductive employees. For one thing, it involves voluminous documentation and it may make the local government subject to possible litigation. When municipal employees are members of unions, elaborate grievance procedures become even more the rule. The time and documentation needed to terminate a worker make the process rather daunting. Some supervisors attempt to arrange transfers for difficult employees, sharing rather than addressing the problem.

Certainly public jobs were not meant to be sinecures. Rather than tolerate chronic absenteeism, lack of productivity, or other on-the-job failures, municipal government ought to utilize improved training and better and more timely evaluatory mechanisms to attempt to lessen problem behavior. In addition, the street-level bureaucracy literature (Lipsky, 1980; Prottas, 1979), which covers police as well as other local government workers, depicts employees who appear uncaring or worse, particularly when dealing with low-income and minority citizens. Local government reinventers will frequently speak of improving customer service with the citizen being the customer. This change in focus does not always make it into the field and requires considerable training as well.

Many municipal governments have turned to the private sector for administration of what had been governmental functions. These have included management of parking lots or municipal golf courses, parking enforcement, refuse collection, and more. Privatization is a continual threat to the security of public jobs. Private employers that take over previously public functions pay less and often offer fewer if any benefits than local government (Kettl, 1993). The possibility of contracting out or privatization can adversely affect workforce morale and productivity.

## CONTEMPORARY INNOVATIONS

### New Public Management

The best approach for the delivery of local government services has been hotly debated. The New Public Management (NPM) philosophy and practices have been accused of creating "hollow states" because they are thinning administrative institutions (Terry, 2005). This refers to the phenomenon by which local governments are contracting out services to both nonprofits and the private firms. The net effect of this has potentially complicated local government managers' work because it eliminates rules and regulations that are needed for institutional memory and simultaneously lessens managers' capacity to respond to local government needs and demands (Terry, 2005). In contrast, Callahan and Gilbert (2003:69) contend that NPM's emphasis on private sector management principles of competition and efficiency of markets enhances service delivery in the public sector. They conducted a study looking at federal, state, and local agencies and found government service users prefer "public agencies characterized by delivery systems that incorporate local planning, end-user choice and an end-user satisfaction focus." Agency design and user satisfaction should be important factors in local government planning.

Although some users may prefer that private sector principles be put in practice in the delivery of local government services, Hague (2001) argues that the shift to market-driven practices in the public sector diminishes the "publicness" or public interest of government services. Similar to Terry (2005), he contends that the capacity of public services has been weakened by recent market reforms. Additionally, Hague argues that NPM lessens the motivation of employees who were drawn to local government work by personal missions to serve their community and who now find their jobs driven more by private market concerns. Hague (2001) further contends that the evidence provided by an increasing distrust in government suggests that public sector work is decreasing in its mission to serve the public interest (Hague, 2001). Two factors that could potentially augment the utility and implementation of NPM or hamper its effectiveness are training and innovations such as e-government, which can be part and parcel of the local personnel function. We will discuss each in turn.

## Training

Faced with the daunting changes in the philosophy and practice of local government HRM, training, and career development will be essential to the successful adoption of new methods to meet public sector needs. In public sector management, the majority of the workforce requires knowledge-based workers. Yet, there are great barriers to making this possible. The barriers tend to be vertical in structure and hierarchical. Innovations in information technology have been credited with enabling worker opportunities to link and share information and experiences horizontally. Training is an area that can foster these processes and linkages but historically has been the first area cut when municipal revenues fall. Additionally, evidence suggests there is already considerably less training in the public sector than the private sector (Shafritz et al., 2001:302–309).

The most common types of training in government are skills training or demonstration; coaching or on-the-job training; formal or informal lecture or classroom training; individual instruction, role playing, job rotation programs, special conferences and seminars, modeling, simulation, and self-paced learning training; and exchange and sabbatical programs (Shafritz et al., 2001:310–312). Although there have been advances, HR managers recognize that the need to meet future challenges will take more than replicating past efforts (West and Berman, 1993). It turns out that those cities that embrace this change "are more likely to implement career development programs, regardless of the city size, type of government or region" (West and Berman, 1993:292).

Career development programs are important components of training. Traditionally, career development was concerned with moving an employee from an entry-level job to the specialist/professional phase to the generalist/team leader phase and culminating in the management/executive phase. Today, learning paths or career models can entail developing individual strengths by having an employee move horizontally to learn new skills and competencies that will be needed at different levels as well as on the more traditional path to career development. The need to invest in training and shepherding career paths becomes apparent as organizations see an increasing demand for new skills. Technology and job-related skills will rank at the top of the list of training needs (Shafritz et al., 2001). Barriers such as merit-system rules, position classification, and other factors embedded in professional pubic personnel administration will need to change. Berman and West (1993:292) note that there is a growing body of literature pointing to the fact that these barriers will not necessarily prevent adoption of new techniques but may make innovations more difficult.

Hays and Kearney (2001) also conducted a study containing projections of 2008 HRM needs based on the anticipated changes due to the reform movements in the public sector. They found technology, workplace expectations, private sector approaches, reinventing government, and political pressures really are changing the recruitment, work, and expectations of HRM in the public sector. They prognosticate that, "[m]uch of the change today and even more of it in the future will be driven by information technology" (2001:595). Technology may very well be making training expected and far less likely to be the first option to be cut when there is a budget crunch. Classroom training has been criticized as the most expensive instructional method. However, innovations in technology such as "virtual" training and other technology-based options may provide more access to training for local government personnel and at a lower cost (Shafritz et al., 2001:331–332).

Before turning to information technology, it is important to mention two other areas in which HR should be playing a role in training and dissemination. The increasing diversity in local workforces requires attention. Civil rights laws and affirmative action have led to a more racially and ethnically diverse public sector as well as one with an increasing number of female employees who are appearing in nontraditional roles. There is also diversity due to sexual preference, disabilities, or recent immigration. Training can assist municipal workers in adapting to an increasingly diverse environment. Human resources staff can play an important role in finding ways to better manage the heterogeneity in so many local governments.

Norma M. Riccucci (2002) has written extensively about managing diversity. She cited a 2000 *New York Times* article, which reported that nooses were placed in public workplaces to harass African American employees. A similar incident occurred in late 2007 at a St. Louis firehouse. After several decades of integration, the department remains divided racially, especially over issues of hiring and promotion. The noose is a reminder that managing diversity is not an academic exercise.

In addition, employers must develop a sexual harassment plan, making clear to all employees that harassment is discrimination and is not to be tolerated. If employers do not have a plan promulgated and a designated place to file complaints (often the personnel department), the city may be liable. This area affects HRM and challenges the previous inaction common to many workforces (Hoyman and Stein, 2005).

## Information Technology

Hays and Kearney (2001) indicate that information technology holds a great deal of promise for innovations that will meet the changing needs and demands in local government personnel administration. The growth of the use of this technology fosters a need for more training. Innovations will take shape through the introduction of e-government. *E-government* refers to the delivery of services via a local government web site. As evidence, a 2000 ICMA survey of 3,749 local governments (city and county) with an 86 percent response rate revealed 42 percent of local governments had a web site and 59 percent used intranet. Additionally, Internet and e-mail access was quite high with 48 percent of localities reporting every department having e-mail access. Fifty-three percent of cities and counties reported every department had Internet access (Smith, 2002:35–36). In 2002, the survey was expanded to 7,005 cities and counties and 53 percent responded (4,123 returns). In 2004, the survey went to 7,944 cities and counties and 3,092 reported back. The 2004 survey found a considerably increased presence of city and county government web sites. Ninety-one percent reported they had a web site in 2004, up from 75 percent in the 2002 survey (Moulder, 2003:39; Coursey, 2005:14).

Clearly, most local governments now have web sites and this has an impact on the services they provide as well as on their own personnel administration practices. In 2000, 86 percent of the cities and counties did not contract out e-government services but, by 2002, in-house web site hosting was down to 55 percent (Smith, 2002:37; Moulder, 2003:42). In 2004, a majority of cities and counties still reported in-house web site management, but the websites have become more complex, necessitating more of a mix of in-house and outsourcing to meet e-government needs. Outsourcing varies by community size. Eighty-one percent of jurisdictions with 250,000 people or more report in-house e-government Web services and a majority with 100,000 or more people also handle their e-government web sites in house. In comparison, 78 percent of smaller communities with populations of 10,000 or less reported that they outsourced their web site services (Coursey, 2005:14).

Norris and Moon examined e-government in their 2005 study and found that e-government was primarily used for information gathering rather than a place to conduct transactions (e.g., obtaining a building permit). In some cases, the web site inadvertently created more work for staff. In other cases, lower administrative cost and staff reductions were reported. Barriers reported to the expansion of e-government web sites included lack of technology, web staff, or financial resources. Ho (2002) also found that insufficient funding and lack of qualified staff were barriers to advancing e-government development. Kim (2004:149–150) noted that in order for managers to retain their information technology staff, they had to address issues of work exhaustion. He suggested the use of more participatory management styles, the need for target dates for project completion, and use of empowerment strategies.

Rocheleau and Wu (2002) found that there are important differences in the way that the public sector and the private sector approach the organizing principles of their information technology systems. The private sector has used the information for internal purposes while the public sector has used recent innovations in information technology for accountability and openness. The private sector also has dedicated more resources and training for information technology. Rocheleau and Wu reported on a survey they had conducted asking elected officials and commissioners about improving information technology. One of the problems they found that affected information technology planning was that the time horizons of local elected officials and commissioners could be too short to accomplish the long-term planning that could maximize the potential of the technology.

The potential for e-government to expand access and create trust and provide services is great but also provides training and resources needs within local governments. West (2004) and Tolbert and Mossberger (2006) found that users of e-government services are more likely to report greater confidence in the online public sector. The potential for public involvement in government may take any of several forms. Thomas and Streib (2005:277, 278) conducted a survey to find out why citizens visit government web sites. They found people use web sites for job-related reasons and personal reasons. In both cases, e-commerce (i.e., transactions with government such as license renewal) ranked highest followed by e-research and e-democracy. E-democracy was the smallest category, and involves citizens expressing a complaint or opinion or possibly wanting a personal response. A greater number of people go to government web sites for information about government or public policy. Although the "internet now serves as major new linkage between society and government" a digital divide—although diminishing—still distinctly exists.

Scott (2006) also studied e-government and the ways governments use technology to get people involved in the process. He (2006:349) found that "very few sites facilitate any online public dialogue or consultation." However, he did find that information, communication, and transactions services on web sites made local governments more accessible as well as more accountable to the citizen. Similar to Norris and Moon (2005), Scott found city size and web site development were positively related. However, Scott noted that cities with a population between 120,000 and 459,000 had web sites that provided the greatest opportunity for public involvement.

The way local governments develop their web sites will have important considerations for e-governance. Brewer, Neubauer, and Geiselhart (2006:492) argued that it cannot be enough to have rote transactions but rather cities should strive for meaningful participation. There should not be a free-for-all vote of pushing buttons on an issue but rather technology needs to be designed to "shape patterns of communication, influence social values, and ultimately affect the common good and public weal."

Taking advantage of recent innovations comes with cautions so that certain populations are not inadvertently left out of the process as noted previously. The digital divide is not inconsequential when we consider that a 2006 study reported that as many as 45 percent of Americans do not have Internet access at home (Mossberger et al., 2006). The study also revealed that race alone is not a statistically significant factor determining access but there is an interaction between race and place. They found that African Americans in areas of concentrated poverty are less likely to have technology access while African Americans residing in wealthier communities are more likely than whites or Asians to have a computer at home. People in areas of concentrated poverty, regardless of demographics, are less likely to have access to a home computer. Internet use rates for Latinos were lower than for non-Hispanic whites. In terms of Internet access then, concentrated poverty is a factor and so is education attainment.

In the end, the NPM is driving the adoption of innovative management practices. The outcomes may be stymied by the engrained personnel practices of the past, but training and innovations in e-government provide mechanisms to obtain practices that increase efficiency and the openness of local government into the future.

Coursey and McCreary (2005) pointed out the implications of information technology for HRM. They noted (2005:201) that "job classification and position descriptions cannot keep pace with rapidly changing technology. Central personnel staffs cannot evaluate these increasingly complex technical skills sets. Traditional tests and evaluation systems quickly become outdated." In addition, public-sector compensation cannot equal that of the private sector. Thus, municipal human resources staff may find it quite difficult to answer the staffing needs created by the increasing use of e-government and information systems technology. This is a challenge for which there is yet no ready remedy.

## IMPLICATIONS

Local government personnel administration conforms to the trajectory of most bureaucracies. For too long, personnel administration has clung to the principles and techniques developed in the Progressive reform era. In more recent years, the standard operating procedures characteristic of many local government personnel systems have frustrated managers, elected officials, and average employees. The emphasis historically has been on control—namely preventing political influence and instead utilizing a scientifically based merit system. Yet, traditional merit techniques have not kept pace with rapidly changing work roles and particularly with new technologies. Venerable personnel practices have come to seem cumbersome, slow, and perhaps irrelevant. The role of organized labor in large city governments has usurped part of the personnel function. Equal employment opportunity and affirmative action have challenged personnel professionals who prided themselves on objectivity and devotion to the merit standard, while confining women to traditional roles and hiring very few members of minority groups. The desire for a representative workforce presented yet another challenge to traditional practice, one accompanied by federal oversight and possible judicial intervention.

In recent years, some have challenged, the very edifice of centralized personnel administration. As Desai and Hamman (1994:391) note,

> Increasing managerial discretion and decentralization are seen as important issues in the debate about improving government performance, productivity, and accountability, and in combating bureaucratic rigidity. The traditional civil service system, characterized by detailed job descriptions and salary schedules, elaborate grievance and disciplinary procedures, appears to leave public managers with very little discretion in managing their human resources.

The desire for devolution of authority to department heads and other managers is a direct by-product of the quest to reinvent government or to move toward Total Quality Management (TQM). Interestingly, just as the Progressives looked at growing corporations as models for their administrative reforms, these latter-day reformers also find their models in the private sector. They are often joined by reformers in other nations who share their enthusiasm for forms of debureaucratization. Whether the enthusiasm and the efforts of these reformers are fully justified is still open to question. For large organizations of people, bureaucracy and the incumbent rules and procedures are not optimal forms but are forms that work in their fashion and for which there is no clearly agreed-upon alternative.

The desire to defuse authority in personnel practice has given birth to radical civil service reform. As Condrey and Battaglio (2007:426) pointed out, "Radical civil service reform is a direct reaction to administrative reform prescriptions that frame government as hamstrung by, among other things, overly bureaucratized civil service systems." Radical reformers wish to end the guarantees of tenure or job security provided by existing systems. They appear to wish to throw out the baby with the bath water "instead of modernizing these systems and their myriad policies and procedures" (Condrey and Battaglio, 2007:428).

Such a radical solution to the crush of standard operating procedures—decentralization—casts doubt on other key concerns of local personnel management. For one, an end to all centralization lessons accountability and the ability to attack equity concerns. It makes affirmative action more difficult and certainly will cause problems regarding compensation with municipal unions.

There is no doubt that the rigid personnel structures developed over a century ago need basic modification to respond to today's needs. They need to adjust classifications to provide for new positions using new technology and in setting up pay scales that realistically reflect national practices as well as local needs. The push for equality for members of minority groups and women helped bring recruitment to modern times. More reform remains highly desirable. The question is whether local elected officials and/or city managers have the will to set about a personnel reform process that examines all aspects of operation and targets smoother, more purposive, and timely administration. To end central personnel administration, particularly in larger communities, is a radical step to take, with consequences of its own. Scholars ought to undertake studies to see whether radical or any other type of reform is actually taking place in local government and under what circumstances. Such study could illustrate the types of cities that reform and why they do.

In the meantime, local government personnel administration appears to be in flux. It is not the old struggle of politics versus merit and efficiency though that is still sometimes present to a certain degree. It is now an issue of bureaucratic reform, major or minor, traditional or radical. In their study of four civil service models, Battaglio and Condrey (2006:118) opted toward "strategic modernization of civil service systems" rather than radical reform. Several years earlier, Ban and Riccucci (1993:99) also saw hope in a number of jurisdictions that had introduced flexibility into their systems. Enhancing recruiting, using multiple measures of abilities, easing selection criteria, and reviewing classifications could make systems more workable. In addition, enhancement of mechanisms for evaluating employees and training on a plethora of topics could assist general performance and provide a greater role for HRM. Enhanced use of information systems technology will provide both challenges and benefits to local government and personnel administration. It is wise to remember that reform movements come and go; time will tell how much local personnel administration will vary from its beginnings in the early twentieth century and how it will adapt to the changing demands of the twenty-first century.

## REFERENCES

Aaron, Henry J., and Cameron M. Lougy. 1986. *The Comparable Worth Controversy.* Washington, D.C.: The Brookings Institution.

Ban, Carolyn, and Norma Riccucci. 1993. Personnel Systems and Labor Relations: Steps Toward a Quiet Revitalization. In *Revitalizing State and Local Public Service.* Frank J. Thompson, ed. San Francisco: Jossey-Bass.

Battglio, R. Paul, Jr., and Stephen E. Condrey. 2006. Civil Service Reform: Examining State and Local Government Cases. *Review of Public Personnel Administration* 26:118–137.

Brewer, Gene A., Bruce J. Neubauer, and Karin Geiselhart. 2006. Designing and Implementing E-Government Systems: Critical Implication for Public Administration and Democracy. *Administration & Society* 38:472–499.

Callahan, Richard F., and G. Ronald Gilbert. 2003. End-User Satisfaction and Design Features of Public Agencies. *American Review of Public Administration* 35:57–73.

Caro, Robert A. 1975. *The Power Broker: Robert Moses and the Fall of New York.* New York: Vintage.

Condrey, Stephen E., and R. Paul Battaglio, Jr. 2007. A Return to Spoils? Revisiting Radical Civil Service Reform in the United States. *Public Administration Review* 67:425–434.

Coplin, William D., and Carol Dwyer. 2000. *Does Your Government Measure Up? Basic Tools for Local Officials and Citizens.* Syracuse, NY: Syracuse University Maxwell School of Citizenship and Public Affairs.

Coursey, David. 2005. E-Government: Trends, Benefits, and Challenges. In *The Municipal Year Book 2005.* Washington D.C.: International City/County Management Association.

Coursey, David H., and Samuel M. McCreary. 2005. Using Technology in the Workplace. In *Handbook of Human Resource Management in Government.* 2nd ed., Stephen E. Condrey, ed. San Francisco: Jossey-Bass.

Desai, Uday, and John A. Hammon. 1994. Images and Reality in Local Government Personnel Practices: Investigating the "Quiet Crisis" Among Illinois City Officials. *Public Administration Review* 4:391–397.

Finegold, Kenneth. 1995. *Experts and Politicians: Reform Challenges to Machine Politics in New York, Cleveland, and Chicago.* Princeton: Princeton University Press.

Haque, M. Shamsul, 2001. The Diminishing Publicness of Public Service under the Current Model of Governance. *Public Administration Review* 61:65–82.

Hays, Samuel P. 1984. The Politics of Reform in the Progressive Era. In *Readings in Urban Politics,* 2nd ed., Harlan Hahn and Charles H. Levine, eds. New York: Longman.

Hays, Steven W., and Richard C. Kearney. 2001. Anticipated Changes in Human Resources Management: Views from the Field. *Public Administration Review* 61:585–597.

Hays, Steven W., and Jessica E. Sowa. 2005. Staffing the Bureaucracy: Employee Recruitment and Selection. In *Handbook of Human Resource Management in Government,* 2nd ed., Stephen E. Condrey, ed. San Francisco: Jossey-Bass.

Ho, Alfred Tat-Kei. 2002. Reinventing local governments and the E-government initiative. *Public Administration Review* 62:434–444.

Hoyman, Michele M., and Lana Stein. 2005. Sexual Harassment in the Workplace. In *Handbook of Human Resource Management in Government,* 2nd ed., Stephen E. Condrey, ed. San Francisco: Jossey-Bass.

Kettl, Donald F. 1993. *Sharing Power: Public Governance and Private Markets.* Washington, D.C.: The Brookings Institution.

Kim, Soonhee. 2004. Factors Affecting State Government Information Technology Employee Turnover Intentions. *American Review of Public Administration* 35:137–156.

Lipsky, Michael. 1980. *Street-Level Bureaucracy: Dilemmas of the Individual in Public Services.* New York: Russell Sage Foundation.

Norris, Donald F., and Moon M. Jae. 2005. Advancing E-Government at the Grassroots: Tortoise or Hare? *Public Administration Review* 65:64–75.

Mossberger, Karen, Caroline J. Tolbert, and Michele Gilbert. 2006. Race, Place, and Information Technology. *Urban Affairs Review* 41:583–620.

Moulder, Evelina R. 2003. E-Government: Trends, Opportunity & Challenges. In *The Municipal Year Book 2003.* Washington D.C.: International City/County Management Association.

Osborne, David, and Ted Gaebler. 1992. *Reinventing Government.* Reading MA: Addison-Wesley.

Prottas, Jeffrey Manditch. 1979. *People-Processing: The Street-Level Bureaucrat in Public Service.* Lexington MA: Lexington Books.

Riccucci, Norma M. 2002. *Managing Diversity in Public Sector Workforces.* Boulder CO: Westview.

Rocheleau, Bruce, and Liangfu Wu. 2002. Public Versus Private Information Systems: Do they Differ in Important Ways? A Review and Empirical Test. *American Review of Public Administration* 32:379–397.

Rodgers, Harrell R., Jr., and Charles S. Bullock, III. 1972. *Law and Social Change: Civil Rights Laws and Their Consequences.* New York: McGraw-Hill.

Schiesl, Martin J. 1977. *The Politics of Efficiency: Municipal Administration and Reform in America: 1880–1920.* Berkeley: University of California Press.

Scott, James K. 2006. "E" the People: Do U.S. Municipal Government Web Sites support Public Involvement? *Public Administration Review* 66:341–353.

Shafritz, Jay M. 1973. *Position Classification: A Behavioral Analysis for the Public Service.* New York: Praeger.

Smith, Russell. 2002. The "Electronic Village": Local Government and E-Government at the dawn of a New Millennium. In *The Municipal Year Book 2002.* Washington D.C.: International City/County Management Association.

Stein, Lana. 1991. *Holding Bureaucrats Accountable: Politicians and Professionals in St. Louis.* Tuscaloosa: University of Alabama Press.

————. 1994. Personnel Rules and Reform in an Unreformed Setting: St. Louis' Politicized Merit System. *Review of Public Personnel Administration* 14:55–63.

Stein, Lana, and Stephen E. Condrey. 1987. Integrating Municipal Workforces: A Study of Six Southern Cities. *Publius* 17:93–104.

Terry. L. 2005. The Thinning of Administrative Institutions in the Hollow State. *Administration & Society* 37:426–444.

Thomas, John C., and Gregory Streib. 2005. E-Democracy, E-Commerce and E-Research: Examining the Electronic Ties Between Citizens and Governments. *Administration and Society* 37:259–280.

Thompson, Frank J. 1975. *Personnel Policy in the City: The Politics of Jobs in Oakland.* Berkeley: University of California Press.

Tobias, Robert M. 2005. Employee Unions and the Human Resources Management Function. In *Handbook of Human Resource Management in Government*, 2nd ed. Stephen E. Condrey, ed. San Francisco: Jossey-Bass.

Tolbert, Caroline J., and Karen Mossberger. 2006. "The Effects of E-Government on Trust and Confidence in Government." *Public Administration Review* 66:354–369.

U.S. Commission on Civil Rights. 1969. For All the People . . . By All the People: A Report on Equal Opportunity in State and Local Government Employment. Washington, D.C.

West, Darrell M. 2004. E-Government and the Transformation of Service Delivery and Citizen Attitudes. *Public Administration Review* 64:15–27.

West, Jonathan P., and Evan Berman. 1993. Human Resource Strategies in Local Government: A Survey of Progress and Future Directions. *American Review of Public Administration* 23:279–297.

# Personnel Recruitment and Retention in the Nonprofit Sector

BETH GAZLEY

Indiana University—Bloomington

## INTRODUCTION

Approximately 1.4 million organizations are recognized under the federal tax code as "nonprofits": exempt entities organized for public or mutual purposes. Two-thirds of these organizations are private foundations, public charities or religious congregations recognized jointly as 501(c)(3) organizations (Pollak and Blackwood, 2007). Overall, more than 12 million paid employees and an estimated 45 million or more volunteers comprise the nonprofit labor force (Leete, 2006).[1] By comparison, all levels of government employ 22 million persons and involve an estimated 15 million or more volunteers (United States Bureau of Labor Statistics, 2007).[2] See Table 6.1.

Although the sector is enormously diverse in terms of its scope of activities, distinct employment patterns emerge. Just 2 percent of nonprofit organizations control three-quarters of the sector's assets. Two fields dominate: health and education, controlling 70 percent of the nonprofit sector's assets and employing 64 percent of its labor force (Leete, 2006; Pollak and Blackwood, 2007). A further 18 percent of the nonprofit labor force is employed in social and legal services, 12 percent in religious organizations, 4 percent in civic and fraternal organizations, and 2 percent in arts and culture (Leete, 2006:160).[3] See Table 6.2.

This chapter's discussion of personnel challenges and opportunities in the nonprofit sector is set against this broad and diverse landscape of civil society organizations. The chapter first discusses the demographic changes that influence nonprofit employment and service provision in the United States, and the economic forces that challenge effective HRM in the nonprofit sector. Second, the chapter focuses on

**TABLE 6.1    Nonprofit Sector Employment in the United States, 1972–2001**

| Year | Nonprofit Sector Employment* | U.S. Civilian Employment | Percentage of Nonprofit Employment |
|---|---|---|---|
| 1972 | 4,576,000 | 82,153,000 | 5.6 |
| 1977 | 5,519,500 | 92,017,000 | 6.0 |
| 1982 | 6,500,000 | 99,526,000 | 6.5 |
| 1987 | 7,400,000 | 112,440,000 | 6.6 |
| 1992 | 9,100,000 | 118,492,000 | 7.7 |
| 1997 | 10,600,000 | 129,558,000 | 8.2 |
| 1998 | 10,900,000 | 131,463,000 | 8.3 |
| 2001 | 11,700,000 | 136,933,000 | 8.5 |

*Includes only organizations registered under Sections 501(c)(3) and 501(c)(4) of the tax code, as well as religious congregations.

*Source:* Reprinted by permission of Yale University Press from Leete, L. Work in the nonprofit sector. Powell, W. W. and Steinberg, R. (Eds.) *The Nonprofit Sector: A Research Handbook,* 2nd ed. 159–179. New Haven, CT: Yale University Press. Copyright 2006 Yale University Press.

**TABLE 6.2    Distribution of Public Benefit Nonprofit* Employment Across Different Types of Organizations in the United States, 1972–2001**

| Year | Health Services | Education/ Research | Religious Organizations | Social and Legal Services | Civic, Social and Fraternal Organizations | Arts and Culture | Foundations |
|---|---|---|---|---|---|---|---|
| 1972 | 42.2 | 21.1 | 19.0 | 10.2 | 6.1 | 1.9 | 0.3 |
| 1977 | 44.5 | 23.2 | 12.3 | 13.0 | 5.5 | 1.2 | 0.3 |
| 1982 | 47.0 | 22.1 | 10.6 | 14.1 | 4.7 | 1.4 | 0.3 |
| 1987 | 45.6 | 22.5 | 8.8 | 16.2 | 5.0 | 1.6 | 0.3 |
| 1992 | 46.6 | 20.6 | 10.5 | 15.6 | 4.6 | 1.8 | 0.3 |
| 1997 | 43.5 | 21.6 | 11.4 | 17.2 | 4.2 | 1.9 | 0.3 |
| 1998 | 42.9 | 21.6 | 11.6 | 17.5 | 4.2 | 1.9 | 0.3 |
| 2001 | 41.9 | 21.9 | 11.8 | 18.3 | 3.9 | 1.9 | 0.3 |

*Includes only organizations registered under Sections 501(c)(3) and 501(c)(4) of the tax code, as well as religious congregations.

*Source:* Reprinted by permission of Yale University Press from Leete, L. Work in the nonprofit sector. Powell, W. W. and Steinberg, R. (Eds.) *The Nonprofit Sector: A Research Handbook,* 2nd ed. 159–179. New Haven, CT: Yale University Press. Copyright 2006 Yale University Press.

recruitment and retention challenges that face HR managers, with attention to both paid and unpaid (volunteer) personnel issues. A summary of the current research on effective personnel practices follows. Where possible, comparative data are offered to put nonprofit personnel management in a broader context.

## ECONOMIC AND DEMOGRAPHIC CHALLENGES

The United States is "simultaneously aging and growing more diverse" (Halpern, 2006:4). Observers also describe a "growing and unhealthy gap between the haves and the have-nots" (Walker, 2006). Increases in health care costs, welfare reform, and fiscal constraints on federal, state, and local governments place new demands on public and private services.

These trends pose both workforce and workplace challenges for the nonprofit sector. As service providers, nonprofit organizations assisting disadvantaged populations report higher demands for their help (Bishop, 2006; Salamon and O'Sullivan, 2004). And as employers, securing and retaining a workforce with the right combination of knowledge, skills and abilities has been a longstanding challenge for nonprofit organizations both within and without the charitable subsector. Increased competition from other sectors for highly skilled employees, high executive management turnover, the labor intensity of some portions of the sector, and limited success in the ability to recruit and retain skilled volunteers all combine to make twenty-first century HRM in the nonprofit sector an enormously demanding activity.

## THE NONPROFIT LABOR FORCE

The employee profile of the nonprofit sector reflects the strong representation of service industries (compared, for example, to manufacturing in the for-profit sector). A greater percentage of nonprofit employees are part-time or temporary workers, and substantially more nonprofit employees are female (67 percent of the nonprofit workforce) when compared to business (44 percent) or the federal government (49 percent). The sector also has a slightly higher educational level and slightly less racial diversity than the national labor force (Leete, 2006). See Table 6.3.

A common assumption is that nonprofits cannot compete with organizations in other sectors on the basis of wages and benefits. In actuality, nonprofit wages vary widely according to geography, occupation, and employee qualifications. Controlling for these factors, organizational size and funding mix are the strongest predictors of salary difference within particular nonprofit industries. Across sectors, average nonprofit wages are slightly lower than those in the government and for-profit sectors (Leete, 2006; Ruhm and Borkoski, 2003). Executive compensation in the nonprofit sector is substantially lower than that of for-profits (Twombly and Gantz, 2001). Governmental comparisons are not readily available.

However, selective controlled occupational or industry studies often erase the disparities. Although governmental comparisons are difficult to make given the way public sector jobs are classified, nonprofit salaries often surpass those in for-profits. The difference tends to occur in industries where both sectors are active, such as childcare, home health care, and teaching (Salamon, 2002). In other words, where wage disparities appear, they tend to be "an industry problem, not a nonprofit problem" (Salamon, 2002:61).

Scholars have wrestled over not only the nature and extent of these pay disparities, but their causes. A combination of internal and external circumstances—particularly, market pressures, government regulation, differences in employer behavior caused by presence/absence of a profit motive, and employee self-selection—explains

TABLE 6.3   Characteristics of U.S. Nonprofit and For-Profit
Sector Workers, 1989 (Not Disabled and Not Enrolled in School)

|  | Nonprofit | For-Profit |
|---|---|---|
| Female | 66.6 | 43.9 |
| Not fluent in English | 1.3 | 3.1 |
| **Race** | | |
| White | 83.8 | 81.5 |
| African American | 9.5 | 9.4 |
| Hispanic | 2.5 | 3.4 |
| Asian | 2.4 | 2.6 |
| Other race | 1.9 | 3.2 |
| **Education Level** | | |
| Eighth grade or less | 2.7 | 5.6 |
| Some high school, no degree | 6.5 | 13.6 |
| High school graduate or GED | 21.7 | 35.2 |
| Some college | 17.6 | 20.5 |
| Associates degree | 9.4 | 6.7 |
| Bachelors degree | 22.6 | 13.5 |
| Graduate degree | 19.4 | 4.9 |

*Source:* Reprinted by permission of Yale University Press from Leete, L. Work in the
nonprofit sector. Powell, W. W. and Steinberg, R. (Eds.) *The Nonprofit Sector: A Research
Handbook*, 2nd ed., 159–179. New Haven, CT: Yale University Press. Copyright 2006
Yale University Press.

many of the observable differences. The great diversity within the sector makes generalizations difficult, but many individual economic studies find evidence of "sorting"
behaviors and a complicated matching process that involves both employer and
employee behavior (Leete, 2006:162). Understanding what attracts employees and
volunteers to the nonprofit labor market therefore becomes an imperative for HR
managers and a principal area of exploration in this chapter.

## A CHALLENGING RECRUITMENT ENVIRONMENT

### A Debate over the Extent of the Problem

A recent report from the Johns Hopkins University Center for Civil Society
Studies was published under the provocative title: *The Nonprofit Workforce Crisis:
Real or Imagined?* (Salamon and Geller, 2007). The title alludes to contradictory
findings on the status of the nonprofit labor force. As Figure 6.1 illustrates, the sector has enjoyed robust employment growth in recent years, outpacing the rate of
growth in the commercial and governmental sectors (Irons and Bass, 2004; Leete,
2006). Selective studies also find nonprofits to be fairly resilient in their ability to

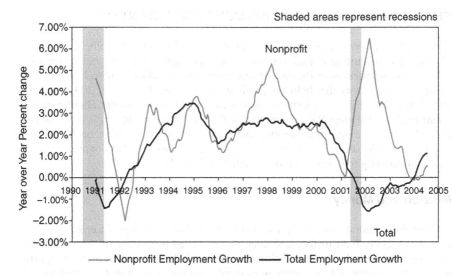

**FIGURE 6.1   Growth in Employment**

*Source:* Reprinted with permission from *Recent Trends in Nonprofit Employment and Earnings: 1990–2004.* Washington, DC: OMB Watch (August 2004).

meet workforce challenges (Salamon and Geller, 2007). However, Figure 6.1 also illustrates the greater volatility of nonprofit employment, where peaks and troughs respond not only to economic trends, but also to policy initiatives or national events that spur an interest in public service.

Yet, many nonprofit organizations report a challenging recruitment environment. And although this is not a phenomenon unique to one sector, nonprofits have higher annual employee turnover than government and business (3.1 percent, compared to 2.7 percent in the business sector and 1 percent in the government sector) (Cappelli, 2005; Weitzman et al., 2002). Some extrapolated analyses project a "leadership deficit" in the tens of thousands based on current growth of the sector, anticipated retirements, and employee transitions to other sectors (Tierney, 2006).

The most pressing ongoing workforce challenges appear to rest on the sector's ability to offer competitive salaries and to recruit qualified staff, particularly in smaller organizations (Ban, Drahnak, and Towers, 2002; Salamon and Geller, 2007). The extent of the labor deficit varies widely according to geography and organizational characteristics. In one statewide study, larger nonprofits and those dependent on government funding report the greatest recruitment challenges (Grønbjerg and Clerkin, 2004).

To the extent that they occur, recruitment challenges experienced by individual organizations have important repercussions. An organization's inability to find the right staff will make the jobs of other staff more challenging. An inability to find staff who reflect the demographic characteristics of clients will make it more difficult to serve particular client populations. Performance quality can also suffer. In one employment survey examining managerial responses to vacancies or turnover, 26 percent of nonprofit organizations reported responding to labor shortages by retaining under-performing staff, and 22 percent postponed or cancelled new programs (Peters et al., 2002).

## EFFECTIVE EMPLOYEE RECRUITMENT AND RETENTION

When staff turnover compromises organizational performance, learning the practices of effective recruitment and retention becomes an organizational imperative. Competitive salaries, benefits, and advancement opportunities represent the principal organizational factors that help nonprofit staff recruitment (Preston, 2002; Salamon and Geller, 2007). Two widespread pieces of conventional wisdom about nonprofit compensation challenge HR managers. The first is that nonprofit employers will have difficulty finding employees because they cannot compete for labor on the basis of salary alone. The second, somewhat competing assumption is that nonprofit workers "are motivated by mission, not money" (Bacon, 2004:1).

### Mission *and* Money

Both of these assumptions hold a kernel of truth. Indeed, nonprofit employers may find it especially hard to find and keep those skilled professionals who can easily cross sectoral boundaries. Nonprofits have lagged behind the business sector particularly when it comes to performance-based compensation. But the problem with these assumptions lies in its suggestion that individuals are motivated by only one or the other of these employment features; that is, either by mission *or* money.

In reality, most individuals make job choices based on a mix of motivating factors, including salary but also including an expectation of other, nonmonetary benefits. Theuvsen (2004:125) observes that "most [employee] actions are in fact extrinsically as well as intrinsically motivated." Nonprofit organizations do well in attracting recruits when they understand the intrinsic motivations of prospective employees, including a desire to produce work of social value, to serve others, to effect change, and to know that they make a difference. Functionally, job design, screening, and interviewing represent the foundations of effective recruitment strategies. Nonprofits will also perform well at recruitment when they are able to communicate the extrinsic rewards of a position in terms of both monetary and nonmonetary benefits. Salient monetary strategies include employee benefits, salary adjustments, and pay-for-performance policies (Ban et al., 2002). Nonmonetary retention strategies focus on job enrichment and advancement opportunities (Day, 2004).

Organizations must also practice managerial techniques that encourage new employees to stay. Studies suggest that many employees join the nonprofit sector for reasons that are distinct from those that keep them in their jobs. The salience of mission may become a less important driver of employee job satisfaction than pay, workplace culture, and opportunities for advancement (Ban et al., 2002; Brown and Yoshioka, 2003). In other words, an organization must understand employee motivations both in terms of what attracts them to nonprofit work (such as mission) and also in terms of what keeps them from leaving (such as benefits, advancement opportunities, and workplace culture).

### Retention Strategies

Small- to mid-sized nonprofit organizations may find themselves particularly challenged in their ability to compete for staff on the basis of pay. Many low-cost strategies are available for them. Retention strategies with a potentially high impact and

low cost include professional development opportunities, family-friendly job benefits such as flextime, telecommuting, family leave time, transportation subsidies,
health benefits, career ladders, and childcare and eldercare subsidies. Supervisors
can be supported with professional development and supervisor support programs.
Managers can recognize exceptional performance through public recognition and
reverse mentoring, and reward longevity through anniversary gifts. Nonprofits can
ensure employees continue to understand their contributions to the organizational
mission by performing outcome evaluations and communicating the results to staff
(Brown and Yoshioka, 2003). In all cases, compensation strategies consistent with
organizational goals, culture, and strategy, and those that can be defended from an
equity basis will be most easily accepted by staff.

Information on the impact of such policies is scarce. It is difficult to assess the
influence of organizational HR strategies on employee retention in isolation from
other external factors that attract individuals to nonprofit work (such as personality) or
cause them to leave (such as family needs). One study of nonprofit executives suggests
that many senior staff, at least, are willing to accept a greater emphasis on non-salary
benefits. Half of those surveyed preferred a salary increase to improve their compensation packages; the remainder suggested retirement contributions, vacation time, and
other monetary and nonmonetary benefits (Bell, Moyers, and Wolfred, 2006). Fewer
than half feel they are making a high financial sacrifice to work where they do—yet
the same number believe the next CEO will expect to earn at least 10 percent more
than they do. These figures suggest that nonprofit executives are aware of their market
value, but willing to negotiate with their boards to create benefit packages that meet
their needs. Similar research for other staff levels would be useful.

## Work and Pay Equity

An additional retention challenge lies in improving work and pay equity. Although
the amount of discriminatory employer behavior appears to be smaller in the nonprofit sector when compared to the for-profit sector (Leete, 2006), pay discrimination according to gender and other demographic characteristics has been found in
many studies of the nonprofit sector (Bell et al., 2006; Grey and Benson, 2003;
Lipman, 2002). Selective occupational analyses find some patterns indicative of
gender discrimination in advancement opportunities, salaries, and performance
bonuses (Gibelman, 2000; Mesch and Rooney, 2008). Although more cross-sectoral
comparisons (e.g., nonprofit/government comparisons) would be helpful, nonprofits are no more immune to discriminatory practices than any other sector. And many
nonprofit employees have minimal legal protection if their employer's small size
restricts employee coverage under federal labor laws. Managers should understand
that a mission with social value does not substitute for a thorough understanding of
employment law.

## Executive Retention: Can Compensation Reduce Turnover?

Across the nonprofit sector, studies also find a high rate of turnover at the executive director level. According to two national studies by the Bridgespan Group
and CompassPoint, three-quarters of nonprofit CEOs plan to leave their job in the
next five years, creating a potential leadership deficit that may limit the ability of
many nonprofits to meet their organizational objectives (Bell et al., 2006; Tierney,

2006). The annual survey of executive compensation and benefits produced by the *Chronicle of Philanthropy* found that nearly one-third of surveyed nonprofits replaced a top executive in 2006 (Barton and Panepento, 2007). Compounding the problem is an absence of succession planning at the majority of surveyed nonprofits (Hrywna, 2007).

It is important to mention that executive turnover has benign features: few CEOs plan to leave the sector entirely; many intend to transition to other nonprofit positions that offer new opportunities, or to related fields such as consulting (Tierney, 2006). Thus, the turnover in executive staff may not represent a heavy loss of institutional knowledge for the sector overall, and may in fact help to disseminate knowledge through and between sectors.

However, the two most commonly cited reasons for leaving are troubling. We first observe that the turnover is only partially due to an aging workforce and planned retirements (DRG, 2006; Teegarden, 2004). Rather, the majority of executive directors point specifically to dissatisfaction with their boards of directors or their compensation package as the factors that will drive them out of their current positions (Bell et al., 2006). Although it is typical for professional staff in any sector to move on to larger organizations in search of better pay or new challenges, even at the largest nonprofit organizations, a substantial minority (41 percent) of executive directors plan to leave within the next three to five years.

Nearly half of those intending to leave report frustration with unsupportive boards (Bell et al., 2006). The dynamic between board and CEO has been addressed widely in the nonprofit management literature, with strong opinions but little general agreement about the best balance of roles and responsibilities between the staff and the governing members of the organization (see, for example, Carver, 2007; Harris, 1993). As a result, both boards and executive staff can impose unreasonable or unacceptable expectations on one another. In no other sector do we find a group of part-time, uncompensated individuals who govern with varying levels of expertise and organizational allegiance but remain nonetheless legally in charge of an organization. Even as the regulatory environment has grown more complex and the amount of information board members are required to understand has increased, it is not at all clear that board members are receiving the training and incentives they need to do their jobs well. Executive turnover may reflect this situation.

Secondly, fundraising pressures place a heavy burden on nonprofit CEOs. The nonprofit fundraising environment has generally grown more challenging over time, fueled by greater donor expectations, heavier regulatory burdens, and increased competition from within and without the sector. Nonprofit CEOs have more to know and more to do to secure organizational resources, and they consequently cite financial stability as their chief internal organizational challenge (Bell et al., 2006).

Both of these causes for executive turnover reflect fundamental characteristics of the sector that may be difficult to address, particularly when understood in the context of legal restrictions on nonprofit executive compensation. It is a common misunderstanding that nonprofit executive pay levels are capped in some way. In reality, boards of directors enjoy great discretion in setting pay levels provided they can justify their decisions with comparable market data and evidence that the decision was made in a way that avoids conflicts of interest. However, the public nature of these salaries (disclosure is required in the 990 tax return since passage of the Taxpayer Bill of Rights) and the amount of press that has been generated about "unreasonable" nonprofit executive pay make many boards conservative in their approach to compensation.

Recent years have seen a slight loosening of the regulations and increased realization by boards of the need to create competitive compensation packages to attract executive talent. The change has been supported by the entry of more business executives into nonprofit employment and board service. Nonetheless, public and donor pressure, legal restrictions that enforce the non-distribution constraint, and other features of the regulatory environment provide strong incentives to boards of directors to minimize risk in setting executive compensation packages. Although salary and benefits, particularly pension payments and bonuses, are likely to continue to improve in the nonprofit sector, they can be expected to do so in a highly stratified way, with the largest organizations initiating the greatest pay increases. Although the nation's largest nonprofits are currently increasing executive salaries faster than their for-profit counterparts, average sectoral salaries for other positions are barely keeping pace with inflation (Barton, Mento, and Sanoff, 2007; Barton and Panepento, 2007; Hrywna, 2007; Schwinn and Wilhelm, 2003). It remains to be seen how small-to mid-sized nonprofit organizations address executive turnover, how the salary push at the executive level translates to mid-level professionals, and what tools and strategies are found to be most helpful.

## VOLUNTEER RECRUITMENT AND RETENTION

Nonprofit organizations can experience labor shortages not only with paid staff but also with volunteers. Nationally, most nonprofit managers report they are ready and willing to take on more volunteers (Hager and Brudney, 2004). Volunteers represent essential resources for many nonprofit organizations. Volunteer service itself has been linked to many other kinds of prosocial behaviors, including greater generosity and higher voting participation.

### Recruiting Challenges with Volunteers

Recruiting sufficient numbers of volunteers is a major problem for one in four (24 percent) of these organizations. Recruiting workday volunteers is their principal challenge (Hager and Brudney, 2004).[4] In a localized study, nearly half (about 47 percent) of Indiana nonprofits with revenues of $250,000 or more report that recruiting and retaining qualified volunteers is a major challenge (Grønbjerg and Clerkin, 2004).

Public policies and programs from the federal level on down have created resources to promote volunteerism, and communicate the societal and personal benefits of volunteering. Myriad programs have been instituted across the United States to encourage civic engagement, from federal stipended service to school and campus volunteer-for-credit programs. It is difficult to tell whether these programs are succeeding in increasing the numbers of volunteers, and in filling the recruitment gap. Trend data are inconsistent, and causal factors are difficult to interpret. The most reliable national data report increases in some specific areas of volunteering and an increase in the numbers of Americans who volunteer, but reflect only a small increase over time in the overall percentage of Americans who volunteer and little change in the hours they contribute (Brudney and Gazley, 2006; Grimm et al., 2006).

There is some hope, however—provided volunteer and HR managers can understand how to capitalize on it. Volunteering among teens and young adults has increased significantly in recent years, no doubt spurred by the focus of many federal and local initiatives on this age group. Recent research on the retirement plans of baby boomers (who currently volunteer at higher than average levels) also suggests that many will continue to volunteer, perhaps even increasing their level of activity post-retirement (Grimm et al., 2006).

## Reducing Volunteer "Churn" with Retention Strategies

Without efforts not only to attract but to *keep* volunteers, volunteer promotional activities do nothing but feed volunteer turnover. One out of every three people who volunteer during a given year does not return the following year (Wilhelm, 2007). This volunteer "churn" results in a substantial drain on organizational resources. Two factors will help organizations to attract and keep more volunteers: more personnel and non-personnel volunteer management resources, and better volunteer management training.

First, nonprofits will be limited in their ability to improve volunteer retention when they are under-resourced. Nonprofit managers cite lack of funds to support volunteers as a principal barrier to volunteer retention, followed by lack of staff time to train and supervise volunteers (Hager and Brudney, 2004). Volunteer management closely parallels HRM in its functions: volunteers are also subject to job design, screening, interviewing, training, supervision, and performance evaluation. National data suggest that while most nonprofits perform these functions with volunteers to some degree, fewer than half perform them to a large degree (Hager and Brudney, 2004). Surprisingly, the frequency of such practices is driven more by organizational size than by the importance of volunteer labor to a particular organization. For example, only one in four Indiana nonprofits (26 percent) has a formal volunteer recruitment program, and only 46 percent of nonprofits involving one hundred or more volunteers do so (Grønbjerg and Clerkin, 2004).

Board members and executive staff are more likely to provide resources for volunteer management when they recognize the value of volunteers to the organizational mission. However, at present, just 30 percent of nonprofits report they annually measure the impacts of volunteers to a large degree, and 32 percent report impact measurement to a small degree (Hager and Brudney, 2004). Staff within organizations that are heavily dependent on volunteers for service provision should be involving their board in planning for volunteers, in thinking through a vision of volunteer involvement for the organization, in integrating volunteer planning with other HR plans, in ensuring the program is designed to be most helpful in achieving a mission, and in assessing how to measure the value of the program (Brudney, 1999; Ellis, 1996).

Present widespread strategies at calculating volunteer value involve simple head counts at the intake level, and calculations of the dollar value of volunteers based on standard wage levels. These provide minimal and incomplete information, and are unlikely to succeed by themselves in convincing executive staff or external stakeholders of volunteer value. Volunteer impact should also be assessed with client feedback, quantification of service increases, measurement of qualitative improvements in services and the social value of volunteer involvement (particularly in preventing other social ills), and measurement of volunteer contributions to staff efficiency and effectiveness (Ellis, 1996).

Second, given the present demographics of U.S. volunteers, volunteer and HR managers and volunteers will succeed in attracting and retaining the new volunteer labor force when they learn how to adjust or improve their recruitment and retention strategies to meet the expectations of this diverse volunteer labor pool. To understand volunteer behavior and expectations takes training (Jamison, 2003). Today's volunteers come with a wider array of skills and expectations than in past generations. They are more likely to work short-term or episodically—this expectation is found particularly with the two most promising demographic groups: baby boomers and young adults (Grimm et al., 2006). They are more likely to volunteer for credit or a learning experience, or to have childcare needs. They have a greater consumer orientation and can be more demanding. They may expect, for example, to have a choice of assignments and to participate in the decision on how they will be deployed. They are more likely to expect recognition and advancement. Penner (2002) argues that effective volunteer retention requires an understanding of a range of internal and external drivers of sustained volunteerism. According to Penner, and much as they do with paid staff, HR managers must understand both the situational factors that lead a volunteer to serve, and also the organizational attributes and management strategies that will encourage them to stay.

In order to address the expectations of present-day volunteers while still meeting organizational objectives, volunteer and HR managers will especially need to learn how to design volunteer assignments to make episodic and short-term volunteering a gateway to more permanent, long-term service, how to screen volunteers effectively in order to place them appropriately, and how to recognize contributions in multiple ways that are meaningful to different kinds of volunteers. They will then need to devise effective means of communicating internally and externally the value of volunteering—internally, to demonstrate to volunteers the importance of their work, and externally, to donors and other stakeholders to communicate the need for volunteer support. Public policymakers, in the meantime, can support volunteer retention by placing greater emphasis and resources not only on recruitment but on the strategies and management capacity that will improve volunteer job satisfaction.

## CONCLUSION: IMPROVING NONPROFIT HUMAN RESOURCE MANAGEMENT CAPACITY

The early years of the twenty-first century present nonprofits with a challenging human capital environment. Competition with other sectors for labor, greater demands for nonprofit services, an aging workforce, and pressures of the executive position are creating higher staff turnover than in other sectors, particularly at executive levels. Many nonprofits are more successful at attracting volunteers than in keeping them. Both paid and volunteer personnel are subject to a great amount of employment "churn", which in turn affects organizational efficiency and service quality. This chapter suggests that the solution lies in great part in finding personnel with the right mix of interests, skills, and motivation to be attracted to the nonprofit sector, and then employing the right HR practices and strategies to retain them.

This environment demands a strategic outlook from HR managers and a strong set of management skills. On the first count, nonprofits can benefit from a holistic approach to HR management embodied in the concept of *strategic human resources management* (Pynes, 2004). SHRM practices are integrated with organizational mission. They are aligned with organizational priorities and attuned to workplace culture and external dynamics. Strategic HR practices occur at the center of the organization rather than the periphery, and are embraced by all supervisors rather than a single HR department. They are proactive in anticipating the impact of market forces, and in designing strategies to take advantage of internal or external strengths and opportunities.

The strategic HR manager must be supported in these activities with adequate resources and knowledge. Beginning at the board level, nonprofit executives must understand the process of employee and volunteer recruitment, motivation, and retention as interrelated activities dependent on all staff for success. The HR function in many nonprofits is under-staffed and under-resourced; boards might profit with a review of their internal functions and an assignment of greater organizational resources to staff and volunteer management. Furthermore, nonprofit jobs are increasingly professionalized, and the rapid increase in graduate programs in nonprofit management offers HR managers new opportunities to broaden their skills and knowledge about volunteer and staff expectations (Pynes, 2004). As educational levels increase, more nonprofit managers can be expected to implement the managerial tools and strategies that support effective personnel recruitment and retention.

To the extent that each organization applies a more strategic approach to HRM functions, the results are bound to support both mission achievement and organizational efficiencies. Effective recruitment, for example, could be supported by disseminating organizational information through web sites, by including employees and board members in recruitment activities, and by being prepared to demonstrate organizational successes to job candidates (Dicke and Ott, 2003). Younger workers can be attracted through internship programs and attention to professional advancement. Careful screening of job candidates and volunteers to understand their expectations and level of interest can assign them appropriately and support retention of both paid and unpaid staff. Career ladders can be developed for volunteers that support long-term volunteer retention by capitalizing on the natural desire of many individuals to progress to more challenging and responsible assignments. Staff and executive compensation strategies can take advantage of—and be justified by—the market research that is now widely available to HR managers. These strategies require a certain mindset from nonprofit managers and board members, one that embraces rather than retreats from the challenges this sector faces. Above all, they require nonprofit managers to understand and be able to capitalize on the powerful attraction of nonprofit work, but in a way that values both employee and volunteer.

## NOTES

1. This figure includes only public benefit nonprofits only [501(c)(3) and (c)(4) organizations].
2. The distribution of volunteers between the nonprofit and government sectors is an estimate because national volunteer statistics have not captured this information since 1992. In that year, approximately one in four Americans volunteered in the public sector (in libraries, fire departments, schools, parks and recreation departments, advisory boards, etc.) (Brudney, 1999). To extrapolate a current

figure, I use the Bureau of Labor Statistics' 2007 estimate of 61 million adult volunteers to arrive at approximately 15 million government volunteers and 45 million nonprofit volunteers. These figures should be considered rough estimates, given lack of current data. Moreover, the number of volunteers is most likely underestimated, given reliance on "formal" (institutional) volunteering in data collection, inconsistent definitions of volunteering, and inconsistent findings across studies.

3. This figure includes the distribution for public benefit nonprofits only [501(c)(3) and 501(c)(4) organizations].
4. These figures are based on a national survey of only 501(c)(3) charities and congregations. Only the responses of charities are reported here.

# REFERENCES

Bacon, Su. 2004. Workers Are Motivated by Mission, Not Money. *The Kansas City Star:* May 18.

Ban, Carolyn, Alexis Drahnak, and Marcia Towers. 2002. *Human Resource Challenges of Human Service and Community Development Organizations: Recruitment and Retention of Professional Staff in the Not-for Profit Sector.* Pittsburgh, PA: The Forbes Fund.

Barton, Noelle, and Peter Panepento. 2007. Executive Pay Rises 4.6%. *Chronicle of Philanthropy.* September 20, 2007. Available at http://www.philanthropy.com/free/articles/v19/i23/23003401.htm. (September 20).

Barton, Noelle, Maria Di Mento, and Alvin P. Sanoff. 2007. Top Nonprofit Executives See Healthy Pay Raises. *Chronicle of Philanthropy.* Available at http://www.philanthropy.com/free/articles/v18/i24/24003901.htm. (September 28).

Bell, Jeanne, Richard Moyers, and Timothy Wolfred. 2006. *Daring to Lead 2006: A National Study of Nonprofit Executive Leadership.* Washington, DC: CompassPoint Nonprofit Services and Eugene and Agnes E. Meyer Foundation.

Bishop, Sheilah Watson. 2006. Nonprofit Federalism and the CSBG Program: Serving the Needs of the Working Poor in the Post-TANF Era. *Administration & Society* 37 (6):695–718.

Brown, William A., and Carlton F. Yoshioka. 2003. Mission Attachment and Satisfaction as Factors in Employee Retention. *Nonprofit Management & Leadership* 14 (1):5–18.

Brudney, Jeffrey L. 1999. The Effective Use of Volunteers: Best Practices for the Public Sector. *Law & Contemporary Problems* 62 (4):219–255.

Brudney, Jeffrey L., and Gazley, Beth. 2005. Moving Ahead or Falling behind? Volunteer Promotion and Data Collection. *Nonprofit Management & Leadership* 16 (3):259–276.

Cappelli, Peter. 2005. Will There Really Be a Labor Shortage? *Human Resource Management* 44 (2):143–149.

Carver, John. 2007. *The Policy Governance Model.* Available at http://carvergovernance.com/model.htm.

Day, Nancy. 2004. Total Rewards Programs in Nonprofit Organizations. In *The Jossey-Bass Handbook of Nonprofit Leadership & Management,* 2nd ed., Robert D. Herman, ed. San Francisco: Jossey-Bass, pp. 660–702.

Dicke, Lisa A., and J. Steven Ott. 2003. Post-September 11 Human Resource Management in Nonprofit Organizations. *Review of Public Personnel Administration* 23 (2):97–113.

DRG. 2006. *2006 Nonprofit CEO Survey Results.* New York, NY: The Development Resource Group, Inc. Available at http://www.drgnyc.com/2006_Survey/Index.htm.

Ellis, Susan J. 1996. *From the Top Down: The Executive Role in Volunteer Program Success.* Philadelphia, PA: Energize, Inc.

Gibelman, Margaret. 2000. The Nonprofit Sector and Gender Discrimination: A Preliminary Investigation into the Glass Ceiling. *Nonprofit Management & Leadership* 10 (2):251–269.

Grey, Samuel R., and Philip G. Benson. 2003. Determinants of Executive Compensation in Small Business Development Centers. *Nonprofit Management & Leadership* 13 (3):213–222.

Grimm, Robert, Nathan Dietz, John Foster-Bey, David Reingold, and Rebecca Nesbit. 2006. *Volunteer Growth in America: A Review of Trends Since 1974.* Washington, DC: Corporation for National and Community Service.

Grønbjerg, Kirsten A., and Richard M. Clerkin. 2004. *Indiana Nonprofits: Managing Financial and Human Resources.* Bloomington, IN: Indiana University School of Public and Environmental Affairs.

Hager, Mark A., and Jeffrey L. Brudney. 2004. *Volunteer Management Capacity in America's Charities and Congregations.* Washington, DC: The Urban Institute.

Halpern, Patrick R. 2006. *Workforce Issues in the Nonprofit Sector.* Kansas City, MO: American Humanics.

Harris, Margaret. 1993. Exploring the Role of the Boards Using Total Activities Analysis. *Nonprofit Management & Leadership* 3 (3):269–281.

Hrywna, Mark. 2007. Nonprofit Times 2007 Salary Survey. *The Nonprofit Times.* Available at <http://www.nptimes.com/07feb/special%20report.pdf>. (February 1).

Irons, John S., and Gary Bass. 2004. *Recent Trends in Nonprofit Employment and Earnings: 1990–2004.* OMB Watch. Available at <http://www.ombwatch.org/article/articleview/2347/1/101?TopicID=3>.

Jamison, Irma Browne. 2003. Turnover and Retention Among Volunteers in Human Service Agencies. *Review of Public Personnel Management* 23 (2):114–132.

Leete, Laura. 2006. Work in the Nonprofit Sector. In *The Nonprofit Sector: A Research Handbook,* 2nd ed., Powell W. Walter and Richard Steinberg, eds. New Haven, CT: Yale University Press, pp. 159–179.

Lipman, Harvey. 2002. Charities Pay Women Less than Men, Study Finds. *Chronicle of Philanthropy.* <http://philanthropy.com/premium/articlas/v14/ i19/19004001.htm>.

Mesch, Debra J., and Patrick M. Rooney. 2008. Determinants of Compensation for Fundraising Professionals: A Study of Pay, Performance, and Gender Differences. *Nonprofit Management & Leadership* 18 (4):435-463.

Penner, Louis A. 2002. Dispositional and Organizational Influences on Sustained Volunteerism: An Interactionist Perspective. *Journal of Social Issues* 58 (3):447-467.

Peters, Jeanne, Anushka Fernandopulle, Jan Masaoka, Christine Chan, and Timothy Wolfred. 2002. *Help Wanted: Turnover and Vacancy in Nonprofits.* San Francisco: CompassPoint Nonprofit Services.

Pollak, Thomas H., and Amy Blackwood. 2007. *The Nonprofit Sector in Brief: Facts and Figures from the Nonprofit Almanac 2007.* Washington, DC: Urban Institute.

Preston, Anne E. 2002. *Task Force Report: Compensation in Nonprofit Organizations.* Alexandria, VA: National Center on Nonprofit Enterprise.

Pynes, Joan E. 2004. *Human Resources Management for Public and Nonprofit Organizations,* 2nd ed. San Francisco: Jossey-Bass.

Ruhm, Christopher J., and Cary Borkoski. 2003. Compensation in the Nonprofit Sector. *Journal of Human Resources* 38 (4):992–1021.

Salamon, Lester M. 2002. What Nonprofit Wage Deficit? *The Nonprofit Quarterly* (Winter):61–62.

Salamon, Lester M., and Richard O'Sullivan. 2004. *Stressed but Coping: Nonprofit Organizations and the Current Fiscal Crisis.* Baltimore: Johns Hopkins University Center for Civil Society Studies and Institute for Policy Studies.

Salamon, Lester M., and Stephanie Lessans Geller. 2007. *The Nonprofit Workforce Crisis: Real or Imagined?* Baltimore: Johns Hopkins University Center for Civil Society Studies and Institute for Policy Studies.

Schwinn, Elizabeth, and Ian Wilhelm. 2003. Nonprofit CEOs See Salaries Rise: Pay Raises Beat Inflation Rate Despite Economic Squeeze. *Chronicle of Philanthropy* 15 (24). Available at <http://www. philanthropy.com/free/articles/v15/i24/24002701.htm>. (October 2).

Teegarden, Paige Hull. 2004. *Change Ahead: Nonprofit Executive Leadership and Transitions Survey.* Baltimore: Annie E. Casey Foundation.

Theuvsen, Ludwig. 2004. Doing Better while Doing Good: Motivational Aspects of Pay-for-Performance Effectiveness in Nonprofit Organizations. *Voluntas: International Journal of Voluntary and Nonprofit Organizations* 15 (2):117–136.

Tierney, Thomas J. 2006. *The Nonprofit Sector's Leadership Deficit.* The Bridgespan Group. Available at <http://www.bridgespangroup.org/kno_articles_leadershipdeficit.html>.

Twombly, Eric C., and Marie Gantz. 2001. *Executive Compensation in the Nonprofit Sector: New Findings and Policy Implications.* Washington, DC: The Urban Institute. Available at <http://www.urban.org/url.cfm?ID=310372>.

United States Bureau of Labor Statistics. 2007. *The Employment Situation: July 2008.* Available at <http://www.bls.gov/news.release/empsit.nr0.htm>.

Walker, David M. 2006. *America at a Crossroads.* Speech Given at Independent Sector's CEO Summit. Minneapolis, Minnesota, October 23, 2006.

Weitzman, Murray S., Nadine T. Jaladoni, Linda M. Lampkin, and Thomas H. Pollak, Eds. 2002. *The New Nonprofit Almanac and Desk Reference: The Essential Facts and Figures for Managers, Researchers, and Volunteers.* San Francisco: Jossey-Bass.

Wilhelm, Ian. 2007. Charities Grapple with Challenges in Keeping Volunteers. *Chronicle of Philanthropy.* Available at <http://www.philanthropy.com/news/updates/index.php?id=2715>. (July 20).

# Section Two

# Techniques

The fifth edition of this book contains seven chapters on various HRM functions. In comparison to previous editions, this edition more clearly emphasizes the "strategic" theme with chapters devoted to strategic human resource management (SHRM), HR performance management (HR metrics), and workforce planning. In addition, it includes several more traditional topics but, as has been the case in previous editions, the content of these chapters is oriented toward change.

Joan E. Pynes' chapter on SHRM defines the approach as "the implementation of human resource activities, policies, and practices to make the necessary ongoing changes to support or improve the agency's operational and strategic objectives." The chapter is punctuated by examples of public employers that have been both successful (e.g., the state of Pennsylvania and its workforce development efforts) and not (e.g., a hospital and its ill-conceived early retirement plan) in implementing HR strategically.

In Chapter 8, "The Trials and Tribulations of Performance Appraisal," Dennis M. Daley reviews the techniques of performance appraisal and their attendant shortcomings. Daley critiques the various rater errors, highlights a number of advancements, and argues that performance appraisal instruments and performance management systems can be designed to meet important organizational purposes. These design enhancements, however, are often stymied by a lack of rater training.

Gary E. Roberts' chapter on employee benefits alerts readers to the "perfect storm" gathering in the public sector. The aging workforce, fiscal stress, increased competition for talented workers, and changing worker needs/expectations are among the forces combining to paint an ominous picture. Employers are struggling to offer competitive benefits packages—introducing family friendly policies, for example—while at the same time containing the spiraling costs of delivering such benefits. Such balancing acts are often undermined by lack of systematic needs assessments and/or calculations of return on investment from benefits.

In their chapter on public sector employee motivation, Gerald T. Gabris and Trenton J. Davis offer up a thorough review of content and process theories of motivation, with considerable attention devoted to public service motivation (or "PSM") theory. The chapter challenges readers to wrestle with the fit between various motivational strategies and current thinking about the nature of public sector work as exemplified in the New Public Management (NPM). The authors argue that the distinctions between public and private-sector work are, at best, blurring and, more likely, disappearing. They conclude by suggesting that the door is wide open in terms of discovering what works to motivate public sector employees.

Following along the theme of knowing what does and does not work, Steven W. Hays and Robert Lavigna's chapter on HR metrics explores current practices and shortcomings of efforts to measure HR's costs and benefits. Though the importance of doing so may appear to be self-evident, the authors note that developing measurement standards for HR functions and practices is in a relatively nascent state. The result, exacerbated by historical neglect of HR as integral to organizational management and performance, is that informed HR decision-making is often compromised. Hays and Lavigna chronicle existing indicators to illustrate their major points.

Willow S. Jacobson's chapter provides a practical discussion of workforce planning. As she and previous chapters suggest, the looming human capital crisis in government and nonprofit organizations would seem to underscore the need for workforce and succession planning. When done correctly, Jacobson observes, workforce planning helps organizations perform strategically in the face of old, and new, challenges. The author explains how to develop and implement successful workforce plans. As she pithily observes, perhaps "The main message is to start somewhere and keep it simple."

In the section's concluding chapter, Jessica E. Sowa takes on the topic of employee grievances, with a focus on state government. Following a discussion of the conventional grievance process and the concept of procedural justice in the workplace, she explores current state practices, reforms, and areas of concern.

# Strategic Human Resources Management

JOAN E. PYNES
University of South Florida

Strategic Human Resources Management (SHRM) is based on the belief that to be effective and able to adapt to changes quickly, agencies need realistic information on the capabilities and talents of their current staff, in essence their *human resources*.

SHRM refers to the implementation of HR activities, policies, and practices to make the necessary ongoing changes to support or improve the agency's operational and strategic objectives. It is an organizational system level approach to HRM, and a concern with the effects of HRM on an agency's or department's performance (Chadwick, 2005). Consider the following. By 2013, nearly half of federal workers will be eligible to retire, including nearly 70 percent of senior managers (Partnership for Public Service, 2005). Montgomery County, VA, estimates that 50 percent of its senior managers will be eligible for retirement in 2010 (Ibarra, 2006; Turque, 2006). Across the United States there is a concern that city manager positions will go unfilled as more city and county managers retire. As far back as 2002, 43 percent of city and county managers were between the ages of 51 to 60. Blumenthal (2007) quotes a fifty-seven-year-old city manager as predicting a "demographic tsunami: Far more managers planning to retire than there are young people to replace them. Whenever city mangers get together for conferences, all you see is gray hair." A survey of New York businesses found that six in ten surveyed reported it is likely that their organizations will face a shortage of qualified workers in the next five years (Bridges and Cicero, 2007).

Impending retirements are not the only reason for public organizations to implement SHRM. SHRM is also important for public agencies facing layoffs and job cuts. Hillsborough County is one of the many local governments in Florida facing cutbacks, but the stress of less revenue has been felt by local and state governments across the country (Salinero and McCartney, 2004; Varian, 2007). Individuals still employed after the layoffs need to possess the requisite knowledge, skills, abilities, and other characteristics (KSAOCs) to keep the county's programs and services operating smoothly. The mayor of Indianapolis has ordered $13 million in property tax cuts from this year's city and county budgets exempting only public safety (O'Shaughnessy and Jarosz, 2007). By 2014, California will need 40,000 more full-time nurses to meet the demands of population growth, including an increase in residents age 65 or older. Public utilities need to recruit and train electrical engineers and skilled linemen to replace those retiring. They are confronted with finding skilled workers from a declining pool of traditional recruits, as well as integrating an ethnically and culturally diverse workforce into a culture dominated by white men (McNabb, Gibson, and Finnie, 2006). Law enforcement and school districts are also falling behind in their staffing goals (Kilgannon, 2007; Peterson, 2006). Today nearly one in every ten U.S. counties has a population that is more than 50 percent minority (U.S. Census Bureau, 2007). U.S. Intelligence agencies are being urged to hire more racial and ethnic minorities. Despite an increase in hiring after September 11, 2001, only 14 percent of the CIA's officer corps are minorities (Hsu and Warrick, 2007). Changing demographics are affecting families, communities, and workforces. Public administrators must meet these challenges amidst pressures for greater accountability.

## DEVELOPING AN EFFECTIVE STRATEGIC HUMAN RESOURCES PLAN

Agency leaders need to understand how their workplaces will be affected by impending changes and prepare for the changes accordingly.

*The Case for Transforming Public-Sector Human Resources Management,* the National Academy of Public Administration (2000); *Federal Employee Retirements: Expected Increase Over the Next Five Years Illustrates Need for Workforce Planning* (GAO, 2001); IPMA-HR's *Workforce Planning Guide for Public Sector Professionals* (2002); and *Human Capital: A Guide for Assessing Strategic Training and Development Efforts in the Federal Government* (GAO, 2004) are just a few of the reports alerting public managers of the need to become proactive and develop a strategic HR plan. The Partnership for Public Service (2006) has developed a process overview for federal executives, but its prescriptions can be used by public managers at all levels of government:

- *Build a Planning Project Team*: When assembling a planning team, include HR professionals, as well as agency leaders. Agency leaders provide sponsorship for the planning process and strategic directions for the plan; while HR professionals bring other expertise. The process must be collaborative. Those charged with responsibility for the plan must be given the necessary time and resources. The planning project team should identify the approach taken, the tasks associated with implementing those tasks, and timeframes in which to complete them. Accountability among team members is important.
- *Review Relevant Inputs*: Once the planning team is in place, collect and analyze information about the workforce; as well as review relevant documents. If available the team

should review agency/department strategic plans; existing human capital plans; retirement, attrition, and hiring projections; staffing and/or recruitment plans; external stakeholder issues and concerns; employee views; and other successful models of SHRM.

- *Engage Managers*: Senior managers should be engaged while developing the plan. There should be a cross-section of senior managers representing the full range of major functions. Managers typically are most aware of the challenges to a unit's mission and its workforce.

- *Assess Challenges and Devise Solutions*: The planning team should collaborate to identify challenges and develop solutions. Quantitative data about the workforce, information that includes retirement, attrition and hiring projections; staffing plans; and employee feedback should be reviewed. Qualitative information that should be considered includes information about strategic goals and priorities, the workforce needed to achieve these goals, and potential challenges to building or maintaining the workforce.

- *Draft the Plan*: Before writing the plan, prepare a comprehensive outline and solicit feedback from agency leaders and managers, employees, and external stakeholders. The plan should also include a timeline for action, the specific tactics, the tasks associated with each change initiative, time frames for completion and the person or persons responsible for each item, and the metrics for assessing success.

In an effort to be proactive, the County of Los Angeles Department of Human Resources has developed a *Strategic Workforce Planning Guide* (County of Los Angeles, Department of Human Resources, 2005). The Guidebook is intended to provide departments with a common definition of strategic workforce planning as it relates to the county's strategic plan; a case study to illustrate an actual strategic workforce plan; a framework for departments to conduct a four-part needs assessment of current and future requirements and developments of their department and a list of strategies, methods, and tools that departments can utilize when developing their workforce plans and be equipped to complete their needs assessment workbook.

HR planning is a critical component of SHRM. It is the process of analyzing and identifying the need for and availability of HR to meet the organization's objectives. Forecasting is used to assess past trends, evaluate the present situation, and project future events. It is not just utility companies having a difficult time finding skilled employees. Public works departments are also facing a shortage of skilled workers (Rexrode, 2007). In Florida, where the unemployment rate hovers around 3.3 percent, public and private agencies that provide public works functions are having a difficult time finding qualified workers. To address this, Pinellas County, FL, developed the Pinellas County's Public Works Academy (PWA). Its Cadet Training Program targets high school seniors nearing graduation. The program runs fourteen weeks and costs approximately $1,000. Students are introduced to more than a dozen disciplines in public works. Environmental lab technology, surveying/mapping design, solid waste management, water treatment, water distribution, wastewater collection, storm-water management, traffic operations, streets maintenance, fleet maintenance, construction services, parks and landscaping, and industrial equipment maintenance are some of the areas in which training is available. Mornings are devoted to classroom instruction at the Pinellas Technical Education Center, and afternoons are reserved for field trips and on-the-job training. There are ten to fifteen cadets in each rotation per year. The participants must have a high school diploma or GED certificate. Toward the end of each rotation, private agencies and city and county departments interview the cadets. Some enter the workforce, others return to school to earn state licenses or for apprenticeship programs. Other PWA programs have trained individuals looking for a career change.

Forecasting HR requirements involves determining the number and types of employees needed by skill level. First, agencies need to audit the skills of incumbent employees and determine their capabilities and weaknesses. Positions must also be audited. In most organizations there are likely to be jobs that are vulnerable, that technology or reengineering are ready to replace. Job analyses must be conducted to provide information on existing jobs. The basic requirements of a job should be defined and converted to job specifications that specify the minimum KSAOCs necessary for effective performance. The skill requirements of positions do change so any changes that occur must be monitored and reflected in the job specifications. It is not enough to monitor changes in positions. Organizations must also keep abreast of the skills that their employees possess. HR planning uses data inventories to integrate the planning and utilization functions of SHRM. Data inventories compile summary information, such as the characteristics of employees, the distribution of employees by position, employees' performance, and career objectives. Specific data that are typically catalogued are age, education, career path, current work skills, work experience, aspirations, performance evaluations, years with the organization, and jobs for which one is qualified. Expected vacancies due to retirement, promotion, transfer, sick leave, relocation, or termination are also tracked. Using a computerized human resource information system (HRIS) to compile these data makes the retrieval of information readily available for forecasting workforce needs.

When forecasting the availability of human resources, agencies need to consider both the internal and external supply of qualified candidates. As noticed in the public utility and public works examples, there is a shortage of skilled workers to meet future demands so recruitment and training programs were developed. Due to changes in Social Security benefits, the erosion of pensions and retiree health benefits, and the elimination of the mandatory retirement age, the labor force participation rates are increasing for those 55 and older (Bridges and Cicero, 2007; Copeland, 2007). Public sector retirement benefits once thought to be secure are not always. Orange County, CA, supervisors voted to reduce the medical benefits for retirees. The county has taken the position that health care coverage for retirees is not a legally protected benefit (Berthelsen, 2007). As a result, many individuals are looking to postpone retirement or make career changes seeking meaningful jobs. Some older Americans have the need to be productive, others may need health benefits and additional income, still others may want to stay mentally and physically active. SHRM would follow these trends and anticipate how they may affect their agencies. For organizations facing a worker shortage is it possible to postpone the retirement of or recruit older workers? Can training opportunities and technology be improved to impart different skills? Can full-time positions be divided into part-time work? Is telecommuting an option? Does your agency have a phased retirement plan? Phased retirements allow workers to reduce their hours or responsibilities to ease into retirement. It provides an opportunity for experienced workers to mentor younger employees and transfer institutional knowledge. Organizations continue to gain benefits from soon-to-be-retiring workers' skills and expertise. Experienced workers often posses valuable knowledge and understand the cultural nuances in organizations.

Unless an organization has a mechanism in place to preserve worker knowledge, knowledge loss can negatively affect the organization. An example of poor SHRM took place in 2007 in Atlanta, Georgia. Grady Memorial Hospital is Georgia's largest public hospital. In an attempt to halt declining revenue and increased expenses, it offered early retirement to 562 employees: 422 took it, twice as many as anticipated. One-third of the departing employees were nurses, nursing assistants, clerks, and other workers in patient care. Another 13 percent came from laboratories and radiology (White, 2007:D11). "The impact of the buyout goes beyond the number of jobs involved," said Dr. Curtis Lewis, chief of Grady's medical staff. "In a cash strapped hospital with aging equipment and a largely indigent patient population, people learn to make things work and maximize resources. In addition, the senior staff developed long-term relationships. Those are the things you lose" (cited in White, 2007:D11).

Strategies that can be implemented to halt the retirements of productive employees are the following: offering part-time work with or without benefits (depending on the employee's need), training employees to develop new skills, transferring employees to different jobs with reduced pay and responsibilities, and addressing any age-bias issues that may exist in the agency.

## SUCCESSION PLANNING

A *succession analysis* should be prepared that forecasts the supply of people for certain positions. Succession plans should be used to identify potential personnel changes, to select backup candidates, and to keep track of attrition. The external supply of candidates is also influenced by a variety of factors, including developments in technology, the actions of competing employers, geographic location, and government regulations. A number of local governments have begun to examine succession planning for their executive positions. They have put together talent banks listing incumbent employees' current skills and areas of expertise, job preferences, and possible new skills the employees may need in order to be promoted. Succession planning becomes more important as the labor supply tightens and the unemployment rates hit low levels. Los Angeles County has developed a training academy to enhance the skills of its current staff. A variety of certificate programs are offered that encompass leadership, problem solving and creativity training. San Diego County examined succession planning for its executive positions. The county put together a talent bank, listing incumbent employees' current skills and areas of expertise, job preferences, and possible new skills the employees may need in order to be promoted.

The Colorado Municipal League (CML) surveyed its members on succession planning. The survey respondents believed it was a critical issue facing local government today, but also indicated that building succession plans were problematic (Reester and Braaten, 2006). When posed the question of how well their organization is handling succession planning for executive levels of leadership, 66 percent responded *poor* or *fair*. The five primary factors identified in the inability to establish a quality succession planning program were: bigger priorities on the horizon every day, easier to deal with today than build your team for tomorrow; lack of money to support a program; lack of knowledge of the issue among career professionals and elected officials; organizational streamlining has created a time-constrained atmosphere where there is little time to invest in professional development; and compensation and benefits are lagging and probable successors will likely seek the non-profit or private sector (Reester and Braaten, 2006:3). Based on the few examples provided earlier it appears that local governments understand the need for succession planning, but not all have the time, resources, or support to implement it. GAO identified the following as reasons why succession planning often fails: lack of ongoing support and interest from leadership; succession planning is not seen as a priority, funding is not sufficient; recruitment and retention, particularly in critical management areas, is perceived to be sufficient to meet organizational needs; resistance from middle managers who already feel overburdened with other "initiatives" not central to their job responsibilities; and employee suspicion toward unsure program goals, poor communication, and organization is too small to sustain a full-scale program (cited in Flynn, 2006:6).

If necessary skills do not exist in the present workforce, employees will need to be trained in the new skills or external recruitment must be used to bring those skills to the organization. The employer must identify where employees with those skills are likely to be found and recruitment strategies must be developed.

In the mid 1990s, the State of Pennsylvania studied the age patterns among its employees to see what skills the state will lose in the next ten years and began targeting recruitment toward acquiring those skills (Helton and Jackson, 2007). The state went on direct recruiting campaigns to hire employees with accounting, budgeting, personnel administration, and computer technology skills. Those candidates were placed in special state-run classes designed to develop their expertise. Six thousand, seven hundred and twelve (6,712) employees retired during fiscal year 2006-07 (Helton and Jackson, 2007). The retirements included social workers, troopers, secretaries, liquor store clerks, park rangers, correction officers, and attorneys, among other administrative job classifications. Due to advanced planning, the residents will not notice a decrease in service. The vacancies caused by retirements are to be filled through promotions. Lower-level vacancies will be filled mostly by external applicants. The state prides itself on offering opportunities for upward mobility. There are opportunities for recent college graduates and entry-level people interested in working for the state (Helton and Jackson, 2007; Mauriello, 2007).

## EMPLOYEE DEVELOPMENT ACTIVITIES

Jobs today are requiring employees to assume more challenging responsibilities. For example, the downsizing of managerial staff in many organizations has required that first-level supervisors possess conceptual and communication skills in addition to their technical and applied skills. Higher-level managers must develop skills that will enable them to scan the external environment and develop organizational strategies. Training and development are used by organizations to improve the skills of employees and enhance their capacity to cope with the constantly changing demands of the work environment. Agencies that wish to be viable must develop strategies to maximize their human resources. As the demands placed on public organizations keep changing, organizations must implement training and development activities to ensure that their staffs have the requisite KSAOCs to confront these new challenges. Training can be targeted to help employees learn new job-specific skills, improve their performance, or change their attitudes. Changes need to be anticipated; training and development needs should be identified, planned for, and budgeted. Developing a comprehensive long-range training program requires SHRM and the recognition that in today's knowledge economy, employees are the most valuable resource. If knowledge is the primary economic enabler, workforce skills are the real capital. Agencies wishing to be viable must develop strategies to maximize their human capabilities. Training and development must be integrated into the core HRM functions. The State of Delaware, Department of Technology and Information's Strategic Plan has as one of its goals to "become the employer of choice with a workforce that is empowered, capable, supportive and accountable." Its strategies include providing consistent opportunity for personal and professional growth, continuing to improve the Performance Management and Compensation Plans, improving communication at all levels of the organization, and deploying and improving the Employee Recognition Plan (Delaware, Department of Technology and Information 2005–2007 Strategic Plan).

Fitzgerald (1992) defines training as "the acquisition of knowledge and skills for present tasks, which help individuals contribute to the organization in their current positions. . . . To be successful, training must result in a change in behavior, such as the use of new knowledge and skills on the job." Career development, however, provides the employee with knowledge and skills that are intended to be used in the future. The purpose of career development is to prepare employees to meet future agency needs, thereby ensuring the organization's survival.

Career development is used to improve the skill levels of and provide long-term opportunities for the organization's present workforce. Career development programs provide incumbents with advancement opportunities within the organization so they will not have to look elsewhere. Taking the time and spending resources to develop employees signals to employees that they are valued by the agency. As a result, they become motivated and assume responsibility for developing their career paths.

The focus of career development plans is to position the agency for the future and allow incumbents to find future job opportunities. Employees and supervisors should produce a development plan that focuses on employee growth and development. The plan should have measurable development objectives and an action plan. For example, supervisors should review their employees' skills with the job descriptions of higher-level positions within the same job family or of positions within the organization to which the employee might be able to cross over. By comparing employees' skills with the skill requirements of other positions, the employees and supervisors can determine what experience and training might still be needed for advancement or lateral movement. Supervisors should direct employees to relevant training opportunities and, when possible, delegate additional tasks and responsibilities to employees so that they may develop new competencies. A number of career development programs can be found in the public sector. Some of them focus on moving employees from paraprofessional positions into more skilled, higher-paying positions. Others focus on developing supervisory and management skills.

Local 1199 of the Service Employees International Union (SEIU), New York's health and human service union, entered into a partnership with City University of New York colleges (CUNY), State University of New York colleges (SUNY), and Rutgers University in New Jersey to offer training programs so union members can obtain nursing degrees or upgrade their skills. Support is provided for pre-BSN (Bachelor of Science in Nursing) courses, RN (Registered Nurse) to BSN programs, RN to Master of Science in Nursing, as well as money for conferences, review courses, and other types of training (SEIU 1199, 2008 & www.1199nbf.org).

Problem-solving skills, initiative, the ability to function as a team player, inter-personal skills, and the creativity to seize opportunities are some of the critical skills managers and executives of public and nonprofit agencies need to guide their agencies. Technical experience and competence is no longer enough; public organizations need leaders with the vision to direct and guide their agencies.

In 2006, the Succession Planning Committee of the City of San Bernardino, California invited city employees to apply for acceptance into its Management Development Program. The goal of the program was to develop its own employees to become future supervisors, division managers, and department heads. Some of the topics participants are exposed to include:

*Understanding the City*

- The role of the mayor
- The role of a city council member
- The role of the city manager
- Agenda item preparation and process
- Review of boards and commissions
- Developing the city budget
- Understanding our city charter and the municipal code
- Police department functions
- Fire department functions
- Workman's compensation
- RFP process

*Training Topics*

- Supervisory skills
- Preventing workplace harassment, discrimination, and retaliation
- Ethics in public service
- Privacy issues in the workplace
- Issues and challenges regarding drugs and alcohol in the workplace
- Personnel issues: Hiring, reference checks, and personnel records
- A guide to labor negotiations
- Public-speaking skills
- Writing skills

## HUMAN RESOURCE COMPETENCIES

For organizations to be successful in implementing SHRM, they need the collaborative effort of agency leaders and HR professionals. HR professionals need the knowledge and skills to undertake a more proactive role. In an article titled "Why We Hate HR,"

Keith H. Hammonds (2005) notes "the human resources trade long ago provided itself, at best, a necessary evil—at worst, a dark bureaucratic force that blindly enforces nonsensical rules, resists creativity, and impedes constructive change. . . . They are competent at the administrivia of pay, benefits, and retirement, but companies are increasingly farming those functions out to contractors who can handle such routines at lower expenses. What's left is the more important strategic role of raising the reputational and intellectual capital of the company—but HR is, it turns out, uniquely unsuited for that." This was written about the HR departments in private for-profit companies, now consider the often archaic public sector regulations as well.

To identify the skills high-performing human resource professionals need, research was conducted by Dave Ulrich and Wayne Brockbank, professors at the University of Michigan, and other partners. The result was the *2007 Human Resource Competency Study* (HRCS). Researchers identified six core competencies: credible activist, cultural steward, talent manager/organizational designer, strategy architect, business ally, and operational executor.

The performance elements of each are provided here.
The *credible activist* is respected, admired, listened to, and offers a point of view, takes a position, and challenges assumptions by:

- delivering results with integrity
- sharing information
- building relationships of trust
- doing HR with an attitude (taking appropriate risks, providing candid observations, influencing others)

The *cultural steward* recognizes, articulates, and helps shape an organization's culture by:

- facilitating change
- crafting culture
- valuing culture
- personalizing culture (helping employees find meaning in their work, managing work/life balance, encouraging innovation)

The *talent manager/organizational designer* masters theory, research, and practice in both talent management and organizational design by:

- ensuring today's and tomorrow's talent
- developing talent
- shaping the organization
- fostering communication
- designing reward systems

The *strategy architect* knows how to make the right change happen by:

- sustaining strategic agility
- engaging customers

The *business ally* contributes to the success of the organization by:

- serving the value chain
- interpreting social context
- articulating proposition
- leveraging business technology

The *operational executor* administers the day-to-day work of managing people inside an organization by:

- implementing workplace policies
- using advanced HR technology

## PROBLEMS AND PROSPECTS OF STRATEGIC HUMAN RESOURCES MANAGEMENT

Research demonstrates the importance of SHRM. Why then is HRM often relegated as a secondary support function rather than a driver of an organization's future? A number of reasons may exist. There are also financial costs associated with SHRM. Some public organizations may be reluctant to spend additional resources on employees, fearing a backlash from its elected officials and citizens. In some instances, leaders may want a greater integration of the HRM function with organizational strategy but often do not understand just what that means. HRM professionals may not have the flexibility to initiate new programs or to suggest new organizational structures. This is especially true when organizational change issues may challenge existing rules and regulations as well as imbedded standard operating procedures.

Another reason why SHRM is neglected is because very often HRM professionals lack the capabilities and skills necessary to move HRM to a more proactive role. To be strategic partners, HRM departments must possess high levels of professional and business knowledge. HRM must establish links to enhancing organizational performance and be able to demonstrate on a continuing basis how HRM activities contribute to the success and effectiveness of the organization. Unfortunately, many HRM departments have spent their time ensuring compliance with rules and regulations, so they lack the skills and competencies to act as a strategic partner. An illustration of this is one local government has a tuition reimbursement program for its employees. Tuition can be reimbursed for undergraduate and graduate college courses. An HR staff person requires employees enrolled in the local the Master of Public Administration (MPA) program to justify the reasons in taking required courses that may not be directly related to their present positions— missing the point that education is not just for the present, but also for the future. Courses such as Public Budgeting, Ethics, and Human Resources Management were challenged. How can these courses not be relevant to public employees at any level of the organization?

Sometimes the political realities of public organizations undermine change. Very often, elected officials and appointed officials have a short-term perspective regarding how they want agencies to operate. Changes in policies and procedures take time to implement and are often not immediately apparent. Elected officials may also be predisposed to favor short-term budget considerations over long-term planning.

## CONCLUSION

SHRM guides management in identifying and implementing the appropriate HR learning activities for resolving organizational problems or adapting to meet new opportunities. HRM professionals must serve as internal consultants working with managers to assess HR needs. Together they must project the demand for services, develop new resources, and determine the appropriate reallocation of services. The SHRM process, once established, can anticipate and prepare for major changes affecting the workplace.

Turnover, including retirements, must be anticipated and planned for. HRM departments must track the skills of incumbent employees and keep skill inventories. Recruitment and training must be tied to the organization's mission. The availability and stability of financial support; the advancement of technological changes, legal regulations, and social and cultural changes; and the evolution of HR requirements must be considered when developing strategic plans.

## REFERENCES

Berthelsen, C. 2007. O. C. Supervisors Raise Current Retirees' Healthcare Costs. *The Los Angeles Times*. August 15, p. B3. or http://articles.latimes.com/2007/aug/15/local/me-retirees15

Blumenthal, R. January 11, 2007. Unfilled City Manager Posts Hint at Future Gap. Retrieved on January 15, 2007, from *The New York Times*, http://www.nytimes.com/2007/01/11/us/11managers.html

Bridges, K., and D. Cicero. 2007. *Preparing for an Aging Workforce: A Focus on New York Businesses*. Washington, DC: AARP.

Chadwick, C. 2005. The Vital Role of Strategy in Strategic Human Resource Management Education. *Human Resources Management Review* 15:200–213.

Copeland, C. June 2007. Labor Force Participation: The Population Age 55 and Older. *Employee Benefits Research Institute Notes*, 28(6).Washington, DC: Employee Benefits Research Institute.

County of Los Angeles, Department of Human Resources. 2005. *Strategic Workforce Planning Guide*. Los Angeles, CA: Author.

Delaware, Department of Technology and Information 2005–2007 Strategic Plan. Available at <http://dti. delaware.gov/strategicplan.shtml>. Retrieved on August 20, 2005.

Fitzgerald, W. 1992. Training Versus Development. *Training and Development Journal* 5:81–84.

Flynn, J. P. 2006. Designing a Practical Succession Planning Program. *PA Times* (May 2006):4, 6.

Grossman, R. J. 2007. New Competencies for HR. Researchers Have Updated the Portfolio of Competencies for High-Performing HR Professionals. *HR Magazine*. Available at <http://shrm.org/hrmagazine/articles/0607/0607grossman.asp>. (June).

Hammonds, K. H. 2005. Why We Hate HR. *Fast Company* 97:40.

Hecht, P. 2007. Nursing Shortage Nears, Analyst Says. *The Sacramento Bee*. Available at <http://www. sacbee.com/111/v-print/story/198563.html/>. (May 30). Instead of URL use The Sacramento Bee, p. A3.

Helton, K. A., and R. D. Jackson, 2007. Navigating Pennsylvania's Dynamic Workforce: Succession Planning in a Complex Environment. *Public Personnel Management*, 36 (4): 335–348.

Hsu, S. S., and J. Warrick. 2007. Intelligence Agencies Urged to Hire Minorities. Diversity Strengthens Efforts, CIA Officials Say. *Washington Post*. Available at <http://www.washingtonpost.com/wp-dyn/content/article/2007/08/14/AR2007081401694.html>. (August 15). p. A09

Ibarra, P. 2006. The Myths and Realities of Succession Planning. *IPMA-HR News* (August):13, 15.

IPMA-HR. 2002. *Workforce Planning Resource Guide for Public Sector Human Resource Professionals.* Washington, DC: Author.

Kilgannon, C. 2007. A Race for Jobs in Police Departments on Long Island. *The New York Times.* Available at http://www.nytimes.com/2007/05/22/nyregion/22cops.html

Mauriello, T. 2007. State Will Be Looking for Lots of Good Men, Women. Upcoming Retirement of About 6 Percent of Commonwealth Work Force Makes Now a Good Time to Apply for State Jobs. *Pittsburgh Post-Gazette* (May 27), p. B-1.

McNabb, D. E., L. K. Gibson, and B. W. Finnie. 2006. The Case of the Vanishing Workforce. *Public Performance & Management Review* 29 (3):358–368.

National Academy of Public Administration. 2000. *The Case for Transforming Public-Sector Human Resources Management.* Washington, DC: Author.

O'Shaughnessy, B., F. Jarosz, 2007. Only Public Safety to be Spared Cuts. *The Indianapolis Star* (July 22), p. A)1.

Partnership for Public Service, 2005. *Federal Brain Drain.* Issue Brief PPS-05-08. Washington, DC: Author.

———. December 2006. *Develop an Effective Strategic Human Capital Plan. A Process Overview for Federal Executives.* Washington, DC: Author.

Peterson, K. 2006. Fewer Choosing Teaching Jobs. *Stateline.* Available at (March 28). http://www.stateline.org/live/details/story?contentId=99537

Reester, K., and M. Braaten. May 2006. Succession Planning Now, Say Colorado Municipal Executives. *PA Times:* (May 2006), 3–4.

Rexrode, C. 2007. A Rich But Hidden Pipeline of Jobs. Public Works Departments—Which Take Care of Roads, Water, Sewers, Traffic Signals and More—Need Capable, Dependable Employees. *St. Petersburg Times:* May 20, pp. 1F, 3F.

Salinero, M., and A. McCartney. 2007. County Plan Eliminated Jobs of 158 Employees. *The Tampa Tribune.* Available at http://www.tbo.com/news/metro/MGBTECDUH4F.html. Accessed on July 24.

San Bernardino. 2006. *Management Development Program,* Interoffice Memorandum, July 21, 2006.

SEIU. 2008. Training and Employment. Available at http://www.1199seiubenefits.org/training/college_degree/Default. aspx.

Turque, B. 2006. Graying of Workforce Troubles County Governments. *Washington Post:* February 26, p. C06.

U.S. Census Bureau. 2007. More Than 300 Counties Now "Majority–Minority." Available at http://www.census.gov/Press-Release/www/releases/archives/population/010482.html

U.S. General Accounting Office. April 2001. *Federal Employee Retirements: Expected Increase over the Next 5 Years Illustrates Need for Workforce Planning.* GAO-01-509. Washington, DC: Author.

———. March 2004. *Human Capital: A Guide for Assessing Strategic Training and Development Efforts in the Federal Government.* GAO-04-546G. Washington, DC: Author.

U.S. Government Accounting Office. 2004. *Human Capital: A Guide for Assessing Strategic Training and Development Efforts in the Federal Government.* GAO-04-546G. Washington, DC: Author.

Varian, B. 2007. County Says It May Cut 480 Jobs. Also on the Chopping Block to Provide Tax Relief: New Libraries, Parks and Fire Stations. *St. Petersburg Times.* Available at https://www.sptimes.com/2007/07/24/news_pf/Hillsborough/County_. (July 24).

Washington State Department of Personnel. 2007. State of Washington Workforce Planning Guide: Right People, Right Jobs, Right Time. Retrieved August 15, 2008 http://www.dop.wa.gov/NR/rdonlyres/D1CADBF4-A744-45E3-9D31-DFECFDEC0294/0/WPGuide.pdf

White, G. July 22, 2007). Resuscitating Grady: Buyouts Leave Hospital with Large Talent Drain. *The Atlanta Journal Constitution* (Metro & State), D1, D10–D11.

# 8

# The Trials and Tribulations of Performance Appraisal
## Problems and Prospects in the Twenty-First Century

DENNIS M. DALEY
North Carolina State University

Building on the development of objective appraisal systems, performance appraisal is poised to undertake major advancements. Various "advanced" versions of the objective appraisal; for example, 360-degree, pass/fail, competency-based, developmental, star, and team appraisal are being discussed. These test our abilities to engage in a process of cognitive ergonomics that will transform our appraisal systems into truly usable instruments. Yet, these new approaches face the same tribulations that past performance appraisal systems had to endure. Advancement is dependent on our abilities to constantly deal with the problems of training, measurement, and inconsistency.

Research on and the practice of performance appraisal resulted in the ability to create highly complex, objective instruments with which to assess employee performance. Whether focused on results or behaviors, the performance appraisal process can map the job terrain (Daley, 1992; Grote, 1996; Latham and Wexley, 1981; Milkovich and Wigdor, 1991; Mohrman, Resnick-West, and Lawler, 1989; Murphy and Cleveland, 1995).

Problems persist. However, it is not the ability to accomplish the performance appraisal process that is in question but the willingness to do it. Performance appraisal does not occur in isolation; it is an integral part of an organization's performance management system. Success depends upon how well processes and people are integrated. In essence, our difficulties are ones of cognitive ergonomics. Adjusting the cognitive fit between processes and people is analogous to the efforts undertaken in the area of physical ergonomics. Improvements enhance productivity. Just as physical materials need to be designed to work in accord with the realities of the human body, administrative processes must incorporate the ways in which the human mind actually functions.

At the beginning of the twenty-first century, we are exploring ways to refine performance appraisal processes to better suit our needs. Following an overview of the performance appraisal techniques used in the twentieth century, this chapter examines six techniques—360-degree appraisal, pass/fail appraisal, team appraisal, competency-based appraisal, star appraisal, and developmental appraisal—currently undergoing trial for use in the twenty-first century. However, these prospects also face problems. The chapter concludes with an examination of the continuing tribulations—training, measurement, and inconsistency—that have previously limited efforts at successful performance management.

## OVERVIEW OF PERFORMANCE APPRAISAL TECHNIQUES

### Subjective Instruments

Essays, graphic rating scales, and checklists are three of the formats that are subjective appraisals. The accuracy of the assessments derived when each of these formats is employed may prove exceedingly high. However, this accuracy flows more from the interactive combination of organization and individual rater than from the merits of the specific instrument being employed.

The *essay appraisal* format is a tabula rosa. Supervisors have a blank space on which they are free to write. Essay appraisals (along with the more modern audio or video log equivalents) are descendant from the traditional duty or fitness report. Almost all appraisals, including today's objective techniques, include an essay component.

The subjective *graphic rating scale* is perhaps still the most pervasive form of performance appraisal (Landy and Farr, 1980:83; Murphy and Cleveland, 1995:434; Milkovich and Wigdor, 1991:55–56). A graphic rating scale consists of a set of items addressing personal traits (trustworthy, loyal, helpful, friendly, courteous, kind, obedient, etc.) and job activities (communication skills, sets realistic goals, keeps files and records up to date, adheres to policies and procedures, knowledge of job, etc.). Employee "performance" on these items is then rated using another set of adjective evaluations (poor, acceptable, fair, good, exceptional, etc.), which are invariably linked to a system of numeric scores. This enables the calculation of an average or overall, summary numeric evaluation or rating.

*Checklist or forced choice* appraisals include sets of items that are linked to the performance of specific jobs; they also include items for which no established relationships have been previously documented (Landy and Farr, 1980:85–86; Mohrman et al., 1989:52–54). In conducting a checklist, performance appraisal supervisors are asked to pick from a series of lists of four those items in each set that are deemed most like and least like an employee. These are then compared against a code sheet and only those that match validated relationships are tabulated into a final score.

### Interpersonal Comparisons

Interpersonal comparisons, such as rankings or forced distributions, may be based on either subjective or objective criteria. However, even when initially based solely on objective, job-related evidence, they experience serious shortcomings. Central to all interpersonal appraisal systems is the comparison or assessment of the individual against other individuals rather than with the specific job to be done.

One method for interpersonal comparisons is that of *ranking*. This is approached in a holistic manner wherein an organization's employees are graded from best to worse. This requires a complete knowledge and understanding of the entire organization—purpose and people. While perhaps feasible only in very small organizations, a number of gimmicks can be used in order to extend its application to larger units.

An alternative ranking process can be employed in which an organization's best and worst employees are designated. The process is then repeated *ad finem* with the remaining employees whereby the next best and next worst employees are so indicated. In the end, this peeling of the onion produces a composite list that ranks employees from best to worst.

*Forced distributions* are another means for making interpersonal comparisons (Mohrman et al., 1989:182–183). Grading on the curve is not a new notion and, unlike rankings, can easily be applied to large organizations. However, it is just as prone to error. Forced distributions assume that employee performance fits some external model or distribution, usually envisioned along the lines of something like a normally distributed, bell-shaped curve. It completely ignores the fact that employees are not randomly selected. Individuals are hired because of their ability or potential; performance should be skewed toward success.

## Objective Instruments

Behaviorally anchored rating scales (BARS) and management by objectives (MBO) essentially involve the same components but approach them with a slightly different focus in mind. Hence, the objective components that are common in both approaches are introduced into the appraisal process in a somewhat different order.

*Behaviorally anchored rating scales* are extensions of the subjective graphic rating scale. They are a clear attempt to translate the graphic rating scale into an objective appraisal system. They address and correct for many of the subjective issues that cloud the validity and inhibit the use of graphic rating scales (Bernardin and Beatty, 1984; Landy and Farr, 1980:83–85; Latham and Wexley, 1981).

Both the BARS and MBO approaches emphasize detailed job analyses. Ideally, performance appraisal should be able to work off the same job analysis system used in the development of an organization's position descriptions and position classification system (and employed as a guide in the selection process and for designing training programs). Unfortunately, many organizations, especially among those in the public sector, employ different systems of job analysis when it comes to selecting people to perform a job and when it comes to assessing their performance on that job.

MBO is more focused on results; however, it obviously can also be adapted to situations in which outputs or processes are more involved than outcomes. MBO originated as a means for managers to translate their strategic plans into implementable programs. It is a basic command and control management system for implementation and monitoring (Odiorne, 1971, 1987; Swiss, 1991:61–127).

## TRIALS

While we can design successful performance appraisal instruments, their use on a day-to-day basis often leads to failure. Our complex appraisal systems often fail to accommodate the work world in which real management occurs. Supervisors and employees balance a myriad of techniques and tasks everyday. This is a world in which neither the time nor energy exists to concentrate on "high maintenance" systems. Hence, performance appraisal must evolve into a more user-friendly version. Six different versions are proposed: 360-degree appraisal, pass/fail appraisal, team appraisal, competency-based appraisal, star appraisal, and developmental appraisal.

With a strong developmental focus, *360-degree appraisal* calls upon the perspectives of supervisors, subordinates, peers, and even self-reviews to form a well-rounded, balanced view. Assuming that most employees are indeed performing well, *pass/fail appraisal* simplifies the appraisal process into a binary yes/no decision. This allows corrective attention to be focused on the few problems rather than wasted on the "busy work" of documenting the obvious. *Team appraisal* introduces an appraisal approach that focuses on the work group itself. While organizations are composed of individuals, their work is accomplished through cooperative teams. Compatible with TQM and gainsharing/goalsharing system, team appraisal assesses this cooperative effort. *Competency-based appraisal* substitutes the difficult to measure behaviors or results with a reduced set of basic skills, knowledge, and abilities that underlie the achievement of those outcomes. *Star appraisal* modifies forced-distribution approaches to focus on recognizing and rewarding the truly exceptional talented performers (without, hopefully, categorizing the other good employees as failures). *Developmental appraisal* jettisons any effort at judgment for a sole focus on coaching employees for growth.

## 360-Degree Appraisal and Development

The combination of information sources (especially supervisor, subordinate, peer, and even self-ratings) is the basis for 360-degree feedback (Murphy and Cleveland, 1995:144–146; Pollack and Pollack, 1996; Edwards and Ewen, 1996; DeLeon and Ewen, 1997; DeNisi and Kluger, 2000; Ghorpade, 2000; Toegel and Conger, 2003). Its effectiveness—which can indeed be great—is based on the sharing and feedback of performance information among an organization's members. The communication of this shared knowledge base ensures a common understanding among organizational members. The 360-degree combination of multiple raters makes this approach complex and costly. With its low hierarchy and professional staff the modern organization is, on the one hand, forced to seek out nonsupervisory sources for appraisal and, on the other, is blessed with highly knowledgeable employees. Hence, 360-degree feedback promises to provide a more balanced and accurate form of appraisal. The 360-degree appraisal is primarily designed to serve as a developmental instrument. When it is transformed into a judgmental appraisal, 360-degree appraisal loses its effectiveness (and often engenders employee distrust).

This technique is especially useful when employed for developmental purposes (Lepsinger and Lucia, 1997; DeNisi and Kluger, 2000; Ghorpade, 2000; Daley, 2001; Toegel and Conger, 2003). However, it is somewhat problematic when incorporated in a judgmental system. Subordinates and peers are especially likely to be concerned with an appraisal that is used judgmentally. When used judgmentally, ratings may suffer from leniency (as individuals are likely to hedge their assessments due to uncertainty) or a fear of retaliation (not wishing to rely upon the enlightenment or benevolent despotism of superiors). Such a transformation is viewed quite negatively and tends to erode employee loyalty. Depending on the purpose (e.g., pay increase, promotion, demotion, etc.), individual ratings may change in up to a third of the cases (Waldman, Atwater, and Antonioni, 1998).

As with any performance appraisal system, 360-degree appraisals must be focused on job-related components. The training for raters (and the possible effects of rater error) is much more important. Since 360-degree appraisal is a highly participative technique, its success or failure has greater symbolic significance and implications (Waldman et al., 1998).

## Pass/Fail and Progressive Discipline

While performance appraisal is one of the most researched aspects of management, it is exceeded by the effort devoted to the staffing process. Recruitment, testing, and selection have been the subject of study and improvement for most of the past century (Gatewood and Feild, 1998). Because of the enormous strides made here, we can propose the introduction of pass/fail appraisal. Since no organization consciously hires people to fail, and our selection devices are indeed rather good, the "average" workforce is, overall, rather exceptional. In addition, as is evident from basic motivational theories, people want their work to make a difference.

Given the presence of employees selected for success and willingness to work, there is little need actually to separate them into various grades (or performance ratings). In fact, most performance appraisal systems report ratings with restricted ranges. Most employees fall into categories that can be designated as "stars" or "superstars," and even these distinctions often prove problematic. Very few employees fail. Hence, for most employees the performance appraisal system is meaningless.

The introduction of a pass/fail appraisal greatly simplifies the endeavor. The vast bulk of the workforce is in actuality exempt from the more burdensome aspects of the process (they pass). Supervisors are then free to devote their efforts not in meaningless documentation but in productive management. Special appraisal processes can be introduced to deal with very specific concerns—problem employees and promotions (Daley, 2001).

The need to establish job-related documentation for undertaking disciplinary action gives rise to its association with the performance appraisal process. Although focused on negative behaviors, discipline fits in with both judgmental and developmental approaches to performance appraisal. However, the ultimate consequences of disciplinary action are clearly judgmental in nature. The requirement to include suggested corrective action provides only a slight developmental cast to this process. A pass/fail system as well as a developmental approach to appraisal would most likely prefer that disciplinary cases be dealt with separately.

In as much as a pass/fail appraisal process readily distinguishes problem employees, it allows the supervisor or manager to interact with most employees on a purely developmental level. Thereby, the supervisor-employee relationship can be virtually freed of the judgmental specter. Such an interpersonal relationship would be conducive to fostering organizational trust and commitment.

A separate disciplinary reporting process can be established. This would be triggered at the occurrence of a critical incident (i.e., a specific and substantive rule infraction or performance failure). Only at this point, would a file be "opened" and a record of the specific event be made. If no other events occur or successful corrective action is undertaken, the file can become "inactive" or "closed" (legally all records must be preserved to document organizational behavior).

Progressive discipline is applied to specific behaviors and is designed to correct them. When an employee who has been subjected to progressive discipline for one behavior exhibits a new disciplinary problem, it is necessary to begin the process anew. Each type of infraction is dealt with separately. To lump all disciplinary infractions together creates an "out to get me" impression among employees and negates any successful or good faith efforts.

Because there are so few problem employees (and those can be dealt with through other means), the popularity of pass/fail systems is rapidly fading. The desire is for performance appraisal to be a means for rewarding and encouraging people. A failure in pass/fail systems is that they do not provide employee feedback that is focused on improvement. Nor are they useful in serving as an indicator for promotional opportunities. Clearly, they are also inappropriate where efforts at pay-for-performance are attempted. Hence, the introduction of systems that discriminate between good and better performance such as in the "Star Appraisals" section (discussed later in the chapter) has begun to eclipse pass/fail systems.

## Team Appraisal and Gainsharing

Performance appraisal of individuals can readily incorporate measures of teamwork and overall team results. Where productivity is derived from the interdependent work of a team, individual incentive pay can be detrimental and divisive. Where success is based on multiple efforts, substantial pay differentials among individuals may not appropriately reflect (and reward) actual accomplishments. Individuals whose efforts are slighted in such an accounting may also harbor ill will toward those unduly/unjustly compensated for the work of others. In such circumstances, a team-based incentive system is more appropriate (Bloom, 1999).

Unfortunately, efforts at team measurements, like results measures in general, have lagged. This has proven especially difficult in the public sector. The widespread disagreement as to the specific goals of programs and the requirement that efficiency/effectiveness results, responsiveness, and equity all be obtained make team measures a difficult task. In addition, the lack of meaningful rewards for such performance distracts from design efforts.

Gainsharing, an instrument for implementing pay for performance, is a synthesis of participatory management and profit sharing (Greiner et al., 1981; Graham-Moore and Ross, 1990; Markowich, 1993; Sanders, 1997; Patton and Daley, 1998; Risher, 1999). With the advent of interest in both pay-for-performance and TQM, gainsharing programs have attracted the attention of public sector organizations. Gainsharing is a means for encouraging or motivating employees through extrinsic expectancy rewards, yet staying within a group or organizational framework. Hence, it combines TQM's emphasis on the advantages derived from teamwork (and away from the distractions of individual competition) with the motivational effect of a strong individual reward system (Swiss, 1992; Cohen and Brand, 1993; Durant and Wilson, 1993; Wilson and Durant, 1994).

## Competency-Based Appraisal

Specific tasks and processes are subject to rapid change; in fact, they are expected to change if the organization is to be successful. Hence, the basic competencies enabling an individual to successfully perform those tasks and to adjust—if not initiate— their changes are focused on. By rewarding these competencies, an organization can reinforce desired behavior (Luthans and Stajkovic, 1999).

Competencies have much in common with personality traits or attitudes. The important difference that transforms a trait or attitude into a competency is job-relatedness. Unfortunately, many organizations do not make the effort to carry out the validation studies that establish the competency link to performance. So far, research efforts have focused primarily on using competencies in job analysis. Yet, the job analysis process is the basic building block for performance appraisal.

By highlighting skills and competencies instead of tasks and behaviors, the organization is targeting the very things it needs to do to succeed. Competencies encompass results; specifically, they indicate the effort necessary for a task or activity to be performed successfully. Individuals think of achieving goals and results rather than narrowly focusing on one specific means of accomplishing an often vaguely defined task. By assuring that the skills and competencies necessary for fulfilling the strategic plan are possessed or provided for through employee training and development, the organization's managers and supervisors concentrate their efforts on the factors essential for success (Pickett, 1998; Brown, 2004).

## Star Appraisal

Star appraisal is an application of pay-for-performance that is weighted toward rewarding those demonstrating exceptional performance. Since 90 to 95 percent of the workforce performs successfully, many organizations desire a performance appraisal process that can distinguish between various levels of good and better performance. A star approach focuses on recognizing and rewarding the truly exceptional performers.

Both pass/fail and forced distribution approaches fail to provide systems that are acceptable to employees. Without employee acceptance, no performance system will be seen as realistic and lead to enhanced productivity. Since nearly all employees pass, pass/fail appraisals fail to discriminate among the successful employees. Since artificial distributions allocated employees, often-through unit or team comparisons, as successful or as failures, forced distributions are not seen as objective. The categorization of employees who are indeed productive as "failures" within their unit comparisons is seen as especially capricious.

A star appraisal approach places limitations on "extremely successful" rankings (between 10 and 15 percent). While this upper limit is not theoretically automatic, given the highly competent workforce it is likely to be met in almost all organizations. Star employees are indeed more productive. Psychologically, star appraisal draws upon the ability of employees to recognize and accept extraordinary performance among their peers. Hence, star performers serve as role models for other employees that can result in better performance across the board. It also sends a clear message to all employees that performance matters and is rewarded.

However, the remaining employees (80 to 85 percent) are not arbitrarily labeled as being unsuccessful. In fact, they are usually eligible for merit pay too (only at a lesser level than the star performers). The difference is that the Star employee is rewarded with a percentage increase that is double that granted the "good" employee. Bonuses are dealt with similarly. For example, instead of a "good" employee getting a 3 percent raise, an "exceptional" employee receiving a 4 percent raise, the Star employee would receive a 6 percent merit increase.

## Developmental Performance Appraisal

Developmental methods take an employee's basic competence for granted (the coordination of recruitment and selection with position or job analysis techniques are deemed sufficient to handle this). Hence, developmental appraisals focus on adding value to the employee. Developmental approaches are humanistic in nature and operate on an intrinsic motivational level (albeit developmental opportunities may also entail substantial present or potential extrinsic rewards). More specifically, the performance appraisal serves as an action device or needs-assessment instrument that triggers employee training. Linking appraisal to training can prove difficult even when used in conjunction with the most objective appraisal instrument (Daley, 2001).

Development focuses on an individual's potential rather than on their current level of skills and capabilities. Hence, it is essential in such assessments to consider the question of *growth for what?* Whether viewed from an organizational or individual perspective, the goal toward which this potential is directed needs examination. Organizationally, the need for developing this potential must be determined. Will the organization accrue some benefit from developing an individual's potential? The HR aspects of an organization's strategic planning process should serve to provide the answers to these questions. If an organization is to provide an employee with enhanced skills and abilities, it is important that the organization perceive what reward it expects to receive from this.

Individuals hope to receive feedback for improving their performance from the appraisal process. They also do not generally perceive an objective assessment as threatening. Largely this latter attitude can be attributed to the relatively high opinion individuals tend to hold with regard to their own abilities. There is even some evidence for managers seeking out negative comments (Ashford and Tsui, 1991; Yeager, Rabin, and Vocino, 1985).

This desire for objective appraisal is, however, intricately tied to an individual's sense of self-identity. In addition, individuals are keenly aware that most appraisals are used for allocating highly desired extrinsic rewards. All of these factors combine to set the stage for an array of potentially divisive individual—organizational conflicts.

Individuals desire development and rewards; organizations desire to develop and reward their employees. Unfortunately, the information necessary for achieving one of these goals may hinder the achieving of the other. If individuals detail their weaknesses so that they can receive needed training in order to improve their performance, they may in the process miss valued rewards. Obversely, in order to efficiently allocate rewards among employees, organizations may miss important considerations that vitally affect their future.

## TRIBULATIONS

As with any performance management system, performance appraisal is plagued by continuous problems focused on maintenance. Regardless of which techniques are employed, including those currently undergoing trial, they will ultimately fail if they do not receive constant attention. These tribulations make the job of management so difficult and so necessary. All systems require that those using them be trained in their use. What we often overlook is that this training needs to be constantly refreshed. While we are sharpening the knife of performance appraisal, we must remember that it can be put to many uses. Finally, performance appraisal is the chief instrument linked to the larger, motivational scheme. Inasmuch as that arena, currently dominated by the concept of pay-for-performance, is inconsistent or unreliable, no appraisal instrument can be successful.

### Training and Rater Error

Performance appraisal is highly dependent upon the skill of the appraiser. With any tool, it is only as good as the individual wielding it. Hence, when things go wrong, it is often considered convenient to blame appraisal problems on rater error. While such a ploy shifts attention from the appraisal system itself, it does not shift responsibility from the organization. Even when problems are indeed due to rater error rather than to environmental or organizational factors, the organization is still responsible for the lack of training or monitoring that contributed to that error's commitment.

Rater errors have been extensively treated in the performance appraisal literature (Landy and Farr, 1980, 1983; Latham and Wexley, 1981:100–104; Murphy and Cleveland, 1995:275–285). Their elimination or alleviation is the focus of most of the efforts at performance appraisal training. In many cases, these errors are corrected through the employment of objective appraisal instruments. In other instances, more thorough supervisory training is recommended. Even though supervisors strive objectively to evaluate employees, rater errors prey on the weaknesses inherent in the process of how humans actually think.

Errors are committed whenever the responsibilities inherent in the job itself are substituted for a measure of the incumbent's job performance (Robbins, 1978). An important and demanding job often implies, and certainly requires, an individual of like stature. Given the effort put into selecting individuals with such capabilities and the basic vagueness or qualitative aspect entailed in most managerial jobs, this is an error easily introduced into the appraisal process.

Similarly, individuals working in a critical unit may benefit from the perceived centrality or significance of their part of the organization. In this case, the importance of the unit to fulfilling the organization's mission is substituted for the job performance of the individual in that unit. In neither instance is the individual's job performance actually measured. Objective appraisals inasmuch as they are focused on job performance, especially in terms of results, are a good check on such errors.

*Contrast errors* arise through interpersonal comparisons. Individuals are not assessed on their job performance but on their performance compared to someone else's performance, or, as is more often the case, someone else's personal traits and characteristics. Personnel profiles tabulating the social and leadership traits, demographic characteristics, or social, ethnic and gender differences of successful employees are compiled. These are then used—often unintentionally, but also explicitly as in the case of interpersonal comparisons such as with forced distribution appraisals—as the norm against which others are compared (Wexley and Nemeroff, 1974; Pizam, 1975; Rand and Wexley, 1975; Bigoness, 1976; Mitchell and Liden, 1982; Mobley, 1982; DeNisi, Cafferty, and Meglino, 1984; Kraiger and Ford, 1985; Shore and Thorton, 1986).

These social differentiation or similar-to-me approaches suffer significant validity problems. While the individuals upon which they are based may be examples of successful employees, the characteristics and traits chosen for the profile may not in any way be related to that success. Concomitantly, even if those traits and characteristics are valid indicators, they may not be the only such indicators. Contrast error excludes people who may be successful or potentially successful from receiving a fair and accurate evaluation. Again, the validation of criteria used in assessing job performance is essential.

*Unidimensional errors* abound. In these instances, one item dominates the evaluation process to such an extent that other, critical factors are ignored. Unidimensional errors can stem from either substantive or mechanical concerns. Such traits and characteristics as age, longevity, or loyalty can be the basis for an overall evaluation even when other factors are formally specified in the appraisal instrument. Admittedly, these factors are desirable. Age and seniority are viewed as indictors of experience (Prather, 1974; Robbins, 1978; Ferris, 1985). On the other hand, loyalty is the trait supervisors often value the most among employees.

The problem here occurs when these measures are used in conjunction with other, supposedly independent factors. The subjective, unidimensional response eliminates the sought-after balance that the intentional introduction of the other factors was designed to achieve. Correlational studies often show this as a problem in the employment of basic graphic rating scales.

Similarly, the vividness of one event can overshadow all other incidents. A halo effect occurs when a good performance in one aspect of a job becomes the basis for overall assessment; a horns effect indicates that an incident perceived as negative was the basis of the evaluation (Odiorne, 1965, 1971, 1987; Murphy and Cleveland, 1995:277–281).

Unidimensional error also occurs with regard to appraisal mechanics. First impression or recency error is introduced when specific events occurring early or late in the rating period are given extraordinary weight in the evaluation. The first impression error leads later performance to be discounted. The recency error places emphasis upon the time nearest the decision at the expense of earlier contributions. Critical incident files (wherein a supervisor notes "good" and "bad" performance as it occurs and places these reminders in a "tickler file" to use later in writing up the formal appraisal) are often a means of countering this cognitive limitation.

Supervisors may also exhibit a central tendency (i.e., awarding everyone middle-range or average ratings) or restricted range (i.e., extremely good and bad ratings are not awarded) problem in which all employees receive the same rating or very close and similar ratings. This problem often emerges when supervisors are required only to justify high and low ratings. It is also likely where supervisors fear that employees would resent an individual who received a higher rating or themselves lose motivation from a lower rating (Glueck, 1978; Bernardin and Beatty, 1984; Murphy and Cleveland, 1995:275–277).

*Constant error* also occurs when supervisors exhibit tendencies toward awarding consistently high or low ratings or are overly lenient or strict in their rating evaluations (Robbins, 1978). While such errors are often applied equally to all employees within the work unit, they make inter-unit comparisons inaccurate. This poses a special problem when employee appraisals are used in determining rewards such as merit pay raises. If one supervisor's rating of a "three" is equivalent to another's "four," the latter employee could well be rewarded and the former not for what is objectively the same level of performance.

*Interpersonal biases* introduce intentional distortions into the appraisal process. The extent to which a supervisor's own performance and career is dependent upon a subordinate's performance, the more likely it is that favorable ratings will be awarded. This interdependence creates a mutual need for maintaining a harmonious relationship (Brinkerhoff and Kanter, 1980; Larson, 1984; Tjosvold, 1985).

Squeaky wheels also benefit from interpersonal bias. They may receive higher ratings than they otherwise deserve in order to avoid any unpleasantness. However, employees deemed difficult as well as those who make use of the organization's grievance process are likely to receive more critical attention in future performance appraisals (Klaas and DeNisi, 1989).

Interpersonal biases are also often found as examples of abuse rather than of errors. They may entail worksite politics wherein ratings are adjusted in order to support or hinder an employee's opportunity for advancement and reward. Supervisors may be influenced by the desires of others—superiors, peers, or subordinates (Robinson, Fink, and Allen, 1996). Lower than deserved ratings can be awarded in an effort to selfishly retain a valued and productive employee; they are also a means for taking-out someone seen as a potential competitor (Teel, 1986; Longenecker, Sims, and Gioia, 1987).

Similarly, appraisal ratings can be affected by factors entirely extraneous to the working relationship. External preferences vis-à-vis politics, religion, and sex may be furthered through the manipulation of the performance appraisal process. Avoiding such abuses is one of the purposes underlying the recommendations for continuously monitoring the appraisal process. Requirements for the automatic review of appraisal by upper level officials and an appeals process are designed with the intention to deter abuse.

Training individuals in the use of these tools is just as important as the development of objective appraisal techniques. Supervisory training requires care. Supervisory training can encompass organizational and employee considerations as well as those related to the appraisal process itself. Performance appraisal is part of an overall performance management system. As such, its interaction with the other systemic aspects is just as an important part of its functioning as are the mechanics of the appraisal process itself.

## Measurement and Goal Displacement

Much of what passes as measurement error (i.e., the inability of supervisors to accurately assess or evaluate individual performance) is in reality supervisory adjustments in response to organizational demands (Daley, 1992:119–121; Longenecker et al., 1987; Murphy and Cleveland, 1995; Bowman, 1999). While the impact of these adjustments may be deemed as negative, they are neither accidental nor totally within the control of the supervisor to correct. Goals may be unclear or misunderstood due to communication problems. A hidden agenda may use performance appraisals as a means of controlling employees rather than for encouraging productivity. The expectations of what can be done may simply be unrealistic. Finally, results may be due to activity of groups rather than of individuals. The supervisors endeavor to coordinate workers and obtain productivity within this system. As such, the performance appraisal is part of the organization's overall management control system (Swiss, 1991; Longenecker and Nykodym, 1996).

Structural problems can also undermine the appraisal instruments themselves. The failure to develop objective appraisal systems can lead to inconsistent or unreliable appraisals. The failure to provide adequate supervisory training in the use of objective systems can also result in a loss of consistency and reliability.

An inability or neglect in goal setting produces similar faults in the appraisal process. Objective appraisal systems operate only if results can be compared against expectations. The failure to establish goals and objectives leaves the system with no expectations. Since managers and supervisors consider an appraisal's specific purpose in making their evaluations, using the appraisal for another, unintended purpose only confounds the process.

The performance appraisal process can also be abused when the decision-making causal process is inverted. Instead of serving as an aid in decisions regarding employee promotion, pay, dismissal, or development, the appraisals are abused in order to justify predetermined decisions.

On a somewhat more technical level, problems arise wherein employees aim to match their behavior to the criteria used in the evaluation. It is difficult to fault employees for doing what is asked of them; yet, for organizations sins of omission are just as deadly as the sins of commission. Ideally, the appraisal system is designed objectively to encompass all the needed tasks. However, in reality important tasks are often ignored or unforeseen. Appraisals may only detail tasks included in out-of-date position descriptions. Tasks that are not easily quantified or are indeed qualitative in nature may be downplayed in favor of those that provide for a more "precise, technical" look. Redesigning the appraisal process is both essential and helpful in such circumstances.

Many organizations accord little priority to the job of administration per se or to the exercise of personnel practices in particular. An organization that is serious about its performance appraisal process incorporates numerous training and support services into its process. The organization also clearly indicates to its supervisors and employees that the supervisors are themselves evaluated on their use of the appraisal system (Mohrman et al., 1989:125–130; Daley, 1992:127–131; Longenecker and Nykodym, 1996).

## Inconsistency and Nonpay-for-Performance

Pay-for-performance incentives take numerous forms. While mostly focused at providing individual incentives (merit pay, bonuses, and skill-based pay), they are readily adaptable to group situations (gainsharing and team/group incentives). While it can be argued that the public sector greatly benefits from emphasizing its intrinsic, public interest or ethos aspects (Perry and Wise, 1990; Naff and Crum, 1999), extrinsic pay-for-performance schemes for enhancing productivity are quite appealing.

The added benefits that can be derived from pay-for-performance are predicated on the existence of an adequate base pay rate that rewards job performance (and is adjusted for inflation and other cost-of-living factors). Failure to maintain this foundation erodes organizational trust and undermines the effectiveness of pay-for-performance incentives (Carnevale, 1995).

Pay-for-performance is also predicated on rewarding employees for desired, productive performance. The pay-for-performance "reward" works because it reinforces desirable employee behaviors. Inasmuch as the organization fails to identify and reward the "correct" behaviors, its pay-for-performance scheme will be less than effective (Luthans and Stajkovic, 1999).

## CONCLUSION

Performance appraisal research and practice during the twentieth century witnessed the development of appraisal instruments from simplistic and subjective adjective checklists into sophisticated devices that can be used objectively to measure the actual tasks that an individual performs. While objective performance appraisal instruments have been developed, training in their use has tended to lag. In addition, research on decision-making has enlightened us on the processes by which the human mind actually functions.

The twenty-first century begins with efforts to synthesize the use of these objective instruments with the functioning of human reasoning. Experiments examining the prospects for such approaches as 360-degree, pass/fail, and team appraisal are underway. The problems of training, accurate measurement, and the human fallibility of rater errors persist. However, these problems no longer go unrecognized. Now, efforts are being consciously made to address them.

## REFERENCES

Ashford, Susan J., and Anne S. Tsui. 1991. Self-Regulation for Managerial Effectiveness: The Role of Active Feedback Seeking. *Academy of Management Journal* 34, 2 (June):251–280.

Bernardin, John H., and Richard W. Beatty. 1984. *Performance Appraisal: Assessing Human Behavior at Work*. Boston, MA: Kent.

Bigoness, William J. 1976. Effects of Applicant's Sex, Race, and Performance on Employer's Performance Rating: Some Additional Findings. *Journal of Applied Psychology* 61:80–84.

Bloom, Matt. 1999. The Performance Effects of Pay Dispersion on Individuals and Organizations. *Academy of Management Journal* 42, 1 (February):25–40.

Bowman, James. 1999. Performance Appraisal: Verisimilitude Trumps Veracity. *Public Personnel Management* 28, 4 (Winter):557–576.

Brinkerhoff, D. W., and R. M. Kanter. 1980. Appraising the Performance of Performance Appraisal. *Sloan Management Review* 21 (Spring):3–16.

Brown, Judith. 2004. Competency-Based Pay . . . Is It Right for Your Organization? *IPMA-HR News* (July):8–9, 11.

Carnevale, David G. 1995. *Trustworthy Government: Leadership and Management Strategies for Building Trust and High Performance.* San Francisco, CA: Jossey-Bass.

Cohen, Steven, and Ronald Brand. 1993. *Total Quality Management in Government: A Practical Guide for the Real World.* San Francisco, CA: Jossey-Bass.

Daley, Dennis M. 1992. *Performance Appraisal in the Public Sector: Techniques and Applications.* Westport, CT: Quorum.

———. 2001. Developmental Performance Appraisal: Feedback, Interview, and Disciplinary Techniques. In *Handbook of Public Management Practice and Reform,* K. Tom Liou, ed. New York, NY: Marcel Dekker, pp. 243–259.

DeLeon, Linda, and Ann J. Ewen. 1997. Multi-Source Performance Appraisals: Employee Perceptions of Fairness. *Review of Public Personnel Administration* 17, 1 (Winter):22–36.

DeNisi, Angelo, and Avraham N. Kluger. 2000. Feedback Effectiveness: Can 360-Degree Appraisals Be Improved? *Academy of Management Executive* 14, 1 (February):129–139.

DeNisi, Angelo, Thomas Cafferty, and Bruce Meglino. 1984. A Cognitive View of the Performance Appraisal Process: A Model and Research Propositions. *Organizational Behavior and Human Performance* 33:360–396.

Durant, Robert F., and Laura A. Wilson. 1993. Public Management, TQM and Quality Improvement: Towards a Contingency Strategy. *American Review of Public Administration* 22 (3):215–245.

Edwards, Mark, and Ann J. Ewen. 1996. *360 Degree Feedback: The Powerful New Model for Employee Assessment and Performance Improvement.* New York, NY: AMACOM Books.

Ferris, George. 1985. The Influence of Subordinate Age on Performance Ratings and Causal Attributions. *Personnel Psychology* 38 (Autumn):545–547.

Gatewood, Robert D., and Hubert Feild. 1998. *Human Resource Selection.* Fort Worth, TX: Dryden Press.

Ghorpade, Jai. 2000. Managing Five Paradoxes of 360-Degree Feedback. *Academy of Management Executive* 14, 1 (February):140–150.

Glueck, William. 1978. *Personnel: A Diagnostic Approach.* Dallas, TX: Business Publications.

Graham-Moore, Brian, and Timothy L. Ross. 1990. *Gainsharing: Plans for Improving Performance.* Washington, DC: Bureau of National Affairs.

Greiner, John M., Harry P. Hatry, Margo P. Koss, Annie P. Millar, and Jane P. Woodward. 1981. *Productivity and Motivation: A Review of State and Local Government Initiatives.* Washington, DC: Urban Institute.

Grote, Dick. 1996. *The Complete Guide to Performance Appraisal.* New York, NY: AMACON.

Klaas, Brian S., and Angelo S. DeNisi. 1989. Managerial Reactions to Employee Dissent: The Impact of Grievance Activity on Performance Ratings. *Academy of Management Journal* 32, 4 (December):705–717.

Kraiger, Kurt, and Kevin J. Ford. 1985. A Meta Analysis of Ratee Effects in Performance Ratings. *Journal of Applied Psychology* 70:56–65.

Landy, Frank J., and James L. Farr. 1980. Performance Rating. *Psychological Bulletin* 87:72–107.

———. 1983. *The Measurement of Work Performance: Methods, Theories and Applications.* New York, NY: Academic Press.

Larson, J. R. 1984. The Performance Feedback Process—A Preliminary Model. *Organizational Behavior and Human Performance* 33 (11):42–76.

Latham, Gary P., and Kenneth Wexley. 1981. *Increasing Productivity Through Performance Appraisal.* Reading, MA: Addison-Wesley.

Lepsinger, Richard, and Anntoinette D. Lucia. 1997. *The Art and Science of 360-Degree Feedback.* San Francisco, CA: Pfeiffer.

Longenecker, Clinton O., and Nick Nykodym. 1996. Public Sector Performance Appraisal Effectiveness: A Case Study. *Public Personnel Management* 25, 2 (Summer):151–164.

Longenecker, Clinton O., Henry Sims, Jr., and Dennis Gioia. 1987. Behind the Mask: The Politics of Employee Appraisal. *Academy of Management Executive* 1 (3):183–193.

Luthans, Fred, and Alexander D. Stajkovic. 1999. Reinforce for Performance: The Need to Go Beyond Pay and Even Rewards. *Academy of Management Executive* 13, 2 (May):49–57.

Markowich, Michael M. 1993. Does Money Motivate? *HRFocus* (August):1, 6.

Milkovich, George T., and Alexandra K. Wigdor, eds. with Ranae F. Broderick, and Anne S. Mavor. 1991. *Pay for Performance: Evaluating Performance Appraisal and Merit Pay.* Washington, DC: National Academy Press.

Mitchell, Terence R., and R. C. Liden. 1982. The Effects of the Social Context on Performance Evaluations. *Organizational Behavior and Human Performance* 29:241–256.

Mobley, W. H. 1982. Supervisor and Employee Race and Sex Effects on Performance Appraisal—A Field Study of Adverse Impact and Generalizability. *Academy of Management Journal* 25 (3):598–606.

Mohrman, Allan M., Jr., Susan M. Resnick-West, and Edward E. Lawler, III. 1989. *Designing Performance Appraisal Systems: Aligning Appraisals and Organizational Realities.* San Francisco, CA: Jossey-Bass.

Murphy, Kevin R., and Jeanette N. Cleveland. 1995. *Understanding Performance Appraisal: Social, Organizational, and Goal-Based Perspectives.* Thousand Oaks, CA: Sage.

Naff, Katherine C., and John Crum. 1999. Working for America: Does Public Service Motivation Make a Difference? *Review of Public Personnel Administration* 19, 4 (Fall):5–16.

Odiorne, George S. 1965. *Management by Objectives: A System of Managerial Leadership.* New York, NY: Pitman.

———. 1971. *Personnel Administration by Objectives.* Homewood, IL: Richard Irwin.

———. 1987. *The Human Side of Management: Management by Integration and Self-Control.* Lexington, MA: Lexington Books.

Patton, Kevin R., and Dennis M. Daley. 1998. Gainsharing in Zebulon: What Do Workers Want? *Public Personnel Management* 27, 1 (Spring):117–131.

Perry, James L., and Lois R. Wise. 1990. The Motivational Bases of Public Service. *Public Administration Review* 50, 3 (May/June):367–373.

Pickett, Les. 1998. Competencies and Managerial Effectiveness: Putting Competencies to Work. *Public Personnel Management* 27, 1 (Spring):103–115.

Pizam, Abraham. 1975. Social Differentiation—A New Psychological Barrier to Performance Appraisal. *Public Personnel Management* 4:244–247.

Pollack, David M., and Leslie J. Pollack. 1996. Using 360-Degree Feedback in Performance Appraisal. *Public Personnel Management* 25, 4 (Winter):507–528.

Prather, Richard. 1974. Extending the Life of Performance Appraisal Programs. *Personnel Journal* (October):739–743.

Rand, T. M., and Kenneth Wexley. 1975. A Demonstration of the Byrne Similar to Hypothesis in Simulated Employment Interviews. *Psychological Reports* 36:535–544.

Risher, Howard. 1999. Are Public Employees Ready for a "New Pay" Program? *Public Personnel Management* 28, 3 (Fall):323–343.

Robbins, Stephen P. 1978. *Personnel: The Management of Human Resources.* Englewood Cliffs, NJ: Prentice Hall.

Robinson, Robert K., Ross L. Fink, and Billie Morgan Allen. 1996. The Influence of Organizational Constituent Groups on Rater Attitudes Toward Performance Appraisal Compliance. *Public Personnel Management* 25, 2 (Summer):141–150.

Sanders, Ronald P. 1997. Gainsharing in Government: Group-Based Performance Pay for Public Employees. In *New Strategies for Public Pay,* Howard Risher and Charles Fay, eds. San Francisco, CA: Jossey-Bass, pp. 231–252.

Shore, L. M., and G. C. Thorton. 1986. Effects of Gender on Self-Ratings and Supervisory Ratings. *Academy of Management Journal* 29, 1 (March):115–129.

Swiss, James E. 1991. *Public Management Systems: Monitoring and Managing Government Performance.* Englewood Cliffs, NJ: Prentice Hall.

———. 1992. Adapting Total Quality Management (TQM) to Government. *Public Administration Review* (July/August):356–359.

Teel, K. S. 1986. Are Merit Raises Really Based on Merit? *Personnel Journal* 65 (3):88.

Tjosvold, Dean. 1985. Power and Social Context in Superior–Subordinate Interaction. *Organizational Behavior* 35 (3):281–293.

Toegel, G., and J. A. Conger. 2003. 360-Degree Assessment: Time for Reinvention. *Academy of Management Learning and Education* 2 (3):297–311.

Waldman, David A., Leanne E. Atwater, and David Antonioni. 1998. Has 360 Degree Feedback Gone Amok? *Academy of Management Executive* 12, 2 (May):86–96.

Wexley, Kenneth, and W. F. Nemeroff. 1974. Effects of Racial Prejudice, Race of Applicant, and Biographical Similarity on Interview Evaluation of Job Applicants. *Journal of Social and Behavioral Science* 20:66–78.

Wilson, Laura A., and Robert F. Durant. 1994. Evaluating TQM: The Case for a Theory-Driven Approach. *Public Administration Review* 54, 2 (March/April):137–146.

Yeager, Samuel J., Jack Rabin, and Thomas Vocino. 1985. Feedback and Administrative Behavior in the Public Sector. *Public Administration Review* 45, 5 (September/October):570–575.

# Employee Benefits

GARY E. ROBERTS
Regent University

## INTRODUCTION

Employee benefits are an essential component of the public sector human resource management system. This chapter will provide an overview of the major types of employee benefits; discuss the major policy, management, and ethical issues surrounding their use; address "best practice" benefits administration attributes; and conclude with a brief discussion of the future of public sector benefits policies.

Government employers provide generous benefits packages for a variety of principle-based and utilitarian reasons. These include enhancing the well-being of employees and their families, increasing employee and hence organizational efficiency and effectiveness, and supporting organizational staffing processes to attract and retain employees. Government employers traditionally have offered generous benefits packages in terms of health insurance, pensions, and paid time off to partially compensate for lower salaries (Reddick and Coggburn, 2007).

Interestingly, data from the Department of Labor's Bureau of Labor Statistics indicate that the overall mean compensation level in the public sector is 51.4 percent higher ($39.50 per hour versus $26.09) than the private sector with the addition of employee benefits (McDonnell, 2008). The main salary disparities are in the executive and professional positions, while for most other occupational categories, such as trades and clerical classifications, government compensation levels are significantly higher (McDonnell, 2008). Overall, benefits consume approximately 31 percent of total compensation in the public sector and 24 percent in the private sector (Reilly, Schoener, and Bolin, 2007). When paid time off is included, compensation reaches 42 percent (Rosenbloom, 2005). Medical benefits assume the greatest percentage of costs (15 percent), followed by paid time off (12 percent), legally required payments (9 percent), and pension benefits (6 percent) (Rosenbloom, 2005).

Employee benefits are becoming more important in employee decision making relative to job and career choice, matching compensation in some surveys (Messmer, 2005; CPA Practice Management Forum, 2007; HR Focus, 2007). Employee benefits such as health insurance, pensions, paid time off, and the flexible workforce initiatives are essential human resource tools for helping public sector employees cope with the stress and strain of the "perfect storm" confluence of complex and elevated service demands, reduced staffing levels, and increasing human capital development requirements. The escalating workplace burdens occur within larger cultural changes that reduce the social support network, including the growth of the dual wage earning family, increased female labor force participation rates, a greater percentage of single parent households, and higher elder care demands. Research clearly demonstrates that employee benefits manifest a host of positive outcomes at the individual employee, work group, and employer levels.[1]

## CATEGORIES OF EMPLOYEE BENEFITS

Figure 9.1 summarizes the two major categories of employee benefits with selected examples that are representative, but not exhaustive, of the range of offerings. The increase in the number, scope, and complexity of employee benefits practices has grown dramatically over the last fifty years, paralleling the rapidly increasing pace of global political, economic, social, and cultural changes. The benefits area is becoming highly differentiated as new categories are added and variants of existing types are altered. For example, traditional indemnity health insurance has been superseded by a host of alternative health care insurance forms, including health maintenance organizations (HMOs), preferred provider organizations (PPOs), and point of service plans (POS). Let us now examine the categories in more detail.

## TRADITIONAL BENEFITS

### Health Insurance

The most costly and important category of benefits are the health, safety, and security benefits, consisting of health insurance, pensions, life and disability insurance, and long-term care insurance. This category provides employees and their families with security against the uncertainties of life. Approximately 90 percent of governmental employers provide health benefits coverage, compared to 60 percent of private employers (see Table 9.1) (The Kaiser Family Foundation, 2007).

There are four major types of health insurance plans. Table 9.2 presents the prevalence of each of the insurance delivery systems, comparing public and private employees (The Kaiser Family Foundation, 2007). The PPO is the most common, covering 50 percent of government employees. The PPO insurance plan uses lower deductibles and coinsurance rates to encourage employees to utilize a designated network of physicians and hospitals (Reddick and Coggburn, 2007). The second most prevalent plan is the HMO which covers 33 percent of governmental employees.

**Traditional Benefits**

1. **Basic Health, Safety, and Security Benefits:**
   * Examples: Pensions, employee and retiree health insurance, prescription drug coverage, mental health benefits, vision, dental, disability insurance, life insurance, and long-term care
2. **Paid and Unpaid Time Off:**
   * Examples: Maternity, family, vacation, sick days, holidays, personal days, compensatory time and bereavement leave, paid lunch and breaks, and family leave

**Work-Life Benefits**

1. **Lifestyle and Employee Well-Being:**
   * Examples: Employee assistance programs, wellness programs and retirement planning, and religious/spiritual friendly workplace
2. **Family-Friendly Benefits:**
   * Examples: On-Site child care, subsidized child care, back-up child care, child care referral, adoption benefits, and elder care
3. **Flexible Workplace:**
   * Examples: Flextime, compressed workweek, job sharing, phased retirement, telecommuting, and virtual workplace
4. **Convenience:**
   * **Examples:** Dry-cleaning, banking, groceries, discounts, parking, and transportation

**Human Capital**

1. **Education:**
   * Examples: Training leave, tuition remission, conference attendance, and sabbaticals

FIGURE 9.1   Benefits Typology

HMOs restrict employees to a primary health care provider who coordinates care within a fixed and restricted network. The POS plan covers 9 percent of employees and is a hybrid of the HMO, with a primary health care physician who coordinates care within a broader network of physician and hospital services (Reddick and Coggburn, 2007).

TABLE 9.1   Comparative Health Care Coverage Rates (percentage)

| Sector of Worker | Sponsor Rate | Eligibility Rate | Participation Rate |
|---|---|---|---|
| Federal | 96.9 | 93.4 | 83.0 |
| State | 96.0 | 88.9 | 80.0 |
| Local | 96.7 | 87.6 | 78.7 |
| Private | 77.6 | 70.9 | 58.1 |

*Source*: Fronstin, 2007.

TABLE 9.2    Comparative Health Care Plan Information (percentage)

| Sector of Worker | Conventional Indemnity | Health Maintenance Organization | Preferred Provider Organization | Point of Service | Consumer Driven Health Plan |
|---|---|---|---|---|---|
| Government | 5 | 33 | 50 | 9 | 2 |
| Private | 3 | 21 | 57 | 13 | 5 |

Source: The Kaiser Family Foundation, 2007.

Traditional indemnity plans service 5 percent of the government employee population. Under indemnity plans, government employers purchase insurance from private carriers that administer the plan and bear all financial costs according to the negotiated terms and conditions. Given the acceleration in health care costs, this form of insurance has decreased dramatically in all sectors (The Kaiser Family Foundation, 2007). The least common form of public sector health insurance is the newest, high deductible (HDHP) or consumer driven (CDHP) plans covering 3 percent of public employees (The Kaiser Family Foundation, 2007). These plans combine high deductibles (typically $3,000) with health savings accounts (pre-tax voluntary employee contributions reserved for health care spending) to provide catastrophic coverage at a reduced cost to the employer. Prescription drug coverage is a basic feature of most governmental health plans, though costs are increasing, given the greater number of drugs prescribed to fight disease and prevent illness. Over 90 percent of local governments provide prescription drug coverage (Roberts, 2004; U.S. Department of Labor, 2000).

## Mental Health Insurance

Mental health benefits are an essential component of a comprehensive wellness system. Almost all governmental employees receive mental health benefits (Roberts, 2004). Mental illness rates are high, with 50 percent of the U.S. population estimated to experience one episode of mental illness in their lifetime, and one out of five persons in any given year (Kessler, McGonagle, and Zhao, 1994; Schott, 1999). Untreated mental illness increases drug and alcohol abuse and physical illness rates (Kessler et al., 1994; Schott, 1999). Given the lingering stigma and uneven coverage levels, only one in three people with mental illness seek assistance (Kessler et al., 1994; Schott, 1999).

A major policy issue is the drive for parity between traditional health insurance and mental health benefits. The Mental Health Parity Act of 1996 provided only partial equality between mental and physical health benefits in the area of annual and lifetime limits (Treatment Online, 2007). The Mental Health Parity Act of 2007 would expand the scope to include deductibles, copayments, out-of-pocket expenses, coinsurance, covered hospital days, and out-patient visits (Treatment Online, 2007). The costs of untreated mental illness are staggering, with estimates of a $150 billion productivity loss, including $43.7 billon for depression alone (Mental Health America, 2007a, b). Hence, mental health parity is an essential element of HR system stewardship and servanthood.

## Dental and Vision

Dental and vision benefits enhance employee and family well-being (Thomas, 2006). Vision and dental problems adversely affect employee quality of life, and with an aging workforce, the negative effects of inadequate dental and vision care are magnified (McQueen, 2006; Bridgeford, 2007; Ophthalmology Times, 2007). Most dental and vision plans only partially cover the full range of expenses. A higher percentage of local governments provide dental (90 percent) than vision benefits (61 percent) (Roberts, 2004).

## Pensions

Pensions provide employees with income security upon retirement. There are two general types of pensions: defined benefit and defined contribution. The defined benefit pension is the most common form in the public sector, covering 90 percent of employees (Reilly, Schoener, and Bolin, 2007). In defined benefit plans, employers provide a fixed guaranteed pension payment based upon a formula consisting of years of service, age at retirement, salary level, and a retirement multiplier of typically 2 to 3 percent (Coggburn and Riddick, 2007). Employees are vested in the pension plan upon a designated number of years of service, usually five to ten years. This attribute enhances retention incentives for long-tenure employees. Defined benefit pensions are becoming less prevalent in the private sector given their higher cost structure. Both public and private employers are required by law to adequately fund defined benefit pension plans, thereby assuming all of the risk for the plan's administrative costs and investment performance. Defined benefits plans have the following advantages for employees: (1) guaranteed lifetime income, (2) regular cost of living adjustments, (3) employer assumption of investment risk, (4) guaranteed designated beneficiary income after the employee's death, (5) employer responsibility for investment decisions, and (6) typically no employee contribution (Papke, 2004). These employee advantages impose significant fiscal pressures upon public employers, however, leading to the movement toward defined contribution plans.

Defined contribution plans are now the norm in the private sector, covering approximately 83 percent of private employees (Reilly, Schoener, and Bolin, 2007). Defined contribution pension plans enable employers to assume none of the risk and obligations associated with a defined benefit plan. Employers contribute a designated percentage (up to a legally defined limit) of the employee's salary into a retirement account that earns interest based upon investment decisions directed by the employee. Employees typically contribute a fixed percentage of their salary, up to the legally defined limit. The advantages of defined contribution plans for employees include contributions portability, no vesting requirements, greater payout flexibility, higher levels of employee autonomy in investment decisions, and a higher rate of return. The major disadvantage is the absence of fixed and secure levels of income given the dependency on portfolio performance. Given the potential risks, most public employees select a defined benefit plan over a defined contribution plan when given a choice (Papke, 2004).

## Life, Disability, and Long-Term Care Insurance

Life insurance policies are provided in two forms, either directly by the employer for all eligible employees or on an elective basis. The amount of life insurance varies depending on the plans but typically ranges from one to two years' salary. From an actuarial standpoint, employees in the 35 to 65 age range are at greater risk of temporary or permanent disability (27 percent for men, 31 percent for women) than they are of premature death (18 percent for males, 11 percent for females) (PR Newswire, 2007; Theodore, 2007). Short and long-term disability policies provide a measure of income security by providing a designated percentage of income, usually 66 percent. Fewer than 50 percent of public and private employers provide disability policies, hence prudent income security planning requires employees to assess income needs and plan accordingly to purchase private insurance (Roberts et al., 2004; U.S. Department of Labor, 2007).

The final type of traditional insurance benefit is a more recent addition, long-term care insurance. Given increases in life span and medical advances, employees are likely to face significant care-giving needs (OxResearch, 2007). Given the great expense of assisted living, increasing numbers of employers (12 percent of private companies) are offering long-term care policies with a variety of options and premium costs (OxResearch, 2007; U.S. Department of Labor, 2007).

## Paid and Unpaid Time Off

While the preceding traditional benefits exemplified basic health, safety, and security benefits, the second broad category of traditional benefits includes paid and unpaid time off. These benefits enable employees to: (1) maintain a reasonable work pace; (2) reduce workday stress and fatigue; (3) provide the time needed to recover from illness and care for ill family members; and (4) refresh the mind, body, and spirit during extended time away from work. These benefits can be divided into three categories: workday paid time off, scheduled time off, and extended absences. Workday paid time off benefits, such as paid lunch hours and breaks, are essential for fatigue reduction and productivity maintenance. Providing paid sick leave enables employees to recover from illness and avoid *presenteeism*, the term used by management researchers to describe working while sick. Presenteeism costs employers an estimated $131 billion annually, given the reduction in workplace effectiveness and the spread of illness among other employees (Hemp, 2004). Sick leave plans vary considerably in terms of the number of days and the provisions for carry-over. Most local government employers provide approximately ten sick days per year (Roberts, 2000). Vacation days provide employees with extended time for rest and relaxation. Most local government workers begin with two weeks of vacation and reach a maximum of five weeks after twenty years of service (Roberts, 2000).

Sick leave abuse is a significant workplace problem, with the most recent Commerce Clearing House (CCH) absenteeism survey indicating a daily mean absenteeism rate of 2.5 percent, costing a typical large employer $850,000 yearly in direct payroll costs (CCH, 2007). CCH research indicates that approximately 35 percent of unscheduled absences are due to illness, with the remainder due to such factors as family issues (24 percent), personal needs (18 percent), work stress (12 percent), and the entitlement mentality that employers "owe" workers more time off (11 percent) (CCH, 2007). To address the issue of unscheduled absenteeism, employers have developed a series of options, including personal leave plans (paid leave banks) that combine sick and vacation days to provide the employee with the flexibility to schedule time off for any reason (CCH, 2007). In addition, some employers will compensate employees for unused leave days (CCH, 2007). The CCH survey also demonstrates that unscheduled absenteeism is considerably higher in workplaces with low morale (CCH, 2007).

The final type of benefit in this group is unpaid family leave, which is required by the Family Medical Leave Act (FMLA) for public and private employers with fifty or more employees. The FMLA permits covered employees to take up to twelve weeks during a year to care for a child, a sick family member, or for personal illness (U.S. Equal Employment Opportunity Commission, 2007). The main weakness from an employee perspective is that most workers are unable to utilize unpaid leave, reducing its effectiveness in supporting work/life balance and ameliorating financial and other life stress (Wisensale, 2001).

## WORK/LIFE BENEFITS

Work/life benefits are becoming an essential element of an effective human resource management system (Roberts, 2004). Work/life benefits are a constellation of employment practices and procedures that support employee mind, body, and spirit well-being. Work/life benefits reject the "wall of separation" view of work that compartmentalizes life domains, isolating labor from the employee's family, community, religious/spiritual, and personal interests (Giacalone and Jurkiewicz, 2003; Hicks, 2003). The overall quality of work/life and the benefits practices that support it are some of the most important employee recruitment and retention factors (Roberts, 2000).

Government is at a crossroads, given the following trends: (1) the graying of the labor force, (2) intense labor market competition, (3) the smaller size of the replacement labor force cohorts, (4) the declining interest and attractiveness of public service among younger employees, (5) the need to find greater levels of transcendence and purpose through intrinsic motivation/accomplishment by performing meaningful work, and (6) a greater interest in life balance (Roberts, 2002; Giacalone and Jurkiewicz, 2003; Hicks, 2003). For example, the work values and life orientation of younger employees are more post-modern, reducing blind acceptance of authority, patience with bureaucratic protocol, and the need to make an immediate impact (Leuenberger and Kluver, 2005). Unless public employers address these factors in a credible and authentic manner, the public sector will be at an increasing disadvantage in the competition for talent.

Figure 9.1 presents a summary of the four main categories of work/life benefits. The presentation is not exhaustive but illustrative of the broad and ever-evolving array of work/life benefits across all employment sectors. Developments in one sector quickly influence the others given the inherent degree of competition in the labor market. Government and other organizations provide work/life benefits for varying motives, including both deontological (principle-based) and teleological (utilitarian) factors. The principle-based servanthood rationale entails an explicit recognition of the public employer's ethical and moral obligation to provide employees with work that is dignified, meaningful, and significant while providing a healthy, safe, and productive workplace environment. The stewardship-based utilitarian motives recognize that a long-term investment in employees is the single most important factor for promoting mission success.

## Employee Assistance Programs and Wellness Programs

The first category of work/life benefits, lifestyle and employee well-being, is designed to enhance the mental, physical, and spiritual health of workers. Employee assistance programs (EAPs) provide crisis and ongoing counseling and drug and alcohol rehabilitation services, among other benefits to distressed employees (Business Roundtable, 2007). These programs are most effective with guarantees of referral and treatment confidentiality/anonymity, along with a workplace culture that values transparency, humility, and problem-solving, which avoids stigmatizing employees who use EAP services as "weak" or sick.

Employee wellness programs are important strategies for improving health through exercise, health risk assessment, weight loss, smoking cessation, nutrition, and stress reduction programs. Wellness programs manifest very high return-on-investment (ROI) ratios in the public and private sectors with significant reductions in health care costs (Chiappetta, 2005; Business Roundtable, 2007). These programs are more effective when they are made convenient for employees (such as on-site fitness facilities), offer monetary incentives and rewards, avoid judging or comparing employees to create self-stigmatization, and are tailored to individual needs and motivations (Winnay, 2004). See Figure 9.2 for a summary of wellness program best-practice attributes.

## Workplace Spirituality and Religious Expression

Wellness and EAP programs address mind and body health, while the religious/ spiritual-friendly workplace addresses the spiritual element. Research clearly demonstrates a favorable relationship between religion/spirituality and mental and physical health (Koenig and Cohen, 2002; Koenig, 2005). The accommodation of employee religious/ spiritual beliefs in the public sector workplace is an area of increasing management, policy, and legal importance (Atkinson, 2000). Barriers to religious/spiritual practice and expression in the workplace are being eroded by global societal changes centering on three major trends: (1) the desire to discover meaning and purpose in work (Mitroff and Denton, 1999); (2) the recognition of the importance of holistic life balance to mental and physical health (Koenig and Cohen, 2002; Koenig, 2005); and (3) world events such as the September 11 terrorist attacks increasing collective individual and institutional vulnerability.

A list of religious-friendly organizational policies and practices include workplace chaplains; respecting dietary or dress restrictions; religious and spirituality-based mental health counseling; liberal leave policies for religious holidays and observations; sensitivity in scheduling meetings and other work events; and providing "quiet time" for prayer, meditation, or scripture study (Digh, 1998; Atkinson, 2000; Cash, Gray, and Rood, 2000; Huang and Kleiner, 2001; Starcher, 2003). Another important component is educating managers and employees on appropriate

---

- Create a culture of wellness within the organization
- Integrate all health care related programs through a case management approach
- Engage in a multimethod communication program on the value of benefits and the relationship of health to benefits costs
- Involve family and spouse in wellness programs
- Engage in targeted incentive strategies to increase buy-in and participation using both positive and negative approaches such as a bonus for completing a health assessment or higher benefits costs for smokers
- Reduce barriers to access and use (on-site fitness center with work release time)
- Role modeling in which chief executives participate in the program in a visible fashion
- Grant work time credits for fitness activities
- Use the Internet and other electronic means of communication to address the needs of remote employees
- Adjust fitness programs to language and cultural values of different demographic groups
- Develop wellness performance metrics linked to management performance appraisal ratings and compensation decisions
- Wellness metrics posted and distributed to employees
- Offer individualized health assessment targeted to needs, motives and lifestyle of employees
- Empower employees to manage their own risks
- Guarantee confidentiality of information
- Provide employee on-line access to health records
- Build a clear business case for wellness through ongoing return-on-investment analysis
- Eliminate stigmatizing employees for disclosing adverse health risk factors

---

*Source*: Business Roundtable, 2007.

**FIGURE 9.2   Wellness Program Best-Practice Attributes**

accommodation strategies (adjustments in workplace duties and policies), religious diversity education, and strategies for preventing religious based discrimination (Digh, 1998; Huang and Kleiner, 2001).

## Family-Friendly Benefits

Family-friendly (FF) benefits include child care in its various permutations (on-site, subsidized, child care referral, sick child care, adoption benefits, etc.). Working families have great difficulty in obtaining affordable child care (Gault and Lovell, 2006). These benefits reduce stress on employees, enabling working parents to spend more quality time with children. The main detriment is the high cost of on-site child care, reducing its efficacy for smaller employers. Given the elevated costs, less than 3 percent of local government public employers offer on-site or subsidized child care in comparison to 5 percent of private employers (Roberts, 2004; U.S. Department of Labor, 2007).

Elder care programs are becoming more important given the increasing number of baby boomers with parent care responsibilities. The greatest pressures are faced by the "sandwich" generation concurrently caring for older children and one or more parents. Approximately 7 percent of local government public employers provide elder care benefits compared to 24 percent in the private sector (Roberts, 2004).

## Flexible Workplace

The third category of work-life benefits is the flexible workplace. These practices enhance employee autonomy in terms of scheduling and work location. Flextime permits employees to select starting and finishing times within designated parameters (e.g., start between 7 and 9 AM and leave between 3 and 5 PM). Approximately 40 percent of local government employers provide flextime benefits compared to approximately 70 percent of private employers (Roberts, 2004). Flextime systems do require higher levels of ongoing scheduling management to ensure adequate coverage.

Compressed workweeks enable employees to work fewer days such as four ten-hour days or three twelve-hour shifts, increasing time spent at home and reducing commuting expenses. Job sharing programs enable working parents to assume part-time work while retaining benefits and seniority. Telecommuting, or the flexible workplace, permits employees to work from home one or more days per week using computer, fax, phone, and other electronic means. The federal government is a leader in telecommuting because of mandated legislative telecommuting requirements. A recent study found that 44 percent of federal employees are eligible for telecommuting compared to only 15 percent in the private sector (Shanks, 2007).

The virtual workplace is the next stage of development in which the employee works 100 percent from a remote location, usually the home. Several private sector companies such as Best Buy are systematically converting entire units to the virtual workplace. Best Buy has shifted almost 60 percent of its 4000 headquarters employees to working from home (Kiger, 2007). The virtual workplace enables employers to retain outstanding employees who move out of the area, increase employee autonomy, and maximize work/life balance (Kiger, 2007).

## Phased Retirement Programs

Phased retirement programs are becoming more common given the labor market pressures associated with the graying of the labor force. As the number of baby boomer employees reaching retirement age increases, governmental employers are faced with serious staffing shortfalls and the loss of institutional knowledge. The need for phased retirement programs is exacerbated by more generous public sector pension policies in which employees can retire on average five years sooner than private sector employees (Reilly, Schoener, and Bolin, 2007). Older employees who are in good health and desiring to extend their working life can remain employed working part-time. Phased retirement programs are most effective when there is no loss of pension benefits.

## Convenience Benefits

The final category of work/life benefits are the convenience benefits designed to reduce employee stress. Examples include on-site dry cleaning, grocery stores, medical and dental care, car repairs, and concierge services, among others. The vast majority of such programs are in the private sector, but they are important to mention given that such benefits are becoming more commonplace and that job applicants will begin to make comparisons between the sectors. The cynical view on the motives for providing this category of benefits is to make it easier for salaried employees to work longer hours for the same compensation level. However, companies such as SAS Corporation offer such benefits as a reward and recognition of the challenges that employees face in their daily lives, even though they restrict work hours to 40 per week (O'Reilly and Pfeffer, 2000).

## Barriers to the Utilization of Work/Life Benefits

There are significant impediments to the utilization of work/life benefits. Research indicates a significant gap between the availability of such benefits and employee participation (Budd and Mumford, 2006). Supervisors resist the flexible and virtual workplace for three reasons: (1) the perceived loss of control over employee behavior/productivity; (2) the presence of "face-time," cultural norms that equate visibility and presence with job effectiveness; and (3) a belief that those who utilize work/life benefits such as job sharing and telecommuting manifest less loyalty and commitment to the organization (Kiger, 2007). The challenge for HR professionals is to renorm the workplace culture to embrace a performance-based value set rather than a personal presence orientation (Kiger, 2007). Another impediment is the "backlash" reaction from single employees given their inability to utilize FF benefits in conjunction with the workload increases that result from such arrangements as flextime, job sharing, and telecommuting. The magnitude of this effect appears to be limited, and researchers recommend the employers publicize the "public good" workplace and societal improvements generated by FF practices (less stress on families) and provide wide access for all employees (flexible workplace, compressed workweek, etc.) (Haar, Spell, and O'Driscoll, 2005).

## Work/Life Benefits: Global Effects

The research literature demonstrates considerable support for the efficacy of work/life benefits, which have been linked to a host of positive workplace outcomes, including higher levels of employee job satisfaction, organizational commitment, loyalty, and lower turnover intention, generating very positive ROI levels (Roberts et al., 2004; Gault and Lovell, 2006). As such, they are becoming a more important component of the total benefits package. A major challenge for government, especially at the local level, is the high cost of such benefits for smaller municipalities. As we will discuss later in the chapter, there are a variety of strategies for cost sharing to promote wider adoption.

## HUMAN CAPITAL BENEFITS

Human capital benefits are assuming increasing importance to employers and employees given the accelerating education, training, and skill requirements of the information age workplace in conjunction with higher rates of labor mobility

(Cantrell et al., 2006). Given that the typical employee will change employers and jobs much more frequently than in the past, employees are more carefully scrutinizing the value-added education, training, and other human capital benefits received from their shorter job tenure (Sullivan et al., 2003). Unless employers can demonstrate human capital benefits' ROI, they will lack a key element for attracting high-quality employees. Key human capital benefits include tuition remission programs for various types of educational endeavors (degrees, certificates, etc.), an individual learning account that provides funds for training activities such as conferences, and sabbatical programs to develop new skills while rejuvenating and refreshing workers by immersion in novel settings (U.S. General Accounting Office, 2003; Carr and Tang, 2005). Approximately 49 percent of private employees have some type of education assistance compared to 52 percent in a survey of local government employers (Roberts et al., 2004; U.S. Department of Labor, 2007).

## BENEFITS COST REDUCTION ISSUES

The focus of this section is to address the serious cost issues surrounding employee benefits and pensions. Health and pension benefits are the two most expensive benefit categories comprising approximately two-thirds of total benefits costs (Rosenbloom, 2005). The cost of health insurance and pensions is a major source of fiscal stress for governments at all levels. For example, a National League of Cities survey found that health insurance (96 percent) and pension plans (93 percent) were leading factors contributing to budget hardships (Pagano, 2004; Reilly, Schoener, and Bolin, 2007). Health insurance premium rate increases exceeded the rate of inflation and worker wage gains for every year since 1999, necessitating a variety of cost reduction measures (The Kaiser Family Foundation, 2007). In the next section, we will address the specific approaches for reducing health and pension plan costs.

### Reducing Health Care Costs

The high rate of increase in health care costs has engendered a wide variety of cost reduction approaches. These strategies include reducing or eliminating retiree health care, increasing employee benefits payments (premiums, copays, deductibles), changing the type of health plan (such as moving to a high deductible or consumer driven plan), and capping future employer contributions to the rate of inflation (Kelley and Ruggieri, 2007). Benefits reductions and cost increases engender negative employee and union reactions given their pocketbook saliency, generating resistance costs outweighing the benefits.

Another strategy is moving toward a self-insured and administered health plan. Self insurance reduces costs and allows health insurance plan attributes and cost structure to be more tailored to the health care needs of employees (Reddick and Coggburn, 2007). Another strategy is to change medical carriers to reduce premium costs. The Kaiser Family Foundation 2007 survey of health care found that about two-thirds of employers have researched changing carriers, with 25 percent making a switch. A final set of strategies address the issues of reducing the demand for health services and/or improving its quality. Wellness programs reduce health care costs through preventing disease and injury, while disease management programs reduce the severity of existing serious health conditions such as back problems, diabetes, cancer, and cardiovascular disease. The ROI levels for well-designed disease management and wellness programs are very favorable (Business Roundtable, 2007). In the health care area, small local governments can reduce costs for health care by joining or forming regional benefits consortiums to realize economies of scale (Gorchow, 2007). This consortium, or regional approach, is another means for reducing the costs of FF benefits such as child and elder care (Roberts, 2000).

Another promising approach for health insurance cost reductions is computerized and portable employee health records, prescription systems, and claims form processing (Bachman, 2007). These reduce medical errors and duplicate billing problems (Thielst, 2007). The Kaiser Family Foundation (2007) recommends developing a tiered or high performance provider network in which health care providers are grouped based upon quality, cost, and the efficiency of provision. This information can be made available to employees, facilitating more effective consumer choice.

## Reducing Pension Benefits Costs

The strategies for reducing pension benefits costs entail moving to a defined contribution plan for new hires, increasing employee pension contributions, and ensuring full actuarial funding to avoid future shortfalls. The State of Michigan's experience provides guidance on how to manage a program to encourage employees to move from a defined benefit to a defined contribution plan (Papke, 2004). The key factor is an ongoing multimethod communication program especially for younger employees given their greater risk tolerance and higher rates of job mobility that contribute to the attractiveness of the portability feature (Papke, 2004).

One of the ongoing issues related to public pension plans, especially at the local level, is chronic underfunding endangering long-term solvency. Research demonstrates that some local governments engage in actuarial assumption manipulation to reduce current budget year pensions contributions (Giertz and Papke, 2007). Sound actuarial assessment provides the foundation for more accurate forecasting, affording pension administrators more lead time in planning strategy and adjusting employer and employee contributions and payouts. The major elements of a sound actuarial analysis include selecting a reasonable discount rate, wage increase levels, employee turnover rates, mortality levels, and inflation factors (Coggburn and Riddick, 2007). For example, a 1 percent decrease in the rate of inflation assumption can reduce pension plan contributions by 20 to 25 percent (Coggburn and Riddick, 2007). Another key element is sage pension plan investing strategies to ensure a reasonable rate of return, including such factors as embracing a long-term approach to smooth out fund performance (five to fifteen years), avoiding high-risk short-term investments, and developing a balanced portfolio (Coggburn and Riddick, 2007).

## Reducing Costs and Increasing Benefits Plan Effectiveness: Needs Assessment

This section will highlight promising, but underutilized, strategies for reducing benefits and pension system costs, some of which can increase the effectiveness of the benefits package as well. The discussion will focus on the areas of needs assessment and flexible benefits including cafeteria plans, benefits communication, and benefits administration.

Best practice benefits plan administration begins with a systematic needs assessment (Roberts, 2003a). The benefits plan must be assessed in terms of its effectiveness in meeting employee needs and expectations. A "one size fits all" policy applied to employee benefits is a very ineffective and inefficient approach. The benefits plan should be designed to meet the demographic and psychographic (values, concerns, and cares) needs of employees. For example, an on-site child care program is very expensive and will not be attractive to a primarily older employee population with elder care needs, while a defined benefits pension plan with a ten-year vesting requirement will exert little motivational or retention value to a younger, more mobile employee.

A systematic needs assessment entails a multiple method and data source analysis of: (1) present and future government fiscal capacity; (2) the present and future labor force profile in terms of age, gender, family status and size, wage rate, income level, occupational category, job experience level, and employment status (full, part-time, contingent, or contract employees); (3) job characteristics including work load, skill mix, working conditions, and work portability; (4) an archival analysis to identify patterns and trends in employee absenteeism, turnover, grievance, accidents, and health care costs; and (5) data from employee attitude/climate surveys, focus groups, and exit and retention interviews including benefits plan administration satisfaction and effectiveness (Roberts, 2003a).

Recent research indicates that less than 20 percent of local governments employ a benefits needs assessment, eroding the ability to make informed benefits plan adjustments (Roberts, 2003a). Based upon the needs assessment and overall mission related objectives, the human resource department should develop clear, specific, valid, and reliable benefits plan performance measures and metrics to provide concrete evidence of the system's success. Such measures include user satisfaction, influence on turnover and absenteeism rates, and employee stress measures, among others.

Employee choice is further enhanced by the adoption of a flexible spending and cafeteria benefits plan that enables employees to select the specific benefits meeting their individual needs (Johnson, 2002; Query, 2003). For example, a married employee whose spouse has health care coverage can decline health insurance and either increase take-home pay or purchase a higher level of another benefit, such as child care.

## Reducing Costs and Increasing Benefits Plan Effectiveness: Communication

Benefits plan communication is another important element. Employees require ongoing education on benefits plan attributes, employer benefits costs, and realistic standards of benefits plan performance (e.g., benefits plan communication standards for responding to questions) through specific metrics (Crosby, 2005; Ackley, 2006; Bottos, 2006). Research clearly indicates that many employees fail to understand basic elements of their benefits package, including the specific benefits they receive, how much they cost the employer, the percentage of pay devoted to benefits, and the market competitiveness of their benefits package (Institute of Management and Administration, 2003; Ackley, 2006; Markowich, 2006). Employees should receive a complete benefits plan orientation supplemented by ongoing communication and updates from the benefits office in both written and electronic form (Crosby, 2005).

Detailed benefits plan summaries written in plain English should be available on the employer's web site and intranet (Bottos, 2006).

Benefits administration should be computerized with 24/7, 365 days per year access to the benefits administration process, including enrollment, current benefits plan summary, change options, and tutorials, among others (Crosby, 2005). For example, most employees are not engaging in the long-term retirement planning necessary to estimate income needs given lifestyle preferences, health care costs, and long-term care needs (Helman et al., 2006). Employees consistently overestimate the value of their retirement plan and the adequacy of their savings (Helman et al., 2006). Ongoing retirement planning information on the web can help educate employees and reduce serious long-term lifestyle maintenance problems. See Figure 9.3 for a complete summary.

## Human Resource Cost Reduction Strategies

If the previously discussed benefits cost reduction strategies are ineffective, the governmental employer may be forced to engage in larger cost-cutting measures by increasing the percentage of uncovered part-time, temporary, or contract labor, eliminating

---

- Leaders should be visible supporters of the benefits change process. Top management should actively participate in benefits information meetings
- Provide a benefits communication realistic preview that accurately describes the strengths, weaknesses, opportunities and threats associated with the benefits packet change
- Tailor the benefits plan change communication message to the needs, interests, and literacy level of the employee
- Approach the benefits plan administration process from the employee perspective. Conduct interviews and focus groups to assess attitudes, irritants, recommendations, and solutions
- Provide a clear and convenient means for filing complaints (hotline, e-mail, etc.)
- Identify the workplace opinion leaders and gain their support
- Begin the change management process early
- Assess employees current level of benefits knowledge and literacy
- Educate employees on the dollar value of benefits and their market competitiveness
- Eliminate jargon and communicate in plain English
- Reduce the clutter by ensuring clear and concise information that avoids overwhelming employees with detail
- Set clear performance metrics that focus on outcomes and process measures
- Avoid blind adherence to "best practices" that may not be appropriate for your unique employee population

---

*Sources:* Hart and Arian, 2007; Crosby, 2005; Markowich, 2006; Ackley, 2006; Goree, 2003; Bilodeau, 2005.

**FIGURE 9.3    Benefits Package Change Management Best Practices**

positions, and engaging in a hiring freeze (Roberts, 2003b; Reilly, Schoener, and Bolin, 2007). All of these approaches entail significant costs, however. The reduction in benefits makes governmental positions less attractive, further attenuating recruitment/retention effectiveness. In addition, there are valid public policy and ethical considerations in providing part-time employees with benefits, including the social justice gains with the reduction in the number of low-income workers and families without health benefits, the public sector recruitment and retention advantages, and lowering status differences between part- and full-time workers (Roberts, 2003b).

## CONCLUSION: THE FUTURE PUBLIC SECTOR BENEFITS ISSUES

The public sector employee benefits finance and delivery system will be under increasing stress and strain from the confluence of ongoing fiscal stress, increased competition from the private sector, and the rapidly changing and evolving area of work/life benefits. Public employers will be scrutinized using standards set in the private sector in such areas as convenience benefits, placing the public sector at competitive disadvantage. Public sector organizations therefore must adopt a greater degree of benefit plan offerings and administrative flexibility. This will require an enhanced management capacity, including the full integration of the needs assessment process in human resources decision making to tailor benefits at the individual and plan level. The challenge will be to develop a "golden mean balance" between standardization and individualization to keep costs manageable and plan administration practical.

Another key element is ongoing benefits package evaluation of efficiency and effectiveness to demonstrate ROI at the individual, work group, and organizational levels. Given the increasing budget share of benefits costs, the human resource system must demonstrate accountability to the key stakeholders (employees, management, legislators, the public). Finally, controversial issues such as coverage of domestic partners (heterosexual and homosexual) will grow in saliency as societal and competitive pressure clash with traditional religious and moral standards (Riddick and Coggburn, 2007). Such issues will serve as litmus tests between increasingly polarized segments of society as a result of the culture wars.

The benefits change management process requires a systematic effort through leveraging traditional human resource practices, such as workforce planning, training needs assessment, compensation and performance management with employee benefits to enhance flexibility, creativity, and innovation. The challenge and stakes are high, but we must continue to support the dedicated and skilled men and women who ably serve our country through the noble calling of public service.

## NOTE

1. There is an ever-growing body of literature demonstrating positive return-on-investment for employee benefits practices. See Roberts, G. E. 2000. An Inventory of Family-Friendly Benefit Practices in Small New Jersey Local Governments. *Review of Public Personnel Administration* 20(2):50–62; Roberts, G. E., J. Gianiakas, C. McCue, and X. Wang. 2004. Traditional and Family-Friendly Benefits Practices in Local Government: Results from a National Survey. *Public Personnel Management* 33(3):307–330; Gault, G., and V. Lovell. 2006. The Costs and Benefits of Policies to

Advance Work/Life Integration. *The American Behavioral Scientist* 49(9):1152–1164; Sands, J., and T. Harper. 2007. Family-Friendly Benefits and Organizational Performance. *Business Renaissance Quarterly* 2(1):107–126.

# REFERENCES

Ackley, D. 2006. Communication: The Key to Putting the "Benefit" Back in Benefits. *Workspan* 49 (2): 32–34.

Atkinson, W. 2000. Divine Accommodation: Religion in the workplace. *Risk Management* 47 (10):12–17.

Bachman, J. 2007. Improving Care with an Automated Patient History. *Family Practice Management* 14 (7):39–43.

Bilodeau, M. 2005. Don't Follow the Herd: Using Data Analysis Tools to Create a Customized Cost Control Approach. *Employee Benefit Plan Review* 59 (12):10–17.

Bottos, L. M. 2006. Mind the Gap: Knowing What Employees Want Is Key. *Employee Benefit Plan Review* 61 (5):20–22.

Bridgeford, L. C. 2007. Sight for Sore Eyes: Older Workers Suffering from Eye Diseases May Change Vision Benefit Landscape. *Employee Benefit News* (April 15):1.

Budd, J. W., and K. A. Mumford. 2006. Family-Friendly Work Practices in Britain: Availability and Perceived Accessibility. *Human Resource Management* 45 (1):23–42.

Business Roundtable. 2007. Doing Well Through Wellness. 2006–2007 Survey of Wellness Programs at Business Roundtable Member Companies. Retrieved on September 25, 2007, from <http://www.businessroundtable.org//publications/publication.aspx?qs=2AC6BF807822B0F19D54F86>.

Cantrell, S., J. M. Benton, T. Laudal, and R. J. Thomas. 2006. Measuring the Value of Human Capital Investments: The SAP Case. *Strategy & Leadership* 34 (2):43–52.

Carr, A. E., and T. L. Tang. 2005. Sabbaticals and Employee Motivation: Benefits, Concerns, and Implications. *Journal of Education for Business* 80 (3):160–164.

Cash, K. C., G. R. Gray, and S. A. Rood. 2000. A Framework for Accommodating Religion and Spirituality in the Workplace. *The Academy of Management of Executive* 14 (3):124–134.

CCH. 2007. *CCH Survey Finds Unscheduled Absenteeism Up in U.S. Workplaces.* Commerce Clearing House. Retrieved on October 9, 2007, from <http://www.cch.com/press/news/2006/20061026h.asp>.

Chiappetta, T. O. 2005. Managing Healthcare Costs. *Public Personnel Management* 34 (4):313–320.

Coggburn, J. D., and C. J. Reddick. 2007. Public Pension Management: Issues and Trends. *International Journal of Public Administration* 30:995–1020.

CPA Practice Management Forum. 2007. Young Professionals Provide Insight on What's Important to Them. *CPA Practice Management Forum* 3 (4):18.

Crosby, A. 2005. Communication: A Key to Effective Benefits Self-Service. *Workspan* 48 (6):56–58.

Digh, P. 1998. Religion in the Workplace: Making a Good-Faith Effort to Accommodate. *HR Magazine* 43 (13):84–91.

Fronstin, P. 2007. EBRI Issue Brief No. 303—March 2007—Employment-Based Health Benefits: Access and Coverage, 1988–2005. Retrieved on September 1, 2007, from <http://www.ebri.org/publications/ib/index.cfm?fa=ibDisp&content_id=3789>.

Gault, B., and V. Lovell. 2006. The Costs and Benefits of Policies to Advance Work/Life Integration. *The American Behavioral Scientist* 49 (9):1152–1164.

Giacalone, R. A., and C. L. Jurkiewicz, eds. 2003. *Handbook of Workplace Spirituality and Organizational Performance.* Armonk, NY: M. E. Sharpe.

Giertz, J. F., and L. E. Papke. 2007. Public Pension Plans: Myths and Realities for State Budgets. *National Tax Journal* 60(2):305–323.

Gorchow, Z. 2007. Granholm Seeks Changes in Prisoner, Public Employee Benefits. *Knight Ridder Tribune Business News* (Washington): June 1, p. 1.

Goree, M. S. 2003. Changing Employee Behavior to Control Health Care Cost. *Workspan* 46 (10):30–33.

Haar, J. M., C. S. Spell, and M. P. O'Driscoll. 2005. Exploring Work–Family Backlash in a Public Organisation. *The International Journal of Public Sector Management* 18 (6/7):604–614.

Hart, D., and M. Arian. 2007. Employee Responsibility in Benefit Change. *Benefits Quarterly* 23 (2): 7–12.

Helman, R., M. Greenwald, C. Copeland, and J. VanDerhei. 2006. Will More of Us Be Working Forever? The 2006 Retirement Confidence Survey. Employee Benefit Research Institute Issue Brief No. 292. Retrieved on September 1, 2007, from <http://www.ebri.org/pdf/briefspdf/EBRI_IB_04-20061.pdf>.

Hemp, P. 2004. Presenteeism at Work—But Out of It. *Harvard Business Review* 82 (10):49–58.

Hicks, D. 2003. *Religion and the Workplace*. Cambridge, UK: Cambridge University Press.

HR Focus. 2007. What Keeps Employees Satisfied? *HR Focus* 84 (8):10–11, 13.

Huang, C., and B. H. Kleiner. 2001. New Developments Concerning Religious Discrimination in the Workplace. *International Journal of Sociology and Social Policy* 21:128–136.

Institute of Management and Administration. 2003. 10 Tips to Improve Your Benefits in the Next 30 Days. *IOMA's Report on Managing Benefits Plans* 3 (11):1.

Johnson, R. E. 2002. *Flexible Benefits: A How-to Guide,* 6th ed. Washington, D.C.: International Foundation of Employee Benefit Plans.

The Kaiser Family Foundation. 2007. The Kaiser Family Foundation and Health Research and Educational Trust Employer Health Benefits 2007 Annual Survey. Retrieved on October 13, 2007, from <http://www.kff.org/insurance/7672/upload/76723.pdf>.

Kelley, A.G., and M. P. Ruggieri. 2007. Municipalities Get a Healthy Dose of Reality on Postemployment Benefits. *The CPA Journal* 77 (4):28–30, 32.

Kessler, R. C., K. A. McGonagle, and S. Zhao. 1994. Lifetime and 12-Month Prevalence of DSM-III-R Psychiatric Disorders in the United States: Results from the National Comorbidity Study. *Archives of General Psychiatry* 51 (1):8–19.

Kiger, P. J. 2007. Throwing Out the Rules of Work: A Workforce Experiment at Best Buy's Headquarters Allows Employees to Decide How, When and Where They Get the Job Done. Retrieved on August 1, 2007, from <http://www.workforce.com/archive/feature/24/54/28/index.php>.

Koenig, H. G. 2005. *Faith and Mental Health.* Philadelphia: Templeton Foundation Press.

Koenig, H. G., and H. J. Cohen. 2002. *The Link Between Religion and Health: Psychoneuroimmunology and the Faith Factor*. Oxford, New York: Oxford University Press.

Leuenberger, D. Z., and J. D. Kluver. 2005. Changing Culture Generational Collision and Creativity. *Public Manager* 34 (4):16–21.

Markowich, M. M. 2006. Combating the Perfect Benefits Storm. *Workspan* 49 (6):22–26.

McDonnell, K. 2008. Benefit Cost Comparisons Betwenn State and Local Governments and Private Sector Employers. *EBRI Notes* 29(6)1–12.

McQueen. M. P. 2006. Health Costs: Getting Dental Coverage. *Wall Street Journal* (*Eastern Edition, New York*): September 24, 2006, p. A.2.

Mental Health America. 2007a. Depression in the Workplace. Retrieved on October 6, 2007, from <http://www.mentalhealthamerica.net/index.cfm?objectid=C7DF951E-1372-4D20-C88B7DC5A2AE586D>.

———. 2007b. Gaining a Competitive Edge Through Mental Health: The Business Case for Employers. Retrieved on October 6, 2007, from <http://nmha.org/go/gaining-a-competitive-edge-through-mental-health-the-business-case-for-employers>.

Messmer, M. 2005. Building Employee Job Satisfaction. *Employment Relations Today* 32 (2):53–59.

Mitroff, I.I., and E. A. Denton. 1999. A Study of Spirituality in the Workplace. *Sloan Management Review* 40(4): 83–93.

Ophthalmology Times. 2007. Health Costs: Getting Dental Coverage; Study: Patients with Poor Vision Incur Greater Medical Costs. *Ophthalmology Times* 32 (6):8.

O'Reilly, C. A., III, and J. Pfeffer. 2000. *Hidden Value: How Great Companies Achieve Extraordinary Results with Ordinary People*. Boston: MA: Harvard Business School Press.

OxResearch. July 19, 2007. *United States: Demand Surges for Long-Term Healthcare*. New York: Oxford Analytica, p. 1.

Pagano, M. 2004. *City Fiscal Conditions in 2004*. Washington, DC: National League of Cities.

Papke, L. E. 2004. Pension Plan Choice in the Public Sector: The Case of Michigan State Employees. *National Tax Journal* 57 (2):329–339.

PR Newswire. 2007. New Study Sheds Light on Americans' Real Risk of Disability: Life Foundation-Sponsored Study Explores Disability Trends by Gender, Age, and Occupation to Coincide with Disability Insurance Awareness Month. *PR Newswire* (New York): May 1, 2007.

Query, J. T. 2003. Flexible Benefits: A How-to Guide, 6th ed. *Journal of Risk and Insurance,* 70 (4):787.

Reddick, G. R., and J. D. Coggburn. 2007. State Government Employee Health Benefits in the United States Choices and Effectiveness. *Review of Public Personnel Administration* 27 (1):5–20.

Reilly, T., S. Schoener, and A. Bolin. 2007. Public Sector Compensation in Local Governments: An Analysis. *Review of Public Personnel Administration* 27 (1):39–58.

Roberts, G. E. 2000. An Inventory of Family-Friendly Benefit Practices in Small New Jersey Local Governments. *Review of Public Personnel Administration* 20 (2):50–62.

————. 2001. New Jersey Local Government Benefits Practices Survey. *Review of Public Personnel Administration* 21 (4):284–307.

————. 2002. Issues, Challenges and Changes in Recruitment and Selection. In *Public Personnel Administration: Problems and Prospects,* 4th ed., S. Hays and R. Kearney, eds. Englewood Cliffs, NJ: Prentice-Hall.

————. 2003a. The Association of Needs Assessment Strategies with the Provision of Family-Friendly Benefits. Research Note. *Review of Public Personnel Administration* 23 (3):241–254.

————. 2003b. Municipal Government Part-Time Employee Benefits Practices. *Public Personnel Management* 32 (3):435–454.

————. 2004. Municipal Government Benefits Practices: Results from a National Survey. *Public Personnel Management* 33 (2):1–22.

Roberts, G. E., J. Gianiakas, C. McCue, and X. Wang. 2004. Traditional and Family-Friendly Benefits Practices in Local Government: Results from a National Survey. *Public Personnel Management* 33 (3):307–330.

Rosenbloom, J. S. 2005. The Future of Employee Benefits. *Journal of Financial Service Professionals* 59 (1):61–65.

Sands, J., and T. Harper. 2007. Family-Friendly Benefits and Organizational Performance. *Business Renaissance Quarterly* 2 (1):107–126.

Schott, R. L. 1999. Managers and Mental Health: Mental Illness and the Workplace. *Public Personnel Management* 28 (2):161–167.

Shanks, J. R. 2007. Federal Telework: A Model for the Private Sector. *Public Manager* 36 (2):59–63.

Starcher, K. 2003. Should You Hire a Workplace Chaplain? *Regent Business Review* 8 (November/December):17–19.

Sullivan, S. E., D. F. Martin, W. A. Carden, and L. A. Mainiero. 2003. The Road Less Traveled: How to Manage the Recycling Career Stage. *Journal of Leadership & Organizational Studies* 10 (2):34–42.

Theodore, D. 2007. *The Changing Face of Mortality Risk in the United States.* Arlington, VA: The Life and Health Insurance Foundation for Education.

Thielst, C. B. 2007. The New Frontier of Electronic, Personal, and Virtual Health Records. *Journal of Healthcare Management* 52 (2):75–78.

Thomas, K. M. 2006. Insurance Gap at Root of Kids' Teeth Troubles: Working Poor Find Costs, Medicaid Restrictions Hurting Dental Care. *Knight Ridder Tribune Business News* (Washington): January 15, 2006, p. 1.

Treatment Online. 2007. The Mental Health Parity Act of 2007 Continues to Move Forward. Retrieved on October 6, 2007, from <https://www.treatmentonline.com/blog/index.asp?blog_id=1200>.

U.S. Department of Labor. 2000. Employee Benefits in State and Local Governments 1998. Bulletin 2531. Retrieved on October 6, 2007, from <http://www.bls.gov/ncs/ebs/sp/ebbl0018.pdf>.

————. 2007. National Compensation Survey: Employee Benefits in Private Industry in the United States, March 2007. U.S. Department of Labor Statistics, Summary 07-05. Retrieved on September 1, 2007, from <http://www.bls.gov/ncs/ebs/sp/ebsm0006.pdf>.

U.S. Equal Employment Opportunity Commission. 2007. Fact Sheet. Retrieved on October 6, 2007, from <http://www.eeoc.gov/policy/docs/fmlaada.html>.

U.S. General Accounting Office. 2003. Human Capital: A Guide for Assessing Strategic Training and Development Efforts in the Federal Government. GAO-03-893G. Retrieved on October 12, 2007, from <http://www.astd.org/NR/rdonlyres/8D3D9012-01F8-4E8C-8EC7-7F9F4BF270AB/0/pp_HumanCapitalPDF. pdf>.

Winnay, S. S. 2004. Are Your Employees Minding Their Behavior? *Employee Benefits Journal* 29 (2): 37–40.

Wisensale, S. K. 2001. *Family Leave Policy.* Armonk, NY: M. E. Sharpe.

# Challenges in Motivating the Public Sector Employee
## Theory and Practice in a Dynamic Environment

GERALD T. GABRIS
Northern Illinois University

TRENTON J. DAVIS
Georgia Southern University

## INTRODUCTION

A colleague once related his father's philosophy regarding the role of a good citizen. He described how his father taught him that a good citizen served either in the military, as an educator, or in government service for part of one's career. Taking up his father's challenge, this colleague worked as an educator before departing for a career in the U.S. Civil Service. To him, public service was noble and honorable; it was simply the "right thing" to do. The significance of this vignette stems from the fact that today a predisposition to serve the public in some capacity, referred to in the public administration literature as "public service motivation" or PSM (Perry and Wise, 1990), while still viable in some quarters, may be diminishing as a motivating factor.

Late in the twentieth and early twenty-first century, traditional public management was routinely criticized as a slow, prone to rowing, and generally ineffective enterprise, incapable of satisfactorily resolving the plethora of issues confronting our society (Kettl, 2000; Light, 1995; Osborne and Gaebler, 1992). According to some scholars, the traditional or Old Public Administration has been pushed aside in favor of the New Public Management (NPM) (Denhardt and Denhardt, 2003). The NPM strives to loosen up inefficient governmental service monopolies primarily through competition and the demands of citizen customers (Barzelay, 2001; Kaboolian, 1998; Pollitt and Bourckaert, 2000). Proponents of the NPM argue that by making governmental organizations more businesslike, as well as more accountable to the citizen-customer, the public sector may relegitimize itself in the eyes of the general population (Denhardt and Denhardt, 2003). Given the emphasis placed on a market orientation, coupled with the thinly veiled superiority of private over public sector management systems, the notion that pursuing a civil service job reflects a noble and honorable vocation is less likely to be heard in the future career deliberations between parents and their children.

The pessimistic and sporadically negative attitude shared by the general populace toward government presents a major motivational challenge for recruiting "the best and the brightest" into the halls of government service (Halberstam, 1972). This chapter examines how the public sector utilizes various theories of motivation for recruiting, retaining, and influencing professional public service employees. Knowledge of motivation theory is strategically important in today's fluid and rapidly changing public sector environment. As such, the following challenges are addressed:

1. How is motivation defined? What general theories of motivation serve as a foundation for motivating public sector employees regarding their job performance, productivity, and job satisfaction?
2. What is meant by PSM and what role might it play in the careers of professional public servants? What motivates individuals to pursue a career in public service or nonprofit management?
3. What techniques do public sector organizations utilize for transforming motivation theory into applied practice?

While the organization of this chapter parallels the flow of topics highlighted earlier, they are each interwoven to some degree. It is difficult to discuss theories of motivation without also considering theories of organizational behavior or specific motivational techniques. Fundamentally, students of HRM should be conversant regarding the rationale and logic of motivation theory, as so much of what we do in practice is tethered to how we think motivation influences human behavior.

## TOWARD A DEFINITION OF MOTIVATION

While there are many theories of motivation, each with its own distinct set of concepts and propositions, there exists an underlying commonality of meaning from which a general definition of motivation might be constructed. Risking oversimplification, we broadly define motivation as the behavioral drive one experiences in relation to satisfying some type of perceived need or needs. This drive induces individuals to engage in conscious action (goal-directed behavior) to resolve felt needs that could be based on rational, normative, physical, or affectual motives.

A college student may need or desire the grade of "A" on an upcoming examination. This perceived need presumably induces the student to study longer prior to the exam. Alternatively, this student may come across a television commercial promoting the thirst quenching benefits of a new brand of beer. This may induce a physical need to drink a beer and even that particular brand. If the student does not act on this need, he or she will likely experience a prolonged state of disequilibrium. Hunger would be another physical need inducing the drive to eat. Finally, our student may "feel" a social obligation to help homeless persons obtain housing. This could lead to the student volunteering to work for a homeless shelter and, after doing such work, experiencing a "good feeling" for acting altruistically, or for doing the normatively "right thing."

This definition, while simple, captures the core rationale embedded in most theories of motivation. Namely, individuals engage in driven behavior (action choices) as a means for addressing one or more felt needs. Obviously, what complicates the motivation process is that individuals may simultaneously experience competing and even contradictory needs of varying intensities. To address these complexities, different motivation theories develop their own nuances and logic that require the student of public administration to think broadly. Given this general introduction, we now turn our attention to several specific theories of motivation that contribute to our understanding of how public service employees behave and perform within their unique organizational milieus.

## MOTIVATION THEORY

For the purposes of this discussion, theories of motivation have been divided into two broad categories: content theories of motivation and process theories of motivation. Content theories of motivation attempt to describe "what" motivates people (Hellriegel, Slocum, and Woodman, 1986). For example, are individuals motivated by extrinsic or intrinsic rewards, or by physical or emotional needs? Process theories of motivation seek to describe "how" content-oriented attributes interact to motivate behavior. Generally, process theories anticipate a more complex sequence of motivation events that eventually result in an outcome.

The specific theories discussed and their respective categorizations are summarized in Table 10.1. Keep in mind that this classification schema is illustrative, and that the clear separation between content and process theories can be vague and permeable. Moreover, while these theories, as well the evidence surrounding their validity, should not be considered exhaustive, they are generally viewed as being foundational to the understanding of employee motivation.

**TABLE 10.1    Classification of Motivation Theories**

**Content Theories**

| Author | Theory | Published |
|---|---|---|
| Abraham Maslow | Hierarchy of needs | (1943) |
| Clayton Alderfer | ERG theory | (1972) |
| Frederick Herzberg | Motivation-hygiene theory | (1959) |
| David McClelland | Achievement needs theory | (1961) |
| Edward Deci and Richard Ryan | Self-determination theory | (1985) |

**Process Theories**

| Author | Theory | Published |
|---|---|---|
| Edwin Locke and Gary Latham | Goal-setting theory | (1984) |
| Edward Lawler, Victor Vroom | Expectancy theory | (1973, 1964) |
| James Perry and Lois Wise | Public service motivation | (1990) |

## CONTENT THEORIES OF MOTIVATION

Content theories of motivation involve attempts to explain the factors within individuals that drive and energize them to engage in goal-directed behavior (Hellriegel, Slocum, and Woodman, 1986). Perhaps the best-known content based theory is the "hierarchy of needs" developed by Abraham Maslow (1943). Maslow argued that humans must first satisfy basic physiological needs, such as hunger, thirst, and sex before moving on to more complex needs, such as security, affiliation, esteem, and self-actualization. Moreover, these latter, more complex needs involve higher psychological forces, where the resolution of the need becomes more intrinsic (value in itself) than extrinsic.

Clayton Alderfer (1972) simplified the Maslowian hierarchy with his more practical ERG model. ERG theory proposes three broad categories of existence needs, relatedness needs, and growth needs. Similar to Maslow's hierarchy, one typically progresses through these need states until a point where growth is no longer possible. In Alderfer's view, when an individual can no longer grow in his or her job, growth needs no longer serve as a motivating factor. Yet, instead of becoming despondent and depressed, individuals regress to lower order needs as their primary source of motivation. For example, maintenance workers within a municipal public works department might be motivated by growth if they think they can get promoted into first-level supervisory positions. However, once this avenue of growth is closed, most likely by persons who have already secured the managerial slots, then the maintenance workers would likely change their behavior to promote stronger interpersonal relationships. In most organizations we call these buddy systems, where workers confide in each other, protect each other from management, develop productivity norms, and strive to gain group recognition and respect. Hence the benefits of being a respected "in-group" member outweigh the less likely payoffs associated with a supervisory promotion. As demonstrated by Hackman and Oldham (1980), if growth needs are stymied long enough, they are unlikely to resurface as motivational forces even if growth opportunities rekindle.

Other content motivation theories include the motivation-hygiene theory of Frederick Herzberg (with Mausner and Snyderman, 1959), and the achievement needs theory of David McClelland (1961). Herzberg argued that two distinct factors separate extrinsic and intrinsic motivational forces, and that only intrinsic factors truly motivate people. Individuals expect extrinsic or hygiene factors, such as pay, equipment, working conditions, and supervisory relations, to be sufficient for carrying out their jobs. If these factors come out of balance, they serve to demotivate workers; however, once they are brought back into check they do not serve as primary motivators. Alternatively, intrinsic factors or motivators, such as achievement, recognition, autonomy, the work itself, responsibility, and advancement appeal to one's higher psychological needs. While research has found that the clear separation of motivational factors is more porous than Herzberg postulates (House and Widgor, 1968), motivation-hygiene theory offers several practical insights regarding how public sector employees might be motivated to perform better.

McClelland's (1961) achievement needs theory takes a slightly different bent. In this approach, individuals are hypothesized as developing dominant need drives, rooted in culture, that strongly influence how they perceive their broader work environments (McClelland, 1961). McClelland's research utilizing the Thematic

Apperception Test (TAT) found that individuals varied in their needs for achievement, affiliation, and power (Stahl, 1983). Achievement motivation is perhaps the most crucial for workers. Achievers prefer to set their own goals and tend to avoid extremes by taking on difficult, but achievable tasks. Achievers also prefer tasks that provide more, rather than less, feedback (Hellriegel, Slocum, and Woodman, 1986). These behaviors parallel the more sophisticated models associated with goal setting theory (Locke and Latham, 1984, 1990), and provide important insights into how such techniques as "management by objectives" may be useful in motivating public sector workers.

One remaining content theory that posits an interesting, yet non-verified, proposition is Edward Deci and Richard Ryan's theory of intrinsic motivation and self-determination (1985). According to Deci and Ryan (1985), intrinsic motivation is related to an individual's need for self-determination (choice) and competence. Self-determination is maximized when an individual is able to choose among courses of action free from external constraints and receives positive yet uncontrolling feedback. Deci and Ryan's contention that monetary incentives may actually lower the intrinsic motivation of an individual when the incentive is withdrawn, more so than if the incentive had never been given in the first place, is well known (Locke and Latham, 1990). When monetary awards are used to control individuals, they may feel that their ability to be self-determining has been reduced and their competency has been called into question. Although Deci and Ryan's proposition regarding how rewards affect individual job performance has not been the subject of empirical research, it does raise questions about the efficacy of merit pay systems.

## PROCESS THEORIES OF MOTIVATION

A second and more complex approach to motivation involves process theory arguments. Theories falling into this category include expectancy theory (Lawler, 1973; Vroom, 1964), goal setting theory (Locke and Latham, 1984), and the Public Service Motivation (PSM) construct (Perry and Wise, 1990).

Expectancy theory is based on three primary assumptions (Lawler, 1973; Vroom, 1964). First, individuals must believe that their behavior is related or will lead to certain outcomes (rewards). This is known as the performance-outcome expectancy. Second, individuals place different values on outcomes. Third, individuals change or alter their behavior based on the perceived probability of success. This is known as the effort-performance expectancy. For example, an employee seeking a raise (outcome) may alter her work ethic (behavior). However, if the employee does not believe that a raise is obtainable or the employee is simply not very motivated by monetary rewards, then she is unlikely to increase her level of motivation.

According to Burke (1994:39), individuals will become "highly motivated" when they believe that their effort will result in outcomes or rewards that are worthwhile and valuable, as well as appropriately set at an attainable level. Thus, the process focus would entail altering both the way an individual's performance is measured, as well as the reward system itself. Such changes would help to ensure that organizational members place an appropriate value on any rewards they may receive, and that the link between their performance and outcomes are clearly defined (Burke, 2002).

Locke and Latham (1990:4) suggest, "Goal setting theory assumes that human action is directed by conscious goals and intentions . . . but does not assume that all human action is under direct conscious control." Goal setting theory makes several important assumptions regarding "how" goals motivate people. First, goals should be difficult but achievable. If a goal is perceived as too difficult, achieving it may be attributed more to luck than skill. Similarly, if a goal is seen as too easy, then anyone can do it, and skill is still not a factor. It is when goals balance skill with extraordinary effort that they convey a sense of genuine achievement for the individual pursuing them. Second, goals should be proximate rather than distal. That is, individuals must feel that by exerting effort a goal can be achieved quickly, rather than ten years later. Third, goals must contain an element of specificity, as goals possessing specificity are more motivational than broad, abstract goals (Locke and Latham, 1984–1990).

A fourth, and more controversial, component of goal setting theory involves the notion of participation. There is some research to support the proposition that participation in goal setting helps motivate workers to exert more effort (Earley, 1985; Erez, 1986; Erez and Kanfer, 1983; Latham and Saari, 1979; Likert, 1967). This implies that goals are more likely to be accepted when they are not imposed by an external authority. Yet, extensive research by Latham and others indicates there is little difference in goal performance between assigned versus participative goals (Carroll and Tosi, 1970; Dossett, Latham, and Mitchell, 1979; Latham, Mitchell, and Dossett, 1978; Latham and Yukl, 1975).

Goal setting theory opens the door to many practical applications for public sector managers. We will touch on such applications later during our discussion of performance appraisal. But first, we close our consideration of process theories of motivation by examining PSM, and the evidence and implications of this construct. Special attention is also paid to explaining how PSM fits within a process-based framework.

In 1990, James Perry and Lois Wise coined the phrase *public service motivation*, where they defined PSM as "an individual's predisposition to respond to motives grounded primarily or uniquely in public institutions or organizations" (1990:368). According to Perry and Wise, there are three motives primarily associated with an individual's decision to enter into public service. First, some individuals may be attracted to public sector work for "rational" motive reasons. For example, they may perceive working for a government agency as a means for implementing public policies that advance their self-interest. Others may exhibit "normative" motives associated with public policies that they feel are ethically correct, such as providing social services to those who are disadvantaged. Finally, some individuals may experience "affective" motives tethered to programs or agencies for which they have a strong emotional attachment.

More recently, Perry (2000) put forth a more comprehensive explanation of PSM. Continuing to argue that a purely "rational" basis for understanding PSM is too limited, thus repositing the proposition that PSM consists of three basic motive sets, Perry has added greater depth and richness to PSM theory through the inclusion of several additional propositions, namely: rational, normative, and affective processes motivate humans; people are motivated by their self-concepts; preferences and values should be endogenous to any theory of motivation; and preferences are learned through social processes.

The key to formalizing a theory of PSM derives substantially from one's socio-historical context (Perry, 2000:480). In this sense, family, schooling, religion, and professional training all combine to influence broader institutions. These institutions reinforce our quickening self-concept and provide a set of self-regulatory processes. It is our self-concept that strongly influences our individual behavior regarding what kind of careers we choose, what kind of rules we follow, and what kinds of obligations and commitments we have toward our sectoral vocations.

One can apply these propositions to a hypothetical situation. A student in the final stages of her undergraduate degree may rationally determine that securing a full-time job is the next logical step toward financial security. This individual strongly believes that social service programs offer a great opportunity to help people and to do the normatively "right thing." So, our nascent public servant applies for a job with a state human services agency. In this instance, the decision to help others in a "normative" motive context may be influenced by her sociohistorical experiences; they congeal to infuse her with a core set of values that she accepts as her own, as well as serve to define her "self-concept." In essence, she views herself as someone who helps others, and as someone who can accomplish this goal by working in a public agency. The longer she works for a human services agency, the more she identifies with its values and preferences. These are learned preferences, which she internalizes and uses to define herself as a member of the nonprofit culture. Ultimately, PSM is the result of a complex series of processes that begin influencing an individual from childhood and continue throughout one's adult life.

## Public Service Motivation: Empirical Research and Evidence

There has been a considerable volume of research devoted to understanding where PSM derives from and what role, if any, it may play within public sector organizations. The empirical research focusing on PSM has been generally supportive; PSM appears to have at least prima facie value for helping us understand why some persons choose public sector careers. A summary of the key themes drawn from this research is provided in the following text. Where appropriate, useful insights for HRM, as well as any weaknesses and limitations of the theory, are also discussed. Finally, we address how PSM fits into our broader understanding of public organizational behavior.

To begin, a substantial amount, but not all, of the empirical research associated with PSM utilizes a measurement scale developed by Perry (1996, 1997). Initially, Perry developed six separate subscales, each incorporating several attitude measures. The original subscales, (1) Attraction to Policy Making; (2) Commitment to the Public Interest; (3) Social Justice; (4) Civic Duty; (5) Compassion; and, (6) Self Sacrifice, have been modified slightly as a result of further analysis and testing. Today, the PSM scale consists of four subscales—the civic duty and social justice components have been removed—and twenty-four attitude measures (Perry, 1997). However, this raises the question of how an individual's score on the PSM scale is related to other important organizational behavior.

In a study of federal employees using a large sample, Naff and Crum (1999) found a significant relationship between PSM score and job satisfaction, performance, and support for various reforms. In another study of federal employees, researchers found a linkage between whistle blowing behavior and PSM score (Brewer and Selden, 1998). Using archival data from the U.S. Merit Systems Protection Board, Brewer and Selden found that whistle blowers behave in ways consistent with the theory of PSM. Namely, these individuals are motivated strongly by the public interest, are high performers, and exhibit high job satisfaction.

More recent research continues to display at least some support for PSM theory. In one non-federal study, Bright (2005) investigated PSM attitudes among employees working for a large county government in Oregon. Similar to other research, he attempted to identify attributes consistent with high PSM scores and uncover how those attributes might influence other administrative issues, such as organizational role, rank, education, and monetary incentives. Generally speaking, Bright's findings were mixed. He found higher PSM scores to be associated with higher levels of education and gender, and not significantly associated with age or minority status. Importantly, Bright found that higher PSM scores were related to managerial status. Hierarchical rank mattered, with higher-ranking managers associating with higher levels of PSM. Finally, a negative relationship between PSM score and monetary incentives was found. These findings, while intriguing, raise some important questions. For example, if PSM is mainly associated with higher-ranking managers, who are well-educated females, what does this say about the remaining segment of employees in the public sector?

Using data drawn from the National Administrative Studies Project (NASP-II), Scott and Pandey (2005) examined whether PSM scores are associated with attitudes toward red tape. In general, they found PSM scores and perceptions of red tape to be negatively correlated. Scott and Pandey (2005) averred that individuals with higher PSM scores are more likely to see rules as legitimate, rather than an impediment to their job. Instead of becoming frustrated, these persons are imbued with a greater determination to pursue what they perceive as the broader public interest, even if this means working through a barrage of rules and procedural obstacles.

Another possibility, however, is that individuals scoring high on the PSM scale are likely to be higher-ranking managers (Bright, 2005) and thus may simply be better situated at evading or gaming red tape obstacles in ways that lower level employees are not. An even more pessimistic interpretation suggests these individuals reach their higher organizational positions not by rocking the boat, but by supporting dubious standard operating procedures and ignoring how red tape burdens may stress those lower in the hierarchy. As any ardent angler knows, dead fish always go with the current.

Moynihan and Pandey (2007) provide yet another glimpse on how organizational variables may associate with and influence PSM. Similar to Perry, they suggest that sociohistorical experiences, such as education, professional group membership, and group culture, influence a person's attitude toward PSM. Specifically, Moynihan and Pandey hypothesize that highly educated individuals, who join professional management associations, are more likely to develop self-concepts that embrace values consistent with PSM. They also claim that organizational institutions related to group culture, red tape, and hierarchy play a role in shaping a person's PSM orientation. Using a national sample of human service administrators, they found empirical support for most of their propositions. Indeed, PSM scores were shown to be positively associated with higher levels of education, having tighter linkages to professional associations, lower perceptions of red tape (which is not surprising since the same dataset was used by earlier researchers), more hierarchical levels, and support for organizational reforms, but inversely to length of tenure (Moynihan and Pandey, 2007).

Finally, research conducted by Coursey, Perry, Brudney, and Littlepage (2008) found further support for the validity of the PSM measurement scale. Using a large sample, consisting of Daily Point of Light and President's Community Volunteer award winners, Coursey et al. report findings similar to other PSM subscale results, indicating that the PSM scale and its subdimensions are highly generalizable. The only issue we have with this approach is that the sample may not be representative of typical public sector employees who choose to work in the public sector. Nonetheless, the consistency of the research on PSM scales is impressive.

While many empirical studies tend to support the existence and instrumentality of PSM, one earlier study conducted by Gabris and Simo (1995) questioned the efficacy, meaning, and value of the PSM construct. They developed their own scale, termed the *Public Service Motivation Survey*, to survey 105 persons in public, nonprofit, and private sector positions. Of importance, this is one of the few studies to actually incorporate private sector respondents as a key component in its dataset. Moreover, Gabris and Simo relied heavily on the "needs" approach to motivation tempered by a cognitive model of psychology (Locke and Latham, 1990; Bandura, 1986). Needs theory contends that individuals are constantly confronted with a panoply of needs, both extrinsic and intrinsic, such as the need for food, sex, affiliation, and achievement that induce drives on the part of individuals to appease them. The tension that a perceived need precipitates cannot be mitigated until some action is taken to satisfy the need. Cognitive psychology assumes that humans make conscious choices to satisfy the continual stream of needs they face, rather than mechanically satisfying only those needs connected with deterministic preconditioning.

Gabris and Simo found little difference between the motivational needs of public, nonprofit, and for-profit employees. For instance, on a battery of twenty separate need variables, ranging from the need for money, authority, responsibility, and community, there were significant differences on only two need items, which were skewed by the nonprofit respondents. However, in a surprising result, public sector respondents perceived the private sector as offering more challenging and rewarding career opportunities. Based on these findings, Gabris and Simo concluded that the PSM construct might exist primarily at the most senior levels of a public organization, where PSM values are continually reinforced and emphasized. For the vast majority of public sector employees, their choice of a career hinges on many competing sets of needs, of which PSM may only play a minor role.

## Public Service Motivation: Implications and Issues

Assuming that the broader public service is moving toward the NPM paradigm, with its emphasis on market competition, smaller and leaner workforces, customer service, and performance measurement, then this transformation has implications for motivating public sector employees. The first implication suggests that the public sector may be adopting and mimicking private business sector practices and techniques to make it more efficient and productive. Even if this is only partially correct, then the rationale that some individuals possess motives that predispose them to want to work in public organizations is diminished. Put another way, the more public sector organizations adopt the techniques and practices of the for-profit business sector, the less difference there is between them, thus reducing the incentive to work in public sector organizations as uniquely special.

As public organizations become more business-like, a second implication is that they may become less PSM friendly. That is, the type of individual likely to succeed and flourish in the "new" public organization may have sociohistorical influences that create a self-concept of competitiveness, performance measurement, winning, and aggressive behavior. An exemplar of this kind of person might be the winner in a "The Apprentice" competition, a reality television show hosted by business tycoon Donald Trump. Thus, there is a need to think carefully about the type of motivation theories and practices that define the work environment that professional public servants face in this era of reform and change that is reconceptualizing how public organizations go about their basic business.

In a recent attempt to explain the tentative linkage between PSM and new models of management, Perry, Mesch, and Paarlberg (2006) considered whether PSM attributes would motivate employees during an era of "new" governance. Perry et al. (2006:89) contended, "Sweeping contextual changes surrounding the way the public's business is conducted suggest a renewed need to visit the drivers of human performance in the public sector." The kinds of contextual forces behind these changes include a greater focus on globalization, demographic shifts exemplified by the surging retirement rates of baby boomers, and, perhaps most significantly, changes in the nature of work itself. The authors acknowledged that the kind of work that the "new" public sector employee will perform would likely be substantively distinct from his predecessors.

Perry, Mesch, and Paarlberg (2006) proceeded to identify thirteen separate propositions regarding what will be expected of future public sector employees. These propositions can be summarized in the following manner: Employees will be expected to function effectively within a "team-based" management system, where group or unit output takes precedence over individual performance. As a consequence, incentive systems that utilize group rewards are likely to become more dominant, where output expectations are tethered to difficult but achievable goals. The team-based system will strongly encourage commitment toward group objectives, facilitated in part by much broader job descriptions where employees are expected to master multiple skills rather than becoming narrow specialists. Employees will also be expected to participate in team decisions on how best to accomplish group tasks and to assume ownership of team objectives. In these new systems, organizations will strive to carefully measure goal achievement, as well as assess the effectiveness of the larger organization in accomplishing a broader mission. In sum, these new public organizations will have flatter hierarchies, less functional specialization, greater reliance on strategic decision making, and less attachment to traditional top-down authority systems. Table 10.2 highlights some of the major characteristic differences between the "traditional" and the newer, emerging "team-based" public management/performance systems.

On balance, we agree with Perry, Mesch, and Paarlberg's (2006) assertion regarding where public organizations are generally heading in terms of how they are modernizing their management systems. At the same time, team-based management strategies are not new. Many of the aforementioned strategies have long been the subject of much attention in the fields of organization development or OD (Dyer, 1987; Golembiewski, 1985, 1995; Golembiewski and Kiepper, 1988; Hackman and Oldham, 1980) and organizational psychology (Blake and Mouton, 1984; Day, Gronn, and Salas, 2004; Lawler, 1984; 1992; Nadler, 1998). The relevant question becomes, *How will an increasing focus on team-based management influence the way in which public organizations design their motivation strategies for public employees now and in the near future?*

TABLE 10.2   Competing Management Characteristics

**Traditional Management Characteristics**

- Steep, top-down, authority hierarchies
- Clear separation between management and labor
- Emphasis on bureaucratic rules and red tape
- Functional specialization of units
- Narrower job descriptions
- Classic civil service pay system; rewards longevity and job tenure
- Formal performance appraisals and individual incentive systems
- Interpersonal relations based on low trust, low openness, high risk, and low owning

**Team-Based Management Characteristics**

- Flatter, less top-down authority hierarchies
- Less separation between management and labor
- Emphasis on collaborative teams and employee autonomy
- Goal oriented and mission driven
- Broader job descriptions
- Compensation based on above-market (i.e., efficiency wage) rates
- No formal performance appraisals and group incentives and rewards
- Interpersonal relations based on high trust, high openness, low risk, and high owning

## PRACTICAL APPLICATIONS OF MOTIVATION THEORY

The potential range of practical public management activities where motivation theory may be utilized is too vast to review here. Thus, to focus the reader's attention, our analysis is limited to three key areas: job design, performance measurement, and compensation systems. This discussion will also compare how practical motivation applications are evolving in relation to changes in the philosophy of public management more generally.

The significance of job design as a potential tool for motivating employees is not a new idea and the classic treatment of this issue by Hackman and Oldham (1980) still has much to offer. Simply put, Hackman and Oldham take job design to a new level. Job design stems from a technique called job analysis, which involves a series of technical processes for developing job descriptions (Bemis, Belenky, and Soder, 1983; Brannick and Levine, 2002). Most traditional job descriptions are narrow, specialized, and consist of a rather limited number of duties and task elements. By simplifying what we expect individuals to do in their jobs, they are far easier to train.

Elemental job design, however, does not motivate employees. Early job design engineers, such as Frederick Winslow Taylor, felt that repetition and simplification of motions made sense, because employees could produce more by working smarter, not harder (Taylor, 1947). Taylor also assumed that workers were principally motivated by extrinsic rewards, namely money. By teaching workers how to produce outputs at a faster pace, which led to greater pay via a piece-rate system, rational workers would see the advantage of repetitive, simplified workflows. The Hawthorne experiments demonstrated, however, that workers wanted more than money; they wanted attention and the feeling that their work was perceived as meaningful (Roethlisberger and Dickson, 1939).

Hackman and Oldham, on the one hand, agree with Herzberg (1966) that job motivation may largely hinge on appealing to an employee's higher psychological needs. Yet on the other hand, they found Herzberg's approach to job enrichment (Paul, Robertson, and Herzberg, 1969), based on vertical and horizontal job loading, too imprecise to utilize as a measurement tool for analyzing the presence of motivational factors in a job (Hackman and Oldham, 1980). Hackman and Oldham argue that three psychological states—meaningfulness of work, experienced responsibility, and knowledge of results—serve as moderators that can result in high internal work motivation, while also providing high growth satisfaction, and job satisfaction.

In order to operationalize job design theory, Hackman and Oldham (1980) created the job diagnostic survey (JDS), which measures such key job characteristics as skill variety, task identity, task significance, autonomy, and feedback, as well as growth need and various contextual issues, such as salary. The beauty of their model is that specific jobs can be analyzed to ascertain how much skill variety, task identity, task significance, autonomy, and feedback is perceived to exist. How employees score their jobs on these indices results in a measure called the motivational potential score (MPS). High MPS scores indicate higher levels of job satisfaction. Voluminous research has been conducted on various MPS measures, and the results have been consistently robust. In short, jobs that expand the variety of skills expected of job incumbents, provide higher levels of responsibility for outcomes, are meaningful, afford broad autonomy, and provide differing kinds of feedback, lead to more motivated employees.

The practical key for the future of job design is clear: employees want more meaningful work, more autonomy, and more feedback. These motivational patterns seem to coalesce well with assumptions of the NPM that advocate broader job descriptions, multitasking, less hierarchy, and fewer rules. This perspective contrasts sharply with the current, narrower job descriptions found in most public sector organizations that reflect a less sanguine view of the employee. Broader job designs with high levels of MPS seem to also provide a much better fit for the kind of team-based management that Perry, Mesch, and Paarlberg (2006) see as emerging.

With the passage of the Civil Service Reform Act of 1978, performance-based (or merit) pay emerged as an impetus for increasing employee performance and productivity. The federal government, and notably President Jimmy Carter, felt that measuring individual performance, and subsequently rewarding or punishing it, would help alleviate the "deadwood," which Carter estimated to be at 2 percent of the federal workforce (Ingraham and Ban, 1984). Expectancy Theory (Lawler, 1973, 1983; Vroom, 1964) is often cited as the theory of motivation justifying performance-based pay. At one level this makes intuitive sense; by setting goals and rewarding preferred behaviors, management is able to inform employees of the kinds of performance expected. Any employee who fails to perform as expected will go justifiably unrewarded, and is given an incentive to improve performance in the future.

Even though the use of performance-based pay at the federal level encountered serious problems (Perry, 1986; Pearce and Perry, 1983; Thayer, 1978), the practice spread rapidly throughout the U.S. public sector (i.e., to most states and many medium- to large-size local governments). To the casual onlooker, measuring individual performance may appear simple. In reality, however, it is complex and difficult. The most common, and easiest to develop, application measures worker traits, such as communication, honesty, judgment, and so forth. Trait instruments, however, are notoriously unreliable. Better designs use goals and objectives based on goal setting theory (Locke and Latham, 1990), and are commonly referred to as *management by objectives*. Other performance appraisal systems use carefully designed, job-related behavioral measures (Latham and Wexley, 1981). We have found that eclectic instruments that incorporate some traits, some objectives, and some job-related behaviors tend to be among the most effective, but are also the most cumbersome to develop. Significantly, even though we have experimented with various performance appraisal designs, problems with accurately measuring individual performance continue to persist.

Another consideration is the ability to apply performance measurement to the kind of team-based management that Perry, Mesch, and Paarlberg (2006) see as emerging. This does not suggest that team-based performance measurement is new. Hackman and Oldham (1980) point out that the creation of work groups requires careful consideration of the design of the group involving composition, norms, and appropriateness of the task. Moreover, for work groups to be successful, they must have a supportive organizational climate, including incentives, training, and clarity of goals, not to mention healthy interpersonal skills. Gabris, Mitchell, and McLemore (1985) and Gabris and Mitchell (1986) found evidence in the mid-1980s that municipal work groups presented an opportunity to reward team productivity, largely because it is easier to measure and visualize the output of groups compared to most individuals.

One technique that shows promise as a motivational tool for intact work groups or teams is called gainsharing (Graham-Moore and Ross, 1995; Hatcher and Ross, 1991). Gainsharing can be defined as a "goal-based" reward program connected with "collective" or intact work group performance. Assume, for example, that a forestry division within a municipal public works department has a budget of $10,000 for planting trees along city parkways. Through careful purchasing coupled with an improved planting technique, the forestry division completes its goal by spending only $5,000; thus, there is a $5,000 savings due to the unit's high level of efficiency. Gainsharing recommends that a formula be devised to reward the efficiency of the work group by sharing a portion of the savings with them. In this way, the organization benefits by rewarding the efficiency of work units, and individuals benefit by working effectively in accomplishing team goals.

Gainsharing does offer intriguing motivational possibilities for public sector work groups. Yet the research on public sector gainsharing, and public sector organizations utilizing it in some format is rare (Graham-Moore and Ross, 1995). Nevertheless, gainsharing has become a widely practiced technique within the private sector; as public organizations become more market driven and private sector-like, the acceptance and application of gainsharing models may also become more common within the public sector.

Skill-based pay is another compensation technique garnering interest in the public sector as a tool for motivating employees (Gupta, 1997; Gupta et al., 1992; Lawler, 1994; Murray and Gerhart, 1998; Thompson and Lehew, 2000). Whereas job-based pay is derived from a mix of duties and responsibilities, skill-based pay rewards employees for acquiring new knowledge, skills, or abilities (KSAs) that provide "value-added" benefits to an organization in a horizontal context, and does not necessarily require vertical promotion. A maintenance worker in a public works department, for example, must master a basic set of job-related KSAs in order to effectively carry out the requirements of the job. As the complexity of the work increases, the mastery of new, more advanced KSAs may be required. Thus, as the maintenance worker increases his skill set he becomes more valuable to the organization. For many public organizations, the practical approach to this situation has been to differentiate nonsupervisory positions into distinct levels where movement from one level to the next is based on more advanced skills, with a corresponding pay increment.

In terms of linking theory to practice, skill-based pay reflects a Herzbergian job enrichment strategy, where the responsibilities of an employee are increased in a way that enhances both their intrinsic and extrinsic motivation (1966). As Hackman and Oldham (1980) argue, job satisfaction is related to skill variety and meaningful work, which can be achieved by enriching traditional job descriptions. When balanced with other motivational techniques discussed in this chapter, we believe skill-based pay is a wise strategy for public organizations to pursue.

One final motivational technique, which dovetails nicely with the market-driven emphasis to public administration espoused by the NPM, involves the "efficiency wage" model. In its simplest description, efficiency wage theory involves the notion that "paying above-market compensation rates might help organizations realize increased effectiveness" (Gerhart and Rynes, 2003:22). An early example of this type of compensation strategy can be seen in Henry Ford's decision in 1914 to double autoworker wages. Yellen (1984) suggested that some organizations might be willing to pay above-average market wages in order to create a psychological expectation among employees that higher pay necessitates harder work. Higher wages may also lead to better applicant pools and longer employee retention. For instance, Krueger (1988) found that the number of applications, as well as the quality of the applicants, for public-sector jobs increased as the ratio of public-to-private-sector pay increased. Holzer (1990), moreover, found that increased wages led to contracted vacancy rates, enhanced the perceived ease of hiring, and reduced the time devoted to informal training. Finally, higher wages may not only lead to better initial applicant pools but may reduce turnover or quit rates compared to organizations paying less (Ehrenberg and Smith, 1988).

Even though many public sector organizations informally practice an efficiency wage rationale, efficiency wage theory has not been the target of much research in the public sector. Recent research by Davis (in press), and Davis and Gabris (2008), however, provides some empirical support for this theory. By targeting several common benchmark positions, the authors were able to identify municipal labor markets, and calculate the average compensation for each position. The most pertinent finding to come out of both studies dealt with a municipality's relative wage position within a labor market and its perceived level of service quality. Perceived service quality was measured by asking city managers or administrators to identify municipalities within their service region known for providing highly innovative, high-quality services. Whether perceived service quality is an accurate predictor of actual service quality is debatable. What can be construed, however, is that many municipalities with a known reputation for providing exceptional services were also found to be leaders in terms of their relative wage position within a labor market.

The potential benefits associated with an efficiency wage system are evident in the City of St. Charles, Illinois (a suburb of Chicago). In 2003, the city implemented a new compensation strategy, based on an efficiency wage model. Specifically, in an effort to recruit, retain, and motivate employees, the city decided to pay its staff at the 75th quartile of its comparable market communities. By way of an annual salary survey, the city recalibrates its pay scale to correspond to any changes with its market comparables. St. Charles also eliminated performance-based pay and cost-of-living adjustments because the city felt that its relative market position, updated annually, mitigated any need for annual cost-of-living increments. In addition, the city abolished its conventional system of formal written evaluations and replaced them with periodic coaching or feedback sessions for all employees. Since 2003, city officials have noted a marked improvement in the size and quality of applicant pools and the city's annual turnover rate is at an all time low. The city enjoys a strong reputation for service quality, as evidenced by the results of an annual citizen survey as well as the measurement of reputational service quality (Davis and Gabris, 2008). Perhaps most importantly, the city's employees appear genuinely satisfied with the organization.

While the efficiency wage model may be a motivational technique for the future of public administration, it does have some drawbacks (Davis and Gabris, 2008). Most notably, not all public organizations have the financial resources to pursue this strategy. Moreover, it may be difficult to convince elected officials that higher wages may actually lead to cost savings (due to lower organizational costs associated with better performance and lower turnover) over the long run. In spite of these drawbacks, the efficiency wage model appeals directly to an individual's extrinsic motives involving money. Though we may rationalize many different reasons why individuals choose to work in the public sector, such as PSM, ultimately, a powerful motivator continues to be extrinsic rewards.

## CONCLUSION

This chapter has attempted to portray varying theories of motivation that challenge and inform public managers. Emerging evidence suggests that some individuals pursue a public sector vocation due to a predisposition to serve the public in some capacity, known as public service motivation (Perry, 2000; Perry and Wise, 1990). Yet, changes in the traditional paradigm of public administration, moving away from traditional bureaucratic moorings toward a more competitive market-driven model, raise the question as to whether there will be any clear distinction between the public and private sectors in the future. We tend to believe that the sectoral differences are disappearing.

This chapter also described more established behavioral theories of motivation that have been used to explain employee behavior, as well as some of the practical applications that support these theories. Fundamentally, these theories suggest that perceived needs drive the goal-oriented behavior of individuals. While many theorists advocate the salience of internal or intrinsic motivators, theories of merit pay and compensation rely more heavily upon extrinsic motivators. In reality, professional administrators will likely need to utilize both intrinsic and extrinsic motivation strategies in order to improve the performance of their agencies. Given that no single theory, model, or technique consistently works indicates that the door is wide open for public administrators to continue exploring human motivation. To that end, finding out what works, at least part of the time, will be a continuing challenge for students of public administration and HRM.

# REFERENCES

Alderfer, C. 1972. *Existence, Relatedness, and Growth: Human Needs in Organizational Settings*. New York: Free Press.

Bandura, A. 1986. *Social Foundations of Thought and Action: A Social Cognitive View*. Englewood Cliffs, NJ: Prentice-Hall.

Barzelay, M. 2001. *The New Public Management*. Berkeley, CA: University of California Press.

Bemis, S., A. Belenky, and D. Soder. 1983. *Job Analysis: An Effective Management Tool*. Washington, D.C.: Bureau of National Affairs.

Blake, R., and J. Mouton. 1984. *Solving Costly Organizational Conflicts*. San Francisco, CA: Jossey-Bass.

Brannick, M. T., and E. L. Levine. 2002. *Job Analysis*. Thousand Oaks, CA: Sage.

Brewer, G. A., and S. C. Selden. 1998. Whistle Blowers in the Federal Civil Service: New Evidence of the Public Service Ethic. *Journal of Public Administration Research and Theory* 8:413–439.

Bright, L. 2005. Public Employees with High Levels of Public Service Motivation: Who Are They, Where Are They, and What Do They Want? *Review of Public Personnel Administration* 25 (2):138–154.

Burke, W. W. 1994. *Organization Development: A Process of Learning and Changing*. Reading, MA: Addison-Wesley.

———. 2002. *Organizational Change: Theory and Practice*. Thousand Oaks, CA: Sage.

Carroll, S. J., and H. L. Tosi. 1970. Goal Characteristics and Personality Factors in a Management by Objectives Program. *Administrative Science Quarterly* 15:295–305.

Coursey, D. H., J. L. Perry, J. L. Brudney, and L. Littlepage. 2008. Psychometric Verification of Perry's Public Service Motivation Instrument: Results for volunteer exemplars. *Review of Public Personnel Administration* 28 (1):79–90.

Davis, T. J. (in press). Playing the External Market: Do Higher Wages "Pay" in the Public Sector? *International Journal of Organizational Theory and Behavior.*

Davis, T. J., and G. T. Gabris. 2008. *Strategic Compensation: Utilizing Efficiency Wages in the Public Sector to Achieve Desirable Organizational Outcomes*. *Review of Public Personnel Administration*. Prepublished August 11, 2008; DOI: 10.1177/0734371X08322872.

Day, D. V., P. Gronn, and E. Salas. 2004. Leadership in Team-Based Organizations: On the Threshold of a New Era. *Leadership Quarterly* 15:857–880.

Deci, E. L., and R. M. Ryan. 1985. *Intrinsic Motivation and Self-Determination in Human Behavior*. New York: Plenum Press.

Denhardt, J. V., and R. B. Denhardt. 2003. *The New Public Service*. Armonk, NY: M. E. Sharpe.

Dossett, D. L., G. P. Latham, and T. R. Mitchell. 1979. Effects of Assigned vs. Participatively Set Goals, Knowledge of Results, and Individual Differences in Employee Behavior When Goal Difficulty Is Held Constant. *Journal of Applied Psychology* 64:291–298.

Dyer, W. G. 1987. *Team Building: Issues and Alternatives*. Reading, MA: Addison-Wesley.

Earley, P. C. 1985. *The Influence of Goal Setting Methods on Performance, Goal Acceptance, Self-Efficacy Expectations, and Expectancies Across Levels of Goal Difficulty*. Paper Presented at the American Psychological Association Meeting.

Ehrenberg, R. G., and R. S. Smith. 1988. *Modern Labor Economics*. Homewood, IL: Richard D. Irwin Publishers.

Erez, M. 1986. The Congruence of Goal Setting Strategies with Socio-Cultural Values, and Its Effect on Performance. *Journal of Management* 12:585–592.

Erez, M., and F. H. Kanfer. 1983. The Role of Goal Acceptance in Goal Setting and Task Performance. *Academy of Management Review* 8:454–463.

Gabris, G. T., and K. Mitchell. 1986. Personnel Reforms and Formal Group Participation Structure: The Case of the Biloxi Merit Councils. *Review of Public Personnel Administration* 6 (3):94–115.

Gabris, G. T., and G. Simo. 1995. Public Sector Motivation as an Independent Variable Affecting Career Decisions. *Public Personnel Management* 24 (1):33–53.

Gabris, G. T., K. Mitchell, and R. McLemore. 1985. Rewarding Individual and Team Productivity: The Biloxi Merit Bonus Plan. *Review of Public Personnel Administration* 4(3):231–245.

Gerhart, B., and S. L. Rynes. 2003. *Compensation: Theory, Evidence, and Strategic Implications*. Thousand Oaks, CA: Sage.

Golembiewski, R. T. 1985. *Humanizing Public Organizations*. Mt. Airy, MD: Lomond Publishers.

Golembiewski, R. T. 1995. *Practical Public Management*. New York: Marcel Dekker.

Golembiewski, R. T., and A. Kiepper. 1988. *High Performance and Human Costs*. New York: Praeger.

Graham-Moore, B. E., and R. A. Ross. 1995. *Gainsharing and Employee Involvement.* Washington, D.C.: Bureau of National Affairs.

Gupta, N. 1997. Rewarding Skills and Competencies in the Public Sector. In *Rewarding Public Employees: A Handbook for Rethinking Government Pay Programs,* H. Risher and C. Fay, eds. San Francisco, CA: Jossey-Bass, pp. 125–144.

Gupta, N., G. E. Ledford, G. D. Jenkins, and D. H. Doty. 1992. Survey-Based Prescriptions for Skill-Based Pay. *ACA Journal* 1 (1):48–59.

Hackman, J. R., and G. R. Oldham. 1980. *Work Redesign.* Reading, MA: Addison-Wesley.

Halberstam, D. 1972. *The Best and the Brightest.* New York: Random House.

Hatcher, L., and T. L. Ross. 1991. From Individual Incentives to an Organization-Wide Gainsharing Plan: Effects on Teamwork and Product Quality. *Journal of Organizational Behavior* 12:169–183.

Hellriegel, D., J. W. Slocum, and R.W. Woodman. 1986. *Organizational Behavior.* New York: West.

Herzberg, F. 1966. *Work and the Nature of Man.* Cleveland, OH: World Press.

Herzberg, F., B. Mausner, and B. Snyderman. 1959. *The Motivation to Work.* New York: Wiley.

Holzer, H. 1990. Wages, Employer Costs, and Employee Performance in the Firm. *Industrial and Labor Relations Review* 43:147–164.

House, R. J., and L. A. Widgor. 1968. Herzberg's Dual-Factor Theory of Job Satisfaction and Motivation: A Review of the Evidence and a Criticism. *Personnel Psychology* 20:369–389.

Ingraham, P., and C. Ban. 1984. *Legislating Bureaucratic Change: The Civil Service Reform Act of 1978.* Albany, NY: SUNY Press.

Kaboolian, L. 1998. The New Public Management. *Public Administration Review,* 58 (3):189–193.

Kettl, D. F. 2000. *The Global Public Management Revolution.* Washington, D.C.: Brookings.

Krueger, A. B. 1988. The Determinants of Queues for Federal Jobs. *Industrial & Labor Relations Review* 41:567–581.

Latham, G. P., and L. M. Saari, 1979. The Effects of Holding Goal Difficulty Constant on Assigned and Participatively Set Goals. *Academy of Management Journal* 22:163–168.

Latham, G. P., and K. N. Wexley. 1981. *Increasing Productivity Through Performance Appraisal.* Reading, MA: Addison-Wesley.

Latham, G. P., and G. A. Yukl. 1975. Assigned Versus Participative Goal-Setting with Educated and Uneducated Woods Workers. *Journal of Applied Psychology* 60:299–302.

Latham, G. P., T. R. Mitchell, and D. L. Dossett. 1978. Importance of Participative Goal Setting and Anticipated Rewards on Goal Difficulty and Job Performance. *Journal of Applied Psychology* 63:163–171.

Lawler, E. E. 1973. *Motivation in Work Organizations.* Monterey, CA: Brooks-Cole.

———. 1983. *Pay and Organization Development.* Reading, MA: Addison-Wesley.

———. 1984. *High Involvement Management.* San Francisco, CA: Jossey-Bass.

———. 1992. *The Ultimate Advantage: Creating the High Involvement Organization.* San Francisco, CA: Jossey-Bass.

———. 1994. From Job-Based to Competency-Based Organizations. *Journal of Organizational Behavior* 15:3–15.

Light, P. 1995. *Thickening Government.* Washington, D.C., Brookings.

Likert, R. 1967. *The Human Organization.* New York: McGraw-Hill.

Locke, E. A., and G. P. Latham. 1984. *Goal Setting: A Motivational Technique that Works!* Englewood Cliffs, NJ: Prentice Hall.

———. 1990. *A Theory of Goal Setting and Task Performance.* Englewood Cliffs, NJ: Prentice-Hall.

Maslow, A. A. 1943. A Theory of Human Motivation. *Psychological Review* 80:370–396.

McClelland, D. 1961. *The Achieving Society.* Princeton, NJ: Van Nostrand-Reinhold.

Moynihan, D. P., and S. K. Pandey. 2007. The Role of Organizations in Fostering Public Service Motivation. *Public Administration Review* 67 (1):40–53.

Murray, B., and B. Gerhart. 1998. An Empirical Analysis of a Skill-based Pay Program and Plant Performance Outcomes. *Academy of Management Journal* 41 (1):68–78.

Nadler, D. 1998. *Champions of Change.* New York: Oliver-Wyman Group.

Naff, K. C., and J. Crum. 1999. Working for America: Does Public Service Motivation Make a Difference? *Review of Public Personnel Administration* 14 (4):5–16.

Osborne, D., and T. Gaebler. 1992. *Reinventing Government.* Reading, MA: Addison-Wesley.

Paul, W. J., K. B. Robertson, and F. Herzberg. 1969. Job Enrichment Pays Off. *Harvard Business Review* (March–April):61–78.

Pearce, J. L., and J. L. Perry. 1983. Federal Merit Pay: A Longitudinal Analysis. *Public Administration Review* 43:315–325.

Perry, J. L. 1986. Merit Pay in the Public Sector: A Case for a Failure of Theory. *Review of Public Personnel Administration* 7 (1):57–69.

———. 1996. Measuring Public Service Motivation: An Assessment of Construct Reliability and Validity. *Journal of Public Administration Research and Theory* 6 (1):5–22.

———. 1997. Antecedents of Public Service Motivation. *Journal of Public Administration Research and Theory* 7(2):181–197.

———. 2000. Bring Society In: Toward a Theory of Public-Service Motivation. *Journal of Public Administration Research and Theory* 10(2):471–488.

Perry, J. L., and L. R. Wise. 1990. The Motivational Bases of Public Service. *Public Administration Review* 50 (3):367–373.

Perry, J. L., D. Mesch, and L. Paarlberg. 2006. Motivating Employees in a New Governance Era: The Performance Paradigm Revisited. *Public Administration Review* 66 (4):89–122.

Pollitt, C., and G. Bourckaert. 2000. *Public Management Reform*. Oxford, UK: Oxford University Press.

Roethlisberger, F. J., and W. J. Dickson. 1939. *Management and the Worker*. Cambridge, MA: Harvard University Press.

Scott, P. G., and S. K. Pandey. 2005. Red Tape and Public Service Motivation: Findings from a National Survey of Managers in State Health and Human Services Agencies. *Review of Public Personnel Administration* 25 (2):155–180.

Stahl, M. J. 1983. Achievement, Power, and Managerial Motivation: Selecting Managerial Talent with the Job Choice Exercise. *Personnel Psychology* 36 (4):775–789.

Taylor, F. W. 1947. *The Principles of Scientific Management*. New York: Harper and Brothers.

Thayer, F. C. 1978. The President's Management Reforms: Theory X Triumphant. *Public Administration Review* 38 (4):309–314.

Thompson, J. R., and C. W. Lehew. 2000. Skill-Based Pay as an Organizational Intervention. *Review of Public Personnel Administration* 20 (1):20–40.

Vroom, V. 1964. *Work and Motivation*. New York: Wiley.

Yellen, J. L. 1984. Efficiency Wage Models of Unemployment. *American Economic Review* 74:200–205.

# Human Resource Metrics in Government
## Measuring the Impacts of HRM

STEVEN W. HAYS
University of South Carolina

ROBERT LAVIGNA
Partnership for Public Service

## INTRODUCTION

One of the most ironic facets of public management is that so little attention is generally paid to measuring the true costs and benefits of the HRM function. Although salaries and fringe benefits can account for 75 percent or even more of a jurisdiction's or agency's budget, the contribution that HRM makes to success or failure is not typically understood. This oddity is compounded by the fact that public managers are generally required to exhaustively justify equipment and other types of purchases, whereas the vast bulk of their budgets—HR—is taken as a given that is rarely analyzed quantitatively. So, when asked seemingly obvious questions such as, *What value are we receiving for our recruitment dollars?* or *Are our training and employee development programs providing a good return on investment?* too often the answers are blank stares, shoulder shrugs, and incredulous expressions.

Triggered largely by the reinvention movement and pressures for increased accountability, only recently has the HR profession begun paying more systematic attention to empirically assessing costs and benefits. This emerging subfield of HRM is generally referred to as *HR Metrics*, or the identification and evaluation of *measurement standards* that can be used to assess the efficacy of HR processes. In addition to providing better ways to assess human resources management, HR Metrics can also enable an organization to assess agency HR issues such as worker motivation, employee potential for promotions, the strength of the leadership "bench" (employees waiting to move into leadership functions), the availability of needed skill sets, and a virtually endless list of related talent management issues.

Although the "science" of HR metrics is evolving—constituting far more of an "art" than a science at this point—significant progress has been made in the last decade in at least identifying and applying some measurement protocols to many workplace variables that impact the HR function, both in the public and private sectors (Bureau of National Affairs, 2005a; Conference Board, 2002; Schneider, 2006). This chapter is intended to provide an overview of the current state of the art in HR Metrics, with the critical caveat that most of the measures are admittedly "proxies." That is, the objects of measurement are complex and ephemeral (e.g., employee job satisfaction is subjective, and can change quickly due to many factors—both internal and external), and therefore HR professionals must often rely on a few concrete indicators to explain worker behavior and/or the impact of various HR procedures. A common example, for instance, is that employee turnover (typically measured by the number of employees who leave as a simple percentage of the existing workforce, often broken out by job category) is one of the most widely used and accepted proxies for such varied results as worker satisfaction, motivation, recruiting and hiring success, supervision, leadership, and an agency's competitiveness in the labor market.

Therefore, there is not yet a generally recognized set of HR metrics that can be applied with confidence. There are, however, plenty of proxies and other measurement strategies that allow HR professionals to do a more effective job of gauging their performance and contribution to agency success than they could just a few short years ago. And metrics methodologies are rapidly evolving.

## WHY HR METRICS?

Stated very simply, the ultimate purpose of HR Metrics is to generate a system of *indicators* that allow public sector managers to accurately assess the status—the "health"—of their workforces and create benchmarks for effective governance. Among the catalysts for this important movement are:

- the ongoing brain drain in public agencies, largely attributable to the imminent retirement of the 78-million-strong baby boomer generation. Government will face this talent challenge before other sectors of the economy because public sector workers are older, on average, than their private sector counterparts (Partnership for Public Service, 2002, 2005);
- a growing realization that government service is too often not an attractive career option for many entry-level (and higher-level) workers (Partnership for Public Service, 2002);
- the corrosive effects of years of inattention to the critical importance of HR (also referred to as *human capital*—HC) to the accomplishment of government agency missions (Cheese and Thomas, 2003);
- increasing pressure on government to operate efficiently and be accountable for results; and
- acknowledgment that the best way to focus attention on HC is to empirically document its contributions, shortcomings, and areas where improvement is needed (Chmielewski and Phillips, 2002).

The logic driving this quest should be self-evident. Given the large expenditures of public revenue for HC, both public managers and the citizens they serve deserve answers to fundamental questions about the quality of the workforce and the linkages (if any) between HR expenditures and government performance. Likewise, it is unwise to invest money in such activities as recruitment, employee training and development, performance management, and the like if it's not possible to conclude with any degree of certainty that the money is being well spent. Moreover, good HR metrics will potentially provide invaluable guidance on both future expenditures and HR strategies. If it can be quantitatively demonstrated that a particular HR technique "works," then resources should be devoted to that practice. A simple example is scheduling flexibility. Every academic study that has ever been conducted on *flextime, compressed workweeks,* and other types of pliable work schedules has definitively shown that they immediately improve worker satisfaction and reduce turnover. Whether higher job satisfaction produces more effective organizations has never been successfully proven; it is possible, however, to empirically link higher satisfaction with lower turnover, a phenomenon that *is* clearly related to organizational efficiency (Finn, 2004). If similar justifications can be developed for other HR practices and innovations, then decision makers are in a much better position to allocate limited resources to maximize public benefit.

## METHODOLOGY

A considerable portion of this study was conducted during the summer of 2006 as part of a Partnership for Public Service project. The Partnership is a nonpartisan nonprofit dedicated to inspiring the next generation to enter public service, and helping government transform itself into an employer of choice. The project was done with the assistance of CPS Human Resource Services, a public agency that does HR consulting.

Much of the information was collected through telephone interviews with decision leaders in the field. These leaders had either written reports or studies on HR metrics, or had reputations for creating innovative measurement strategies in their agencies. In all, the study team interviewed (by phone or e-mail) thirty-five experts from academia, nonprofits, and public agencies. The respondents include most of the key figures in public administration who have written about HR metrics and/or HRM generally, a sampling of well-informed federal managers, and leaders of HR metrics research projects from state and local government. We also gleaned additional information from the massive amount of literature (reports, documents, and surveys) emanating from such sources as the U.S. Government Accountability Office (GAO); U.S. Office of Personnel Management (OPM); and U.S. Merit System Protections Board (MSPB); Partnership for Public Service (PPS); National Association of State Personnel Executives (NASPE); International Public Management Association for Human Resources (IPMA-HR); and other state, local, and nonprofit organizations. The study team also surveyed academic literature to identify the types of HR metrics that stand up to empirical testing and which offer the greatest potential to use as meaningful indicators.

Subsequent analysis has been ongoing by organizations that include the PPS (www.ourpublicservice.org), the GPP (www.gpponline.org), OPM (www.opm.gov), and the International City/County Management Association Center for Performance Measurement (www.icma.org/performance). In essence, many organizations are working to quantify both the *inputs of the HR function* (measures that have always been fairly easy to gather), and to juxtapose that information with a relatively new focus—the *outputs and outcomes of the HR function*. Attention has thus turned not only to measures such as turnover rates, but the reasons for turnover. Similarly, hiring data continue to be analyzed in terms of yield rates and success in acquiring needed skill sets, but it is now supplemented by such measures as the *managers' satisfaction with quality of new hires*. Likewise, when the impact of training is being assessed, managers look not only at the absolute number of workers who receive instruction, but how participation in the program affected job performance (i.e., what are the actual outcomes of training?). This approach to public sector HRM is admittedly somewhat tardy—arriving about forty years after the advent of *program budgeting* and other output-oriented measurement efforts—but its late arrival in no way diminishes the critical role that it will ultimately play in future decision making.

## STUDY FORMAT

In order to simplify the presentation of a lengthy list of trends in HR measurement, we present much of the material as lists and/or bulleted items. We use narrative discussions to explain topics that are either controversial (even iconoclastic) or require additional explanation for better understanding. Because many of the actual metrics are self-explanatory, they are presented largely as bulleted points organized around HR areas typically of interest to the entire public administration community. Therefore, some of the indicators address relatively cosmic concepts such as citizen attitudes about public service (an important measure due to the inherent linkage between recruitment success and attitudes toward government). Other indicators are more down-to-earth, dealing primarily with the impacts of individual HR approaches or the health/quality of HC.

### Public Support for Government Service and the Recruitment Conundrum

One of the most troublesome trends in government today is the apparent lack of interest potential employees have in public service. For nearly two generations, the nation has been bombarded by a cacophony of government bashing rhetoric from politicians and (to a lesser extent) the media. Not surprisingly, this has dampened interest in government careers.

However, although the public sector continues to trail the private sector as an employer of choice among most Americans, some data trends show that the tide could well be turning. Recent surveys of job satisfaction in corporate America reflect growing discontent. During the past four years, for instance, the percentage of *private sector* workers who report that they are happy or content in their jobs dropped from 59 percent to about 48 percent according to a Conference Board poll. Possible explanations must include the increasing tendency of corporate America to renege on pension promises, the lack of loyalty that corporate America has shown to long-term workers, and the "everyone for him/herself" ethic that supposedly typified the 1980s and 1990s and which has subsequently experienced a downturn (Bureau of National Affairs, 2005b).

In addition, a 2006 Gallup Poll showed that fully 20 percent of workers in the private sector are *actively disengaged*—i.e., fundamentally disconnected from their jobs. It is estimated that this problem costs the U.S. economy over $300 billion annually in lost productivity.

While this scenario is unfortunate, it creates opportunities for the public service. Disenchanted private sector workers (and new entrants to the workforce interested in "doing good") represent a target of opportunity for government. According to many studies (Laurent, 1999; Light, 2002; U.S. Merit Systems Protection Board, 2002a, 2002b), a large portion of the public workforce is attracted to government because of a "public service ethic." That is, they are motivated by a desire to serve, to make an impact, and "do good"—touch the lives of citizens (clients). Recent polling by the PSP shows that there is relatively strong interest in public service work among both younger and older workers, but a low level of knowledge about how to apply for and obtain government jobs (Partnership for Public Service, 2006). The challenge for public agencies is to close this gap, and translate interest into job applications.

While there appears to be a sizable pool of Americans who want to "do good," many also want to "do well." And this creates a talent challenge for government around another HR metric—compensation—which is a potential hurdle to recruiting new workers. According to empirical analyses of government's struggles to recruit employees in certain job fields, salary is often the problem. One business student who recently responded to an online survey about interest in government described the salary as "laughable." Barriers include the base salary itself (relative to competing private sector jobs), rigid compensation systems that lack flexibility, and the steep cost of living in areas that have high concentrations of public employees (Washington, DC is an obvious example) (See, e.g., U.S. General Accounting Office, 1992; U.S. Office of Personnel Management, 2004; Young, 2003). And, as widely recognized, the salary gap becomes more pronounced as an employee climbs the organizational ladder.

A comprehensive analysis of public opinion concerning *federal* employment was conducted by the PPS (the Hart-Teeter Study). The findings of this study reinforce the conclusion that college graduates do not typically consider the federal government an employer of choice. Specifically, only 16 percent of the college-educated expressed much interest. Those without college degrees were about twice as likely to express favorable impressions of federal employment (30 percent), and blue-collar workers were the most eager to seek work in public agencies (35 percent). Perhaps the most important labor group—professional and managerial workers—was among the most disinterested (only 17 percent interested in pursuing a federal job). The only positive news in the report is that younger workers were far more likely to have favorable views about federal employment. Some of the oft-mentioned impediments to a federal career include salary (as noted), "bureaucracy," and a lack of information. Indeed, later iterations of the Partnership study of younger workers reinforce the notion that, although interest in public employment may be increasing among both old and young (college-age) workers, their entry into government service is inhibited by limited information about how to gain public employment (Partnership for Public Service, 2006, 2008). There is an apparent lack of readily accessible information to encourage those with public service aspirations to follow through and actually apply for work.

There have been few studies that analyze citizens' perspectives on state and local professional opportunities. Logic would dictate, unfortunately, that the federal data are largely transferable to other levels of government. The Partnership for Public Service, in two surveys, found that college undergraduates and older (age 50–65) workers are less interested in state and local government work than in federal government service (Partnership for Public Service 2006, 2008). This discrepancy may be due, in part, to lower prestige that many might ascribe to nonfederal jobs.

Consistent with this concern, HR metrics that are potentially useful in assessing the public's attitude toward civil service employment are often recruiting-related. The inference is that higher confidence in government is linked to more interest in government employment. For example (Cornell, 2004; CPS Human Resource Services, 2005; Phillips, 2003; PriceWaterhouseCoopers, 2006):

- the absolute number of job applicants with critical skill sets (e.g., engineers, RNs, and/or information technology experts), relative to their presence in the general population;
- the percentage of job offers *accepted*, and reasons why desirable applicants decline;
- vacancy rates by job category, compared to similar positions in the immediate labor market;
- the amount of time required to fill vacancies, coupled with the applicant yield (number of candidates per position) and cost per hire;
- the diversity of the applicant pool by race, national origin, gender, and age.

Now that just about everyone agrees that simply "counting noses" is insufficient, the new approach is to measure recruiting success using more sophisticated quantitative techniques. For example, one strategy is to track the number of "first offers" accepted (i.e., how many of the #1 candidates for various jobs joined the agency?). Another theme in the literature is the need to view recruitment as a *labor supply chain*. This supply chain approach argues that managers should consider the skill and employee mix needed to accomplish the mission (e.g., the skill needs and mix of full-time, part-time, contract, or other workers). Data should then be collected and analyzed on which supplier of labor (university program, type of worker) has the best track record for producing good performers who advance and stay with the organization. Unfortunately, to do this well, an agency must thoroughly analyze at least five years' worth of historical data using mathematical algorithms which identify turnover and performance trends by unit, location, position type, salary, tenure, program assignment, etc. The objective is to view recruitment as a "talent pipeline" in which both the incoming talent and outgoing talent can be forecast and planned for. Given the high costs of turnover (Sasser, 1997; Schneider and White, 2003; Sloper, Linard, and Paterson, 1999), the necessity to assess *both* inputs (hires) and exits (retirements and resignations) is paramount.

Understandably, this level of evaluation and quantitative sophistication will not come naturally to many HR practitioners. This dilemma is amusingly characterized by the Scott Adams' *Dilbert* cartoon that has Catbert, the evil HR director, saying, "If I could do math I wouldn't be working in human resources." Fortunately, this is far more representative of the old (antiquated) HR model. Today's HR managers must either "get with the program," or be left behind. The IPMA-HR has been a leader in articulating a competency model for HR professionals. The IPMA-HR model lists twenty-two different competencies including:

- Possess good analytical skills, including the ability to think strategically and creatively
- Creatively understand business process and how to change to improve efficiency and effectiveness

- Possess the ability to be innovative and create a risk-taking environment
- Know business system thinking
- Apply information technology to HRM
- Design and implement change processes
- Link HR to the organization's mission and service outcome

## Beyond Recruiting: More Workforce Indicators

While recruiting new employees is critically important, so is keeping and developing the good performers already employed. Each good employee represents a tremendous investment, so figuring out if the current employees are satisfied, competent, and likely to hang around is a major concern.

One vast source of useful information concerning the status of the current workforce is available in the federal government. The OPM has a rich repository of demographic data on the federal workforce (*Demographic Profile of the Federal Workforce*, an annual report). As anyone who has glanced at the dataset knows, the information includes detailed breakdowns by pay (and other) level, full-time/part-time, average salaries, gender, average years of service, time toward retirement eligibility, total years of service, type of retirement plan, educational level, age, occupation, disability status, veteran status, etc. These data are available *by agency*. OPM also publishes a bimonthly summary of federal trends in employment, payroll, turnover, and other important indicators.

Both OPM and the MSPB also track recruitment in executive agencies, identify "targeted occupations," and track the success of various recruiting and hiring programs (e.g., USAJOBS, internship programs, campus recruiting, the use of recruitment bonuses, on-the-spot hiring authority, etc.). However, the agencies' success in building a qualified workforce is subjected to very little formal evaluation (U.S. Merit Systems Protection Board, 2005; U.S. Office of Personnel Management, 2006a, b, c).

Regular and larger-scale employee attitude surveys of the federal workforce provide another important data source. The most recent OPM biennial employee survey (2006a) included more than 220,000 responses from employees in hundreds of federal agencies and their subcomponents. Although a few agencies have tapped this reservoir, many have not. They haven't used the information to analyze why their employees feel the way they do and whether they are any danger signs that should be addressed. The problem, of course, is that a great deal of time and effort would be required to mine the depths of the attitudinal responses. Were agencies to do so, however, they could make significant strides in such obvious areas as employees' commitment to the agency's mission, the quality of leadership and supervision, and the degree of alignment between employees' expectations and their agencies' cultures and objectives. Information of this type would be quite valuable in identifying problem areas, and perhaps in generating suggestions concerning where HC investments might best be made. And some, but not all, agencies have begun to mine the data.

A related benefit of analyzing the data might be to provide insights into *how HC is linked to agency performance*. This is perhaps the greatest conundrum facing organizations and managers, yet some important insights into the nuances of the problem may well be sitting at their fingertips.

In sum, there is virtual unanimity among both academics and federal managers that the federal government produces a large amount of HC data. That is, the problem is *not* that there is insufficient data about the status of the workforce. Rather, observers usually agree that not all data are systematically organized, integrated, evaluated, "mined," or made available in a meaningful fashion to decision makers (Stephenson, 2006; Sullivan, 2004; ; U.S. General Accounting Office, 2004; U.S. Government Accountability Office, 2004). A related opinion is that, many high-level decision makers are not sufficiently concerned about HC issues to use whatever data might be provided to them.

At all levels of government, HR metrics that can help address "state of the workforce" issues include the following types of indicators (Ammons, 2006; Applied Skills and Knowledge Group, 2005; Schay et al., 2002):

- Turnover among new hires (e.g., first year, or first three years)
- Reasons for attrition (exit interview data)
- Turnover in mission critical positions, among high performers, and/or among employees with critical skills and competencies
- Attrition rates by retirement eligibility (in other words, are experienced people voting with their feet as soon as they can?)
- Annual grievances per hundred employees; percentage of grievances upheld

## Performance Evaluation: The Potential Keystone to Performance Metrics

Another major source of data—employee performance appraisals—has potential to help gauge the quality and performance of the public service. Once hired, a worker's value to the organization becomes *the* primary concern. Is the person performing up to expectations? Does he or she demonstrate the skills that were originally sought during the hiring process? Is the employee developing critical new skills? And, most fundamentally, is the person making an important contribution to agency performance?

Unfortunately, it is commonly recognized that individual performance appraisals are not very accurate sources of information. Although they serve as the cornerstone of most efforts to implement pay-for-performance and support other important HRM decisions (e.g., training and development, promotions), it's well documented that evaluations in most organizations, public and private, are subjective, inflated, and often unrelated to actual performance.

There is no "silver bullet" to solve this problem (in fact, the federal government has experimented with dozens of performance assessment strategies dating back to the 1920s). However, there are ways to improve the utility of performance evaluations, both as a measure of employee performance and as a metric.

Measures of group performance are one possible alternative, as are attempts to tie assessments to measurable job indicators (see Barber, 2004; Hatch, 2006; Huselid and Becker, 2005; Mercer Human Resource Consulting, 2003, 2005). Another approach gathering steam in the private sector is to "weight" both jobs and the people in them. Jobs can be separated into categories based on their contribution (importance) to the core mission. SAS and other technology firms sometimes have identified three classes of jobs based on their impacts—low, medium, and high. Individual employees are then graded as A, B, or C, based on their job performance and advancement potential. While admittedly simplistic, this approach does give organizations a tool to help decide where to spend their resources (e.g., where to focus on succession planning, which jobs to downgrade if they become vacant, and which employees need cross-training to prepare them for the next promotion).

Another key—and problem—in effective employee performance evaluation is dispersion of scores. Managers who assign inflated evaluations to everyone, or who fall victim to "central tendency," are not doing their jobs. To make performance appraisal meaningful, managers must distinguish among performance levels. While this does not mean a forced distribution or bell curve, it does mean documenting and explaining justifiable variations.

Yet another complicating factor, particularly in the federal government, is the increasing use of noncivil service workers (referred to as the *multisector* or *shadow workforce*)—contractors, grantees, state employees paid by federal agencies, temporary workers, seasonal employees, etc. (Light, 2002). Outsourcing work to private sector contractors is a big part of this. This large and growing federal "workforce" often flies under the radar of HR metrics. To adequately account for the multisector workforce, there must be a careful alignment of an overall HC plan with the mission and strategic goals of the agency. This overall plan should focus on creating a results-oriented culture and reliable accountability systems that include the shadow workforce.

The increasing use of contractors also affects the permanent workforce. For example, a 2004 MSPB study reported that "job security" has become one of the most critical concerns of federal workers (U.S. Merit Systems Protection Board, 2004). This has important implications for job satisfaction, organizational commitment, and other important aspects of worker confidence. Because job security has traditionally been one of the chief advantages of government employment, job uncertainty resulting from the multisector workforce may affect potential metrics in areas such as turnover and recruitment. Outsourcing has workforce implications for state and local governments too.

Although the accurate measurement of performance continues to be a maddeningly elusive goal for HR managers, there are a few HR metrics that serve as proxies. These include:

- Surveys of managers on their satisfaction with subordinate staff and the quality of new hires
- Comparisons of agency objectives, by program, with performance of critical staff (i.e., are there obvious laggards or achievers in different parts of the organization?)
- Percentage of managers and workers who are promoted from within compared to the percentage hired from outside
- Overall percentage of workers who must be referred to remedial training programs to address deficiencies
- Multiphased evaluations—including 360-degree techniques—to provide a more accurate snapshot of worker performance
- Worker surveys aimed at evaluating the evaluation process—that is, to what extent do the employees perceive the assessment protocol to be valid and reliable; if there is disagreement (and there almost certainly *will* be), advice should be solicited from the workgroup on more concrete indicators of actual achievement

## LEADING WORKFORCE METRICS: A MIXED BAG

The literature on HR metrics suggests that the amount of measurement taking place is exhaustive. Although it would be reassuring to draw such a conclusion, we fear that the reality is less optimistic. Instead, various organizations, people, and study groups have advanced proposals for HR metrics, which are used "somewhere." Too often, these remain good ideas but not realities. Using HR metrics is not yet a standard HR practice, but HR managers and professionals should apply in their own settings (Krell, 2004; National Academy of Public Administration, 2002; National Association of State Personnel Executives, 2006).

In this context, we present additional indicators and measurement protocols that essentially comprise a compendium of "what's being done in government." Where appropriate, short descriptions are provided. The reader should keep in mind that we are not endorsing the actual effectiveness or suitability of these HR metrics, largely because very few of these measures have been systematically evaluated and, when used they must be adapted to individual situations. There is no one-size-fits-all solution to measuring HR effectiveness.

However, it is reassuring that the high level of energy being devoted to this topic virtually ensures that HR metrics will be part of the HRM conversation for decades to come. And, despite the challenges and complexities of measuring workforce "quality," there are some leading workforce metrics. According to current practice and literature, some of the most widely used and important HR metrics are:

- **Quality of recruitment.**   There is a growing sense that simply measuring recruitment by counting noses is not enough. Instead, measuring recruiting success is critical. For example, as listed earlier, one strategy is to track the number of "first offers" accepted (i.e., how many of the "#1 candidates" were actually hired?). In addition, there is the talent "supply chain" approach, also described earlier, in which both the incoming and outgoing talent are forecast and planned.

- **Employee satisfaction and attitudes.**   are usually based on employee surveys and analysis (such as the *Partnership's Best Places to Work in the Federal Government* project). Creating a system-wide set of benchmarks on employee attitudes should be a high priority, and is within reach with already existing data. Moreover, norms could be compared with data on employees in other levels of government and the private sector.

- **Organizational commitment/engagement.**   This measure goes beyond job satisfaction and includes the extent to which employees identify with organizational mission, goals, philosophy, values, policies, and practices. This is measured by questionnaires/surveys such as Organizational Commitment questionnaires, the Gallup Q12 survey, and the PPS "Best Places to Work" ratings. Other less direct ways to measure this include turnover rates, grievance rates, and aggregate performance appraisal statistics (e.g., a low average rating probably reflects poor organizational commitment).

- **Turnover and retention.**   The best way to measure this metric is not only by comparing it to historical rates, but also to best practice organizations. Perhaps even more critical is measuring the quality of turnover—the percentage of high-performing workers who leave and whose departure could have been prevented. In other words, agencies should focus on whether they're losing good performers. Another approach is to measure "excellence in retention" (the ability to hold onto top performers). In the private sector, this has been linked to financial success in Fortune 500 companies (Welbourne, 2004).

- **Average job tenure.** This is most meaningful when tracked within key job groups where greater tenure is a true asset, and where expertise is critical to success.
- **HR investment.** This is the cost of providing HR services, usually measured as a cost per employee compared to a norm or benchmark, or ratio of number of HR staff to total number of employees. These measures exist in state and local government, but are not widely used in the federal government.
- **Competency level (mastery).** refers to the extent that employees develop key competencies in particular areas tied to core mission, strategy, and programs. Employee development programs and training that are not linked to agency mission and goals are only tangentially relevant (except if they improve satisfaction and commitment). Logically, then, the goal is to assess training and development ROI by measuring competency gains, and linking them to program outcomes. Old measures like training budgets, training hours attended, and course evaluations are inadequate.
- **Educational levels.** (by occupational specialty).
- **Leadership quality.** is a measurement challenge, but has been assessed through 360-degree evaluations, assessment centers, and also through mobility. Managers who move from agency to agency, often with promotions at each stop, can be more valuable than those whose entire experience has been in a single agency. In general, private sector leadership development programs have been shown to produce ROI of 200–500 percent. Similar government programs should also generate ROI, as discussed later, but this is difficult to document.

    Another emerging indicator of leadership quality is the extent to which managers develop and advance their best performers. In particular, this metric is intended to identify and reform "talent hoarders" who keep talented subordinates with them rather than helping them progress. This dimension could be included in supervisory ratings.
- **Innovation and creativity.** Because every organization needs to adapt to change, employees' level of creativity is critical. Unfortunately, this is difficult to measure. Primary data sources are improvements based on employee suggestions and input from employee focus groups, surveys of managers, recognition of employees by professional groups, employee publications, patents granted, etc.
- **Productivity (agency-specific).** The enduring challenge in government is to document results in the very imperfect world of politics, policymaking, abstract goals, "fuzzy numbers," and even fuzzier measures of results. Yet, despite these obstacles, measurement of agency (or program) productivity has preoccupied the public management literature for over twenty years. This reflects efforts by government organizations to identify concrete (albeit imperfect) outcomes and outputs.

Virtually every issue of publications such as *Public Productivity and Management Review* contains examples of public agencies that have identified measurable objectives. These range from the simple (e.g., police response times and crime clearance rates, how long it takes to fix potholes) to the complex (e.g., assessing the Federal Trade Commission's economic contribution by calculating the financial benefit to consumers of lawsuits that reduce unfair trade practices). Critical to making HR metrics meaningful is that they be linked—to the extent feasible—to agency goals and objectives. In other words, the contributions of agency employees need to be tied to organization missions and goals—and results (Brookings Institution, 2002; Hackman, 1985; National Academy of Public Administration, 1996).

## OTHER MEASURES

There are also a series of other commonly used measures. Some are losing significance in both the public and private sectors but, in general, these "secondary measures" continue to be used by many public agencies.

- **Workforce profile data.**   include demographic characteristics such as age, race, retirement eligibility, salary level, position, average job tenure, educational level, etc. To be used effectively, this information needs to be analyzed by agency, program, occupation, etc. It also needs to be put into context, by comparing to previous time periods, other agencies, the private sector, etc. The average age of employee by program and/or occupation is a standard (however imperfect) way to track likely bulges and shortages of workers, predict attrition, and identify recruiting priorities.
- **Compensation and benefits.**   In government, the usual formula for measuring and comparing compensation and benefits is to compute the percentage of the budget "invested" in pay and benefits. Adequate measurement also means analyzing labor market statistics to ensure that compensation is competitive.
- **Work/life balance.**   Recent research reveals that workers are increasingly unwilling to sacrifice their personal lives for their jobs. Specific measures of work/life balance usually include computations of overtime, weekend work, amount of travel, and other tangible measures. This information is supplemented with attitudinal surveys, and collected in exit interviews to analyze why employees quit.
- **Health and safety.**   In general, public agencies "assess" the literal health of their workforces by tracking employee sick leave usage over time, by position, and job category. Insurance costs, disability rates, and mortality figures also enter the equation. Safety is often assessed by the U.S. Occupational Safety and Health Administration (OSHA) compliance and accident rates.
- **Labor management relations.**   This metric can range from "number of employees terminated successfully," to the outcome of a contract negotiation (length of time to reach contract agreement, level of pay increases, and/or reduced employer costs for benefits). Workplace conflict, as measured through adverse actions and other forms of complaints, can be used as a proxy measure for the state of labor management relations.

## SPECIFIC EXAMPLES FROM THE FEDERAL GOVERNMENT

Several specific public agencies are using distinctive approaches to collect, analyze and use metrics. In the federal government, for example, the Tennessee Valley Authority (TVA) projects, assesses and manages turnover. TVA begins by identifying key positions and then assigns each a "position risk factor" (i.e., an estimated measure of difficulty in hiring replacements). These scores range from 1 to 5; 1 means that there are available candidates with the needed skills; 5 means it takes up to five years to master key skills and there aren't replacements available.

Employees are then asked to estimate when they think they'll actually retire (not just when they're eligible). Each employee is scored according to a "retirement probability index" (1 means the incumbent is likely to stay on for five or more years, while a 5 means that retirement is less than one year away).

TVA then calculates an "attrition factor" by multiplying the risk factor and the retirement probability. The result is a score from 1–25. Positions that score 20 or higher require immediate action—a specific replacement plan. Positions that score 15–19 are "priority," which triggers the development of a staffing plan. Lower-risk jobs (10–14 points) are handled through longer-term strategies such as training and college recruitment programs, while low-risk jobs (1–9 points) receive less immediate attention.

The GAO, consistent with its efforts to help federal agencies address HC challenges, developed a set of metrics to take the pulse of its own workforce. The measures are:

- New hire rate—ratio of new employees hired to the number of planned hires.
- Acceptance rate—ratio of acceptances to offers made.
- Retention rate—percentage of staff onboard who stay with the agency (calculated with and without retirements).
- Staff development—based on staff responses to four questions on the annual employee survey. These questions ask employees to rate the impact of internal training, computer-based training, external training, and on-the-job training.
- Staff utilization—based on the responses to three questions in the employee survey. Questions include "my job makes good use of my skills," "GAO provides me with opportunities for challenging work," and "in general, I was utilized effectively."
- Leadership—another measure based on responses to the survey. In this case, ten questions related to leadership are analyzed, focusing on topics such as "my immediate supervisor gives me the opportunity to do what I do best," and "my supervisor provides meaningful incentives for good performance."
- Organizational climate—also derived from the employee attitude survey, focusing on five survey questions such as "my morale is good," "I am satisfied with my job at GAO," and "I am treated fairly."
- "Help get job done"—employee satisfaction with internal operations, based on employee ratings of twenty-one administrative services (e.g., Internet and intranet systems, IT support, customer support services).
- Quality of work life—assesses employee satisfaction with ten internal GAO "services" such as pay and benefits, building maintenance, and workplace safety.

Another example is the metrics approach the U.S. Army uses for civilian employees. The *Civilian Forecasting System* uses data from the previous five years to develop a seven-year forecast of workforce distribution (age, location, classification, skill category, all cross-tabulated with turnover), turnover by tenure, projected vacancies and the available supply of candidates (measured, in part, by the number of resumes in hand and past recruitment experience for that job category), and "what if" scenarios. This latter feature tries to answer questions such as *what would happen if the Army offered a hiring bonus to engineers; what impact would that have on hiring success?*

## METRICS FROM STATE GOVERNMENT

With no pun intended, the general state of HR metrics in state government is poor; many states can't provide even the most basic demographic figures. To fill this gap, the NASPE (National Association of State Personnel Executives, 2005, 2006) is developing a set of measures and benchmarks for key HR functions. This work in progress has identified the following measures:

- Recruitment and selection
  - Percentage of hires who complete their probationary periods, excluding those who leave voluntarily.
  - "Job fit" as measured by a survey that asks supervisors three questions: "Does your new hire's competence fit with the job requirements as needed and expected? "Does your new hire display the behaviors and work ethic needed?" "Overall, is your new hire a good fit for your work unit and the job he or she is assigned?"
  - Number of job offers required before an acceptance, qualitative evaluations of the applicant pool, and the percentage of protected group hires in managerial positions.
- Retention, defined as "voluntary turnover of key performers in key jobs," and protected group attrition as a percentage of total turnover. Worker engagement has been folded into this construct, to be measured by surveys to determine the percentage of employees who "look forward to coming to work."
- Compensation and benefits
  - Average percentage difference in pay and benefits between top-rated and average employees.
  - Percentage of employee pay "at risk" based solely on performance.
  - Percentage of workers whose average pay is at or above market. This should be correlated with turnover (i.e., to determine if turnover is linked to noncompetitive wages).
- Employee relations
  - Percentage of turnover among poorly performing managers and employees (based on annual performance appraisals).
  - Percentage of employees placed on performance improvement programs.
  - Percentage of administrative actions (e.g., EEO complaints, grievances, etc.) overturned by reviewing bodies.
  - Correlations between diversity and pay, and diversity and adverse actions (i.e., discrepancies among protected and unprotected demographic groups).
- Training and development. Instead of typical indicators (training costs per worker, number of training hours, and number of employees trained), NASPE has opted to survey attitudinal responses:
  - Percentage of employees who report they are satisfied with their learning opportunities (over time).
  - Percentage of employees who report a lack of training that affects their performance.

Individual states are also mounting their own metrics programs, in some cases relying on the U.S. OPM employee attitude survey. For example, Washington and Oregon have administered surveys to samples of workers. These data may provide a potential set of norms (benchmarks) against which to compare federal employees.

In Texas, the University of Texas *Survey of Organizational Excellence* is a large-scale effort to assess employees' views of the state government working climate. The University has administered the survey since the 1980s, and the survey is now used by both public and private organizations.

In state government, the survey is administered online to state employees every two years. The questions focus on five "workplace dimensions:"

1. Work group (e.g., supervisor and team effectiveness)
2. Accommodations (e.g., pay, benefits, and physical work space)
3. Organization features (change and goal orientation)
4. Information (communication)
5. Personal demands (job satisfaction and empowerment)

Each of the more than seventy-five participating agencies receives a report that summarizes trends in that agency, as well as comparisons with other agencies of similar size and mission, and with all respondents. Each area is rated (e.g., as a "strength" or "area of concern").

In Pennsylvania, HR staff take a more targeted approach by calculating a "retirement probability factor" to project and prepare for turnover in critical positions. By relying on a decade's worth of attrition data, the state calculates the probability of retirements for key job classes based on when employees become eligible to retire, and historical retirement trends for one, two, and three years after retirement eligibility. The result is a relatively accurate predictor of future retirement based on past trends.

At a more macro state level, the ongoing GPP periodically assigns "grades" to state programs in five functional areas, including HR (people). Sponsored by the Pew Charitable Trusts, the GPP assigns A, B, C, D, and F grades to states (as well as some cities and counties, in earlier versions of the project). The people dimension covers areas such as hiring, training and development, and workforce planning. Grades are largely tied to results such as conducting workforce planning, decentralizing decision-making authority, improving timeliness, and simplifying administrative functions. The GPP could provide a basis of comparison to the federal workforce. For the most recent example of a GPP report card, see "Grading the States" (Government Performance Project, 2008).

## METRICS AND BENCHMARKS FROM LOCAL GOVERNMENT

Local governments are a diverse group and therefore use a wide range of metrics and benchmarks. This shows that local agencies are attempting to quantitatively assess workforce activities. On the other hand, what local governments are measuring often doesn't link to workforce outcomes (e.g., fast hiring doesn't necessarily mean good hiring).

The specific metrics (and benchmarks in parenthesis) given in the following list have not been statistically validated, but are typical of the approaches cities and counties are using. Some were developed by the International City/County Management Association (ICMA) as part of its larger local government metrics program. The benchmarks shown are averages or ranges (see Ammons, 2006):

- Grievance rates (2 per 100 employees)
- HR "staff efficiency" measures

- ○ (0.7 HR employee per 100 FTEs)
- ○ (HR operating costs less than 3 percent of entire payroll)
- ○ (92 percent of routine HR requests cleared in two days or less)
- ○ (Average approval time for routine request is four hours)
- Job postings (98 percent posted within two days of approval)
- Applicant screening (90 percent of applicants screened within two days of receipt)
- Benefits processing (all benefits requests handled in two days)
- Overall turnover rates (1–15 percent, depending on jurisdiction)
- Recruitment yields (at least fifteen qualified applicants per vacancy; at least two candidates rated "highly qualified" for each vacancy)
- Time to recruit and create eligibility list (40–120 days for professional applicants, 14–56 days for lower-level workers)
- Prompt position audits/reclassifications (95 percent completed in less than fifteen days)
- Prompt dispute resolution (hearing scheduled within three weeks, final decision in sixty days)
- Favorable resolution rates for grievances (jurisdiction wins 75–96 percent)

## ROI—THE NEXT FRONTIER?

HR metrics, particularly in the private sector, are also now intertwined with discussions of ROI, or mathematical efforts to document both the costs and the returns of HR activities (Rohm, 2002; U.S. Department of Labor, 2000). For example, turnover reduction has been estimated to generate a ROI of between 50 and 1,000 percent of the departing employee's base salary, depending on value to the organization, time required to hire a replacement, lost productivity attributable to the learning curve of the new worker, recruitment costs, etc. Another estimate of the cost of lost productivity from turnover is 1 to 1.5 times base salary, not including the "senioritis" phenomenon that occurs while a worker prepares to leave the organization ("retiring in place").

ROI is also estimated in some organizations through a "rookie count"—the percentage of workers with less than two years experience. A benchmark is that over 20 percent is too high; the workforce is too "green."

Table 11.1 shows other ROI metrics and benchmarks (Bureau of National Affairs, 2005b).

## CONCLUSION

We hope the preceding discussion has provided some new ideas about how to approach HR, and measuring HR effectiveness. Personnel administration is not simply a hackneyed set of techniques (Wallace Sayre's famous "triumph of technique over purpose" condemnation dating back to 1948).

Each HR function has real-world *consequences* that directly influence agency performance, and the well-being of the citizens the agency serves. To the extent that HR practitioners can identify and quantify the impacts of their activities, they will enhance their professional reputations and greatly improve the usefulness of their

TABLE 11.1   ROI Metrics and Benchmarks

| Metric | Benefit or Benchmark |
| --- | --- |
| Rookie ratio | Not more than 20 percent |
| Percentage of employees eligible to retire in five years | Less than 17.5 percent |
| All positions filled within two weeks | Linked to higher ROI |
| 100 percent of HR transactions online | Linked to higher ROI |
| At least one-third of new employees recruited from employee referrals | Linked to higher ROI |
| Job offers accepted by first choice candidates a majority of the time | Linked to higher ROI |
| Balanced allocations of internal promotion and external recruitment for management positions | High ROI (varies by setting). Depending upon the type of industry, companies at either extreme (all lateral entry or all internal promotion) lag behind companies that balance promotions. |
| "Poor quality" hires | Less than 6 percent |
| New hire voluntary separations | Less than 3.3 percent |
| Improving worker competencies incrementally (see ROI calculation: Kravetz, 2005). | Linked to higher ROI |
| Reducing time to reach competent performance level (for new employees, through orientation and training) | Linked to higher ROI |

activities to line managers. Those who ignore this imperative are at risk of having their functions outsourced to service providers that are more proficient at justifying HR expenditures. Therefore, the choice is simple. The transition to becoming more adept at identifying and applying sophisticated data collection techniques is truly one of the most critical challenges faces public sector HR managers in the new millennium. Hence, Catbert's cynical assertion that, "If I could do math I wouldn't be working in human resources," no longer applies.

## REFERENCES

Ammons, David. (2006, May 5). Odds and Ends in Human Resource Administration: Selected Cities. HR Metrics provided by email exchange.

Applied Skills and Knowledge Group. October 2005. *Measuring Human Capital.*

Barber, Jamie. 2004. *The Numbers Game: Nine Steps to Making the Most of Your HR Metrics.* Intronet: The Total Resourcing Solution.

Brookings Institution. June 2002. *Troubled State of the Federal Public Service.* Center for Public Service, Washington, D.C.

Bureau of National Affairs. August 2005a. *2005–2006 Recruiting Metrics & Performance Benchmark Report.* Washington, D.C.

————. September 2005b. *Workforce Strategies: Quantifying Human Resources: How to Convert HR Metrics into Dollars and Cents.* Washington, D.C.: BNA Inc.

Cheese, Peter, and Bob Thomas. 2003. *Human Capital Measurement: How Do You Measure Up?* Chicago: Accenture.

Chmielewski, Todd, and Jack Phillips. (2002, July–August 31). Measuring Returns-on-Investment in Government: Issues and Procedures. *Public Personnel Management.*

Conference Board. 2002. *Value at Work: The Risks and Opportunities of Human Capital Measurement and Reporting.* www.conference-board.org

Cornell, Christopher. September 2004. Metrics by the Expert at HR Technology Conference. Workindex. com.

CPS Human Resource Services. 2005. *Building the Leadership Pipeline.* Sacramento, CA.

Finn, R. February 2004. Five Steps to Effective Human Capital Measurement. *Strategic HR Review.*

Government Performance Project (2008). The Pew Center on the States. http://www.pewcenteronthestates.org/gpp_report_card.aspx

Hackman, R. 1985. Doing Research That Makes a Difference. In Lawler et al., eds. *Doing Research That Is Useful for Theory and Practice.* San Francisco: Jossey-Bass.

Hatch, James. 2006. *The HR Scorecard: The New Way to Measure Your Human Capital.* PriceWaterhouseCooper, Saratoga Institute.

Huselid, M. A., and B. E. Becker. 2005. *The Workforce Scorecard.* Boston: Harvard Business School.

Krell, Eric. October 2004. Human Capital Management: How CFOs Manage Investments in Their Companies' Biggest Asset. *Business Finance.*

Laurent, Anne. February 1999. Extreme Measures. *Government Executive.*

Light, Paul. June 2002. *The Troubled State of the Federal Public Service.* Washington, D.C.: Brookings.

Mercer Human Resource Consulting. November 2005. *Tempered by Fire: Where HR Is. Where It Needs to Go.* Boston: Mercer Human Resource Consulting.

————. July 2003. *HR Professionals Report Widespread Use of Metrics.* Boston: Mercer Human Resource Consulting.

National Academy of Public Administration. June 1996. *A Competency Model for Human Resources Professionals.* Washington, D.C.: National Academy of Public Administration.

————. July 2002. *Summary of Human Resources Management Research for the National Commission on the Public Service.* Washington, D.C.: National Academy of Public Administration.

National Association of State Personnel Executives. May 2006. *Preliminary Draft: HR Metrics for State Governments.* Columbia, South Carolina: National Association of State Personnel Executives.

————. June 2005. *2005 Survey of the States HR Metrics.* Lexington, KY: NASPE.

Partnership for Public Service. June 2002. *Insights on the Federal Government Human Capital Crisis: Reflections of Generation X.* Washington, D.C.: Partnership for Public Service.

————. October 2004. *New Partnership for Public Service Report Finds Federal Government Is Using the Wrong Methods to Assess and Select Its Employees.* Washington, D.C.: Partnership for Public Service.

————. 2005. *Federal Brain Drain.* http:www.ourpublicservice.org/research_show.htm?doc_id=320870.

————. 2006. *Back to School: Rethinking Federal Recruiting on College Campuses* (Washington, D.C.: May).

————. 2008. *A Golden Opportunity: Recruiting Baby Boomers Into Government.* (Washington D.C.: January)

Phillips, Jack. December 2003. Human Capital Measurement: A Challenge for the CFO. *Chief Learning Officer.*

PriceWaterhouseCoopers. 2006. *Saratoga Metrics.* Chicago: PriceWaterhouseCoopers.

Rohm, Howard. (2002, May 16). *Developing and Using Balanced Scorecard Performance Systems.* Balanced Scorecard Institute.

Sasser, W. E., L. A. Schlesinger, and J. L. Heskett. 1997. *The Service Profit Chain.* New York: The Free Press.

Schay, Brigitte, Mary Beach, Jacqueline Caldwell, and Christelle LaPolice. 2002. Using Standardized Outcomes Measures in the Federal Government. *Human Resources Management* 41 (3).

Schneider, Craig. February 2006. The New Human-Capital Metrics. AICPA: CFO.com. [also published in *CFO Magazine*].

Schneider, B., and S. S. White. 2003. *Service Quality.* Thousand Oaks, CA: Sage Publications.

Sloper, Phil, Keith Linard, and David Paterson. April 1999. Toward a Dynamic Feedback Framework for Public Sector Performance Management. *Public Performance Productivity.*

Stephenson, Ed. (2006, May 13). Response to Email Inquiry Relating to HR Metrics.

Sullivan, John. 2004. *Rethinking Strategic HR.* San Francisco: CCH Incorporated.

U.S. Department of Labor. June 2000. *Testing and Assessment: An Employer's Guide to Good Practices.* Washington, D.C.: U.S. Department of Labor.

U.S. General Accounting Office. March 1992. *Federal Recruiting: Comparison of Applicants Who Accepted or Declined Federal Job Offers.* Washington, D.C.: U.S. General Accounting Office.

———. March 2004c. *Human Capital: A Guide for Assessing Strategic Training and Development Programs.* Washington, D.C.: U.S. General Accounting Office.

U.S. Government Accountability Office. (2004, July 20). *Human Capital: Building on the Current Momentum to Transform the Federal Government.* Washington, D.C.: U.S. Government Accountability Office.

U.S. Merit Systems Protection Board. February 2002a. *Competing for Federal Jobs—Job Search Experiences of New Hires.* Washington, D.C.: U.S. Merit Systems Protection Board.

———. September 2002b. *Making the Public Service Work: Recommendations for Change.* Washington, D.C.: U.S. Merit Systems Protection Board.

———. May 2004. *What's on the Minds of Federal Human Capital Stakeholders.* Washington, D.C.: U.S. Merit Systems Protection Board.

———. 2005. *Managing Federal Recruitment: Issues, Insights, and Illustrations.* Report to the President. Washington, D.C.: U.S. Merit Systems Protection Board.

U.S. Office of Personnel Management. April 2004. *Draft: OPM's Guiding Principles for Civil Service Transformation.* Washington, D.C.: U.S. Office of Personnel Management.

———. May 2006a. *The Human Capital Assessment and Accountability Framework (HCAAF): Systems, Standards, and Metrics* Washington, D.C.: U.S. Office of Personnel Management.

———. May 2006b. *Required Outcome Metrics for HCAAF.* Washington, D.C.: U.S. Office of Personnel Management.

———. May 2006c. *What Constitutes Strong Evidence of a Program's Effectiveness?* Washington, D.C.: U.S. Office of Personnel Management.

Welbourne, Theresa. August/September 2004. HR Metrics for HR Strategists. *IHRMI.link.*

Young, Mary. 2003. *The Aging-and-Retiring Government Workforce: How Serious Is the Challenge?* Lexington, MA: Linkage, Inc.

# 12

# Planning for Today and Tomorrow
## Workforce Planning

WILLOW S. JACOBSON
University of North Carolina, Chapel Hill

## INTRODUCTION[1]

Over last two decades it has been recognized that HR should be a strategic partner with management because HR can help organizations achieve their strategic and organizational goals (Daley, 2006; Pynes, 2003; Down et al., 1997). Strategic human resource management (SHRM) has begun to be recognized as an important role for HR departments. With the move to SHRM, HR departments are shifting their focus from short-term to long-term workforce needs that are integrated with the strategic planning process (Roberts, 2003; Selden and Jacobson, 2007).

In addition to the rise of SHRM as a goal for HR departments and agencies, both organizational and broader social trends provide important justifications for workforce planning. The impending exodus of baby boomers from the nation's workforce, coupled with the increasing competencies and skills required of public-sector employees to provide quality services, sets the stage for a key challenge that governments will face in the coming years. They will compete with private and non-profit organizations, as well as one another, for talented workers.

In short, the nation is poised for a workforce crisis, and governments are likely to feel the crisis first because of their high proportion of older employees and their high demand for knowledge workers. People with the required skills and knowledge will become harder to recruit and retain, especially if governments are not clear about the skills that they seek. Workforce planning can help governments perform strategically in the face of increasingly complex governmental demands made even more challenging by the impending changes in and demands for human capital.

Governments must have the resources to achieve the goals and objectives outlined in their strategic plans. Moreover, simply continuing basic service provision requires resource planning that incorporates and addresses changing demographic and social demands. Techniques such as performance budgeting help governments plan for and track the level at which they are accomplishing their goals (Rivenbark, 2004). Just as organizations need to determine if the appropriate financial and capital components are in place for achieving organizational objectives, they also need to consider whether the appropriate human capital is in place. Identifying a funding source for a position is not enough. Workforce planning enables governments to determine their need for human resources to meet their objectives, and the availability of those resources.

*Workforce planning* is a process designed to ensure that an organization prepares for its present and future needs by having the right people in the right places at the right times. This chapter examines the importance of workforce planning for governments. It addresses how national demographic trends are creating a workforce crisis and highlights the particular challenges that this crisis will create in the public sector. Further, the chapter discusses common steps and considerations for the workforce planning process.

## IMPORTANCE OF WORKFORCE PLANNING

Strategic planning within all levels of government is becoming more common[2]. Commonly these plans involve the creation of an organizational or governmental mission statement, identification of core values, and specification of organizational goals by the organization's stakeholders (Rivenbark, 2004). To accomplish these goals and directions, governments must properly align their financial and human resources. Workforce planning aims to create a systematic assessment of the content and composition of a government's workforce to determine what actions the government needs to take to respond to current and future demands to achieve organizational goals and objectives, also discussed as Human Resource Planning (HRP) (Shafritz et al., 2001; Selden and Jacobson, 2007).

In much the same way that financial issues are not the sole responsibility of the finance office, workforce planning is not the lone responsibility of the HR department. HR staff are key players in supporting and assisting the development of a workforce plan, but the ownership of workforce planning belongs to all managers, top administrators, and governing boards (IDHR, 2007; Pynes, 2003). As Daley notes "integrating the use of human resources/personnel practices into the strategic planning process enables an organization to better achieve its goals and objectives" (2006:163). He goes on to comment that improving human capital offers the most promise for improving organizational effectiveness.

Workforce planning is important because, simply put, the numbers do not lie. The large number of aging baby boomers in the workforce considered in relation to the much smaller number of younger workers available to replace them sets the stage for a crisis (Young, 2003). A recent *Harvard Business Review* article notes, "The most dramatic shortage of workers will hit the age group associated with leadership and key customer-facing positions" (Dychtwald, Erickson, and Morison, 2004:48;

Byham, 1999). Many governments expect retirements of 50 percent or more among their senior managers in the next five to seven years (Young, 2003). For example, a 2008 United States Office of Personnel Management study finds that by 2016 60.8 percent of the federal full-time permanent workforce will be eligible to retire, though it is unlikely all those eligible will opt for retirement the numbers are still staggering (USOPM, 2008). Turnover without planning can lead to increased costs, lack of continuity, and immediate negative effects on organizations.

Given the current demographics of the national workforce, the potential for turnover is great. Baby boomers (people born between 1946 and 1964) now make up 45 percent of the workforce, and Matures (people born before 1946), 10 percent. The proportion of older workers (defined as those fifty-five years old and up) is projected to increase an average of 4 percent per year through 2015 (Young, 2003). The rapid increase of people in the workforce who are aged 45–69 years has been referred to as the *age bubble* (see Figure 12.1).[3] As the population ages, employers will have to determine how best to replace the growing number of retiring workers from a much smaller pool of rising workers.

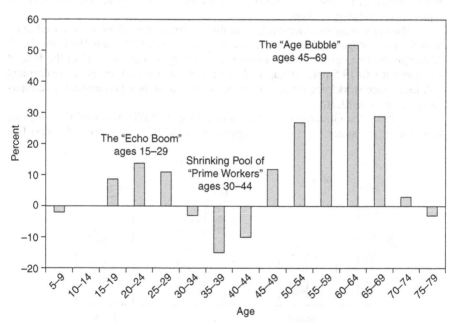

**FIGURE 12.1    Percentage Change in Population by Age Group, 2000–2010 (Estimated)**

*Source:* From Mary B. Young, The Aging-and-Retiring Government Workforce: How Serious Is the Challenge? What Are Jurisdictions Doing about It? 31. Report sponsored by CPS Human Resource Serv. (Burlington, Mass.: Ctr. for Org. Research/A Div. of Linkage, Inc., 2003), available at http://www. wagnerbriefing.com/downloads/CPS_AgeBubble_ExecutiveSummary.pdfpdf (last visited August 19, 2008). Reprinted by permission.

## HIGH STAKES AND PRESSING DEMANDS
## FOR THE PUBLIC SECTOR

Stakeholders at all levels of government may find it more difficult to lead and govern their communities and serve their citizens as they face the added challenge of large retirement numbers in the next decade (Young, 2003). As Miracle (2004:449) notes: "Rapidly evolving technology, dramatically shifting workforce demographics, ever-increasing globalization, and a maturing workforce have combined to challenge human resource professionals of the 21st century. Government agencies large and small have begun to analyze their workforces carefully to consider how best to prepare their workers to meet tomorrow's challenges."

The demographic transitions that are occurring nationwide pose particular challenges for the public sector: the average age of public workers is higher; the levels of specialization of knowledge, skills, and training are greater; and access to available resources, such as training funds, recruitment bonuses, and financial incentives, often is more constrained. Regarding relative ages, on average, 46.3 percent of government workers are forty-five years old or older, whereas in the private sector, just 31.2 percent fall in this age range (Abbey and Boyd, 2002). Federal, state, and local governments will face a great challenge in the next decade as they strive to replace these retiring workers.

The percentage of older workers in the government workforce increased more than the percentage of older workers in the private sector between 1994 and 2001. Although the local government numbers are slightly less dramatic than the federal government's (a 19.5 percent gap with the private sector), all levels of government will likely face workforce retirement issues sooner than their private-sector counterparts (see Figure 12.2).[4]

In 2005, the Government Performance Project (GPP) reported that in more than half of the states, one in five employees would be retiring over the next five

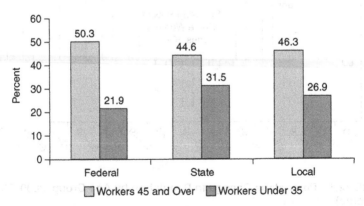

**FIGURE 12.2   Younger and Older Workers By Level of Government, 2001**

*Source:* From Craig W. Abbey & Donald J. Boyd, *The Aging Government Workforce* (Albany, N.Y.: Nelson A. Rockefeller Inst. of Gov't, 2002), available at http://www. rockinst.org/publications/welfare/archives.aspx (last visited August 19, 2008). Reprinted by permission.

years. "In Tennessee, the number is a boggling 40 percent; Maine and Nebraska are close to that. 'We call it the brain drain,' says Michael Willden, director of Nevada's social services department. 'I have nine major divisions, and the head of all but one of the divisions could leave tomorrow.' Clearly, there needs to be planning for the future or else the future will be bleak for anyone who relies on state services" (Barrett and Greene, 2005:27).

A 2007 report by the United States Government Accountability Office raised similar concerns for the federal government: "In 2006, OPM reported that approximately 60 percent of the government's 1.6 million white-collar employees and 90 percent of about 6,000 federal executives will be eligible for retirement over the next 10 years" (USGAO, 2007:6). These issues can be seen in specific agencies and job types as well. For example, the FAA in their planning process recognized that between fiscal year 2006 and fiscal year 2015, approximately 70 percent of the agency's controller workforce will become eligible to retire. And, as Barr notes, "Crunch time for the federal acquisition workforce hits in 2015. That's when 54 percent of contracting officers will be eligible to retire, according to a recently released report by the Federal Acquisition Institute. That is a sharp jump from fiscal 2005, when only 13 percent were eligible" (2006:1).

As a large percentage of the workforce prepares for retirement, federal, state, and local governments will have to replace a greater percentage of knowledge workers than the private sector. These knowledge workers require specialized training and education that enable them to fill roles such as health care worker, legal professional, natural scientist, engineer, educator, and manager (Benest, 2003; Greenfield, 2006).[5] More than 50 percent of all government jobs are in occupations that require specialized training, education, or job skills, compared with 29 percent in the private sector (Abbey and Boyd, 2002). Occupations that require specialized education, training, or skills are dominated by older workers in the public sector. Therefore, finding skilled replacements for government employees will be made difficult not just by the demographic challenges of aging workers but also by the nature of the work performed by these workers, and by competition for younger workers from other sectors.

Training budgets have faced many cuts and freezes that have hampered government's ability to prepare future leaders for advancement (Young, 2003). "Recession[s] in the 1980s and then the early 1990s were textbook examples of how state and local organizations drastically cut training in order to meet emergency budget cutback targets . . . Consequently, training was hard-pressed to maintain any continuity, much less identity." Despite this traditional and lasting challenge, "public sector organizations have increasingly placed more emphasis on training and development. Surface acceptance has progressed to increasing commitment to training and development programs by many private and public sector organizations." Nonetheless, the public sector lags. "As an industry wide survey taken in the late 1990s reveals about plans for training budgets, the public sector is still 'trailing edge' compared to the private sector, but at least 85 percent of the agencies surveyed were planning on maintaining or increasing funds" (Shafritz et al., 2001:304–306). As the 2005 GPP results report "One potent device that serves both to retain employees and build a staff for the future is employee training. Unfortunately, in hard budget times training is often the first thing cut. In Maryland, for example, Andrea Fulton, executive director of the Office of Personnel Services and Benefits, had a $350,000 fund designated for employee training. That fund has been wiped out" (Barrett and Greene, 2005).

Factors that exacerbate the situation include past trends and employment practices, such as periods of rapid growth, downsizing, imposition of hiring freezes, and offering of early retirement incentives. Public employers also are hampered by the declining appeal of public service and continued competition for talent.

On the bright side, many experts believe that a few moderating variables will soften the blow of an aging public-sector workforce. First, the declining value of retirement investments and the rising cost of retiree health benefits may influence retirement-eligible employees to continue working (Young, 2003). Second, the recent economic downturn actually increased the appeal of government employment because of its relative job security. Finally, although it is too early to measure the full impact, large-scale disasters such as 9/11 and Hurricane Katrina have highlighted the vital role that government plays in serving and protecting citizens, and thus may have made public service careers more attractive.

Though this chapter focuses on workforce planning, it is important to note that very closely related to workforce planning—and a term that is often used for associated practices—is *succession planning*. Daley notes that "[w]hile succession planning highlights and identifies individuals who may succeed in key leadership positions, workforce planning is concerned with identifying key competencies that the organization will need and assuring that necessary training and development are provided" (2006:169). Ritchie (2007:26) defines succession planning as "a systematic effort to project future leadership requirements, identify leadership candidates, and develop those candidates through deliberate learning experiences. It is part of the broader concept of 'workforce planning,' which provides a 'framework for making staffing decisions and related investments based on an organization's mission, strategic plan, budgetary resources, and desired workforce competencies.' Succession planning is the leadership planning piece of that framework, focusing on leadership positions at every level of the organization."

## WORKFORCE PLANNING: A CRUCIAL TOOL

Workforce planning is not a panacea for the demographic changes that governments will face, but this crucial tool allows governments to be better prepared and more responsive. Also, it helps align current and future workforce needs with the organization's strategic objectives, helps leverage HR practices to affect performance and retention, and increases opportunities for current and future workers. Workforce planning or Human Resource Planning is a means to achieve a competitive advantage through the effective use of an organization's human resources (i.e., SHRM).

### Aligning Needs with Objectives

By gaining a more complete picture of the skills and competencies of their current workforce, organizations can fill vacant positions more efficiently as well as maintain service proficiency in the face of increased turnover, labor market shortages, and limited compensation levels. At the same time they can inform future needs. Having the appropriate workforce in place contributes to implementing a strategic plan and determining the skills needed to achieve long-term goals and objectives (USOPM,

2005). Also, it helps improve employees' ability to respond to changing environmental demands by clarifying what skills the organization has in place, to be tapped when needed. For example, the Department of Human Resources in Johnson County, Kansas notes in its annual workforce planning report that "By systematically and routinely analyzing workforce data to assess employee's attributes, monitoring and understanding social, economic, and political trends, then aligning that information with the current and projected needs and goals of the organization, the organization is able to have the right people with the right competencies in the right jobs at the right time—now and in the future" (2006:5).

## Leveraging Practices

Workforce planning helps focus a government's workforce investment on employee training, retraining, career counseling, and productivity enhancement, while ensuring that staff development efforts fit within the available budget. It also can help maintain and improve diversity, cope with effects of downsizing, and mitigate effects of employees leaving the organization (Pynes, 2004; USOPM, 2005).

## Increasing Opportunities

Two major benefits of workforce planning are increased opportunities for high-potential workers and enlargement of the talent pool of promotable employees. Workforce planning can provide clear avenues for employees to pursue their career plans. Such avenues will help attract and keep valued employees, and that in turn will ensure a continuing supply of capable successors for key positions.

## Summary

A well-developed workforce plan integrates training and development activities to provide a continuing supply of well-trained, broadly experienced, well-motivated people who are ready and able to step into key positions as needed. Also, it determines the key skills and characteristics needed for recruitment and selection. Having a plan can increase staff retention, tailor training goals and needs, provide leadership opportunities, clarify hiring priorities, increase employees' satisfaction, enhance employees' commitment to work and the workplace, and improve the organization's image (USOPM, 2005).

## CONSIDERATIONS AND ACTIONS IN WORKFORCE PLANNING

As governments prepare to undertake workforce planning, there are some preliminary considerations that they may want to first attend to and clarify.

## Preliminary Considerations

Before undertaking workforce planning, governments should review the following list and consider attending to the tasks identified in it.

- *Gain the support of top leadership.* It is necessary to obtain resources and continued commitment for the planning process. This means gaining the support of elected officials, managers, and department heads.
- *Assess what you have already accomplished in workforce planning.* Many governments have processes or practices in place that are key elements of a workforce plan but have not been strategically aligned.
- *Develop communication strategies.* How will communication with organizational heads, HR staff, program managers, and supervisors work? (Commonwealth of Pennsylvania, 2007)
- *Learn from others.* There is no need to reinvent the wheel.

## A Workforce Planning Model

Organizational success depends on identifying and developing the best people for key organizational roles (Ibarra, 2005). Although there are different models of workforce planning, most include similar basic steps and issues for consideration. "Regardless of the instrument or model used, any workforce planning approach must be flexible and visionary in order to prepare for changing needs and produce meaningful solutions." (Helton and Soubik, 2004:462). Following are four phases consistently identified as needed to develop a workforce plan (USOPM, 2005):[6]

1. Review organizational objectives.
2. Analyze present and future workforce needs to identify gaps or surpluses.
3. Develop and implement HR strategies and a plan.
4. Evaluate, monitor, and adjust the plan.

These phases inform and draw from one another and lack rigid delineations. Workforce planning is a fluid and cyclical process (see Figure 12.3) (Anderson, 2004)[7].

*1. Review organizational objectives.*    An important first step in workforce planning is to coordinate strategies. Most organizations have an annual strategic plan, which can be the foundation for workforce planning strategies (IDHR, 2007). There should be a clear understanding of organizational objectives and the link between workforce planning and other strategic objectives. Leaders will want to consider questions like the following:

- What are our strategic goals and objectives? Does this plan address the future that we have identified? (IDHR, 2007)
- Do we have the skills and the people to achieve our objectives over the next two years? The next five years?
- Do our current and future organizational needs take into account workforce demographics, mission, goals, position allocations, and workloads? (IDHR, 2007)
- Are the skills and the people truly aligned with the needs of our organization?
- Are alternative workforce strategies available to accomplish our goals and objectives?

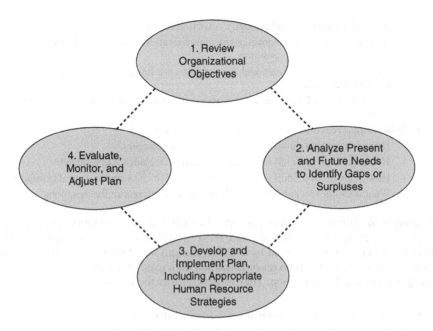

**FIGURE 12.3   Basic Workforce**

***2. Analyze present and future workforce needs to identify gaps or surpluses.***   The next phase of workforce planning is to analyze current and projected workforce needs and then identify gaps between them. Governments must gain a strong understanding of the composition and characteristics of their present workforce to aid them in determining current conditions and highlighting areas that may need additional planning to meet future needs. For example, they will need to identify what skills will be lost and also anticipate how workforce needs in the future may change. Agencies will need to determine how to anticipate expansions and reductions in programs or other changes that may affect the organization. The analysis phase can be broken into three steps: (a) analyze the current workforce profile; (b) analyze the future workforce profile; and (c) determine gaps and surpluses.

***a. Analyze the current workforce profile.***   The first step is to establish a "snapshot," or baseline, of where the organization is now. This process is crucial for the entire organization, various departments, and even specific organizational functions or classifications to undertake. This step is also commonly referred to as *supply analysis.*[8] Leaders might consider the following as they go through this phase:

- Demographic data on the workforce: age, gender, race, tenure, and education levels
  - Retirement eligibility statistics and patterns
  - Employees' skills, knowledge, and competencies
  - Employees level of performance (this includes accurate and appropriate performance evaluations)[9]

- ○ Salary data and contract/temporary costs (IDHR, 2007)
- ○ Supervisory ratios and management/employee ratios, including projected retirement of people in leadership positions
- ○ The extent to which functional requirements are linked to meeting the objectives identified in phase 1
- ○ The extent to which turnover has reduced the skill set of certain occupational groups
- Which employees are likely to retire in the next five years?
  - ○ How many of these individuals are key leaders/managers?
  - ○ How many of these individuals have specialized technical knowledge?
  - ○ How many of these individuals are in the same job class and/or same department?
  - ○ What does our recent history say about our ability to recruit for these jobs?

*b. Analyze the future workforce profile.*   Leaders must next identify future workforce needs, composition, changes, and skills in order to outline job requirements. This is also commonly referred to as *demand analysis* (Anderson, 2004)[10]. When done well this phase can help an organization anticipate and prepare for the major changes affecting the workforce. They might consider the following:

- What new skills will we need in order to accomplish our goals and mission?
  - ○ How many employees will be needed to meet future service needs?
  - ○ What factors affect the demand for our services?
  - ○ How might new technologies change how the service is provided?
  - ○ Which are critical positions?
  - ○ Which critical positions are essential to the achievement of the mission and goals of the agency?
  - ○ What skills or positions are needed in emergency situations?
  - ○ How is the workforce going to change?
  - ○ What external workforce trends, such as skill availability in the labor market, will affect us? (Pynes, 2003)[11]
  - ○ What are the potential impacts of legislative changes?
  - ○ What are the impacts of social and economic trends?
  - ○ What will be the competition for future skills?
- How will our workforce be different in five years?
  - ○ Which generations will still be working? Which will be retiring? Which will be coming into the workforce? What are the characteristics of each of these generations?
  - ○ How will the racial and ethnic backgrounds differ from today?
  - ○ How will the gender balance differ?
  - ○ How will educational backgrounds be different?
- How will our HR needs be different in five years?
  - ○ What role will technology play? Will it be able to replace some workers? Will we need a higher level of training in technology? Will we need to replace our technology in order to attract and retain new workers?
  - ○ How do the jurisdiction's growth and development patterns play a role in HR needs?
  - ○ How will the jurisdiction's demographics play a role in HR needs? (e.g., older populations requiring different city services and housing?)

- What should we be doing now to prepare for our changing needs and changing workforce?
  - ○ What strategies should we employ? What are some possible solutions to workforce shortages and changes? Do the solutions require outside assistance or legal authority?
  - ○ What are the constraints against implementing strategies? What are some possible solutions to those constraints? (League of Minnesota Cities, 2007)

These efforts at collecting and working with the data can help the organization conduct appropriate forecasting efforts, which brings us to the next step of gap and surplus analysis.

*c. Determine gaps and surpluses.* The materials gathered in steps *a* and *b* provide the data necessary to analyze resulting gaps and surpluses. "Gap analysis" is the process of comparing information discovered through the "current workforce profile and the future workforce profile to identify 'gaps' or surpluses in the current staffing levels and organizational skills, and the staffing levels and skills that are anticipated for the future workforce needs" (League of Minnesota Cities, 2007:6). Gap analysis helps provide the information necessary to develop strategies and solutions for current as well as future needs.

In determining gaps and surpluses, the most important question is: What is the gap between the projected need and the projected supply? Additionally it is useful to consider these questions:

- Do we currently have the skills that we anticipate needing?
- Are there areas in which future needs exceed current resources and projections?
- What skill gaps are critical for future goal accomplishment?
- Are there areas in which the current workforce exceeds the projected needs of the future?
- Are there areas in which the current supply will meet the future needs, resulting in a gap of zero?
- Are there existing employee skills, qualifications, or short- and long-term competencies required for the proposed organizational objectives?

Once gaps are identified, management and leadership should consult to prioritize the gaps that will have the most impact on organizational goal attainment (Commonwealth of Pennsylvania, 2007).

An important component of conducting workforce planning is having access to and utilizing comprehensive information and data about employees. Many governments, particularly cities, are struggling to keep technology up to date (Selden and Jacobson, 2007). These steps yield a lot of information that needs to be managed. Workforce planning often utilizes data inventories to integrate the planning and utilization function of SHRM (Pynes, 2003). Data inventories compile summary information, such as the items identified in steps *a* and *b*. Using a computerized Human Resources Information System (HRIS) to compile these data makes the retrieval of information readily available for forecasting workforce needs (Pynes, 2003). An example of this comes from the City of Virginia Beach. As Miracle (2004:449) reports, the city's Human Resources and the Communications and Information Technology departments collaborated to develop Workforce Planning and Development (WorkPAD) software, which won the 2003 E-Town State and

Local Government Award for government agency best practices. WorkPAD "enables planners to pull data from the Human Resources Information System (HRIS) database, the Virginia Retirement System, and numerous other resources to enhance workforce planning efforts. Managers can query this system to produce reports detailing projected retirement statistics, workforce demographics, vacancy reports, and much more. This innovative software also features an online KSA and Competency Assessment piece that enables employees and supervisors to tailor career development paths" (Miracle, 2004:449).

**3. Develop and implement HR strategies and a plan.**  When the organization clearly understands present and future needs, including the gap between them, it can develop and implement strategies and responses to give it a cohesive strategic workforce plan for effective service delivery. Workforce planning strategies aim to affect the entire life cycle of employees, from selection to training to turnover. Governments will need to determine the components to be included in the workforce plan; these are likely to involve changes in recruitment, development, and retention methods, and outsourcing strategies. Strategies might include addressing the organization's position on specific skill groups, such as information technology professionals or engineers, including what work model the organization would like to employ relative to these groups (retention, new hires, retraining, or outsourcing).

In selecting and implementing strategies, it is important to consider issues such as the following:

- *Time*
  - Is there time to develop staff internally for upcoming vacancies and skill shortages, or is specialized recruitment the best option? (IDHR, 2007)
- *Resources*
  - What resources (staff, money, technology, etc.) are currently available to provide assistance in developing and implementing the selected strategies?
  - Does the cost of providing the resources justify the result?
  - Are adequate resources available for implementing the selected strategies?
- *Internal Depth*
  - Do current staff demonstrate the potential and interest to develop the skills necessary to be promoted to new or modified positions, or will external recruitment be needed? (IDHR, 2007)
  - How will people be identified for future training and development? (Commonwealth of Pennsylvania, 2007)
- *Alignment with Goals*
  - Are selected strategies aligned with the organization's mission and goals?
  - Are there clear objectives for the strategies selected?
  - How do different workforce strategies affect outcomes?

Although an organization may not have a formal workforce plan in place, it already may be undertaking some commonly employed strategies through its HR services (IDHR, 2007).

Most commonly considered strategies relate to training and development efforts as well as recruitment and retention. While the strategies may vary somewhat by organization, there are a number of strategies commonly employed in workforce planning.

- Career development programs
- Personal development consultation
- Leadership development
- Mentoring
- Provision of training and learning opportunities and resources
- Provision of opportunities to develop career paths
- Organizational structure
- Job design
- Classification flexibility
- Cross-training
- Knowledge capture
- Process changes and streamlined work
- Recruitment plans
- Identification of critical skills (with up to date job descriptions)
- Internship programs and volunteers
- Specialized or targeted recruitment and selection
- Retention programs
- Flexplace or telecommuting
- Alternative work schedules
- Employee training
- Employee recognition
- Employee performance incentives[12]
- Special projects/job rotations
- Work–life balance
- Workplace allocation
- Staff training and retraining
- Interagency transfers

Training and development activities are essential to the effective use of an organization's HR and are an integral part of HR planning (Pynes, 2003). Despite often limited training budgets, states such as Arizona have placed a premium on training. In addition to in-house training and tuition reimbursement, the state spent $6.5 million in 2003 on outside training, conferences, and seminars for employees (Barrett and Greene, 2005). Many other organizations are in the process of developing specific training in the area of leadership development as they have identified this as a critical area of future need. For example in Plano, Texas, in an effort to "develop current managers and prepare the next generation of leaders, the city launched an intensive new training effort called the Management Preparation Program of Plano (MP3). Adapted from private and public-sector programs, the program was customized to fit Plano's priorities and to complement existing programs. 'Leadership for the 21st Century,' for example, is a nine-month course for employees who are interested in becoming supervisors and managers and for people already in those roles who want to hone their skills" (Young, 2005:25).

Pennsylvania has had a program in place since 1998. "Pennsylvania's Management Associate Program (PMAP) has recruited state residents with a master's degree to participate in a developmental program that grooms them to become candidates for mid- and upper-level management jobs in state government. Each Associate is sponsored by a state agency, who pays his or her first-year salary" (Young, 2005:48). The United States Coast Guard has been seen as a strong federal sector example in the area of public-sector leadership development. Their central Leadership Development Center, which is designed to be like a corporate education center in the public sector, is located on the grounds of the Coast Guard Academy. They have also developed the Commandant's Leadership Advisory Council (Young, 2005:89).

In addition to these specific examples of leadership development activities, there is a greater recognition that leadership development is not just for the top level but is important throughout the organization. As Young notes, organizations are expanding their leadership pipelines by "[d]efining leadership as a competency that employees at all levels are expected to develop and demonstrate. A number of organizations we interviewed, such as the Coast Guard and the Virginia Beach, Virginia Police Department, have decided to ingrain certain elements of leadership development throughout their organization. By providing everyone with common frameworks and language, they hope to make leadership an ongoing topic of conversation among employees at all levels" (Young, 2005:8).

Many of the strategies for workforce planning, including training, focus on providing individuals with specific skills and knowledge as well as organizational information. The effective transfer of knowledge from one set of employees to another helps an organization not only retain needed information but also to minimize the transition time in a new position (Kiyonaga, 2004). Knowledge that may be considered for transfer can include not just the technical knowledge related to how to do the job, but also institutional knowledge, tips and habits, and knowledge about relationships. Greene (2001:1) notes that "Effective management of intellectual capital requires that the critical knowledge be created/captured, organized/analyzed, disseminated and applied to produce the desired results, thereby enabling the organization to know what it needs to know to remain viable."

Kathryn Tyler (2005:60), in writing about knowledge management, relates the story of Raytheon and their approach to knowledge transfer:

> "In 2004, Marilyn Weixel, SPHR, woke up to a looming mass exodus of experienced workers at her organization. She realized that more than 35 percent of her workforce at Raytheon Vision Systems, a national defense contractor in Goleta, Calif., would be eligible to retire by 2009. 'In many situations, the person [set to retire] was the only one in the whole nation who knew how to do something. They invented it,' says Weixel, who is senior manager of HR.
>
> Raytheon was in need of a dynamic solution. So Weixel created a training program called Leave-A-Legacy, which formally pairs employees who have vital knowledge—subject matter experts—with high-potential subordinate employees. Since it began, she has heard anecdotally from management that the program has successfully encouraged near-retirees to share knowledge on a daily basis, and it has also given them a sense of purpose. As one retiring employee said, 'This program is the first time I believed I was really valued—after nearly 20 years [at Raytheon].' In addition, the program is securing the commitment of high-potential employees by giving them higher-level work."

Although training and development and retention efforts play a critical role in workforce planning, as can be seen from the previous list, they are only part of the strategy. There are times when there will just not be the resources within the organization to develop, and as a result the organization may consider gaining the needed staff through hiring. This requires the organization to examine its hiring practices. Efforts at the U.S. Patent and Trademark Office (USPTO) program have included the development of a year-round recruiting program in which they made offers based on projected attrition. Additionally, they established summer office tours to enhance the summer hiring program (National Academy of Public Administration, 2006b:141).

In addition to the common efforts to train for the skills that will be needed as the organization loses people or gains new responsibilities, an alternative is to consider how to reinvent or retool positions and departments. For example the organization might ask the question, "Is it possible that we could decide to discontinue this service?" This might occur, for example, in a city that currently provides a fall leaf-removal service for residents, but whose primary person in charge of that service is getting ready to retire. The city may want to ask itself, "Is this a core service?" "Is this service of high importance to our residents?" "Are there other entities—public or private—that already provide this service?" "What would happen if we discontinued this service as far as liability, public relations, legal compliance, etc.?" (League of Minnesota Cities, 2007).

If a service is determined to nonessential but discontinuing it is not an option, an organization might consider if there are other ways to accomplish the service. For example, suppose a city employs its own City Assessor who is retiring in three years. Assessments can't be discontinued entirely; they are needed to determine property taxes. However, is there another way to accomplish this service for city residents? Will the County be willing to handle assessments for the city and, if so, how much would they charge? Could the city hire an outside consultant to do the assessments? Should the city consider a joint powers arrangement or consider sharing an employee with another city? (League of Minnesota Cities, 2007).

The League of Minnesota Cities' "City Employees & Workforce Planning: Getting Started" proposes that if contracting out does not seem to be a good option, a city might want to consider some nontraditional approaches such as:

- *Splitting up jobs*
  *Example.* The City Engineer retires and is hired back on a part-time basis with no supervisory duties; all supervision is assigned to a different department director or to a lower-level supervisor.
- *Teamwork (several different departments join together to accomplish various aspects of a job)*
  *Example.* The Fire Marshall retires and the various duties are reassigned to the Fire Chief and the Building Inspection Department.
- *Using volunteers*
  *Example.* The city is unable to recruit a sufficient number of park maintenance workers to maintain the city's parks. The city establishes a volunteer program in which the city's garden club takes over flower planting and other duties for all city parks.
- *Working outside of job class*
  *Example.* The city is unable to recruit a utility billing clerk with an appropriate level of computer skills. However, there is a part-time public works employee who is very good

with computers. The city hires and trains the public works employee to handle utility billing duties on a part-time basis and public works duties on a part-time basis.

The strategy chosen should be done so based on the needs and the goals of the organization. As well as keeping in mind that it is important to consider approaches that allow the organization to plan for controlled and uncontrolled events that may affect the organization's workforce (Helton and Soubik, 2004).

**4. Evaluate, monitor, and adjust the plan.**    Just as strategic plans undergo an annual review, workforce plans need regular evaluation and adjustment. By reviewing the workforce plan, an organization has the opportunity to assess what is working and what is not, and make necessary adjustments. Doing so will ensure that the plan and related strategies are in line with the agency's mission, goals, initiatives, strategic plan, and vision, and that they address new workforce and organizational issues and developments (Commonwealth of Pennsylvania, 2007).

Some important dimensions to consider in this area are as follows:

- What goals or objectives have we met?
- Have our strategies achieved the intended results?
  - The strategies relate to a number of HR practices all of which it is important to monitor and consider how well it is performing, from selection methods to training initiatives.
- Have our projections been on target?
- Are we getting the necessary feedback from program managers and supervisors?
- What is the budgeting impact of the planning process, and what resources are available?
- Have there been indicators of change and a need to realign workforce planning efforts?

As governments work on developing these plans and strategies that may also want to be sure to consider some additional issues such as how these plans impact:

- Workers' compensation insurance: this kind of issue arises when employees are telecommuting or sharing a job.
- Equal Pay Act and pay equity: the more jobs and duties are shared, the more complicated addressing the issue of equal and equitable pay becomes.
- Liability issues: experimenting with new job duties or hiring less experienced workers can mean increased training requirements and safety concerns.
- Unemployment insurance: whenever jobs are eliminated or hours reduced, this kind of insurance can become an issue.
- Age discrimination in Employment Act: the more a city uses older workers, the more likely it is that age discrimination issues can arise.

## STATUS OF GOVERNMENT WORKFORCE PLANNING AT FEDERAL, STATE, AND LOCAL LEVELS

Although increased attention and dialogue have been focused on workforce planning, a proportional increase in action and implementation has not occurred. The following briefly summarizes efforts in federal, state, and local governments.

At the federal level, the GAO has drawn attention to the risk faced by the nation's government because of its lack of strategic human-capital planning (U.S. General Accounting Office, 2003).[13] Federal agencies have been required to undertake some human-capital planning as part of the Government Performance and Results Act, but meeting this requirement often falls far short of the detail, and focus is needed in a full workforce plan. The level of sophistication and the comprehensiveness of workforce planning efforts vary across federal agencies (Whitehouse, 2006).[14] Agencies such as the Department of Energy, the Department of Labor, the Office of Personnel Management, the Social Security Administration, the Department of Transportation, and the Department of Veterans Affairs have been identified as having promising practices in place (Whitehouse, 2006).

Workforce planning activities have been increasing on the state level, though not on a scale appropriate to address the looming challenges. In 1998 the majority of the states did no workforce planning, with only five having implemented a comprehensive, formal plan. By 2005 more than half of the states had workforce plans in place (Selden and Jacobson, 2006). As noted by Barrett and Greene (2005:27) "A reasonable number of states are doing a solid job at this kind of future-oriented thinking. In Georgia—which may well have the best-managed HR operation in the country—agencies' personnel plans are included as a module of their strategic and budget plans, which are submitted annually and look out three to five years. Agencies look at their trends and gaps, conduct assessments and highlight the strategic plan areas where they have the greatest need or concern. The cumulative data from those agencies are reported to state leaders so they can consider budgeting to fill those needs." Many of the state HR departments offer tools and online resources for the agencies to use. For example, Wisconsin (2006) offers an online webcast training that is provided in their tools and resources section of their web site along with information on HR metrics and how to use them. Virginia's Department of HRM offers online tools to agencies as well as access to the HR Data Warehouse that allows agencies to analyze staffing, projected attrition and replacement needs. "New York has done a good job of engaging its agencies in this process. The training office of the Department of Environmental Conservation, for example, worked with each division to help identify who might retire in the next 10 years and to set up formalized exit interviews to gain insight into key aspects of a retiree's job, documenting critical processes and procedures" (Barrett and Greene, 2005:27).

"But many others have not come very far, either because of the recent budget crunch or simple lack of interest. 'It's really a hit-or-miss process right now,' says Wyoming HR director Brian Foster'" (Barrett and Greene, 2005:27–28). Among local governments, many cities and counties have not invested in formal workforce planning (Selden and Jacobson, 2007; Johnson and Brown, 2004).[15] Only about 20 percent of the cities in 1999 and 19 percent of the counties in 2001 reported that they conducted government-wide formal workforce planning (Selden and Jacobson, 2007). A 2004 survey by the IPMA-HR found that only 37 percent of the responding members had a workforce plan. More than 50 percent of the respondents represented local governments. Among those indicating that they were developing a workforce plan, there was substantial variation in where they were in the planning process. Only 6 percent reported that they had had a plan in place for more than five years (Johnson and Brown, 2004).[16] This finding of a low number of local governments performing workforce planning is consistent with the findings of other studies.[17]

Although few local governments have formal workforce plans, research in this area has demonstrated that, as part of their HR activity, many governments are undertaking practices or strategies that are components of workforce planning and provide a good starting point for these governments to build upon (Jacobson, 2007).

## Barriers Faced

Despite the identified benefits of conducting workforce planning, few organizations have formal plans in place. Results from the IPMA-HR national survey provide an initial understanding of common barriers. Survey results indicate that the most common barriers to creating timely and complete workforce plans included preoccupation with short-term activities, insufficient staffing, lack of funding, and lack of executive support (see Table 12.1).

Agency uncertainty, given no mandate for workforce planning, was found to be an often noted reason amongst North Carolina municipalities (Jacobson, 2007). Changes in administration and fiscal constraints on supporting new initiatives also can act as barriers (Johnson and Brown, 2004). Additionally, "many jurisdictions feel pulled in two directions: Their workforce-planning process shows them there are serious challenges ahead due to an aging workforce and retirements, but their budgets are severely cut. There's pressure to choose a short-term fix, such as early retirements, layoffs, and reduced training" (Young, 2003:6).

Also, although many managers claim they want greater integration of the HRM function with organization strategies, often they do not understand what this entails (Pynes, 2003). They are reluctant to give HRM professionals the flexibility to initiate new programs or to suggest new organizational structures such as might result from workplace planning strategies. Additionally, some HRM professionals may lack the capabilities and skills to move such initiatives forward. HRM professionals may need to be trained in the skills that are necessary to align the organization's strategy with its core competencies.

Workforce planning initiatives often require levels of coordination across functions and departments (some organizational cultures may not be open to this). Additionally, sometimes the political realities of public organizations undermine

**TABLE 12.1    Barriers to Planning for IPMA-HR Participants**

| Barriers | Percentage |
| --- | --- |
| Preoccupation with short-term activities | 39.2 |
| Insufficient staffing | 34.0 |
| Lack of funding | 25.8 |
| Lack of executive support | 18.0 |
| Restrictive merit system rules on hiring | 13.4 |
| Insufficient marketing effort | 6.2 |
| Lack of confidence in planning technique | 6.2 |
| Resistance to change | 1.0 |

*Source:* From Gilbert L. Johnson & Judith Brown, *Workforce Planning Not a Common Practice, IPMA–HR Study Finds,* 33 Public Personnel Management 379, 386 (2004), text available as a PDF at http://unpan1.un.org/intradoc/groups/public/documents/IPMA-HR/UNPAN017926.pdf. Reprinted by permission.

change, both in terms of elected and appointed officials who often have a short-term perspective. They may want a quick fix and not be patient enough for systemic changes to occur. Elective officials may be predisposed to favor short-term budget considerations over long-term planning.

## RECOMMENDATIONS AND CONCLUSION

The message that workforce changes are coming is not new. Neither is concern about government's readiness to address them successfully. In the early twentieth century, Henri Fayol, a management scholar, wrote about the fourteen points of management, among them, that management has a responsibility to ensure the "stability of tenure of personnel" (Fayol, 1984). If that need was ignored, Fayol believed, key positions would be filled by ill-prepared people.

As noted earlier, it is important when undertaking workforce planning that top management set overall direction and goals. Obtaining managerial and supervisory input and commitment is important in development and implementation of work-force planning strategies. Also essential is establishment of a communication strategy to create shared expectations, promote transparency, and report progress. During workforce planning, communicating with and involving managers is necessary, for they will be crucial in many steps of the process, including data acquisition and analysis, selection of strategies for change, implementation of strategies, and evaluation of the plan's impacts (Johnson and Brown, 2004).[18] Additionally, communicating succession needs and opportunities to staff is crucial. However, staff should recognize that succession plans are not guarantees of long-term employment or advancement.

Despite the obstacles to and the complexity of good planning, governments should begin to consider how they might use workforce planning. A wise and manageable first step is to gather relevant information in order to understand the current workforce better, and to begin a dialogue on the matter within the organization. Another helpful step is to consider the connection between workforce planning and the organization's larger strategic planning initiatives as leaders think about what they will need from the workforce in the coming years.

Like all major changes and initiatives, workforce planning requires long-term and significant commitment throughout an organization. It is not easy and will not occur overnight. The plan should have a five- to ten-year time horizon and commitment from those who lead the organization and those who implement the plan. There are many aspects and dimensions to consider in undertaking this process, including time, resources, internal depth, "in-demand" competencies, workplace and work-force dynamics, and job classifications. Formulating all aspects of a good plan might take several years and involve long-term culture change by the organization (Fountaine, 2005).

Workforce planning initiatives will need to be vertically integrated with the strategic planning process and horizontally integrated with other HR functions such as training and development, compensation and benefits, recruitment and selection, labor relations, and evaluation of the HR planning process (Pynes, 2003). Consider how this process links and needs to be integrated with other HR practices that fill the chapters of this book. Mary Young writes about the integrated approach in which she notes that, "In the Integrated Model, any or all of an organization's talent-management activities may serve to build the leadership pipeline. And because these varied activities are all aligned with the strategic plan and . . . they are connected to each other" (2005:6). "Workforce planning should be the framework—the glue—that integrates all HR practices" (Young, 2005:13).

Leadership has consistently been found to be a crucial element in successful organizational change. A guiding coalition of "change champions" must help lead major changes (Jacobson, 2003). Managers, elected officials, and representatives from throughout the organization need to be involved and committed to workforce planning. Working together helps managers and employees gain a better understanding of HRM issues. Likewise, HRM staff becomes more informed about the needs of the employees and departments. Through planning and better understanding of current and future workforce needs, an organization not only becomes more effective in the present but also positions itself for the future. Government leaders, who are stewards of the public trust, provide a great gift when they think beyond their tenure and leave their organizations readier to face the future.

It will be important to be clear who has authority and resources must be assigned to the person(s) responsible for the planning and implementation. Often this will involve establishing a HR planning taskforce composed of managers and/or staff from a variety of departments and staff that is in charge of identifying the trends and challenges that will impact the agency (Pynes, 2003). In the National Academy of Public Administration report, "Transforming the FBI: Roadmap to an Effective Human Capital Program," one of the first recommendations was to appoint a Human Capital Implementation Team (National Academy of Public Administration, 2006a).

Although a limited number of public sector organizations have formal workforce plans, as part of their HR activity, many are undertaking practices or strategies that are components of workforce planning and provide a starting point.

Workforce planning must start somewhere—possibly with conversations between leaders and department heads or with gathering of relevant data and indicators. The main message is to start somewhere and keep it simple. If the organization wants line managers to do regular workforce planning, it must make such planning uncomplicated for them and integrate it into other processes, such as strategic planning or budgeting (Young, 2003).

"Forewarned is forearmed. And forearmed is *confident*. One of the most striking benefits of thorough, ongoing workforce planning is the level of calm it provides—even in jurisdictions facing significant numbers of retirements" (Young, 2003:6–7).

## NOTES

1. Much of this section has been adapted from Jacobson, Willow. Preparing for Tomorrow: A Case Study of Workforce Planning in North Carolina Municipal Governments. *Public Personnel Management,* Forthcoming.
2. A recent study of medium- and large-sized North Carolina municipalities found that 100 percent of respondents were conducting strategic planning in some form. Additionally, federal efforts such as Government Performance and Results Act require agencies to conduct strategic planning.
3. "The Age Bubble is the balloon effect created by the baby boom generation (people born between 1946 and 1964) whenever it does anything en masse—whether it's starting school (which led to overcrowded classrooms and double-sessions, followed by a building boom in new schools), becoming teenagers, going to college (another spate of professor-hirings and expanded campuses), becoming

parents, turning 50 (the AARP reinvented itself to become more attractive to 'young elders'), or retiring (the focus of this report). The sheer number of baby boomers who will become eligible for retirement between now and 2015, coupled with the much smaller pool of younger workers who can take their place, make[s] the Age Bubble a critical human resource challenge for employers." Young, 2003: 32. "According to the Bureau of Labor Statistics (BLS), workers age 25–44 will decline by 3 million, dropping from 51 percent of the labor force in 1998 to 44 percent in 2008, while, over the same period, workers age 45+ will increase from 33 percent to 40 percent of the workforce, an additional 17 million workers." Dohm as cited in Young, 2003:32.

4. *Id.* at 5. "Only about 1 in 5 federal government workers is below 35 years of age. The gap between older and younger federal government workers is 28.4 percentage points. While slightly less pronounced, a similar pattern holds for local government workers[,] with a difference of 19.5 percentage points . . . The state government workforce has a more even distribution of workers than the other two levels of government. Only 13.1 percentage points separate older state government workers (43.6 percent) from younger state government workers (31.5 percent)." *Id.*

5. There has been increased attention to the issue of preparing the next generation of local government managers. The International City/County Management Association has begun to tackle this issue actively. For example, *see* Benest, 2003.

6. The U.S. Office of Personnel Management suggests the following five steps as part of its Workforce Planning Model: Step 1: Set strategic direction; Step 2: Analyze workforce, identify skill gaps, and conduct workforce analysis; Step 3: Develop action plan; Step 4: Implement action plan; and Step 5: Monitor, evaluate, and revise. USOPM, 2005.

7. Anderson (2004) argues that across the many workforce planning models there are four essential steps that are reoccurring: (1) supply analysis, (2) demand analysis, (3) gap analysis, and (4) solution analysis. The model presented here incorporates these same elements but uses slightly different language. These steps are included in the model presented here but under different labels.

8. Supply analysis "examines the current and future composition of the workforce and workload" (Anderson, 2004:367).

9. "Equally critical as adequate training is assessing how well individual employees are performing. While almost all states have some kind of annual performance review, their utility varies widely. Indiana has trouble getting its managers to complete the appraisal forms. And Wyoming's managers are disinclined to create adequate employee evaluations because—as with so many other states—there's no money to be awarded even for super-performers. "We struggle with that," says HR director Foster. "We're trying to get managers to understand that appraisals are about more than just pay adjustments." (GPP, 2007).

10. Demand analysis "examines future activities, workloads and the competency set your workforce of the future will need" (Anderson, 2004:368).

11. Agencies need to consider internal and external supply of qualified candidates. Internal supply might be influenced by training and development, transfer, promotion, and retirement policies (Pynes, 2003). The external supply of candidates is also influenced by a variety of factors, including development of technology, the actions of competing employers[,] geographic location, and government regulations (Pynes, 2003).

12. For more information, *see* David N. Ammons & William C. Rivenbark, *Gainsharing in Local Government*, **Popular Government**, Spring/Summer 2006.

13. U.S. Government Accountability Office 2005 report found that in a 2002 Federal Human Capital Survey, more than one out of every three federal employees said that they were considering leaving their jobs. Research by the PPS found that by 2004, 53 percent of federal civil servants and 71 percent of federal senior executives had achieved retirement eligibility. Further, about half of the federal government's information technology workforce will be eligible for retirement in the year 2010. As cited in Liebowitz, *Bridging the Knowledge and Skills Gap.*

14. Scores for human capital on the President's Management Agenda: Scorecard demonstrate this variation. See www.whitehouse.gov/results/agenda/scorecard.html (follow "The Scorecard September 30, 2006" hyperlink) (Accessed on Nov. 22, 2006).

15. This conclusion is supported by data and findings from the GPP and the IPMA-HR. Selden and Jacobson, 2007. Johnson and Brown, 2004.

16. These may well be inflated percentages. Probably a much lower percentage of participants actually had a workforce plan (Johnson and Brown, 2004) In 2004, IPMA-HR issued a survey to its 5,700 members designed to measure the extent to which public agencies use workforce plans and have a formalized workforce planning process in place. The response rate to the workforce planning

section of the survey was low (only 97 responses were received). The authors of the survey report conducted a follow-up telephone survey using a random sample of nonrespondents. It found that these people did not have workforce plans and thus did not return the survey. Thirty-nine percent of the 2004 IPMA-HR survey respondents indicated that they were actively involved in succession planning, and 51 percent identified themselves as city, town, or village governments. *Id.*

17. For example, a 1996 survey conducted by the National Academy of Public Administration's Center for Human Resources Management revealed that only 28 percent of government respondents had, or planned to have, a succession management program (National Academy of Public Administration, 1997).

18. This point is drawn from GAO report, which identified numerous lessons and strategies that can help agencies successfully implement strategic workforce plans based on the human capital experiences of leading organizations. As cited in Johnson and Brown, 2004.

# REFERENCES

Abbey, Craig W., and Donald J. Boyd. 2002. *The Aging Government Workforce.* The Nelson A. Rockefeller Institute of Government. Albany, NY. Retrieved on February 3, 2005, from http://www.rockinst.org/publications/welfare/archives.aspx.

Anderson, Martin W. 2004. The Metrics of Workforce Planning. *Public Personnel Management* 33 (4): 363(16).

Barr, Stephen. 2006. Another Warning of a Retiring Workforce. *Washington Post.* Monday, August 14, 2006; D04. http://www.washingtonpost.com/wp-dyn/content/article/2006/08/13AR2006081300573_pf.html. Accessed last on August 6, 2007.

Barrett, Katherine, and Richard Greene. 2005. Grading the States: A Management Report Card. *Governing: Special Issue* (February):24–95.

Benest, Frank. 2003. "A Call to Action" in Preparing the Next Generation: A Guide for Current and Future Local Government Managers. Frank Benest, ed. ICMA Press. Washington, D.C.: Int'l City/County Mgmt. Ass'n, 2003), available at jobs.icma.org/documents/next_generation.cfm?cfid=283007&cftoken=25103158 (last visited Oct. 31, 2006).

Byham, William C. 1999. Grooming Next Millennium Leaders: Start Now to Identify and Develop the Next Generation of Leaders. *HR Magazine,* February.

Commonwealth of Pennsylvania's Office of Administration. *Workforce and Succession Planning: Workforce Planning Model Detail.* Retrieved on August 19, 2008, from http://www.portal.state.pa.us/portal/server.pt?open=512&objID=1442&PageID=266293&mode=2

Daley, Dennis M. 2006. Strategic Human Resource Management. In *Public Personnel Management: Current Concerns, Future Challenges,* 4th ed., Norma M. Riccucci, ed. Longman: New York.

Down, James W., Walter Mardis, Thomas R. Connolly, and Sarah Johnson. (1997), "A strategic model", *HR Focus,* Vol. 74 No.6, pp. 22–4.

Dychtwald, K., Erickson, T., and B. Morison. 2004. It's Time to Retire Retirement. *Harvard Business Review:* March, 48–57.

Fayol Henri. 1984. General and Industrial Management 62 (Irwin Gray rev., New York: Inst. of Electrical and Electronics Engineers).

Federal Aviation Administration. June 2006. A Plan for the Future 2006–2015: The Federal Aviation Administration's 10-year Strategy for the Air Traffic Control Workforce.

Fountaine, Dave. 2005. Human Resources: What's Your Plan. *Public Management,* January/February.

Government Performance Project. Retrieved on November 6, 2006, from http://results.gpponline.org.

Greene, Robert J. 2001. Effectively Managing Intellectual Capital: Critical Challenge for Human Resources. SHRM White paper. March 2001.

Greenfield, Stuart. 2006. Focus on Labor: Government Agencies, You Have a Problem. *IPMA-HR News.* February 2006, 19–23.

Helton, Kimberly A., and John A. Soubik. 2004. Case Study: Pennsylvania's Changing Workforce: Planning Today with Tomorrow's Vision. *Public Personnel Management* 33 (4): 459(15).

Ibarra, Patrick The Mejorando Group Presentation, City of Wilmington Regional Workshop (June 15, 2005).

Idaho Division of Human Resources. *Workforce Planning Guide.* Retrieved on July 2, 2006, from http://www.dhr.idaho.gov/Portals/14/Documents/HRInfo/WorkforcePlanningGuide.pdfJacobson,

Willow. 2003. Receptivity to Change in the Public Sector: Two Federal Case Studies. *Dissertation.* Syracuse University.

————. 2007. Who Will Be There to Serve? Workforce Planning. *Popular Government* 27, 2 (Winter 2007).

Johnson County Department of Human Resources. 2006. Johnson County Government, Kansas: Annual Workforce Planning Report, FY 2007.

Johnson, Gilbert L., and Judith Brown. 2004. Workforce Planning Not a Common Practice: IPMA-HR Study Finds. *Public Personnel Management* 33 (4):379(10).

Kiyonaga, Nancy. 2004. Today Is the Tomorrow You Worried About Yesterday: Meeting the Challenges of a Changing Workforce. *Public Personnel Management* 33 (4).

League of Minnesota Cities, City Employees & Workforce Planning: Getting Started 1 (working draft, St. Paul: the League, n.d.).

Miracle, Krise. 2004. Case Study: The City of Virginia Beach's Innovative Tool for Workforce Planning. *Public Personnel Management* 33 (4):449(10).

National Academy of Public Administration. 1997. Center for Human Resources Mangement., Managing Succession and Developing Leadership: Growing the Next Generation of Public Service Leaders (Washington, D.C.: the Academy, 1997).

National Academy of Public Administration. Fall 2006a. "Creating A Roadmap to an Effective Human Capital Program: The Experience of the FBI" *gov.* pp. 32–36.

National Academy of Public Administration. Fall 2006b. "Finding and Retaining the Best Workforce: The Experience of the U.S. Patent and Trademark Office" *gov.* pp. 37–43.

Pynes, Joan E. 2003. Strategic Human Resource Management. In *Public Personnel Administration: Problems and Prospects,* 4th ed., Steven W. Hays and Richard C. Kearney, eds. Prentice Hall: Upper Saddle River, New Jersey.

————. 2004. The Implementation of Workforce and Succession Planning in the Public Sector. *Public Personnel Management* 33 (4).

Ritchie, Christina. 2007. Succession Planning: The Alarm Has Been Sounded, But Is Anyone Listening? *Popular Government* 72 (2):26–33.

Rivenbark, William C. 2004. Defining Performance Budgeting for Local Government. *Popular Government* 69 (2).

Roberts, Gary E. 2003. Issues, Challenges, and Changes in Recruitment and Selection. In *Public Personnel Administration: Problems and Prospects*, ed. Steven W. Hays and Richard Kearney, 4th ed. (Upper Saddle River, NJ: Prentice-Hall, 2003), pp. 89–104.

Selden, Sally, and Willow Jacobson. 2007. Government's Largest Investment—Human Resource Management in States, Cities, and Counties. In *Pursuit of Performance: Management Systems in State and Local Government,* Patricia Ingraham, ed. John Hopkins Press.

Shafritz, Jay M., David H. Rosenbloom., Norma M. Riccucci., Katherine C. Naff., and Albert C. Hyde . *Personnel Management in Government: Politics and Process.* New York: Marcel Dekker, *2001,* 5th edition.

Tyler, Kathryn. 2005. Training Revs Up: Companies Are Realizing That Enhanced Performance Requires a Bigger Training Engine. *HR Magazine* (April).

U.S. General Accounting Office. 2003. *High-risk Series: An update.* GAO-03-119, January. (Washington, D.C.: GAO, Jan. 2003). Available at www.gao.gov/new.items/d05207.pdf. Accessed on Oct. 31, 2006.

U.S. Government Accountability Office 2005, GAO-05-207, High-Risk Series: An Update (Washington, D.C.: USGAO, 2005) http://www.gao.gov/new.items/d05207.pdf

U.S. Government Accountability Office. Testimony before the Subcommittee on Financial Services and General Government, Committee on Appropriations, House of Representatives. Human Capital Federal Workforce Challenges in the 21st Century. Statement of J. Christopher Mihm, Managing Director, Strategic Issues. GAO-07-556T (2007).

U.S. General Accounting Office, GAO-01-509, Federal Employee Retirements: Expected Increase Over the Next 5 Years Illustrates Need for Workforce Planning (Washington, D.C.: USGAO, 2001)

U.S. Office of Personnel Management. March 2008. An Analysis of Federal Employee Retirement Data: Predicting Future Retirement and Examining Factors Relevant to Retiring from the Federal Service. Retrieved on August 21, 2008 from https://www.opm.gov/feddata/RetirementPaperFinal_v4.pdf

U.S. Office of Personnel Management. 2005 Workforce Planning Model (Washington, D.C.: OPM, Sept. 2005), Retrieved on November 22, 2006, from www.opm.gov/hcaaf_resource_center/assets/Sa_tool4.pdf

Young, Mary B. 2005. "Building the Leadership Pipeline in Local, State, and Federal Government: The Second in a Series of Research Studies on Leading Issues in Public-Sector Human Resource Management." Sponsored by CPS Human Resource Services and the International Public Management Association-Human Resources. Published by the CPS Human Resource Services.

Young, Mary B. 2003. *The Aging-and-Retiring Government Workforce: How Serious Is the Challenge? What Are Jurisdictions Doing About It?* The Center for Organizational Research A Division of Linkage, Inc. Report sponsored by CPS. http://www.wagnerbriefing.com/downloads/CPS_AgeBubble_ExecutiveSummary.pdf

# Employee Rights to Address Wrongs
## Trends in State Government Grievance Practices

JESSICA E. SOWA

Maxine Goodman Levin College of Urban Affairs
Cleveland State University

## INTRODUCTION

Significant administrative reforms have been occurring across state governments in the United States, with many of these governments making significant changes to the structures and practices affecting their public employees (Coggburn, 2000, 2001; Hou et al., 2000; Kellough and Nigro, 2006; Hays and Sowa, 2006). These reforms, including decentralization of personnel authority and the reduction of or removal of civil service protections from state government employees, have raised questions concerning the nature of the employee/employer relationship in state government today.

As public employees have often sacrificed many of the extrinsic rewards that they would receive from private industry to work for government, these employees assumed that government, operating as a "model employer," would make certain concessions to account for these sacrifices. Primarily, the operating assumption for these employees was that they would be protected in their work from various forms of intrusion, including political or partisan intrusion, and treated with fairness if problems arose in the completion of their duties. The administrative reforms in government today have challenged these assumptions. As state governments continue down the path of deregulation of the personnel function, it is important to examine whether this deregulation has changed the nature of employee rights in state government and explore the ramifications of these changes for public employees.

This chapter examines employee rights in state government, focusing on a central employee right, the ability to seek redress for wrongful action (perceived or actual) through a structured process of grievance or complaint. For government employees, structured procedures through which they can seek relief for personnel actions taken against them can be conceived of as a necessary procedural safeguard, providing an intrinsic "security blanket" that allows them to be active in the performance of their duties without fear of retribution (Kearney, 2001). Reform of grievance policies and procedures in state governments is not something that should be taken lightly by politicians and other reformers, as changes to these procedures could result in significant alterations to employee choices and actions and possibly have a chilling effect on employee creativity and innovation. This chapter will:

- Define employee grievances and discuss the classic model of grievance procedures in government.
- Discuss the concept of procedural justice as applied to grievance policies and procedures.
- Explore the current practices of state governments with reference to their grievance or complaint procedures, highlighting different trends in grievance procedures.
- Highlight areas of concern and explore the implications in grievance procedures for employees in state government.

## GRIEVANCE PROCEDURES: THEORY AND PRACTICE

### Classic Model of Grievance Procedures

Classical labor relations practices provide a starting point for examining the development of grievance policies and procedures. Formally defined, an employee grievance is "an employee or union complaint (or, albeit infrequently, a management complaint) arising out of dissatisfaction with some aspect of the contract or work environment" (Kearney, 2001:298). When establishing the employee/employer relationship, whether through civil service procedures or through a union contract, the power generally rests with management, and the structures and practices surrounding this relationship often favor the needs of management. Therefore, for employees to agree to this relationship, they must be assured that management will keep up their part of the bargain. If management fails to uphold their agreement, grievance procedures provide workers with a way in which to seek redress with a guarantee of fair treatment.

In determining what aspects of the employee/employer relationship are subject to the grievance process, Richardson (1977:162) states that the inclusion of actions in the grievance process is "limited only by the variety of circumstances that might arise in the employee relationship and by the real or imagined grievances arising therefrom." In a sense, if one can perceive a slight or wrong in any aspect of the employee relationship with management, they could formally complain about that wrong through the grievance process. Therefore, government agencies have been careful in defining the boundaries of formal grievance processes for fear of becoming overwhelmed with employee complaints or for fear of reducing the autonomy or the rights of managers to act toward and direct their employees. While grievance procedures vary greatly across jurisdictions, some common personnel issues of subjects included under grievance procedures are job assignments, layoffs, reductions in force, discrimination, reprimands, suspensions, and discharges (Kearney, 2001).

While grievance procedures vary across and within state governments, the traditional model of the grievance process generally involves three main steps, with the steps focused on addressing and resolving the grievance in the most expeditious way possible. These steps are the following:

1. *Initial complaint:*   The grievance process begins when an employee brings a complaint to a supervisor. This complaint generally is initiated orally and the supervisor will seek to resolve the complaint in an informal fashion.

2. *Written complaint:*   If the complaint is not resolved informally between the supervisor and the employee, the "formal" grievance process begins, with the grievance detailed in written form, signed by the grievant, and forwarded up the management structure. Depending on the structure of the grievance process in the jurisdiction, the grievance may be handled and resolved by the next management level from the immediate supervisor of the employee filing the grievance. If the grievance is not resolved, the next step becomes necessary.

3. *Higher management involvement:*   Depending on the structure of the grievance process, when the grievance is unresolved at the lower management level, the grievance may then be referred for resolution to a higher level of management, including a department head or a labor relations manager. In addition, an external committee, such as an employee relations board, may also become involved in resolving the grievance.

If these steps fail to produce a resolution, many grievance procedures will include a final step for arbitration, involving a neutral third party. In most grievance procedures, specific time limits are associated with each of the steps of the grievance process in order to foster expeditious treatment of the employee complaints (Kearney, 2001). While the classic grievance procedure model is employed in many jurisdictions, it is important to examine why such procedures or processes are included in these jurisdictions' personnel practices; in particular, an important question is why both state governments and state government employees should care about the presence of grievance procedures.

## Grievance Procedures and Procedural Justice

Grievance procedures are inherently about procedural justice, with procedural justice defined as judgments associated with the fairness of the way in which employees are treated in the workplace (Folger and Konovsky, 1989; Blader and Tyler, 2003). Procedural justice includes many different components of how employees are treated in the work setting, including justice associated with decision-making procedures, justice associated with the treatment of the employee overall in the organization, and the source of this justice, such as the rules in place in the organization and the nature and operation of organizational authority (Blader and Tyler, 2003). Research has shown that procedural justice is an important concept or practice in organizations, as procedural justice influences numerous components of the employee relationship, including commitment to work, compliance with organizational rules, and employee retention (Kim and Mauborgne, 1993; Schaubroeck, May, and Brown, 1994; Blader and Tyler, 2003) In particular, employees are more likely to accept personnel decisions that are unfavorable to their interests as long as those decisions are made and reviewed with a fair and transparent procedure (Rubin, forthcoming).

If they are to be attentive to procedural justice as a method of retaining their employees, states must consider the policies and procedures in place for their employees to voice their reactions to personnel actions. While the grievance resolution process can impose costs on management in terms of time and attention, the overall benefits associated with the perceptions of the employees concerning how they were treated through the process, the procedural justice benefits, may outweigh the costs. State governments must consider whether providing policies that foster procedural justice among their employees are worth the associated costs to management. The following section explores the current processes in place in state governments in relation to how these governments address and process employee complaints.

## STATE GOVERNMENT GRIEVANCE OR COMPLAINT RESOLUTION PROCESSES

For this chapter, existing state laws, policies, and procedures were examined to determine current trends in the practices of state governments in employee complaint or grievance procedures. Across the fifty states, there is significant variation, including the subjects or issues covered by grievance procedures, the structure of the grievance procedures, and the processing of and resolution of employee complaints. Exploring practices across state governments in the United States highlights particular trends or common methods of structuring and resolving employee complaints, including the role of union representation and collective bargaining in grievance procedures, decentralization of grievance procedures across agencies in state government, the scope of grievance procedures, and the use of counseling and dispute resolution mechanisms to reduce the volume of formal grievances.

### Collective Bargaining and Grievance Procedures

In state governments with significant union representation among state employees, the structure of grievance procedures is mostly drawn from collective bargaining agreements. As the collective bargaining agreements structure the employee relationship—from leave and vacation policies to salary structure—for many of these state employees, grievance procedures are focused on resolving complaints of employees pursuant to the implementation of the respective collective bargaining agreements. If employees believe that provisions of the collective bargaining agreement have been misapplied or violated, they are allowed to initiate a grievance under state law and/or under the provision of their contracts.

Generally, in states with a strong union presence, state law governs labor relations for state employees, addressing the right to union representation, recognition of employee organizations, and the manner in which disputes surrounding collective bargaining can be resolved. For example, Division 4, Chapter 10.3 of the Government Code of California, "State Employer–Employee Relations," governs disputes between the state government and public employee organizations (California, 1995). Chapter 150E of the General Laws of the Commonwealth of Massachusetts allows for inclusion of formal grievance procedures in any collective bargaining agreement, with the grievance procedure designed for resolving differences in the interpretation of the collective bargaining agreement (Massachusetts, 2004). Chapter 89 of the Hawaii Revised Statutes addresses collective bargaining in public employment, allowing that public employers will enter into written agreements with the representatives of public employee organizations to establish grievance procedures (Hawaii, 2007). Therefore, in states with significant collective bargaining presence, state law specifies the role of employee organizations in structuring the grievance process.

In these states, the grievance procedures generally follow the classic model, with specified steps to follow in order to resolve the grievances, such as the case of Delaware (see Exhibit 13.1).

As stated, the collective bargaining agreements, while varying depending on the particular employee organization, generally allow for grievances surrounding the interpretation of the collective bargaining agreement. However, some states have established procedures alongside the contractual grievance procedures or have established provisions to protect those employees not included within collective bargaining agreement. For example, Section 18 of the State of Delaware Merit Rules allows

---

**Exhibit 13.1**

---

### State of Delaware State Employee Merit Rules Chapter 18 Grievance Procedures

18.6 Step 1:  Grievants shall file, within 14 calendar days of the date of the grievance matter or the date they could reasonably be expected to have knowledge of the grievance matter, a written grievance which details the complaint and relief sought with their immediate supervisor. The following shall occur within 14 calendar days of receipt of the grievance: the parties shall meet and discuss the grievance and the Step 1 supervisor shall issue a written reply.

18.7 Step 2:  Any appeal shall be filed in writing to the top agency personnel official or representative within 7 calendar days of receipt of the reply. The following shall occur within 30 calendar days of the receipt of the appeal: the designated management official and the employee shall meet and discuss the grievance, and the designated management official shall issue a written response.

18.8 Step 3:  Any appeal shall be filed in writing to the Director within

14 calendar days of receipt of the Step 2 reply. This appeal shall include copies of the written grievance and responses from the previous steps. The parties and the Director (or designee) may agree to meet and attempt an informal resolution of the grievance, and/or the Director (or designee) shall hear the grievance and issue a written decision with 45 calendar days of the appeal's receipt. The Step 3 decision is final and binding upon agency management.

18.9   If the grievance has not been settled, the grievant may present, within 20 calendar days of receipt of the Step 3 decision or of the date of the informal meeting, whichever is later, a written appeal to the Merit Employee Relations Board (MERB) for final disposition according to 29 Del.C. §5931 and MERB procedures.

---

*Source:* State of Delaware. 2007. Chapter 18 of the State Merit Rules. Office of Management and Budget. Available at <http://www.delawarepersonnel.com/search/mrules.asp?page= Sections&ID=18.0>. Accessed on August 8, 2007.

employees to file grievances concerning the application of state merit rules or law. The section states that employees covered by collective bargaining agreements should follow the procedures outlined in the agreements, but allows for the use of the merit grievance procedure if the subject being grieved is not covered by the collective bargaining agreement (State of Delaware, 2007).

Connecticut, through the Department of Labor Relations, provides a grievance and appeal process for classified employees not included in a collective bargaining agreement, which includes the ability to grieve dismissals, demotions, suspensions, and misinterpretation of state personnel statutes or rules (State of Connecticut, 2007). Wisconsin also provides for a comprehensive grievance procedure for employees not covered by collective bargaining agreements (State of Wisconsin, 2007). In addition, Alaska provides for a complaint procedure for employees not covered by collective bargaining agreements, with the complaint procedure governing issues other than dismissal, demotion, or suspension. However, this complaint procedure only allows employees to pursue the complaint up to the Commissioner of Administration, with the commissioner's decision or findings considered the final administrative decision. For dismissal, demotions, or suspension, Alaska employees not covered by collective bargaining are provided with an appeal process to the state personnel board (State of Alaska, 2007).

Therefore, states with strong collective bargaining agreements and significant union presence generally provide the most comprehensive grievance procedures. However, the challenge in these states is for those employees not covered by collective bargaining agreement. As seen, some states provide for comprehensive grievance procedures through merit rules or other state processes. Others, such as Alaska, provide more limited complaint procedures for employees not covered by collective bargaining agreement. Overall, one can conclude that state government employees covered by collective bargaining agreement generally have access to the most formal and structured grievance policies.

## Decentralization of Grievance Procedures

A common practice across state governments is the decentralization of personnel practices to individual agencies, moving away from central control by a single statewide personnel agency. This decentralization also extends to the employee complaint process, with many states decentralizing grievance procedures to the agency level. While many state governments provide language in their laws and personnel regulations concerning the minimum level of grievance procedures that should be afforded employees, these governments allow individual agencies to further specify the protections and processes that employees can use to address personnel actions taken against them. For example, Missouri, through the Code of State Regulations, has decentralized all grievance procedures to the individual agency level, covering those personnel actions not subject to appeal to the Personnel Advisory Board. Each agency is required to construct written procedures that are approved by the personnel director, with these written procedures addressing certain minimum provisions, including time frames for each step in the process, provisions for prohibiting retaliation, and or discrimination surrounding the filing of a grievance, and a method for informing employees of the grievance procedures (State of Missouri, 2007).

Similarly, Article 12 of the Kansas Administrative Regulations allows each agency to develop their own grievance procedures (Kansas, 2007). South Carolina and Arkansas are other states that allow for individual agencies to develop their own grievance procedures. Tennessee also does not provide for standard grievance forms, but allows for individual agencies to develop their own forms for the grievance process. Arizona, while decentralizing the authority to develop grievance procedures to individual agencies, provides a detailed list of issues and practices that must be addressed or included in each agency's grievance policy (see Exhibit 13.2).

---

**Exhibit 13.2**

## State of Arizona Grievance Procedures
## R2-5-702. Grievance Procedures

Content. The grievance procedure established in each state agency shall include as a minimum:

1. A requirement that the grievant have an oral discussion with the immediate supervisor in an attempt to resolve the problem, prior to initiating the written grievance procedure.
2. A requirement that the employee file the grievance in writing with the immediate supervisor within 10 working days after the occurrence of the action being grieved. The date of occurrence of a suspension is the first day of suspension.
3. A requirement that the grievance contain a complete statement of all the facts and circumstances involved in the alleged violation and the specific redress sought.
4. A requirement that a grievance alleging noncompliance with these rules shall specify the precise rule alleged to have been violated.
5. A requirement that all employees presenting a grievance in which the issues and redress sought are identical will sign the grievance and designate a contact person from the group.
6. A provision that the employee or group of employees filing a grievance may select a representative at any step in the procedure after the oral discussion with the immediate supervisor.

7. A provision that a grievant must be allowed a reasonable amount of work time to prepare and process a grievance and that the use of such time shall be approved in advance by management.
8. A requirement that a state service employee who serves as the representative of a grievant must receive approval for annual or compensatory leave to represent the grievant.
9. A requirement that the grievant must have a minimum of five working days after receipt of a response to forward the grievance at any step, must sign the grievance at each step, and must state the reasons why the response at the previous step was unsatisfactory.
10. A requirement that the agency head will respond to the grievant not later than 40 working days after receipt of the grievance at the first step. Within the 40 working day period, the time for any step may be extended by the agency head with the concurrence of the grievant.
11. A statement that the decision of the agency head is final on all grievances except those that allege discrimination or noncompliance with these rules. For Department of Administration employees, the decision of the Director is final on all grievances except those that allege discrimination or noncompliance with these rules.

---

*Source:* Arizona State Government Grievance Procedures. Arizona Department of Administration. <http://www.hr.state.az.us/Employeerelations/grievance.htm>. Accessed on October 10, 2007.

As states decentralize personnel authority across a wide variety of policies and practices, it is not surprising that many states decentralize grievance procedures. This decentralization could be positive in some instances; certain agencies may deliver services that require significant discretion on the part of their employees and therefore may require more stringent protections for their employees. However, state governments should be attentive to whether this decentralization of grievance procedures could lead to disparate policies across agencies. While providing a minimum of protection in the policies, as evidenced by Arizona, will ensure that all employees are afforded basic procedures, significant differences across agencies in decentralized states could reduce the degree to which the grievance procedures create a sense of procedural justice on the part of employees, and could lead to the perception that certain agencies are not the "best" in which to work or fail to provide adequate protection for their employees.

## Scope of Grievances

In designing grievance procedures, one of the states' central challenges rests with determining what personnel issues should be included. Across the fifty states, there exist significant differences concerning which personnel actions are subject to grievances, with some states, such as those with strong collective bargaining agreements providing an expansive range of grievable issues, and others providing a restricted list of grievable issues. In establishing the range of personnel issues that fall under grievance procedures, state governments generally focus on addressing certain issues.

First, most states, even those with the most restrictive grievance procedures, provide a certain minimum level of coverage. For example, Georgia, one of the states most often discussed with reference to significant personnel reform and the reduction of civil service protections for state employees, still provides a minimum level of coverage for employees in the unclassified service.* The issues explicitly available for grievance by these employees include:

1. Allegations of unlawful discrimination because of race, color, sex, national origin, disability, age, or religious or political opinions or affiliations.
2. Allegations of sexual or other forms of harassment.
3. Retaliation for using this grievance procedure.
4. Erroneous, arbitrary, or capricious interpretation or application of personnel policies and procedures.
5. Unsafe or unhealthy working conditions (State of Georgia, 2007).

North Carolina, another state with restrictive grievance procedures, specifies a minimum level of protection for different employee classifications (see Exhibit 13.3).

Therefore, most states, even when seeking to make their grievance procedures as narrowly drawn as possible, provide a minimum level of protection. This protection generally centers on ensuring that government employees (even those not

*The unclassified service in Georgia includes all new employees after July 1, 1996. See Rules of the Georgia State Personnel Board. <http://www.spa.ga.gov/employees/rules/rule1.asp#100>. Accessed on October 20, 2007.

---

**Exhibit 13.3**

---

## State of North Carolina Employee
## Appeals and Grievances

---

| Covered Persons | Grievable Issues |
|---|---|
| Career State employees or former career State employees | • Dismissal, demotion, or suspension without pay without just cause<br>• Denial of promotion due to failure to post<br>• Failure to give promotional priority over outside applicants<br>• Failure to give RIF reemployment consideration<br>• Failure to give policy-making/confidential exempt status priority reemployment consideration<br>• Failure to follow systematic procedures in reduction in force (not alleging discrimination)<br>• Denial of veteran's preference in connection with RIF |
| Any State employee or former State employee | • Denial of request to remove inaccurate or misleading information from personnel file<br>• Policy-making designation<br>• Discrimination in denial of promotion, transfer, or training; or retaliation in selection for demotion, RIF or termination |
| Any applicant for State employment | • Denial of veteran's preference in initial State employment<br>• Denial of employment on the basis of illegal discrimination |
| Any State employee | • A false accusation about political threats or promises<br>• Violation of the FLSA, Age Discrimination Act, FMLA or ADA (except for employees in exempt policy-making positions). |

---

*Source:* State of North Carolina. 2007. State Personnel Manual. Office of State Personnel. <http://www.osp.state.nc.us/manuals/dropmenu.html>. Accessed on September 6, 2007.

considered part of a classified, civil service, or collective bargaining employment contract) who suffer adverse personnel actions based on clear claims of discrimination have a formal avenue of recourse. State governments understand that while reducing the formal personnel rules governing public employment may be desirable to free up managerial flexibility, it is still necessary to offer clear procedures in the event of unfair or unlawful discrimination in the employer/employee relationship, such as discrimination covered by the Americans with Disabilities Act, Title VII of the Civil Rights Act of 1964, and other equal employment opportunity laws.

When states seek to narrowly draw their grievance procedures, with the focus on ensuring that the government is not unduly subject to a large number of employee complaints, most grievance procedures exclude matters that are outside of the purview of individual government agencies or constitute central government actions. For example, many grievance procedures explicitly place retirement systems, health insurance, life insurance, the classification system, and reductions in force outside of the structured grievance process. As decisions on statewide policies and practices such as health insurance and retirement systems cover a significant amount of employees, opening up these parts of the employment relationship to the grievance process could create an avalanche of complaints and grievances. For example, if a state government changes health care coverage in order to save the state government money during a fiscal crisis, if employees were allowed to grieve such changes, these employees could organize and produce a flurry of grievances, fundamentally frustrating any other action while agencies worked to resolve the large volume of new grievances. Therefore, state or systemwide policies or practices are often excluded from grievance policies and procedures.

In addition, in constructing grievance procedures, state governments are attentive to protecting the rights of their managers to make managerial decisions concerning their employees in the process of carrying out the statutory goals of their agencies. Managers often have to make hard decisions concerning the assignment of employees to various tasks and evaluation of their performance, decisions that even the most rational employee may have a hard time accepting as just if these decisions conflict with the employee's opinion of their role or performance. States are attentive to protecting this discretion on the part of managers in the grievance process, because allowing grievances of fundamental managerial actions could result in a complete stalemate between managers and employees, in effect bringing state government operation to a standstill.

Some particular management actions excluded from the grievance process include: directing employees in the operation of the agency's mandate, and hiring, promoting, transferring, and retaining employees. However, this does not imply that managers can make capricious decisions concerning their employees, transferring employees they do not like or penalizing particular employees on their performance reviews. While these managerial actions are exempt from the grievance process, many state grievance procedures do allow complaints or grievances concerning the manner of administration of these actions. For example, Wisconsin's Human Resources Handbook states "management possess the sole right to operate an agency to carry out the statutory mandate and goals assigned to the agency and all management rights repose in management, however, such rights must be exercised consistently" (State of Wisconsin, 2007). Therefore, if an employee believes a personnel action was taken against them in a manner that is inconsistent with current practices or was undertaken for a discriminatory reason, these employees can grieve the manner of administration of the action, rather than the action itself.

An interesting example of a state seeking to manage their grievance process is Louisiana. In its human resource handbook, Louisiana defines *grievance* as an internal agency procedure to resolve personnel actions that are not appealable to the State Civil Service Commission (State of Louisiana, 2007). Louisiana employs a decentralized model of grievance procedures, with each agency determining its own grievance policy and procedures. These policies and procedures can include as many personnel actions as desired by the agency, but again, they are handled entirely within the individual agencies. Outside of agency grievance procedures, Louisiana then allows certain personnel actions to be appealable to the Director of Civil Service and the Civil Service Commission, actions similar to the aforementioned examples of Georgia and North Carolina (layoffs, discrimination, etc.), but also reassignment and suspensions (State of Louisiana, 2007). By differentiating between a grievance and an appeal, the State of Louisiana allows most employee complaints to be resolved within agencies, reserving the more formalized process of appeal to the most serious of personnel actions.

It is clear that many states have designed their grievance policies and procedures with specific attention toward ensuring a balance of employee protection with limits on employees' ability to undermine managerial action and discretion. Even states with expansive grievance policies understand that managers must often take difficult action against employees, so grievance procedures often protect managers from unnecessary employee reactions to criticism or discipline surrounding employee performance. In addition, state governments realize that governmentwide policies and practices should be removed from grievance policies to ensure that employees cannot frustrate governmentwide policies designed to serve the good of the overall system.

## Early Resolution of Grievances

State governments acknowledge that the initiation of formal grievances can sometimes be a cumbersome and contentious process. The formal grievance process can require significant paperwork and time investment on the part of both the employer and the employee and may prolong conflict between the two parties. Therefore, more states are instituting mediation and alternative dispute resolution processes to resolve employee complaints before these complaints enter the formal grievance process.

Colorado provides a State Employee Mediation Program, designed to be a "facilitated problem-solving approach to resolving disputes" (State of Colorado, 2007). This confidential program can be initiated either before a grievance has been filed to resolve differences between the employee and manager or it can be used after the grievance process has been initiated. If the grievance process has been initiated and mediation is requested by either party involved in the grievance, the deadlines associated with the various steps are suspended during the mediation process (State of Colorado, 2007). Kentucky, Nevada, Ohio, Virginia, Wyoming, Washington, and Oregon are among the many states that have instituted such programs. In general, while mediation or dispute resolution programs can help resolve conflicts between employee and manager and perhaps reduce or eliminate the desire of the employee to file a formal grievance, these programs generally are voluntary and do not preclude employees from still filing a formal grievance or complaint. In addition, mediation programs are generally designed to quickly and economically resolve disputes in the workplace: employee complaints involving complex personnel issues or claims of illegal discrimination in a personnel action, mediation programs may not be appropriate.

An additional method to resolve employee complaints before these complaints transform into formal grievances is to require oral discourse between employees and managers. For example, Arizona requires agency grievance procedures to include a provision for mandatory oral discourse prior to the filing of the grievance. Employees are required to inform their manager of their complaint and their intention to file a grievance. The purpose of the oral discourse is to provide a final, informal opportunity for the manager and the employee to communicate before entering the formalized grievance process. The Arizona policy also states that employees cannot file the grievance unless they have completed this step. This is a useful mechanism for resolving personnel issues that may arise from miscommunication or failure to understand a personnel action on the part of either the employee or the manager. A manager may not be aware that a personnel action has created a problem for an employee. Requiring the employee to inform the manager may provide an avenue for the manager to clarify the action and/or apologize for a miscommunication, thereby avoiding a time-consuming formal grievance procedure.

Both mediation processes and mandatory informal or formal discourse as part of the grievance process represent sound strategies to seek to reduce the need to initiate formal grievance procedures. However, in utilizing such strategies, state governments should be careful to inform employees of their rights under the state policies. Employees should recognize that they still have recourse if a resolution is not achieved through these processes. If not, the procedural justice associated with complaint and grievance procedures would be significantly reduced and employees could believe that management prefers expeditious resolution of complaints over the "fair" resolution of complaints.

## STATE COMPLAINT AND GRIEVANCE PROCEDURES: SUMMARY AND CONCLUSIONS

Significant reforms are sweeping the state government landscape with reference to the status of and treatment of state government employees. Scholars have raised concerns about the dramatic changes to states such as Georgia and Florida and to the more subtle changes occurring in other states, concerns that highlight the need to avoid wholesale reduction or elimination of employee protections. Public employees charged with the business of government often have to make challenging and unpopular decisions; providing these employees with protection in the execution of their duties enables them to adopt a sense of equity and procedural justice in how they are subsequently treated by their employers. Grievance policies and procedures are inherently about providing this procedural justice to government employees. Employees are aware that they are provided with recourse if necessary to seek redress for wrongful personnel actions, and these employees may accept adverse personnel actions as long as they perceive that they have been treated fairly. Therefore, grievance policies and procedures should not be reformed without serious attention to the possible negative ramifications for the employee relationship to state government.

Through a review of state government laws and policies, several trends in state government grievance procedures were highlighted. These trends include:

1. State governments with strong union presence and collective bargaining agreements for their employees tend to provide the most comprehensive grievance procedures centered on the implementation of the collective bargaining agreements. However, these states generally also provide separate protection for those employees not covered by collective bargaining agreements.

2. More state governments, along with the decentralization of other personnel policies and authority, are decentralizing the creation of grievance procedures to the agency level. These governments generally provide a minimum of requirements for the agency policies.

3. Many states are explicitly detailing what personnel actions fall outside of grievance procedures. In particular, state policies are attentive to removing managerial actions associated with the accomplishment of agency goals from the scope of grievable issues.

4. States are increasingly creating mediation programs and other methods of promoting discourse in order to reduce the filing of formal grievances.

The trend for increasing and protecting managerial authority at the agency level and protecting managerial action is particularly important. One of the classic complaints concerning civil service systems has been the frustration that the associated rules and regulations have produced for managers in these systems. Attention to the need for managers to police the performance of their employees without fear of being swamped in grievances is a trend that should produce positive impacts for these agencies. However, in doing so, the associated policies should ensure that employees can challenge the administration of these decisions, if not the content, to protect against discrimination in many forms.

For state governments seeking to reexamine their grievance procedures, the advice would be to seek to balance the needs of management to manage with the rights of employees to be treated in a fair and equitable manner. Providing employees with recourse to address adverse personnel actions, whatever the outcome of this recourse, is inherently necessary for the well-being and satisfaction of these employees. Implementing innovations such as mandatory oral discourse and mediation services can supplement these policies and hopefully reduce formal grievances. However, if employees believe they have no formal recourse for adverse personnel actions, the impact of this on state government employee performance and morale could be serious, making these grievance policies and procedures still a necessary part of personnel regulation and policy in state government.

## REFERENCES

Blader, S. L., and T. R. Tyler. 2003. What Constitutes Fairness in Work Settings? A Four-Component Model of Procedural Justice. *Human Resource Management Review* 13:107–126.

California. 1995. *Annotated California Code: Government Code.* St. Paul: West Group.

Coggburn, J. 2000. The Effects of Deregulation on State Government Personnel Administration. *Review of Public Personnel Administration* 20 (4):24–39.

———. 2001. Personnel Deregulation: Exploring Differences in the American States. *Journal of Public Administration Research and Theory* 11:223–244.

Folger, R., and M. A. Konovsky. 1989. Effects of Procedural and Distributive Justice on Reactions to Pay Raise Decisions. *Academy of Management Journal* 32:115–130.

Hawaii. 2007. *Michie's Hawaii Revised Statutes.* Charlottesville: Lexis Law Publishing.

Hays, S. W., and J. E. Sowa. 2006. A Broader Look at the 'Accountability Movement': Some Grim Realities in State Civil Service Systems. *Review of Public Personnel Administration* 26 (2):102–117.

Hou, Y., P. W. Ingraham, S. Bretschneider, and S. C. Selden. 2000. Decentralization of Human Resource Management: Driving Forces and Implications. *Review of Public Personnel Administration* 20:9–22.

Kearney, R. C. 2001. *Labor Relations in the Public Sector,* 3rd ed. New York, NY: Marcel Dekker, Inc.

Kellough, J. E., and L. G. Nigro. 2006. Dramatic Reform in the Public Service: At-Will Employment and the Creation of a New Public Workforce. *Journal of Public Administration Research and Theory* 16 (3):447–466.

Kim, W. C., and R. A. Mauborgne. 1993. Procedural Justice, Attitudes, and Subsidiary Top Management Compliance with Multinationals' Corporate Strategic Decisions. *Academy of Management Journal* 36:502–526.

Massachusetts. 2004. *Massachusetts General Laws, Annotated.* St. Paul: West Group.

Richardson, R. C. 1977. *Collective Bargaining by Objectives.* Englewood Cliffs, NJ: Prentice-Hall.

Rubin, E. V. (Forthcoming). The Role of Procedural Justice in Public Personnel Management: Empirical Results from the Department of Defense. *Journal of Public Administration Research and Theory.*

Schaubroeck, J., D. R. May, and F. W. Brown. 1994. Procedural Justice Explanations and Employee Reactions to Economic Hardship. *Journal of Applied Psychology* 79:455–460.

State of Alaska. 2007. Alaska Department of Administration, Division of Personnel and Labor Relations. <http://dop.state.ak.us/website/>. Accessed on October 10, 2007.

State of Arizona. 2007. Arizona State Government Grievance Procedures. Arizona Department of Administration. Available at <http://www.hr.state.az.us/Employeerelations/grievance.htm>. Accessed on October 10, 2007.

State of Colorado. 2007. Employee Handbook. Colorado Division of Human Resources. Available at <http://www.colorado.gov/dpa/dhr/pubs/docs/emphandbook.pdf>. Accessed on September 7, 2007.

State of Connecticut. 2007. Office of Labor Relations. Available at <http://www.ct.gov/opm/cwp/view.asp?a=3006&Q=386312&opmNav_GID=1386>. Accessed on October 10, 2007.

State of Delaware. 2007. Chapter 18 of the State Merit Rules. Office of Management and Budget. Available at <http://www.delawarepersonnel.com/search/mrules.asp?page=Sections&ID=18.0>. Accessed on August 8, 2007.

State of Georgia. 2007. Policy: Employee Grievance Procedure (Unclassified Service). Office of the Governor. Available at <http://www.spa.ga.gov/pdfs/compensation/cb.grievance_policy.pdf>. Accessed on November 30, 2007.

State of Kansas. 2007. Article 12, Kansas Administrative Regulations. Available at <http://www.da.ks.gov/ps/documents/regs/default.htm>. Accessed on September 6, 2007.

State of Louisiana. 2007. Human Resources Handbook. Louisiana Department of State Civil Service. Available at <http://www.civilservice.la.gov/HRHandbook/Grievances/procedures.htm>. Accessed on August 1, 2007.

State of Missouri. 2007. Code of State Regulations. Available at <http://www.sos.mo.gov/adrules/csr/current/1csr/1csr.asp>. Accessed on September 6, 2007.

State of North Carolina. 2007. State Personnel Manual. Office of State Personnel. Available at <http://www.osp.state.nc.us/manuals/dropmenu.html>. Accessed on September 6, 2007.

State of Wisconsin. 2007. Wisconsin Human Resources Handbook. Office of State Employee Relations. Available at <http://oser.state.wi.us/docview.asp?docid=1484>. Accessed on August 8, 2007.

# ᚑ᚜ᚅᚅᚅᚅᚅᚐ **Section Three** ᚆᚅᚅᚅᚅᚅᚐ

# The Issues

To draw an old saw, in public sector HRM, change is constant. The traditional, technical tasks remain important, of course, but increasingly, HR managers are involved in policy concerns such as diversity, information technology, ethics, labor relations, privatizing and outsourcing, and many others. Wise agency and department administrators bring top HR people into organization-wide decision making because ultimately, all problems and challenges involve the organization's employees.

Chapters 14 and 15, the first two chapters in this section, address diversity issues. Chapter 14, by J. Edward Kellough, presents a comprehensive overview of how governments and courts have responded to historic patterns of discrimination in public employment and personnel processes. The affirmative action controversy is analyzed from the perspective of intent, high stakes, and justifications. Kellough explains how attacks, such as California's Proposition 209 and similar state initiatives, as well as Supreme Court decisions, contributed to a transition of affirmative action preferences to "diversity management." He concludes with a glimpse at the future of affirmative action and diversity.

In Chapter 15, Mary E. Guy and Susan Spice explore gender issues in the workplace. The critical role of gender differences is examined, from their societal and economic origins to specific impacts in the workplace. Guy and Spice then examine how gender makes a difference in workplace concerns such as balancing family and work and accommodating women's traditional role as family caregiver. The authors advocate a reshaping of the male-dominated workplace to a gender neutral environment.

Chapter 16, by new contributor Robert T. Wooters, shifts the reader's attention to the issue of information technology (IT) in HRM systems. Through summarizing the results of the GPP on IT systems in state government, the author provides an assessment of the states' IT systems and applications and compares the states to large private sector employers. Contrary to popular belief, Wooters finds that the states' IT systems are ahead of corporate systems in many respects.

An enduring HRM issue is ethics. The HR manager is uniquely situated to advance ethical principles and behaviors for public employees. In Chapter 17 Jonathan P. West reviews the responses and strategies of public organizations to the ethics challenge. He then brings ethics to bear on specific HRM functions, from hiring and performance appraisal to benefits and privatization. West concludes that HR managers must recognize the importance of ethics as a precondition of good government.

Another new contributor, Patrice M. Mareschal, reviews recent developments in public sector labor relations in federal and state government, including changes in the legal environment and vicious attacks on federal unions by the George W. Bush administration. Mareschal's Chapter 18 next employs state case studies to examine current trends. She concludes with an evaluation of "the political scorecard" for unions in the states, finding that the labor movement remains viable, particularly in the public sector.

The last chapter in this section, Chapter 19 on outsourcing HR, is contributed by Jerrell D. Coggburn. He examines why public organizations consider outsourcing of HRM functions, describes common problems with outsourcing, and contemplates the prospects for HR outsourcing, concluding that such activity is likely to increase in the coming years. Coggburn issues a call for additional research on HR outsourcing, so we can develop a better understanding of its true impacts.

# 14

# Affirmative Action and Diversity in the Public Sector

J. EDWARD KELLOUGH
University of Georgia

## INTRODUCTION

It is widely known that discrimination directed against racial, ethnic, and other minorities and women has a long and distressing history. This chapter is about the ways in which government organizations in the United States have responded to historic patterns of discrimination in public personnel systems. Obviously, there are many reasons why government should be involved in combating discrimination in public employment. Fundamental notions of merit and justice, for example, require that the public service be free from prejudice. As Hays (1998) notes in a broad discussion of civil service selection procedures, "public jobs are public resources, to which everyone has a potential claim." The process by which those valuable resources are distributed must not be closed to specified groups of people identified by factors such as sex, race, or ethnicity. In addition, government has a responsibility, through its own employment practices, to provide an appropriate example for nongovernmental organizations (Krislov, 1967). If government cannot protect women and minorities from discrimination within the ranks of its own workforce, how can we reasonably expect it to counter discrimination in private employment or other endeavors? Finally, government efforts to open the public employment process to underrepresented groups are desirable also because we know that a governmental bureaucracy reflective of the public it serves, in terms of such characteristics as race, ethnicity, and sex, can help to ensure that all interests are appropriately considered in policy formulation and implementation processes. There is a growing body of empirical research to demonstrate that a more representative public bureaucracy promotes greater governmental responsiveness to a variety of public interests (e.g., see Meier, 1993; Meier and Stewart, 1992; Selden, 1997; Selden, Brudney, and Kellough, 1998; Wilkins and Keiser, 2006).

## EARLY ACTION IN RESPONSE TO DISCRIMINATION

Despite strong arguments for equal employment opportunity, and not withstanding constitutional guarantees of equal protection of the laws and merit system rules designed to ensure that applicants for public employment would be judged only on the basis of their abilities, discrimination in the public sector was extensive and openly practiced well into the twentieth century. Rosenbloom (1977) notes, for example, that during the administration of William Howard Taft, a policy of segregation of whites and African Americans was initiated within the Census Bureau, and African American appointments were reduced in areas of the country such as the South where whites objected to their employment. Under the subsequent administration of Woodrow Wilson, other discriminatory practices were encouraged or condoned, such as the segregation of offices, rest rooms, and lunchrooms. It was also under Wilson that a photograph was for the first time required to accompany applications for federal employment. Although that requirement was eventually dropped, at the time, it was apparent that "the color of one's skin had become a test of fitness for federal employees" (Rosenbloom, 1977:54).

It was not until the 1940s that the most egregious discriminatory practices were first confronted by the federal government, and then, meaningful action was taken only after early civil rights advocates, led by A. Philip Randolph, threatened a mass rally in the nation's capital to protest discrimination by the government and defense industry contractors. The Roosevelt administration was decidedly cool to the idea of such a public expression of African American sentiment. The Administration feared that a massive protest rally in Washington D.C., designed to call attention to racism within the United States, would divide the country along racial lines just as we were being forced to contemplate the possibility of war against Nazi Germany and its racist ideology. There was speculation that the march would turn violent, that social unrest would spread across the country, and that military discipline would be disrupted.

Nevertheless, efforts by Roosevelt to dissuade Randolph and other leaders of the March on Washington movement failed until the president agreed to establish, through issuance of a new executive order (No. 8802), an administrative organization with authority to investigate allegations of discrimination by defense contractors and federal agencies (Kellough, 2006). This organization, known as the Fair Employment Practices Committee (FEPC), was the first federal government agency designed to protect minority interests since the period of reconstruction following the Civil War (Reed, 1991:15). Following the issuance of Roosevelt's order creating the FEPC on June 25, 1941, the anticipated protest march was canceled, just days before it was scheduled to occur. The order rested on the president's ability to act independently of Congress to set the terms and conditions of executive agency contracts and to regulate the federal personnel system under existing civil service law. At this point in American history and politics, there was no chance that a substantive antidiscrimination program would come from Congress since numerous key leadership positions in that institution were filled by conservative southern Democrats committed to racial segregation. Consequently, reliance on executive authority was essential if a policy of nondiscrimination was to be pursued. To avoid the need to ask Congress for funding to support the FEPC, money for the Committee's operations came from a presidential discretionary fund appropriated for the operation of agencies within the Executive Office of the President.

The FEPC soon established itself as a serious force in the struggle against discrimination. The Committee held highly publicized hearings to investigate alleged discriminatory practices and began a process of directing public attention to the plight of minorities in important segments of the labor market. But as might be expected, this work generated substantial opposition, especially among influential southern Democrats whose support Roosevelt needed on a number of other issues, and as a result, the Committee placed the president in a politically difficult position. Congress eventually refused to appropriate money for operation of the Committee, and on June 28, 1946, the FEPC filed its final report and officially went out of business. During the years of its operation, however, the Committee achieved considerable success in documenting discriminatory practices by a number of defense contractors and federal agencies.

In the years immediately following abolition of the FEPC, there was no administrative agency to implement a policy of nondiscrimination in the federal civil service. President Truman urged Congress to act, but when it became clear that congressional action would not be forthcoming, he found it necessary to respond by issuing yet another executive order (No. 9980) creating a Fair Employment Board (FEB) within the Civil Service Commission. The responsibilities of the FEB, which was established in 1948, were limited to the investigation of complaints of discrimination arising from within federal government agencies. It could hold hearings and make recommendations, but it could not force agencies to comply with its opinions. Truman later created another committee to perform similar work with regard to government contractors. That organization, known as the Committee on Government Contract Compliance, was established by Executive order 10308 of December 1951.

In 1955, Eisenhower abolished Truman's FEB and established, by executive order, a new committee independent of the Civil Service Commission. Eisenhower's new organization was known as the President's Committee on Government Employment Policy (PCGEP). The PCGEP was set up as an agency-funded entity, so that direct appropriations from Congress for its operation were not needed. The Committee continued the work of investigating complaints of discriminatory practices within federal agencies—work that had been undertaken earlier by the FEPC and the FEB—and, as was the case with its predecessors, it could not compel agencies to change employment decisions, even if it found convincing evidence of discrimination. Its opinions were merely advisory. The effectiveness of the program rested to a considerable extent, therefore, on the persuasive abilities of Committee members. The enforcement of nondiscrimination policy regarding government contractors was also reorganized under a new contract compliance committee.

## THE DEVELOPMENT OF A PROACTIVE APPROACH

During the Truman administration, staff members from the FEB realized that a policy resting primarily on the investigation of complaints might not be the most effective means of confronting discrimination. It was suspected that the extent of discriminatory practices was much broader than what was suggested by the number of formal complaints filed. Many minority group members, it was found, were hesitant to register complaints because they feared retaliation or retribution if they spoke out. As a result, the FEB initiated a very limited and experimental program of "constructive action" to counter discrimination. This program, which Rosenbloom (1977:64) describes as somewhat "ill-defined and ineffective," consisted of "conferences with fair employment officers and outside organizations, periodic surveys and appraisals, and the adoption of some new recruitment techniques, better training programs, and steps toward further integration" (Rosenbloom, 1977:64). Eisenhower's PCGEP maintained this program, although it apparently did little to emphasize the approach.

Dramatic change was to occur, however, when John F. Kennedy entered the presidency. At the very beginning of the Kennedy administration, the president fundamentally reorganized the federal antidiscrimination effort. Executive Order 10925, issued on March 6, 1961, consolidated programs regarding government contract compliance and the federal civil service under a newly established authority known as the President's Committee on Equal Employment Opportunity (PCEEO). The committees that had operated during the Eisenhower years were dissolved. The PCEEO received and investigated complaints as the earlier committees had done, but Kennedy's order required substantially more than what had been mandated earlier. The new order required that the positive program of recruitment and outreach to the minority community, begun under Truman, be a primary and integral part of the federal effort. Under Kennedy, this approach became known as "affirmative action."

Kennedy's program placed a substantial new burden or obligation on federal agencies. Earlier efforts were focused primarily on prohibiting federal employers from engaging in discriminatory behavior. That is, agencies were directed, for the most part, *not to do* certain things. They were not to disadvantage minority job applicants or employees because of race or ethnicity. Kennedy maintained these requirements, but in addition, he stressed that federal organizations were *to do* other things, that is, they were to undertake and emphasize certain actions such as minority recruitment and the provision of training to promote greater equality of opportunity. The difference between the two approaches is that between a negative prohibition on the one hand and an affirmative requirement on the other. The PCEEO under the direction of Vice President Johnson, who Kennedy selected as chairman of the Committee, was very aggressive in pursuing this strategy, but all of the Committee's work was grounded firmly on the principle of nondiscrimination. Affirmative action in the form of minority recruitment and outreach certainly did not mean that agencies stopped recruiting nonminorities, and since training and upward mobility programs were made available to all lower-level employees regardless of race, ethnicity, or sex, such efforts served to reinforce a doctrine of equal opportunity.

Following Johnson's rise to the presidency in 1963, a number of additional developments occurred regarding the structure and operation of the federal program. First, Congress finally acted to prohibit discrimination by private employers and organizations receiving federal assistance through passage of the Civil Rights Act of 1964. That legislation marked a fundamental shift in the government's approach to the problem of discrimination, but significantly, its provisions did not initially apply to the federal civil service. Also, there was no requirement under the law that employers engage in affirmative action. Consequently, the PCEEO which was continuing its program of requiring affirmative action by federal agencies (and federal government contractors), came under strenuous attack by some members of Congress who argued that the Committee's work was no longer needed since the Civil Rights Act had established the Equal Employment Opportunity Commission (EEOC) to implement a policy of nondiscrimination, and contractors would fall under the jurisdiction of the EEOC (Graham, 1990). Of course, that argument completely ignored the issue of discrimination within federal agencies. In order to save the federal affirmative action program, President Johnson, through Executive Order 11246 of 1965, transferred authority for the nondiscrimination effort within the federal civil service to the Civil Service Commission and gave the Department of Labor (DOL) authority with respect to federal contractors. In 1967, through Executive Order 11375, Johnson added language prohibiting discrimination on the basis of sex to existing affirmative action programs.

Progress in the employment of minority group members was slow throughout the remainder of the 1960s, however, and the social unrest characteristic of much of that decade helped to persuade many people that additional action to strengthen the campaign against discrimination was needed. Urban rioting in the largely black ghettos in many metropolitan areas had risen to unprecedented levels. In the African American community there was a growing sense of black nationalism and a feeling that we should move from simple equality of opportunity to equality of results. In this context, and in the face of unrepentant discrimination against minorities in private sector construction trades, the DOL in 1967, through its Office of Federal Contract Compliance Programs, began a program in the City of Philadelphia requiring that federal construction contractors establish goals for minority employment as a condition of receiving federal contract dollars (Graham, 1990). The Nixon administration subsequently strengthened this program, which became known as the "Philadelphia Plan," and eventually required this type of action by all major federal contractors. This approach to affirmative action placed an increased positive burden on employers by forcing them to establish realistic objectives for minority employment and plan for their accomplishment. In 1971, this type of affirmative action was endorsed by the chairman of the U.S. Civil Service Commission, Robert Hampton, who issued a memorandum on May 10 of that year authorizing federal agencies to establish numerical goals and timetables for minority employment (Rosenbloom, 1977:107–110). Under this method, numerical goals were targets for the representation of women and minorities in an organization. Timetables were dates or timeframes within which specified goals were planned to be accomplished. Although goals and timetables required no organization to accept individuals who did not possess necessary qualifications, they did allow for the consideration of race, ethnicity, and sex in selection or placement decisions.

The policy decision to authorize goals and timetables marked another dramatic shift in the nature of the federal EEO program. An employment goal, if it is meaningful, may imply that a limited preference will be extended to minority group members or women when they possess requisite qualifications. That is to say, an employer who has established a goal for increasing the employment of minorities or women, who then subsequently locates qualified minority or female job applicants, will likely prefer those individuals over equally qualified nonminorities or men. To do otherwise would suggest that the goal is essentially meaningless. This situation indicates, however, that the use of goals and timetables may transcend a strict or literal interpretation of nondiscrimination, in that selection policies may not be purely neutral. This orientation to affirmative action, which eventually came into wide use, was authorized, however, only when minority group members or women were measurably underrepresented in an organization. Nevertheless, affirmative action in this form spawned substantial controversy and judicial activity. In fact, so much attention has been focused on numerical strategies for affirmative action in public employment and elsewhere, that goals and timetables, and the preferences they can imply, now form the dominant paradigm of affirmative action policy in the minds of most people.

With the establishment of affirmative action goals and timetables, the federal government's EEO program rested on several distinct elements. The earliest initiatives, begun under Roosevelt, consisted of executive orders prohibiting discrimination and procedures for the investigation of complaints. The first affirmative action programs emerged later under Kennedy in the form of recruitment efforts, training programs, and other positive measures designed to promote the employment of minorities and women. Eventually, goals and timetables were authorized which implied preferences for minority group members and women under specified circumstances. Table 14.1 illustrates these components of the program. In general, it should be clear that by the early 1970s, affirmative action could take many specific forms, and implications for the principle of nondiscrimination were different for different approaches. In all cases, however, affirmative action involved, and still involves, efforts to promote the employment of members of groups that have historically suffered discriminatory treatment.

As the nation was dealing with the social tumult of the 1960s, other important developments occurred with respect to equal employment opportunity. One of the more important of these was passage of the Age Discrimination in Employment Act (ADEA) of 1967. Congress had considered prohibiting discrimination on the basis

**TABLE 14.1   Equal Employment Opportunity and Affirmative Action Programs**

| Individual-Based "Reactive" Policies | Group-Based "Proactive" Policies (Affirmative Action) | |
|---|---|---|
| Approaches that Pre-Date Affirmative Action: <br><br> • Executive orders and other laws prohibiting discrimination <br> • Procedures for the investigation and resolution of complaints | Early Approaches to Affirmative Action: <br><br> • Work force analysis <br> • Removal of artificial barriers to minority and female selection <br> • Career development and upward mobility programs <br> • Recruitment and outreach efforts | Preferential Approaches to Affirmative Action: <br><br> • Voluntary goals and timetables for the selection of members of targeted groups <br> • Consent decrees specifying selection goals and timetables <br> • Court-ordered selection goals and timetables |
| Equal employment opportunity programs based on a strict interpretation of the principle of nondiscrimination | | Programs that transcend equality of opportunity and nondiscrimination in a strict sense by permitting preferences |

*Source:* Kellough, 2006.

of age earlier when it debated and passed Title VII of the Civil Rights Act of 1964, but it was decided that legislative action on that issue should wait until after the DOL had investigated the problem and issued a report. The ADEA, which was passed three years later, prohibits employment discrimination against persons aged 40 years or older. When it was first enacted, protection was extended only through age 65, but through subsequent amendments, that restriction was eliminated. More significantly for our purposes, the law was also amended in 1974 to cover all state, local, and federal government organizations.

Another major development in the growth of EEO law and affirmative action was the decision by the U.S. Supreme Court in 1971 in *Griggs v. Duke Power Company*. In that case, the Court unanimously ruled that Title VII of the 1964 Civil Rights Act proscribed not only intentional discrimination but also actions that were "fair in form, but discriminatory in operation." This ruling meant that an employer, whose actions might not be intentionally discriminatory, could still be in violation of Title VII if its employment practices screened out a disproportionate number of minorities or women, and those practices could not be shown to serve a legitimate business necessity. An examination for employee selection, for example, could not be used if it eliminated disproportionate numbers of minority applicants, and there was no evidence that it was a valid measure of ability to perform on the job.

This concept of unintentional discrimination eventually became known as *disparate impact*, and the idea was elaborated by the court through subsequent decisions. It is contrasted with *disparate treatment* which is the term used to describe purposeful or intentional discrimination. In a disparate impact case, according to guidelines originally laid out by the court, a minority plaintiff, for example, would first bear the burden of demonstrating through the use of appropriate statistics that an employer's practices had resulted in a substantial disparity between minority and nonminority selection or promotion rates. At that point, the burden would shift to the employer to demonstrate that the practices that produced the disparity served a legitimate business purpose. If the employer was successful in demonstrating that point, then no violation of Title VII would have occurred, unless the plaintiff could demonstrate that there were other, less discriminatory, practices that would serve the identified business interest equally well.

In 1989, this application of the burden of proof in disparate impact cases was overturned by a more conservative Supreme Court in the controversial decision in *Wards Cove Packing Company v. Atonio*. In that case, the Court ruled that the burden would remain on plaintiffs throughout the process, and that plaintiffs would need to show that employers selected challenged employment practices because of their discriminatory effect. Thus, the concept of disparate impact was substantially undermined. Congress responded to this and other Court decisions from the 1989 term with the Civil Rights Act of 1991 which, among other things, amended Title VII to specifically incorporate the standards associated with disparate impact analysis as they had been originally articulated in *Griggs*. The implications of the *Griggs* case and the concept of disparate impact have been substantial. Except for the period between the *Wards Cove* decision and passage of the Civil Rights Act of 1991, employers have had a strong incentive to engage in employment practices, including affirmative action in its various forms, to help ensure that minorities and women are not denied opportunity. In other words, one way for an employer to be shielded from claims of discrimination under disparate impact theory is to make certain that its work force is sufficiently integrated to make any claim of statistical disparity along racial, ethnic, or gender lines impossible.

This incentive for affirmative action provided by disparate impact theory was made applicable to the public sector with passage of another important piece of federal legislation, the Equal Employment Opportunity Act of 1972, which brought all state, local, and federal government agencies under coverage of Title VII of the Civil Rights Act of 1964. This legislation gave the EEOC direct responsibility for monitoring state and local government employment practices. Under EEOC guidelines, state and local governments were required to collect and report data on minority and female employment, and by the mid-1970s goals and timetables and the preferences they imply were well established as a part of the affirmative action process at these levels of government. With respect to the federal government, the 1972 law reaffirmed the program implemented by the Civil Service Commission, but a reorganization order by President Carter coinciding with the 1978 Civil Service Reform Act transferred authority for supervision of federal EEO and affirmative action practices to the EEOC (Kellough and Rosenbloom, 1992). In issuing guidelines for the federal program, the EEOC initially placed great emphasis on numerical goals and timetables in agency affirmative action plans, but during the Reagan years (1981–1988), the agency backed away from that approach. Subsequent EEOC regulations permitted but did not require agencies to develop numerical goals for minority and female employment in instances where those groups were underrepresented.

In the 1970s, the federal government also began to address the problem of discrimination against the disabled. The Rehabilitation Act of 1973, for example, prohibited discrimination against "otherwise qualified handicapped individuals" by any organization receiving federal financial assistance or by federal contractors or agencies. The purpose of the law was to ensure that no qualified individual who also happened to have a disability would be subject to discrimination under any program or activity supported by the federal government. The provision that recipients of federal funding be barred from discrimination essentially meant that all state and local governments would be covered by the law. Provisions prohibiting discrimination by federal contractors and federal agencies also required "affirmative action" by those organizations, which has involved recruitment, outreach, and training.

In 1990, Congress addressed the problem of discrimination against the disabled once more through the Americans with Disabilities Act (ADA). This new law was based on principles established by the Rehabilitation Act of 1973 and the regulations that had been issued to implement that earlier legislation (Kellough, 2000). The ADA is comprehensive in that it extends prohibitions on discrimination against the disabled to private employers without federal contracts but it also applies directly to state and local governments, although affirmative action is not mandated. Federal agencies are not covered by the ADA, however, because it was reasoned that they are sufficiently governed by the Rehabilitation Act and its affirmative action requirements.

## THE AFFIRMATIVE ACTION CONTROVERSY

As previously noted, affirmative action policies, especially those involving preferences for minorities and women, have engendered significant debate. The dispute over affirmative action is best understood, however, when we realize that such policies are intended to have the effect of redistributing opportunity from those who have been historically advantaged to groups that have suffered disadvantages because of race, ethnicity, sex, or other traits or circumstances (Edley, 1996). In the context of government affirmative action, this redistribution of opportunity involves highly valued jobs. Thus, the stakes are high, and the outcomes can be extremely important for people on both sides of the issue. Employment, after all, provides the means by which most individuals support themselves and their families financially. Beyond that, employment can be an avenue to self-fulfillment, a way of defining who we are and what we do. We should expect, therefore, that policies operating to alter the distribution of employment opportunities will very likely be opposed by individuals who prefer the earlier distribution.

We should also realize that affirmative action involving the use of limited preferences is more vulnerable to criticism than other approaches such as recruitment or outreach. This is true simply because the existence of preferences appears to contradict the concept of equality of opportunity. It is difficult for anyone to oppose efforts based firmly on the principle of nondiscrimination, such as broader recruitment or upward mobility programs, but numerical approaches including goals and timetables are more easily opposed by those who argue that a strict interpretation of equal opportunity should prevail. From the viewpoint of those opposed to affirmative action, preferences amount to reverse discrimination; numerical goals, often referred to as *quotas* by opponents, have the effect, it is argued, of illegitimately discriminating against nonminority males and sometimes nonminority women.

The key question is whether the racial-, ethnic-, and sex-based distinctions drawn by affirmative action goals and the accompanying preferences can be justified. Those who equate affirmative action with reverse discrimination argue that such distinctions cannot be defended. They suggest that selection decisions should be based solely on individual merit without consideration of factors such as race, ethnicity, or sex.

However, others remind us that precise measures of individual merit or qualifications are often beyond our reach. They argue that limited advantages for women and minorities in such personnel actions as selection, promotion, assignment, and transfers should be allowed to make up for past or current discrimination. Usually, this view rests on an idea known as compensatory justice, which is the notion that groups, such as minorities or women, who have suffered discrimination and have been denied opportunity as a result, should be given certain advantages to compensate for that injustice. Proponents of affirmative action draw a distinction between discrimination motivated by racial or gender animus, on one hand, and limited minority or female preferences, on the other, that are sometimes present in affirmative action programs intended to assist those who have historically been the victims of racism, ethnocentrism, or sexist attitudes. Opponents of affirmative action counter that while the compensatory argument may hold for identifiable victims of discrimination it should not be applied across-the-board to groups, since some group members may not have suffered discriminatory treatment. But it can be very difficult or impossible to determine whether any particular individual has or has not been victimized by discrimination.

It should also be remembered that affirmative action is not intended to benefit particular individuals, but rather, it is a means of requiring employers or other institutions to ensure that their employment processes give consideration to all qualified people. Additionally, arguments for race-, ethnic-, and sex-based affirmative action are not limited to remedial justifications alone. Such programs are also often defended in more utilitarian terms in that they work to integrate society more rapidly than other approaches, reduce income inequalities, further distributive justice, and promote efficiency by ensuring that the talents of all individuals are used (Taylor, 1991).

The emergence of a Republican majority in Congress in 1994, as well as conservative gains in state legislatures across the nation at that time, helped to push the issue of preferential affirmative action to a very prominent position on the public agenda. In 1995, the Republican leadership in Congress advocated efforts to eliminate the use of affirmative action (Holmes, 1995). In response, the Clinton administration conducted a complete review of federal affirmative action programs and concluded that such approaches should be continued (Stephanopoulos and Edley, 1995). Considerable debate over the issue has also taken place at the state level, with California figuring prominently in the struggle. A Republican governor of California, Pete Wilson, campaigned vigorously against affirmative action on his way to reelection to a second term in 1994, and in 1995 the Regents of the University System of California voted to prohibit the consideration of race or gender in decisions regarding admissions to state universities. More significant, however, was passage of Proposition 209 by California voters in November 1996. Proposition 209 was a ballot initiative that amended the state constitution to prohibit the use of preferences based on race, ethnicity, or sex associated with affirmative action by the state and local government jurisdictions within the state. The success of Proposition 209 indicated that citizen initiatives could be effective tools against affirmative action, and a similar initiative was undertaken in the state of Washington. The Washington initiative (1-200) appeared on the ballot in November 1998, and passed with the support of 58 percent of the voters, making Washington the second state to prohibit racial-, ethnic-, or sex-based preferences in state employment, contracting, or higher education. In the Fall of 2006, a similar measure (known as Proposal 2) was approved by voters in the state of Michigan by a margin of 58 percent to 42 percent.

As the controversy over affirmative action grew in the 1990s, new programs emphasizing "diversity management" emerged (Kellough, 2006:67–71). Proponents of diversity management argued that such programs would be less controversial than affirmative action because they were based on the idea that we should welcome all individuals and value their differences. In contrast to the preferences associated with affirmative action, diversity management strategies focused on inclusiveness and suggested that we should work to ensure that all employees succeed to the fullest extent of their abilities. In practice, however, many diversity management efforts looked very much like older affirmative action programs. A study from 2004, for example, found that 88 percent of federal agencies claimed to have a diversity management program by the year 1999, but 25 percent of those agencies had established their programs by simply changing the name on the door of the affirmative action office (Kellough and Naff, 2004).

Other agencies from that same study, however, noted that their programs did contain activities not usually associated with affirmative action. Such activities included training to promote an understanding of and appreciation for diversity, the provision of mentors for new employees, and the development of internal advocacy groups for employees drawn from underrepresented categories including women and minorities. Nevertheless, even in those agencies, diversity programs also typically included traditional affirmative action recruitment efforts (Kellough and Naff, 2004).

In practice, therefore, diversity management efforts appear to have two meanings. From one perspective, diversity management means that we should manage diversity within an organization so that we promote understanding and harmony across groups and thereby enhance organizational productivity. The second view, however, is that diversity management means that we should manage organizations in such a way as to increase diversity, and this latter orientation is practically indistinguishable from traditional affirmative action. These twin perspectives are reflected in the writings of R. Roosevelt Thomas, the advocate who coined the phrase *diversity management* in the early 1990s. Interestingly, Thomas argued that diversity management was distinct from and should replace affirmative action, since it would be less divisive, but at the same time he advocated for minority recruitment and outreach efforts as a part of those programs (Thomas, 1990).

There is little empirical evidence that diversity management focused on creating welcoming environments within organizations has been effective. An examination of the strength of diversity management programs within seventy-two federal agencies found, for the most part, that programs which were stronger terms of diversity training and other activities did not also exhibit increased promotion opportunities for women and minority group members, or diminished dismissals or voluntary separations for African Americans (Naff and Kellough, 2003). Detailed case studies of two agencies with highly developed diversity management programs came to largely the same conclusion (Naff and Kellough, 2003:1324–1332). While these findings should not be considered the final word on the impact of diversity management efforts, they do raise serious questions about the effectiveness of some aspects of those programs. In contrast, elements of diversity management strategies focused on creating or increasing organizational diversity should be evaluated as we would evaluate any affirmative action effort. It is interesting to note, however, that the debate on affirmative action has taken place without much attention to questions about the impact of the policy.

Has affirmative action been successful? Much of the difficulty we face in trying to answer that question stems from our inability to demonstrate conclusively that affirmative action is the cause of observed growth in the employment of minorities and women. In general, trends in minority and female employment in government have been upward, but it is difficult to separate the impact of affirmative action from that of innumerable other forces that could be driving such change. It is true, nevertheless, that significant increases in the employment of minorities and women in the federal civil service did occur following the initiation of affirmative action in the 1960s, and it appears that at least part of those increases are due to affirmative action (Kellough, 1989). Indeed, there are a number of well-constructed studies that find evidence of the effectiveness of affirmative action throughout the public and private sectors (e.g., see Goldstein and Smith, 1976; Leonard, 1985; Hyclak and Taylor, 1992; Price, 2002; Kellough, 2006).

## THE SUPREME COURT AND PREFERENTIAL AFFIRMATIVE ACTION: EXAMINING THE LIMITS OF LEGAL PERMISSIBILITY

From a legal perspective, preferential affirmative action arises in three ways. It may be the result of (1) a court order, (2) a consent decree sanctioned by a court to settle litigation, or (3) a voluntary decision by an organization. Affirmative action required by court order is authorized by Title VII of the 1964 Civil Rights Act when a federal court has found evidence of discrimination. Standards for the review of court ordered preferential affirmative action are articulated by the Supreme Court in *Firefighters Local v. Stotts,* 1984 and *United States v. Paradise,* 1987. Guidelines for permissible preferential affirmative action embodied in consent decrees are similar to those for voluntary affirmative action and are established in *Firefighters v. City of Cleveland,* 1986. Voluntary affirmative action, consisting of race- or sex-conscious practices established by an organization without external persuasion or compulsion arising out of litigation, includes preferential programs such as numerical goals and timetables set by a government agency for the employment of specified numbers of minorities or women (Selig, 1987).

Because most affirmative action is voluntary, in the sense that the term is used here, a closer look at the legal parameters of such action is warranted. In general, preferential affirmative action programs voluntarily adopted by government organizations are limited by the prohibitions on discrimination contained in Title VII of the Civil Rights Act of 1964 (as amended) and constitutional guarantees of equal protection of the law. Section 703 of Title VII of the 1964 Civil Rights Act defines as unlawful any employment practice that discriminates against any individual on account of race, color, religion, sex, or national origin. Thus, race- or sex-based affirmative action implemented by public institutions must be reconciled with those Title VII prohibitions on discrimination. Likewise, the equal protection clause of the Fourteenth Amendment forbids states to deny any person within their jurisdictions the "equal protection of the laws," and distinctions established by states and their local subdivisions on the basis of race and gender incorporated into affirmative action plans must therefore be reconciled with that equal protection guarantee. Because the Fourteenth Amendment applies only to actions of the states; however, its restrictions do not limit the federal government. The due process clause of the Fifth Amendment, which applies to the federal action, has been interpreted by the Supreme Court as requiring equal protection of the laws (*Bolling v. Sharpe*), and thus constitutional constraints are also imposed on federal affirmative action.

Statutory limitations on affirmative action established by Title VII have been interpreted by the Supreme Court in two important cases (Kellough, 1991, 2006). The first was *United Steelworkers of America v. Weber,* 1979. At issue was the legality of a plan negotiated as part of a collective bargaining agreement between Kaiser Aluminum and Chemical Corporation and the United Steelworkers of America, which reserved for African Americans 50 percent of the openings in an in-plant craft training program until the black proportion of craft workers in the plant approximated the proportion of blacks in the local labor force. The Supreme Court upheld the legality of the affirmative action plan arguing that although Title VII, as indicated in Section 703 (G), cannot be interpreted as requiring preferential treatment to overcome a racial imbalance, it does not preclude voluntary efforts to overcome such an imbalance. In view of the legislative history and purposes of Title VII, the Court held that the prohibition on discrimination could not be read literally to proscribe all race-based affirmative action plans. Writing for a majority of the Court, Justice Brennan noted that if Congress had meant to prohibit all race-conscious affirmative action, it easily could have done so "by providing that Title VII would not require or *permit* racially preferential integration efforts" (*Steelworkers v. Weber,* 1979 p. 205, emphasis in original).

Because *Weber* addressed the legality of voluntary affirmative action by a private employer, the question remained as to whether its outcome would guide the statutory review of similar programs undertaken by a public employer. This question was addressed in 1987 in *Johnson v. Transportation Agency, Santa Clara County, California.* The Court applied the criteria outlined in *Weber* to a voluntary race- and sex-based affirmative action plan adopted by the Transportation Agency which provided that, in making employment decisions within traditionally segregated job classifications where women or minorities were significantly underrepresented, the Agency could consider the sex or race of a job candidate along with the individual's qualifications. No specific number of positions was set aside for minorities or women, but the eventual objective was to have minorities and women employed in positions roughly in proportion to their representation in the relevant local labor force. Following the *Weber* precedent, the Court upheld the agency's affirmative action plan, and with the announcement of the *Johnson* decision, a relatively clear set of standards emerged for judging the statutory legality of voluntary preferential affirmative action programs by government employers. When challenged under Title VII, such programs must be designed to address a manifest racial or gender imbalance in traditionally segregated job categories. Further, when considering whether a manifest racial or gender imbalance exists, the employer must consider the proportion of minorities or women in traditionally segregated positions relative to their proportions with the requisite qualifications in the local labor force. Affirmative action must also be constructed as a temporary strategy, and race or sex may be only one of several factors included in the decision process.

Constitutional restrictions on voluntary affirmative action by government organizations evolved through a series of cases beginning in the 1980s and are considerably more rigorous than the constraints imposed by the Court in *Weber* and *Johnson.* Consequently, these restrictions establish the effective operational limits for governmental affirmative action. As was noted earlier, the issue turns on judicial interpretation of the concept of equal protection of the laws. In most circumstances, the courts apply one of two analytical standards when deciding whether government actions that create classifications among people violate the equal protection components of the Fifth or Fourteenth Amendments. The first standard simply requires that a rational relationship exist between the distinctions imposed and a legitimate governmental end. Under this standard, individuals challenging governmental policies bear the burden of showing that classifications or distinctions drawn by government between people are irrational. In practice, few laws reviewed under this standard of scrutiny are found in violation of equal protection (Grossman and Wells, 1988).

But when government classifications limit fundamental freedoms or rights, or force distinctions based on race or national origin, the second major standard requiring a heightened level of scrutiny, commonly known as strict scrutiny, is usually applied. Under the application of strict scrutiny, the government must defend the validity of its actions by demonstrating that they serve a compelling governmental interest, and are narrowly tailored to meet that interest in that there are no less-intrusive or less-drastic alternatives available to meet the government's end. This is the standard by which affirmative action by government is judged. In 1986, in *Wygant v. Jackson Board of Education,* a plurality of the Supreme Court endorsed the principle that strict scrutiny should be the basis for review of affirmative action by state or local government, and later, in 1989, in *City of Richmond v. Croson*, a majority endorsed the application of strict scrutiny to review affirmative action by subnational governments.

Strict scrutiny also became the appropriate level of review for federal government affirmative action programs as the result of the Supreme Court's ruling in 1995 in *Adarand v. Pena*. Following that decision, any racial classifications incorporated into voluntary affirmative action programs by state, local, or federal employers must be shown to serve a compelling governmental interest in order to achieve Constitutional legitimacy. Exactly what type of interest will be sufficiently compelling to permit such action is unclear, but it is likely that the correction of past discrimination by the government employer involved may be one such interest. Once a compelling governmental interest is identified, the method used to achieve that interest must be narrowly tailored. This means that affirmative action should not impose any undue burden on innocent third parties, that is, the government must use the least intrusive means available to achieve its end. Affirmative action that compromises a bona fide seniority system during times of layoffs, for example, will not withstand constitutional scrutiny if it places an undue burden on nonminorities. Affirmative action in the form of hiring or promotion goals and timetables may be less intrusive than a program that violates seniority rights (see *Wygant*), and given evidence of past discrimination by government, such an approach would presumably be acceptable, although there is no way to know with certainty how the Court will respond to such a case.

Since the mid-1990s, affirmative action programs reviewed under strict scrutiny were struck down by the Fifth and Eleventh Federal Circuit Courts of Appeal and upheld by the Sixth and Ninth Circuits (see *Hopwood v. State of Texas*, 1996; *Johnson v. Board of Regents of the University System of Georgia*, 2001; *Smith v. University of Washington School of Law* 2000; *Grutter v. Bollinger*, 2003). All of those cases, however, involved challenges to affirmative action in public college or university admissions rather than public employment. The *Grutter* case involved a preferential affirmative action plan at the University of Michigan, School of Law. The Supreme Court heard an appeal of *Grutter* along with a companion case (*Gratz v. Bollinger*), also from the University of Michigan, and decisions by the Court in those cases in 2003 helped to settle questions of the constitutionality of preferential affirmative action in university admissions. In *Grutter* (539 U.S. 306, 2003) and *Gratz* (539 U.S. 244, 2003), a majority of the Court held for the first time that student body diversity at a state university was a compelling interest of government. In *Grutter*, the court found that the affirmative action program at the Law School was also narrowly tailored and was therefore constitutional. In *Gratz*, however, the Court found that an undergraduate admissions program involving minority preferences was not narrowly tailored, and consequently was not constitutional.

For proponents of affirmative action in the public employment context, these opinions were not directly helpful, but the reasoning underlying the Court's finding that student body diversity served a compelling state interest could be relevant. In essence, the Court found that diversity within a student body was compelling because it enhanced the ability of the university to do its job. That is, the Court was persuaded that diversity improves the learning environment within a university of college. To the extent that a similar rationale could be developed in support of affirmative action in public employment, the constitutionality of affirmative action in that context might also be strengthened. Such an argument could conceivably be built from the literature on representative bureaucracy and the fact, as noted at the beginning of this chapter, that a representative public workforce helps to ensure that all interests are reflected in policy-making and implementation processes. Of course, the composition of the Supreme Court has changed since 2003. Justice O'Connor, who was instrumental in the Court's decision in *Grutter*, was replaced by John G. Roberts, who is now the Chief Justice and is not likely to be as sympathetic to affirmative action as was Justice O'Connor.

## EQUAL EMPLOYMENT OPPORTUNITY AND AFFIRMATIVE ACTION IN THE FUTURE

Will affirmative action survive long into the twenty-first century? If the employment of minorities and women continues to increase in areas where they are currently underrepresented, it will eventually become difficult to sustain political support for preferential forms of the policy. Ultimately, then, such practices may come to an end. But, of course, the debate will focus, and to a considerable extent has already focused, on the question of how much progress for minorities and women is sufficient. At this time, women and minorities remain underrepresented in higher-level positions in many government agencies, so we can expect the issue to remain on the agenda for some time to come, provided there is no action by the Supreme Court to tighten current Constitutional limitations imposed on preferential programs. Such a ruling by the Court could come, however, in the form of a very restrictive interpretation of the circumstances that would comprise a government interest sufficiently compelling to enable preferential affirmative action in public employment to survive strict scrutiny. Of course, preferential affirmative action by the federal government could be curtailed also through Congressional action, and states may move to prohibit such policies, as has already been done in California, Washington, and Michigan.

What will be left of affirmative action if goals and preferential policies are eliminated? In that situation, future programs might resemble affirmative action typical of the early 1960s, based largely on minority outreach or recruitment efforts. Employers, for example, could still work to attract minorities or women into their pool of applicants, but actual selection decisions would be required to be free from the consideration of race or sex. Whether such policies will be effective in overcoming discrimination against women and minority group members is open to question. One factor that may work to the advantage of minorities, however, is the ever-increasing racial and ethnic diversity in the United States. As minorities become a larger segment of the population nationally, many organizations may find increased advantages in drawing on the talents and abilities of all people, regardless of racial or ethnic background. The manner in which this factor will ultimately operate, and the effectiveness of future efforts to combat discrimination, will be revealed in the coming years.

With respect to federal law and the regulation of state equal employment opportunity programs, there have been several significant rulings by the Supreme Court since the mid-1990s. In 1996, for example, in *Seminole Tribe v. Florida*, the Court ruled that Congress does not have power under Article I of the constitution to abrogate a state's sovereign immunity in federal court. In other words, state governments cannot be sued in federal court for a failure to implement provisions of federal law enacted pursuant to the authority of Congress contained in Article I. The

Supreme Court's decision in this case rested on an expansive interpretation of the Eleventh Amendment to the constitution, and it could have grave implications for state employees seeking relief from alleged state violations of a wide variety of federal statutes that presumably would include the Civil Rights Act of 1991 and the Equal Employment Opportunity Act of 1972 which establish and outline state government responsibilities under Title VII of the Civil Rights Act of 1964. In effect, these and other laws may apply to the states, but state employees may not have the ability to sue states to seek enforcement unless, of course, the states wave their rights to immunity. In 1999, in a similar case, *Alden et al. v. Maine*, the Court ruled that Congress also lacks the power to abrogate a state's sovereign immunity in state court. This ruling, based on the same reasoning as that in *Seminole*, has the effect of preventing state employees from suing a non-consenting state in its own courts to force compliance with federal law. Finally, in what to date may be the most significant development along these lines, the Court ruled in January of 2000 in *Kimel v. Florida Board of Regents* that the application of provisions of the Age Discrimination in Employment Act of 1967, which would allow state government employees to sue their employers under the law, also represented an unconstitutional abrogation of state sovereign immunity by Congress, acting under authority of the Fourteenth Amendment. Though practical implications of these decisions are not entirely clear, they raise fundamental questions about the effectiveness of federal statutory law as a mechanism to combat discriminatory behavior by state governments, and it may well be that state law itself will become the primary check against discriminatory behavior by state government institutions in the future.

## REFERENCES

*Adarand v. Pena*, 515 U.S. 200 (1995).
*Alden et al. v. Maine*, 527 U.S. 706 (1999).
*Bolling v. Sharpe*, 347 U.S. 497 (1954).
*City of Richmond v. Croson*, 488 U.S. 469 (1989).
Edley, Christopher, Jr. 1996. *Not All Black and White: Affirmative Action, Race, and American Values.* New York: Hill and Wang.
*Firefighters v. City of Cleveland*, 478 U.S. 501 (1986).
*Firefighters Local v. Stotts*, 467 U.S. 561 (1984).
Goldstein, M., and R. S. Smith. 1976. The Estimated Impact of the Antidiscrimination Program Aimed at Federal Contractors. *Industrial and Labor Relations Review* 29 (4):523–543.
Graham, Hugh Davis. 1990. *The Civil Rights Era: Origins and Development of National Policy, 1960–1972.* New York: Oxford University Press.
*Griggs v. Duke Power Company*, 401 U.S. 425 (1971).
Grossman, J. B., and R. Wells. 1988. *Constitutional Law and Judicial Policy Making.* New York: Longman.
*Grutter v. Bollinger*, 539 U.S. 306 (2003).
Hays, Steven. 1998. Staffing the Bureaucracy: Employee Recruitment and Selection. In *Handbook of Human Resource Management in Government*, Stephen E. Condrey, ed. San Francisco: Jossey-Bass, pp. 298–321.
Holmes, S. A. 1995. Programs Based on Sex and Race Are Under Attack: Dole Seeks Elimination. *New York Times:* March 16, p. 1A.
*Hopwood v. State of Texas*, 78 F. 3d 932 (5th Cir., 1996).
Hyclak, T., and L. W. Taylor. 1992. Some New Historical Evidence on the Impact of Affirmative Action: Detroit, 1972. *The Review of Black Political Economy* 21 (2):81–98.
*Johnson v. Board of Regents of the University System of Georgia*, 263 F. 3d 1234 (11th Cir. 2001).
*Johnson v. Transportation Agency, Santa Clara County, California*, 480 U.S. 616 (1987).

Kellough, J. Edward. 1989. *Federal Equal Employment Opportunity Policy and Numerical Goals and Timetables: An Impact Assessment.* New York: Praeger.

———. 1991. The Supreme Court, Affirmative Action, and Public Management: Where Do We Stand Today? *The American Review of Public Administration* 21, 3 (September):255–269.

———. 2000. The Americans with Disabilities Act: A Note on Personnel Policy Impacts in State Government. *Public Personnel Management* 29, 2 (Summer):211–224.

———. 2006. *Understanding Affirmative Action: Politics, Discrimination, and the Search for Justice.* Washington D.C.: Georgetown University Press.

Kellough, J. Edward, and Katherine C. Naff. 2004. Responding to a Wake-Up Call: An Examination of Federal Agency Diversity Management Programs. *Administration and Society* 36 (1):62–90.

Kellough, J. Edward, and David H. Rosenbloom. 1992. Representative Bureaucracy and the EEOC: Did Civil Service Reform Make a Difference? In *The Promise and Paradox of Civil Service Reform,* Patricia W. Ingraham and David H. Rosenbloom, eds. Pittsburgh: University of Pittsburgh Press, pp. 245–266.

*Kimel v. Florida Board of Regents,* 528 U.S. 62 (2001).

Krislov, Samuel. 1967. *The Negro in Federal Employment: The Quest for Equal Opportunity.* New York: Praeger.

Leonard, Jonathan S. 1985. What Promises Are Worth: The Impact of Affirmative Action Goals. *Journal of Human Resources* 20 (1):3–20.

Meier, Kenneth J. 1993. Representative Bureaucracy: A Theoretical and Empirical Exposition. In *Research in Public Administration,* James L. Perry, ed. New Greenwich, Connecticut: JAI Press, pp. 1–35.

Meier, Kenneth J., and Joseph Stewart, Jr. 1992. The Impact of Representative Bureaucracies: Educational Systems and Public Policies. *The American Review of Public Administration* 22, 3 (September): 157–171.

Naff, Katherine C., and J. Edward Kellough. 2003. Ensuring Employment Equity: Are Federal Diversity Programs Making a Difference? *International Journal of Public Administration* 26 (12): 1307–1336.

Price, Vivian. 2002. Race, Affirmative Action, and Women's Employment in U.S. Highway Construction. *Feminist Economics* 8 (2): 87–113.

Reed, Merl E. 1991. *Seedtime for the Modern Civil Rights Movement: The President's Committee on Fair Employment Practice, 1941–1946.* Baton Rouge: Louisiana State University Press.

Rosenbloom, David H. 1977. *Federal Equal Employment Opportunity: Politics and Public Personnel Administration.* New York: Praeger.

*Seminole Tribe v. Florida,* 517 U.S. 44 (1996).

Selden, Sally Coleman. 1997. *The Promise of Representative Bureaucracy: Diversity and Responsiveness in a Government Agency.* Armonk, New York: M. E. Sharpe.

Selden, Sally Coleman, Jeffery L. Brudney, and J. Edward Kellough. 1998. Bureaucracy as a Representative Institution: Toward a Reconciliation of Bureaucratic Government and Democratic Theory. *American Journal of Political Science* 42, 3 (July):717–744.

Selig, Joel L. 1987. Affirmative Action in Employment: The Legacy of a Supreme Court Majority. *Indiana Law Journal* 63:301–368.

*Smith v. University of Washington School of Law,* 233 F. 3d 1188 (9th Cir. 2000).

Stephanopoulos, George, and Christopher Edley, Jr. 1995. *Affirmative Action Review: Report to the President.* Washington D.C.: U.S. Government Printing Office.

*Steelworkers v. Weber,* p. 205 (1979).

Taylor, Bron Raymond. 1991. *Affirmative Action at Work: Law, Politics, and Ethics.* Pittsburgh: University of Pittsburgh Press.

Thomas, R. Roosevelt. 1990. From Affirmative Action to Affirming Diversity. *Harvard Business Review* 68 (2):107–117.

*United States v. Paradise,* 480 U.S. 149 (1987).

*United Steelworkers of America v. Weber,* 443 U.S. 193 (1979).

*Wards Cove Packing Company v. Atonio,* 490 U.S. 642 (1989).

Wilkins, Vicky M., and Lael R. Keiser. 2006. Linking Passive and Active Representation by Gender: The Case of Child Support Agencies. *Journal of Public Administration Research and Theory* 16 (1):87–102.

*Wygant v. Jackson Board of Education,* 476 U.S. 267 (1986).

# 15

# Gender and Workplace Issues

MARY E. GUY
University of Colorado Denver

SUSAN SPICE
Florida State University

## INTRODUCTION

Gender is a significant influence in the workplace. It shapes career choices, job opportunities, mentoring networks, promotions, and salary. These consequences combine to affect career ceilings, the degree to which a position affords autonomy and discretion, and the amount of retirement benefits. How can gender affect so many issues? This is the subject of the chapter. We explain the effect of gender in the workplace and how the HR function factors into the equation.

To start, we look at how employment for women in government compares to employment in private industry. Figure 15.1 shows that the workforce is almost half women and half men. In 1960, the workforce was predominantly male, with men comprising two-thirds of all workers. By now, men comprise only 52 percent.

In contrast to the civilian labor force as a whole, the public sector workforce shows a similar trend but the degree of parity lags somewhat. Figure 15.2 shows that while almost 48 percent of workers in business establishments are women, only 43 percent of federal workers are women and 45 percent of workers in state and local governments are women.

It is likely that some of the difference between the private and public sectors results from contracting out service delivery. Women predominate in the health and human services occupations and much of this work is contracted out to nonprofits and private businesses. There is no way to tell how many women and men are employed by nonprofits and private businesses but whose salaries are paid through government contracts.

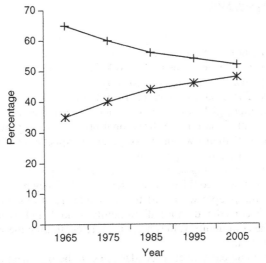

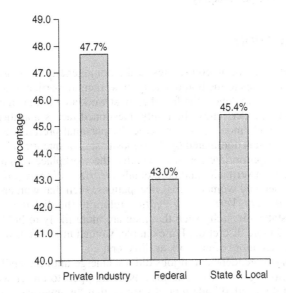

Source: U.S. Department of Labor, 1998; U.S. Equal Employment Opportunity Commission, 2000, 2005b.

**FIGURE 15.1   Gender Composition of Civilian Labor Force**

Source: U.S. Equal Employment Opportunity Commission, 2005a,b, 2006.

**FIGURE 15.2   Percentage of Female Workers in Private Industry Compared to Government**

## EMBEDDED PATHWAYS

To understand the dynamics of gender, per se, and how girls are reinforced for one set of choices while boys are reinforced for another, we describe the confluence of forces that create gender differences in the workplace. There are, for lack of a better term, embedded pathways that diverge for boys and girls and result in different career trajectories. These pathways result from the messages that they receive as children. As if scripted, girls are steered to one set of behaviors while boys are steered to another. This is not a one-directional process. The pathway reflects the combined influences of their own interests, parental expectations, individual skills and abilities, and occupational preparation.

Organizations are nothing more than a group of people who come together to achieve a mission that none could achieve independently. They reflect the mores and cultural values of the people who staff them. Gender relations within an agency reflect that which is considered "normal" in family, school, and social settings. The more egalitarian the community values are, the more egalitarian the workplace practices are, and vice versa.

Roles in the home carry over to gender roles in the organization. Women and men who behave in traditional gender roles are the norm. Those who bend accepted stereotypes are outliers and perturb the "comfort zone" of the organization. Hires and promotions that defy the "normal" are unusual and must withstand heightened scrutiny from peers, subordinates, and superiors. HR processes usually reinforce the norm. This gives rise to job segregation, status differentials between female-dominated and male-dominated jobs, and pay inequity.

## JOB SEGREGATION

Just as housing segregation contributes to the homogeneity of neighborhoods, job segregation contributes to the homogeneity of workers in particular jobs. We use the term *job segregation* to denote the fact that most workers work primarily with members of their own gender. Thus, the rarely questioned fact is that there are de facto "women's jobs" and "men's jobs." Whether by personal preference, tradition, discomfort in a job that is dominated by the opposite sex, or intentional "lockout" from jobs not thought appropriate for one's gender, the workplace remains segregated. This is the case both vertically and horizontally. *Horizontal segregation* refers to the distribution of men and women across occupations, such that women are clerks and men are truck drivers. *Vertical segregation* refers to the distribution of men and women in the status hierarchy such that men are more likely to hold jobs at higher ranks that afford more discretion. For example, women more often work as assistant directors while men more often work as directors.

The theory of gender-neutral jobs did not emerge until the civil rights era. Up until 1969 it was legal to advertise jobs as being open to either women or men. Newspaper "Help Wanted" ads would specify that "women need not apply" for men's jobs, and vice versa. Though EEOC guidelines issued in 1969 put an end to publicly announcing which gender would fill the job, there remain informal expectations among hiring authorities as well as job applicants. This holds true for administrative posts as well as lower-level jobs.

Holdovers from overt job segregation are still apparent in the workplace. It is rare that a job title will have about half women and half men. It is more likely to be skewed in one direction or the other. There are exceptions to the pattern, but by and large, an office will be predominately male or predominately female. Women's jobs include a narrower range of occupations than men's. They dominate in clerical jobs and low-end service occupations; as professionals they are most likely to be teachers, nurses, or social workers. Because "women's" jobs pay less, women are more likely to work in "men's" jobs than vice versa. On average, jobs for which men are thought more capable pay about 24 percent more than jobs for which women are thought more capable (Guy and Killingsworth, 2007). About three-fourths of all paraprofessionals are women and an even higher percentage of support jobs are held by women. Though these jobs require skills of a level comparable to the skills required of craft workers, an occupational category that is 95 percent male, they are compensated at lower rates because they are "women's work."

Table 15.1 shows the pattern of employment in states, counties, cities, and special districts. If there were no job segregation, each of these categories would have about 45 percent female employees and 55 percent male employees because 45 percent of the state and local government workforce is female. Instead, for other than professionals and technicians, the categories are lopsided—the jobs are held either by women or by men.

Vertical segregation is perpetuated by preconceived notions about masculinity and femininity. Leadership is often equated with masculinity, and followership is often equated with femininity. Likewise, communication styles that accompany leadership, such as directness, forthrightness, assertiveness—are congratulated in men but criticized when practiced by women. This makes it difficult for women to advance into leadership posts and excel. This difficulty is made obvious by looking at the gender composition of federal ranks, especially at the highest levels. Table 15.2 demonstrates that women are concentrated at the lower ranks in the federal workforce while men are concentrated at the upper ranks. The lowest federal grade is GS 1 and the highest is GS 15. The Senior Pay Levels rank above the grade classifications. In this highest rank, although there are few women, there are no differences between their responsibilities and those of their male peers (Dolan, 2004).

### TABLE 15.1   State and Local Government Employment, 2005

| Job Category | Percentage Held by Women |
|---|---|
| Administrative support | 86 |
| Paraprofessionals | 74 |
| Professionals | 56 |
| Technicians | 43 |
| Officials/administrators | 38 |
| Service/maintenance | 24 |
| Protective service | 19 |
| Skilled craft | 5 |
| Total | 45 |

Source: U.S. Equal Employment Opportunity Commission, 2005a.

**TABLE 15.2   Percentage of Women Workers in Federal Employment, 2004**

| Grade Grouping | Percentage of Women | Percentage of Men |
|---|---|---|
| GS 1–4 | 64 | 36 |
| GS 5–8 | 65 | 35 |
| GS 9–11 | 49 | 51 |
| GS 12–13 | 39 | 61 |
| GS 14–15 | 31 | 69 |
| Senior pay levels | 26 | 74 |

*Source:* U.S. Office of Personnel Management, 2005a,b,c.

## GENDERED JOBS/GENDERED WAGES

According to 2004 data, women who work in public administration earn about 76 percent of what men earn. This is about 4 percent lower than the average wage differential across all occupations, which is 80 percent (U.S. Bureau of Labor Statistics, 2005:57). Why does this difference persist forty years after the Equal Pay Act? It would seem that job segregation holds the answer. However, this answer may be wishful thinking. There is no occupational category reported by the Department of Labor (DOL) in which men's and women's wages are at parity. The wage differential across all job categories ranges from a low of 58 percent in finance and insurance jobs to a high of 95 percent in the construction industry.

Today it is common to find agencies whose lowest paid workers are predominantly women and whose highest paid workers are predominantly men. It is common to find that men hold most of the jobs that provide autonomy and administrative discretion and most of the women hold jobs that are routine, dead-end, and rule bound. For example, only about 15 to 20 percent of city managers are women and the preponderance of these are in smaller jurisdictions. Moreover, there is some evidence that women managers are typically accorded less policy-making discretion than their male peers (Zhang and Yang, 2007; Zhang, 2007).

In the job market, women and men start out fairly even when they enter the workforce but their paths soon diverge. For workers ages 16 to 24, women earn 95 percent as much as men. Then women's wages begin to plateau while men's continue to rise. In the age range of 25 to 34 years, women earn 88 percent of their male peers. By the time they reach their peak earnings years, ages 45 to 54, women earn 73.5 percent of what men earn. As their careers unfold, men can expect to move higher up the career ladder, to hold jobs that afford more discretion and autonomy, and to enjoy higher career earnings (U.S. Bureau of Labor Statistics, 2007).

Why is this the case? Two reasons account for most of the difference. First, many HR practices that are taken for granted were designed decades ago for married men whose wives did not work out of the home. These practices are the legacy of the 1800s when it was thought fair to pay less to women than to men. Second, the type of work that women predominately perform—because women do it—is compensated at lower rates. The following discussion of emotional labor explains this.

## Emotion Work in Public Service Jobs

A recently recognized element in public service jobs is emotional labor. It is that work which requires the engagement, suppression, and/or evocation of the worker's emotions in order to get the job done. The performance encompasses a range of personal and interpersonal skills, including the ability to evoke and display emotions one does not actually feel, to sense the affect of the other and alter one's own affect accordingly, and to elicit the desired emotional response from the other. It is required in jobs that require face-to-face or voice-to-voice communication. Thus, most street-level workers—counter clerks, caseworkers, call takers, police officers—must perform it in order to do their jobs (Guy, Newman, and Mastracci, 2008; Norsby and DeHart-Davis, 2007).

Emotional labor can be characterized as falling into two categories, caritas and macho. *Caritas* represents expressions of caring, nurturance, empathy, and supportiveness. *Macho* represents "tougher than tough" emotional expressions, characteristic of law enforcement and corrections officers. Although there are few gender differences when women and men in the same jobs are compared in terms of the degree to which they perform emotion work, there are significant differences in the types of jobs that require emotional labor, with those requiring macho expressions more likely to employ men and more likely to pay higher wages. It matters not that workers self-select into, and out of, jobs where the emotional labor demands exceed their comfort level. What does matter is that those jobs that require more caritas pay less because they treat feminine caritas as less worthy than masculine toughness.

Traditional "women's work" (such as casework, education, and health care) has been undervalued in part because it is thought of as an extension of women's family and household responsibilities, and therefore does not require any special or additional skills. The performance of caritas remains invisible because it is rare for annual appraisals to include ratings that reflect its performance. Because it is not rated as a skill, it does not factor into salary considerations. In other words, such work is "essentialized" and treated as a "comes with" rather than as a compensable job-related performance.

Workplace patterns are a microcosm of societal norms. These norms change ever so slowly and remnants of a bygone era remain. Classification and compensation schemes reward "men's" jobs with higher wages, more autonomy, and more discretion, while "women's" jobs are accorded lower pay, less autonomy, and less discretion. A look at the past helps to explain this. Paul Van Riper's history of the U.S. civil service details the "otherness" of women as they sought federal government jobs and gradual integration into the workforce.

## HISTORY OF WOMEN IN CIVIL SERVICE

The first jobs held by women in the federal government were as postmistresses in small towns or as "female clerks" within agencies such as the Treasury Department (Van Riper, 1958). It was routinely assumed that women should be paid less than men since the latter were supporting their families and it was considered morally questionable for a woman to work outside the home. After years of debate about whether women should be hired and, if so, whether they should be paid and how much, legislation was passed in 1864. It set the salary of female clerks at $600 a year, about half that of men's salaries who performed similar work. This was considered positive social policy for preserving the traditional family unit while still providing income for those women who would be destitute if not employed (Van Riper, 1958).

Although this is hard to believe now, at the time it was seen as a constructive compromise. Women were *supposed* to be wives and mothers and men were *supposed* to be the breadwinners. Employment practices were designed to perpetuate the gender balance where men worked outside the home and women worked inside the home.

A more substantial rise in the number of women in the civil service occurred after the passage of the Pendleton Act in 1883, which established merit system employment based on competitive exams, tenure, and political neutrality. About this time, the typewriter was invented. This labor saving invention allowed employers to standardize clerical duties and the job of typist was born (Goldin, 1990). Though the job classification was static and not designed to provide opportunities for upward mobility, the work was an improvement over the manufacturing jobs that were available to women at the time. By 1904 women in federal civil service counted for 7.5 percent of the total service (Van Riper, 1958). This was a dramatic increase in the proportion of women workers in government offices following the 1864 legislation that had required that they be paid for their work, if only at half the rate of men's pay.

With the outbreak of World War I, government needed an influx of women workers. During that time, women received the majority of new appointments and their numbers leapt to 20 percent of civil service employees. The growing strength of women's political activism, coupled with the rapid increase of women college graduates, prompted the Civil Service Commission to act when the DOL's Women's Bureau issued a report in 1919 indicating that women were being denied access to 60 percent of civil service exams. In response, later that year the Civil Service Commission opened all tests to both women and men (Van Riper, 1958). This victory was followed by the Classification Act of 1923, which required that men and women federal employees receive equal salaries for doing the same work. This was a significant advance from the 1864 legislation that provided for women to be paid at half the rate of men.

On the heels of the suffrage movement, an era that produced unparalleled gains for women's political equality, women attended college at the same rate as men until about 1930. From then until the 1960s, though, social forces discouraged women from venturing outside the home except during the labor shortages of World War II or in cases of dire financial straits (Woloch, 1994). Despite the bubble of educated women, HR policies continued to relegate women to second-class status. A private sector example demonstrates this: Ginzberg (1966) surveyed women who had earned graduate degrees during the 1920s and quotes a respondent who held a Ph.D. in economics and worked for a leading oil company. She reported that the company "would not allow women economists to make formal reports to directors. All had to be relayed through a man" (p. 104). Though such blatant bias is rarely found today, remnants of these practices remain threaded through HR practice, especially when one looks at the number of executive posts that have never, in the history of the agency, been held by women.

This cursory history brings us back to current times and the question of why women's earnings continue to lag behind men's. In addition to the reasons already mentioned, the difference between women's and men's educational attainment is usually cited.

## EDUCATION

One explanation for why women lag behind men in earnings and promotions is that women workers do not have as much education as men. Although this was the case in the past, it no longer prevails. The past forty years have seen women achieving bachelor's and master's degrees in increasing numbers. As of 1985, the number of degrees awarded to women matched those awarded to men. Table 15.3 shows that since that time, women have steadily surpassed men in college and graduate education. The question is how does information about degrees conferred translate into workforce statistics? The answer is that in 1970, 15.7 percent of male workers and 11.2 percent of women workers held bachelor's or graduate degrees. By 2004, 32.3 percent of male workers held bachelor's or graduate degrees and 32.6 percent of women workers held bachelor's or graduate degrees. This means that there is educational parity among workers, thus negating the explanation that lack of education accounts for the inequity in pay.

The educational level of women who do not go to college also closely matches the level for men. Among workers with high school educations who did not go on to college, 28 percent are women and 31 percent are men. Among workers who have less than a high school education, 7 percent are women and 11 percent are men (U.S. Bureau of Labor Statistics, 2007:7).

The significance of women's higher educational attainment is that it takes away the ready explanation for why women's salaries lag behind men's. This parity in educational attainment levels the playing field and removes "lack of education" as a plausible explanation for pay and promotion inequities.

If there is one thing we know about higher education, it is that it instills in college graduates a desire for autonomy and discretion on the job, which are two attributes that are missing in most "women's jobs." It should come as no surprise that work conditions that used to be shrugged off as inescapable now are challenged by young women who expect nothing less than equal opportunity across the board. For this reason we can predict a growing number of legal challenges to the wage gap and other work conditions that provide less opportunity for women.

**TABLE 15.3   Percentage of College Degrees Awarded to Women, 1960–2004**

| Degree | Year | | | | | | | | | |
|---|---|---|---|---|---|---|---|---|---|---|
| | 1960 | 1965 | 1970 | 1975 | 1980 | 1985 | 1990 | 1995 | 2000 | 2004 |
| **Bachelor's** | 35.3 | 42.8 | 43.1 | 45.3 | 49.0 | 50.5 | 53.2 | 54.7 | 57.2 | 57.5 |
| **Master's** | 31.6 | 32.9 | 39.7 | 44.8 | 49.2 | 50.1 | 52.6 | 55.0 | 58.0 | 58.9 |

*Source:* U.S. Department of Labor, 1998; U.S. Census Bureau, 2006:183.

## WORKPLACES DESIGNED FOR MEN BUT INHABITED BY WOMEN

From an HR perspective, the core of the problem is that women are not men. How could a fact so obvious be a problem? The policies that govern the workplace were designed when men were the primary out-of-home workers. The standard full-time workweek was arbitrarily defined as forty hours, and benefits packages, designed for men to support their families, were attached to full-time jobs to aid in recruitment and retention. With wives to run errands, pick children up after school, shop for groceries and household items, and handle miscellaneous tasks, men were free to pursue their careers and have leisure time after work and on weekends. Concerns about workers' family obligations were not the employer's concern.

The demographics of the workforce have changed faster than the HR practices that govern classification, compensation, and benefits. As social and economic conditions evolved, women entered the workforce and remained even after they married and had children. Even the proportion of married-couple families with children under 18 in which the mother is employed grows each year. In 2004 almost two-thirds (65 percent) of mothers in traditional families where the fathers are present and there are children under age 18, were in the labor force. Additionally, increasing numbers of women are heads of households with children to support. Table 15.4 demonstrates the rapid growth of mothers in the workforce. Currently at 73 percent, the increase is gradual but continuous and shows no sign of stopping. This high proportion of mothers in the workforce means that the pressure on employers to respond to their childcare needs will continue to grow. It also negates another explanation for why women's salaries are lower—that women are paid less because they are workforce "transients," leaving the workplace for long periods while their children are young and then re-entering once children have left home.

The bottom line from these facts about women's educational levels and commitment to careers is that the wage disparity between women and men is not explained by a lack of either. The prevalence of men in higher ranks and women in lower ranks is also not explained by education or childcare responsibilities. Women's elevation to positions that afford autonomy and discretion is rife with obstacles. Metaphors are best used to capture the dynamics that result in job, pay, and promotion disparities.

### Glass Ceilings, Glass Walls, Sticky Floors, and Trap Doors

*Glass ceilings* is a term used to capture the fact that although women and men entering the workforce start out relatively even, men rise in rank at faster rates than women. While there is no obvious failing in their credentials, experience, or performance,

**TABLE 15.4    Percentage of Married Women in the Labor Force Who Had Children, 1960–2004**

| Year | | | | | | | | |
|------|------|------|------|------|------|------|------|------|
| 1960 | 1965 | 1970 | 1975 | 1980 | 1985 | 1990 | 1995 | 2004 |
| 27.6 | 32.2 | 39.7 | 44.9 | 54.1 | 60.8 | 66.3 | 70.2 | 72.8 |

*Source:* U.S. Department of Labor, 1998; U.S. Bureau of Labor Statistics, 2005:16.

women watch their male colleagues ride the escalator to higher ranks while they plateau. Tables 15.1 and 15.2 are emblematic of this. Even when controlling for years of education and experience, this dynamic prevails.

*Glass walls* refers to job segregation that frequently detours women. For example, if a woman begins her career in a staff position and excels at it, she may believe that she is eligible for promotion into a post with administrative line authority. It is likely, however, that because her work experience is in a staff function, such as legal counsel, she will be turned down for promotion into a line position because she does not have sufficient supervisory experience. Or, she may have begun work in the HR department. Although an essential function, her work experience may be treated as ancillary to, rather than central to, the service mission of the agency. Although she excelled at the glass walled job, it stands in the way of gaining the kinds of experiences that she will need to compete for top-level administrative posts.

*Sticky floors* is a metaphor that captures the situation when a woman is excellent in a staff position or as a lower-level manager and is passed over for promotion because of it. She is so good at getting people to work together and she is such a good facilitator that she is viewed more as a team member and less of a leader. Her occupational floor is "sticky," holding her down and preventing her from moving into more autonomous positions.

*Trap doors* are those events that have a significant deleterious effect on a woman's career. Primary among these is sexual harassment. Despite the presence of legal protections, a woman who becomes a victim of sexual harassment will encounter difficulty. If she allows it to continue by not filing a formal complaint, she is thought to be enabling the harassment or perhaps even inviting it. If she files a formal complaint, supporters line up either behind the harasser or her. News of the complaint travels like wildfire through the grapevine. Even when resolved in her favor, the firestorm that surrounded the complaint sticks in people's memories and a negative halo surrounds her. She often will elect to leave the agency and go to work elsewhere to silence the rumor mill and repair her reputation. This slows down what may have been, prior to the harassment, a rapid ascent up the chain of command.

These four dynamics—glass ceilings, glass walls, sticky floors, and trap doors—are roadblocks that slow women's integration into the workforce. Education serves as a ticket out of the glass ceilings, glass walls, and sticky floors. Legislation and case law attempt to bolt the trap doors.

## Plenty of Laws, Too Little Enforcement

What are the prospects for tailoring the workplace to fit the lifestyles of both women and men? Since 1963, a number of laws have been passed by Congress that should serve as levers to flatten the playing field and provide opportunities for women that match those available to men. Demands for these laws resulted from discrimination in a variety of forms: unfair salary disparities, denial of promotion opportunities, penalties for pregnancy, childbearing and childrearing, and sexual harassment. These problems have arisen because workplace policies have treated all employees as if they were men and have penalized women for their non-male characteristics, including childbearing, childrearing, and gendered roles.

Laws have been on the books for decades that require equal pay for equal work but they have been honored in the breach more often than not. The following discussion enumerates the major laws affecting women in the workplace. The Equal Pay Act of 1963 was an amendment to the Fair Labor Standards Act of 1938. It requires that employers pay equal wages for work that is substantially equal unless the employer can show that a difference in wages is attributable to a factor other than gender.

The Civil Rights Act of 1964, Title VII, makes it illegal for employers to refuse to hire or to discharge any person on the basis of sex. It outlaws discrimination with respect to compensation, terms, conditions, or privileges of employment. It also makes it unlawful to limit, segregate, or classify employees or applicants in any way that deprives them of employment opportunities or otherwise adversely affects their employment status.

Executive Order 11375, issued in 1967 extended the protections to women that had been afforded to minorities in Executive Order 11246, which was issued in 1965. It requires nondiscrimination and positive action by federal contractors on behalf of women, including recruitment, training, employment, and upgrading.

The Equal Employment Opportunity Act of 1972 was an amendment to the Civil Rights Act of 1964. It strengthened the EEOC and gave it the ability to go to court for direct enforcement action. EEOC guidelines regarding sex discrimination barred hiring based on stereotyped characterization of the sexes, classifying jobs as men's or women's, and advertising under male and female listings. As amended in 1972, the law covers federal, state, and local governments, and most companies of at least fifteen employees.

The Pregnancy Discrimination Act of 1978 prohibits discrimination on account of pregnancy. It requires that women affected by pregnancy, childbirth, or related medical conditions shall be treated the same for all employment-related purposes, including receipt of benefits under fringe benefits programs, as other persons not so affected but similar in their ability or inability to work.

The Civil Rights Act of 1991 sets standards for employers when they attempt to justify discriminatory actions or policies based on business necessity, shifts the burden of proof to the employer after the plaintiff has established a prima facie case, and provides the right to a jury trial, and compensatory and punitive damages.

The Family and Medical Leave Act of 1993 covers all employers with fifty or more employees who are employed for at least twenty weeks during the year. Employees are entitled to twelve weeks of unpaid leave during any twelve-month period for the recent birth or adoption of a child; to care for an ill child, spouse, or parent; or for the employee's own health condition that precludes working.

In combination with one another, these laws should pry open the doors of economic parity. Despite more than forty years of laws, though, conditions persist. Why? The laws are only as strong as the will to enforce them.

## PROBLEMS AND PROSPECTS

This chapter began with a discussion of how gender makes a difference in a number of workplace issues. The future will bring changes as the workplace continues to adjust to accommodate the needs of women and as employers compete for the best workers. One would be naive to assume that the embedded pathways of men and women would merge. It is reasonable to foresee adjustments to accommodate these pathways, however. Current efforts to implement more family-friendly policies is one such initiative. Employers are pressed to make the workplace more attractive to women in order to recruit and retain them.

## Balancing Family and Work

In 1950, only 34 percent of women ages 25 to 34 were in the workforce. By 1990, 74 percent were in the workforce. It is this huge increase that drove Congress to pass the Family and Medical Leave Act and President Clinton to sign it shortly after his inauguration in 1993. A recent evaluation of its impact concludes that few employees take advantage of it. In 1995, only 3.6 employees for every 100 used it. Five years later, in 2000, 6.5 per 100 employees were taking advantage of it. This amounts to about 16 percent of workers. Why so few? Fewer than two-thirds of the women who used it for leave received any pay and only 70 percent of men received pay. In essence, the act simply assures employees that they do not have to fear job loss if they take leave for family or personal medical reasons (U.S. Department of Labor, n.d.).

Increasing numbers of women in the workforce are also driving reconsideration of how, where, and in what time frame, work gets done. The proliferation of telecommuting, flextime, and contingent workers is due in large part to the numbers of women who enter the workforce and remain there throughout their childrearing years. Doing double duty—at work and at home—necessitates changes in the traditional 8 AM to 5 PM format.

Dual benefits accrue when employers become family friendly. Not only do mothers benefit, but fathers also enjoy the advantage of being able to tailor their work life to their family life rather than vice versa. Expanded leave arrangements, dependent care, choice of benefits, telecommuting, and flextime, advantage both genders. Slowly but surely, HR policies are adjusting to accommodate employees who must balance family obligations with work demands.

**Part-Time Employment.**  The definition of full-time versus part-time is important for its economic consequences. Unlike their full-time compatriots, part-timers are usually ineligible for benefits, such as paid vacation; personal and sick leave; health, disability, and life insurance; and retirement. This arbitrary custom has a disparate impact on women, who hold 68 percent of all part-time jobs (U.S. Bureau of Labor Statistics, 2007). Because of the cultural burdens of caregiving, women work a double shift, on call at both the office and home. To help them cope with double demands on their time, many women elect to work part-time jobs so that they can "manage" both shifts.

**Flexible Schedules.**  Greater flexibility in work schedules, with greater choices for where work is conducted and when the workday begins and ends, is becoming more common. The Internet has made telecommuting from home a reasonable alternative for many knowledge workers.

The proportion of full-time workers on flexible schedules rose sharply in the 1990s (Bureau of Labor Statistics, 1998). In 1991, 15.1 percent of full-time workers were on flexible schedules; by 1997, 27.6 percent were. In 1997, 28.8 percent of private sector workers had flexible schedules while only 21.7 percent of government

TABLE 15.5    Percentage of Workers with Flexible Schedules, 2004

| Type of Business Establishment | Women | Men | All Workers |
|---|---|---|---|
| Public sector | 18.4 | 22.6 | 20.3 |
| Federal | 30.0 | 28.0 | 28.8 |
| State | 26.6 | 30.7 | 28.4 |
| Local | 12.0 | 16.1 | 13.7 |
| Private sector | 28.9 | 29.0 | 27.5 |

*Source:* U.S. Bureau of Labor Statistics, 2004.

workers did. Flexible work schedules were not distributed evenly across all levels of government then, nor are they now. In 1997, federal employment offered the highest amount at 34.5 percent of workers; 29.4 percent of state workers had it, and 13.1 percent of local government workers had it. Table 15.5 shows the status of flextime in 2004. The rapid advances of the 1990s have plateaued and the percentage of workers with flextime is actually somewhat smaller than it was in 1997 except in local government.

**Expanded Concepts of Paid Leave.**    For full-time workers, an increasing array of leave benefits has developed to accommodate employee needs. The old standbys of sick leave and vacation leave have given way to personal leave, leave for family sickness, family leave for childbirth and adoptions, unpaid sabbaticals, and more. An expanded concept of sick leave is also on the horizon. On June 10, 2000, President Clinton announced family sick leave for federal employees. In the past, federal employees were allowed to use up to thirteen days of sick leave each year for family care purposes. Now, employees may use up to twelve weeks of sick leave each year to care for a family member with a serious health condition. The definition of family includes an employee's spouse and parents-in-law; children and their spouses, parents, siblings and their spouses, and "any individual related by blood or affinity whose close association with the employee is the equivalent of a family relationship" (*Federal Times*, 2000:10).

**Benefits.**    Benefits packages are being reworked to compensate for the fact that workers from dual career households require options rather than take-it-or-leave-it benefits. For example, if a husband works for an agency that offers good family health insurance and the wife also works for an employer that provides good family health insurance, there is no need for both to subscribe. The worker who opts not to subscribe to an offered benefit has nothing to substitute for it and foregoes the benefit. A cafeteria plan, on the other hand, provides each worker with a choice of benefits. Benefits are offered for selection as if on a buffet line. Workers are allotted a set number of dollars worth of benefits. It is up to them to select the combination of benefits within the prescribed dollar amount that best suits their needs. This is more equitable than the traditional practice of employees opting either in or out of specific benefits with nothing to substitute for the benefits declined. Included in the new buffet of benefits are funds to cover child care and elder care costs, medical expense accounts, pension alternatives, and insurance for legal services.

**Childcare.**   Childcare is a concern from both the benefits standpoint and the classification and compensation side of the coin. As a benefit for parents, it is a valuable component of a compensation package. For public entities that provide day care services, training and compensation of childcare workers is an emerging concern. The wages of childcare workers are notoriously low. As a result, turnover among workers is high, which jeopardizes quality and raises operational costs. Many states impose minimum training and education requirements for childcare workers and this will grow as quality problems catch the public eye (Kimmel, 2000).

An added dimension to childcare is the time that mothers take off from work immediately following childbirth. A recent study in the State of Minnesota reveals that new mothers with paid maternity leave take approximately four more weeks off than new mothers whose leave is unpaid. This is a substantial difference and suggests that the mere availability of unpaid maternal leave works better in theory than in practice for women who are economically vulnerable (McGovern et al., 2000). Many women have no choice but to forego maternity leave if it means foregoing income.

**Eldercare.**   By the year 2030, the percentage of the population age 65 and older will rise to 20 percent of the total U.S. population (Weinberg, 2000). Eldercare is becoming a major concern for working adults and for women in particular. At their peak earnings years, women find themselves pulled away from their jobs to care for frail parents and in-laws. The more that employers can do to accommodate the time and energy demands of eldercare, the less likely it is that they will endure productivity slumps or, worse, lose valuable employees.

**Work/Life Specialists.**   Leave policies, innovations in benefits packages, and accommodating child and eldercare concerns come under the heading of work/life issues. Work/life professionals are HR specialists who focus on workplace innovations that ease the tensions between family obligations of workers and the employer's concern for productivity. Those who study productivity and are sympathetic to the cross-cutting pressures of family and work argue that work/life innovations reduce stress and absenteeism. It is up to work/life specialists to assess the effectiveness of innovations and determine which have the greatest impact on retention and productivity.

Employee benefits, altered work arrangements, and a process for introducing and monitoring family-friendly HR practices, are innovations that are employed in dots and dashes around the country. The prospect for full-scale accommodation to the difference that gender makes—and the time frame for reaching it—still awaits.


## CONCLUSION

This chapter has touched on a number of issues that differentiate men from women in the workplace. The pay gap, job segregation, and forfeiture of benefits in part-time work, all disadvantage women. Despite a variety of federal laws and the fact that more women achieve college degrees than men, the workplace is not a level playing field. The chapter also touches on HR practices that advantage both women and men. The expanding concept of paid leave and accommodation to family responsibilities frees men to play a more active role in the family than their fathers could. In order to have enduring change, alterations in the standard way of doing things must advantage both women and men. Otherwise, a backlash occurs and women's gains will be imperiled. The national effort to do away with affirmative action provides a case in point.

Though affirmative action has not closed the pay gap, it has opened doors for women. First, it raised people's consciousness about fairness and giving women a chance in jobs that had formerly shut them out. Now there are women working on public works crews, as police officers and firefighters, and as agency heads. Many have line authority where they used to occupy only staff positions. The anti-affirmative action trend across the country puts many of these gains at risk. The door slammed shut to women once before—in the 1930s. If history is a predictor, social forces are likely to push back some of these advances in a pattern of "three steps forward, two steps backward" (Guy, 1993). Women's integration into the workforce has been by fits and starts rather than by continuous, steady progress.

## Workplace Changes

What shape would a gender neutral work environment take? A gender neutral workplace would mean that people no longer take note when a woman is appointed to head an agency. At this point, it still makes headlines when a woman is named to the top job. Deil Wright and his colleagues have tracked the rate at which women have been appointed to head agencies across the states (Bowling et al., 2006; Bowling and Wright, 1998; Wright, 1999). Their work indicates that there has been a steady increase in the proportion of agencies headed by women. In 1964, only 2 percent of agencies were headed by women. By 1998, 22 percent of agencies were headed by women. By now, about one out of three agencies are headed by women. There have been a number of new agencies established and this growth in state government is the largest contributor to the increasing number of women agency heads. The greatest inroads have been in the newest agencies, such as Elder Affairs, Victims Advocacy, and agencies that focus on arts, history, and cultural events.

At the federal level, workforce planners project that the demand for secretaries, administrative assistants, and clerks, will continue to decline (Partnership for Public Service, 2007). Currently, women occupy the vast majority of these jobs. As these typecast jobs disappear and newer jobs are developed, they will probably be more gender neutral. This gradual transformation of the workplace will continue to flatten the playing field.

Employers will be faced with fewer and fewer applicants for predominantly female jobs unless they change their wage-setting practices to make sure they are paying equal wages for work that is of equivalent value. Job evaluation studies are a useful tool for comparing all positions within a jurisdiction, despite job dissimilarity. These studies measure several factors including the skill, effort, responsibility, and working conditions of each job. They can head off expensive litigation by identifying and correcting HR practices that have a disparate impact.

In summary, the prognosis is mixed. Judging from history, women periodically make significant inroads into positions once open only to men. Progress continues for a couple of decades, only for a backlash to occur. During the backlash, women recede into less desirable jobs that offer lower pay. When the problem regains public visibility, doors open once again and women regain opportunities for the more desirable jobs. An important function of the HR department is to monitor patterns of employment in the agency or jurisdiction and take note of those areas where job segregation is keen. Succession planning and staff development programs can be used to help promising workers advance out of less desirable jobs. Constant vigilance is required to ensure that the embedded pathways of women and men bring advantage rather than disadvantage.

## REFERENCES

Bowling, Cynthia J., and Deil S. Wright. 1998. Change and Continuity in State Administration: Administrative Leadership Across Four Decades. *Public Administration Review* 58 (5):429–444.

Bowling, Cynthia J., Christine A. Kelleher, Jennifer Jones, and Deil S. Wright. 2006. Cracked Ceilings, Firmer Floors, and Weakening Walls: Trends and Patterns in Gender Representation Among Executives Leading American State Agencies, 1970–2000. *Public Administration Review* 66 (6):823–836.

Dolan, Julie. 2004. Gender Equity: Illusion or Reality for Women in the Federal Executive Service? *Public Administration Review* 64 (3):299–308.

*Federal Times.* 2000. Sick Leave for Family Care. June 26, p. 10.

Ginzberg, Eli. 1966. *Life Styles of Educated Women.* NY: Columbia University Press.

Goldin, Claudia. 1990. *Understanding the Gender Gap: An Economic History of American Women.* Oxford: Oxford University Press.

Guy, Mary E. 1993. Three Steps Forward, Two Steps Backward: The Status of Women's Integration into Public Management. *Public Administration Review* 53 (4):285–292.

Guy, Mary E., and Jennifer Killingsworth. 2007. Framing Gender, Framing Work: The Disparate Impact of Traditional HRM Practices. In *Strategic Public Personnel Administration: Building and Managing Human Capital for the 21st Century,* vol. 2, A. Farazmand, ed. Westport, CT: Praeger, pp. 399–418.

Guy, Mary E., Meredith A. Newman, and Sharon H. Mastracci. 2008. *Emotional Labor: Putting the Service in Public Service.* Armonk, NY: M. E. Sharpe, Inc.

Kimmel, Jean. 2000. Employment-Related Child Care Issues: What We Know and What We Do Not. *Employment Research* 7 (1):5–6. Available at W.E. Upjohn Institute, 300 S. Westnedge Avenue, Kalamazoo, MI 49007-4686, <www.upjohninst.org>.

McGovern, Patricia, Bryan Down, Dwenda Gjerdingen, Ira Moscovice, Laura Kochevar, and Sarah Murphy. 2000. The Determinants of Time Off Work after Childbirth. *Journal of Health Politics, Policy and Law* 25 (3):527–564.

Norsby, Douglas J., and Leisha DeHart-Davis. 2007. *Gender Differences in Emotional Labor Processes.* Paper Delivered at the Public Management Research Association Conference. Tucson, AZ, October 25–27, 2007.

Partnership for Public Service. 2007. *Where the Jobs Are: Mission Critical Opportunities for America,* 2nd ed. Available at <http://www.ourpublicservice.org>. Accessed on November 7, 2007.

U.S. Bureau of Labor Statistics. (1998, March 26). Workers on Flexible and Shift Schedules in 1997 Summary. USDL 98-119. Available at <http://stats.bls.gov/news.release/flex.nws.htm>. Accessed on July 8, 2000; no longer available.

———. 2004. Table 2. Flexible Schedules: Full-Time Wage and Salary Workers by Sex, Occupation, and Industry, May 2004. Available at <http://www.bls.gov/news.release/flex.t02.htm>. Accessed on September 2, 2008.

———. (2005, May). *Women in the Labor Force: A Databook.* Report 985. Washington, DC: Government Printing Office.

———. (2007, September). *Highlights of Women's Earnings in 2006.* Washington, D.C.: Government Printing Office. U.S. Department of Labor, Bureau of Labor Statistics. 2007. *Highlights of Women's Earnings in 2006,* p. 16. Available at <http://www.bls.gov/cps/cpswom2006.pdf>. Accessed on October 23, 2007.

U.S. Census Bureau. 2006. *Statistical Abstract of the United States: 2007,* 126th ed. Washington, D.C.: Government Printing Office.

U.S. Department of Labor. n.d. Chapter 8 Summary and Conclusions. Available at <http://www.dol.gov/esa/whd/fmla/chapter8.htm>. Accessed on September 2, 2008.

———— (Women's Bureau). (1998, June 10). *Equal Pay: A Thirty-Five Year Perspective.* Washington, D.C.: Government Printing Office.

U.S. Equal Employment Opportunity Commission. 2000. Occupational Employment in Private Industry by Race/Ethnic Group/Sex, and by Industry, United States, 2000. Available at <http://www.eeoc.gov/stats/jobpat/2000/national.html>. Accessed on October 30, 2007.

————. 2005a. National Employment Summary: State and Local Government Information (EEO-4), 2005. Table 6: State Summary by Job Category. Available at <http://www.eeoc.gov/stats/jobpat_eeo4/2005/us.pdf>. Accessed on October 30, 2007.

————. 2005b. Occupational Employment in Private Industry by Race/Ethnic Group/Sex and by Industry, United States, 2005. Available at <http://www.eeoc.gov/stats/jobpat/2005/national.html>. Accessed on October 30, 2007.

————. 2006. Table A-1: Ten Year Trend, Government Wide Employment of Workers in the Federal Work Force. Available at <http://www.eeoc.gov/federal/fsp2006/aed/table_a_1.html>. Accessed on October 30, 2007.

U.S. Office of Personnel Management. 2005a. Trends by General Schedule and Related (GSR) Grade Groupings (All Employees) 1994–2004, Table 1-5. Available at <http://www.opm.gov/feddata/demograp/table1-6.pdf>. Accessed on November 5, 2007.

————. 2005b. Trends by General Schedule and Related (GSR) Grade Groupings (Men Only) 1994–2004, Table 1-6. Available at <http://www.opm.gov/feddata/demograp/table1-6.pdf>. Accessed on November 5, 2007.

————. 2005c. Trends by General Schedule and Related (GSR) Grade Groupings (Women Only) 1994–2004, Table 1-7. Available at <http://www.opm.gov/feddata/demograp/table1-7.pdf>. Accessed on November 5, 2007.

Van Riper, P. 1958. *History of the United States Civil Service.* Evanston, IL: Row, Peterson and Company.

Weinberg, Joanna K. 2000. The Past, Present, and Future of Long-Term Care—A Women's Issue? *Journal of Health Politics, Policy and Law* 25 (3):566–582.

Wright, Deil S. (1999, December). Summary of ASAP Results. Available from author c/o American State Administrators Project (ASAP), Odum Institute for Research in Social Science, The University of North Carolina, Chapel Hill, North Carolina 27599-3355.

Zhang, Yahong. 2007. *2006 Florida City Manager Survey.* Unpublished paper.

Zhang, Yahong, and Kaifeng Yang. 2007. *2007 Georgia City Manager Survey.* Unpublished paper.

# HR Information Technology Systems in State Government
## Findings from the 2007 Government Performance Project

ROBERT T. WOOTERS[*]
Lynchburg College

## INTRODUCTION

The use of information technology (IT) systems is undoubtedly on the increase in the public and private sectors. Since 1970, IT spending in the U.S. economy has grown at least hundred-fold (Mistry, 2006). Software vendor SAP reports an expected increase of around 17 percent (taking currency fluctuations into account) in software and software related service revenues for the full-year 2007, compared to the full-year 2006 (*SAP Announces 2007 Preliminary Results*, 2008). Similarly, the use of information systems in the human resource (HR) function has grown steadily over the past several years (Ngai and Wat, 2006). Organizations can realize a wide range of benefits through the use of HR information systems, including reduced HR transaction times, a more efficient HR operation overall, and the increased use of the HR function in achieving the strategic goals of the organization (Beckers and Bsat, 2002). This chapter discusses the use of IT systems in the HR management function in state governments by summarizing the relevant results from the 2007 survey performed by the Government Performance Project (GPP), a research project of The Pew Center on the States.

---

*Produced by Robert Wooters in partnership with the Government Performance Project of the Pew Center on the States. The views expressed are those of the author and do necessarily reflect the views of the Government Performance Project, the Pew Center on the States or The Pew Charitable Trusts.

## OVERVIEW

Advances in IT have clearly altered the nature of the services that are provided by the HR function, changing both the types of activities that can be automated, and the point of access for users of the services provided by HR departments (Florkowski and Olivas-Luján, 2006). By handing over administrative tasks to automated systems, not only can cost savings be realized, but HR staff can be freed up to perform other functions. As an example of cost savings, consider the use of information systems for time and attendance management. According to *HR Magazine*, these types of tools often cut labor costs by between 5 and 10 percent in organizations that employ a significant percentage of hourly employees (Robb, 2004). Moreover, through the automation of these mundane administrative activities, HR employees are able to shift their focus to performing tasks that are more tactical in nature, tasks that help to achieve the strategic goals of the organization. In turn, this strategic planning can become easier and more powerful through the use of additional IT systems for functions such as succession planning, recruitment, knowledge management and HR data analysis.

Another benefit of the use of IT systems in HR is that employees are no longer required to engage in face-to-face meetings with HR staff for simple information or transaction-based activities. They are instead able to use telephone or computer interfaces to receive these HR services (Florkowski and Olivas-Luján, 2006). An example is the management of employee benefits. According to human capital and financial management consulting firm Watson Wyatt Worldwide (2007), the increased complexity of health benefit plans has resulted in many companies using technology to give employees access to information about their options and tools to manage their benefit plans. Through the use of HR portals, companies can provide information about multiple benefit providers in an easy-to-use format.

In 2007, the GPP investigated the ways in which state governments across the United States are benefiting from the use of IT systems as part of their HR management, with a particular interest in how these tools are helping the states to address an impending wave of retirements from state service.

## 2007 GOVERNMENT PERFORMANCE PROJECT

The Government Performance Project (GPP) is a nonpartisan, independent research project of The Pew Center on the States. Established in 1998, the GPP evaluates how well state governments perform the basic management of money, people, infrastructure, and information—four areas critical to developing and implementing public policy—every three years. This is accomplished through the use of a web-based survey, analysis of publicly available documents, and journalistic interviews. The "People" section of the GPP investigates how well states manage their employees, including the implementation of hiring, retention, development, and performance management systems. In June of 2007, states were asked to complete an extensive online survey; by December of 2007, forty-two states had completed the survey (an 84 percent response rate).

Although the subject of Human Resource Management Information Technology (HRMIT) systems had been examined in previous iterations of the GPP survey, the 2007 survey expanded the scope of the questions that addressed this topic.[1] One of the most dramatic findings of the 2004 iteration of the GPP survey was that the percentage of the workforce that was within five years of retirement eligibility exceeded 20 percent in more than half the states. The results of the 2007 survey are even more alarming: in twenty-three of the forty states that responded to this survey question, the percentage of the workforce within five years of retirement eligibility now exceeds 25 percent, with one state reporting nearly 55 percent. With this in mind, we chose to focus here on functions of IT systems that help states to recruit employees, to serve current employees more efficiently, to share and retain organizational knowledge, and to engage in strategic workforce planning.

As we will discuss shortly, HRMIT functions fall into two broad categories: those that involve the distribution of information or the automation of processes ("administrative") and those that help to achieve the strategic goals of the organization ("strategic"). We will first provide an overview of how comprehensive the states' HRMIT systems are in both of these categories, and then spotlight the following four issues:

1. *The use of hiring web sites for state government employment.* This function falls into the administrative category. Prospective applicants are able to obtain a significant amount of information about a potential employer, and the application process is somewhat automated and streamlined. This research was done through a study independent of the online GPP survey in order to more objectively evaluate the web sites.

2. *The implementation of self-service functionality through HR web portals.* This function is also categorized as administrative. HR portals offer a highly customizable, personalized, web-based point of access where employees can find essential information, tools, and services that they need to engage in HR transactions (Florkowski and Olivas-Luján, 2006). This not only frees up HR professionals from fulfilling information requests and processing transactions, but serves employees better by speeding up the transactions and giving them flexibility in when and where to use these tools. There is evidence that the availability of self-service applications increases employee satisfaction (Paetsch, 2002). Managers and HR professionals can benefit from self-service functionality as well.

3. *The use of IT systems for training and knowledge management.* Conceptually, this falls within the realm of both the administrative category and the strategic category. The online publication of training information, as well as the standardization and automation of the registration process is obviously administrative. Knowledge management, however, in the context of retaining organizational knowledge, is a critical strategic issue, especially in light of the fact that in the next ten years a full 43 percent of the U.S. workforce will be eligible for retirement (Eucker, 2007). Managers in the private and public sector alike are already engaging in emergency measures such as rehiring retired employees in order to keep institutional knowledge from walking out the door (Goldberg, 2007).

4. *The comprehensiveness and availability of the states' workforce data.* This clearly falls within the strategic category. Strategic workforce planning is the "process by which a business ensures that the right people are in the right place and at the right time to accomplish the firm's mission" (Kazan, 2005). It involves addressing the current state of the workforce, assessing future workforce needs, identifying the gap between the current and future workforce, and planning for how to fill that gap. Accurate workforce data are necessary to take the first step. Again, in light of the aging workforce, it is crucial that organizations in both the private and public sector proactively plan for their future workforce needs.

We begin the discussion with an evaluation of the comprehensiveness of the HRMIT systems that state governments have in place.

## OVERALL COMPREHENSIVENESS OF HRMIT SYSTEMS

One goal of the GPP survey was to determine how comprehensive the states' HRMIT systems are. The survey presented a checklist of various components that any organization might have as part of their HRMIT system, which was drawn from both academic literature and feature lists for commercial HR software. States were asked to indicate whether these components were currently implemented, planned for implementation in the next two fiscal years, or not implemented and not planned. As indicated earlier, functions that are implemented in an HRMIT system fall into two broad categories: administrative functions (including electronic distribution of information), and strategic functions. In order to identify those states that have implemented, or plan to implement, the most administrative and strategic components as part of their HRMIT systems, we computed two "comprehensiveness indexes" based on these two categories. These indexes were computed by assigning a value of 2 to a component if it is currently implemented, a value of 1 if the response indicates that the state plans to implement the component in the next two fiscal years, and a value of 0 if the component is not planned for implementation. These values were then summed to form each index. As shown in Table 16.1, the states that had the highest scores on the strategic index also had high scores on the administrative index[2].

The seven components considered strategic in this analysis are: career planning, competency management, knowledge management, salary planning, skills database, succession planning, and workforce planning. All other components fall into the administrative category. Reliabilities (as shown with Cronbach's alpha) for both of these factors were very high: 0.89 for the strategic grouping, and 0.88 for the administrative grouping.[3]

Six states—Georgia, Virginia, Michigan, Utah, North Carolina, and Louisiana—had a strategic index of 10 or more. These states also had high scores on the administrative index; they are capitalizing both strategically and administratively from their use of IT. They are not only taking advantage of IT systems to disseminate information and automate processes such as benefits management and payroll, but are also leveraging these systems as part of their strategic human capital management in areas such as workforce planning, knowledge management, and succession planning.

- **Georgia,** with a strategic index of 14, reported having the most components in its HRMIT system of any respondent in the survey. Every item queried on the survey is included in their system, except for labor relations management, which they do not plan to implement.
- **Virginia,** also with a strategic index of 14, reported having all but two of the components listed, indicating plans to implement attendance management as part of the HRMIT system over the next two years, and no plans to implement organizational charts. The state does note that an organizational chart tool is available elsewhere.
- **Michigan,** with a strategic index of 13, indicated that they have implemented all but three of the components, and noted plans to implement career planning and health and safety information in the next two fiscal years. The state has no plans to implement

TABLE 16.1   HRMIT Comprehensiveness Indexes

| State | Administrative | Strategic |
|---|---|---|
| Alabama | 23 | 6 |
| Arizona | 32 | 6 |
| Arkansas | 23 | 7 |
| California | 20 | 7 |
| Colorado | 12 | 0 |
| Connecticut | 21 | 0 |
| Delaware | 29 | 7 |
| Georgia | 32 | 14 |
| Idaho | 24 | 0 |
| Illinois* | n/a | n/a |
| Indiana | 26 | 6 |
| Iowa | 23 | 2 |
| Kansas | 27 | 2 |
| Louisiana | 32 | 10 |
| Maine | 18 | 4 |
| Maryland | 32 | 9 |
| Massachusetts | 15 | 6 |
| Michigan | 31 | 13 |
| Minnesota | 26 | 4 |
| Mississippi | 30 | 7 |
| Missouri | 23 | 4 |
| Montana | 28 | 9 |
| Nebraska | 22 | 2 |
| Nevada | 26 | 3 |
| New Hampshire | 22 | 2 |
| New Jersey | 17 | 7 |
| New Mexico | 33 | 7 |
| North Carolina | 30 | 11 |
| North Dakota | 19 | 0 |
| Ohio | 19 | 6 |
| Oklahoma | 16 | 0 |
| Oregon | 14 | 8 |
| Pennsylvania | 25 | 0 |
| South Carolina | 24 | 6 |
| Tennessee | 26 | 9 |
| Utah | 29 | 13 |
| Vermont | 21 | 3 |
| Virginia | 31 | 14 |
| Washington | 23 | 0 |
| West Virginia | 15 | 9 |
| Wisconsin | 33 | 7 |
| Wyoming | 15 | 7 |
| Mean | 24.07 | 5.78 |
| Standard Deviation | 5.94 | 4.06 |
| Minimum | 12 | 0 |
| Maximum | 33 | 14 |
| N | 41 | 41 |

*Note: Illinois did not respond to this survey question.

retirement planning as part of their internal HRMIT system, but indicated that retirement planning services are provided by a third-party administrator.

- **Utah,** also with a strategic index of 13, lacks four of the components listed, and has plans to implement competency management and organizational charts. The state does not plan to implement health and safety information or labor relations management.
- **North Carolina,** with a strategic index of 11, lacks six of the components listed, but plans to implement five in the next two fiscal years: career planning, performance management, recruitment, skills database, and workforce planning. The state does not plan to implement health and safety information.
- **Louisiana,** with a strategic index of 10, lacks only five of the components listed, and plans to implement four over the next two fiscal years: career planning, competency management, skills database, and succession planning. The state does not plan to implement labor relations management.

A few states reported "other" components as part of their HRMIT system. Note that all of these fall into the administrative category. Kansas reported the use of an automated position management system. New Mexico uses a commitment accounting system to manage position funding. Arizona reported several current and planned "other" components, including two innovative applications that are worth noting here.

Arizona currently uses an automated system to ensure the timely granting of permanent status to probationary employees. A reminder e-mail is sent to the employee's supervisor within thirty days of the end of probation. The reminder e-mails are sent every Friday until the supervisor grants the employee permanent status or extends the employee's probationary period. The state also uses an automated system for the filing and processing of I-9 forms.

In addition, Arizona plans to put into service an innovative application designed to expedite the onboarding process for new employees by automating the processes from the time that an applicant has been identified as a preferred candidate until that candidate becomes an employee. The *Onboard Arizona* system enables the online creation of a job offer and electronic routing of that offer for agency approval, provides a web site for the prospective employee to review and validate employment information, produces pre-filled new hire forms, automatically transfers new hire information into the HR information system, and assigns an employee identification number on the employee's first day of work. This system is intended to reduce the time and cost to hire a new employee, and to improve the quality of that employee's initial days of employment.

## HIRING WEB SITES

We now examine the use of IT in the administrative function of recruiting employees for state employment. Independent of the online survey, the GPP research team conducted a study of states' hiring web sites in June 2007. The increasing availability of the Internet has changed not only the way that people work, but also the way that people search for employment (Kumar, 2003). According to The Pew Internet and American Life Project, 71 percent of adult Americans are at least occasional Internet users, and 94 percent of these have a connection at home (Horrigan and Smith, 2007). Job hunters find that it is much faster to use the Internet to search for employment than it is to use more traditional routes, and that more information about companies and specific career opportunities is available online, giving prospective applicants a better foundation to decide whether or not they wish to apply (Kumar, 2003).

Using a rigorously constructed rubric, GPP researchers evaluated the states' hiring web sites on both usability and content (see Appendix B). Factors that influenced the usability score include clarity and consistency of navigation, job search functionality, and the ability to apply online. Factors considered in the content score include information about state employment (e.g., benefits information and career development opportunities), recruiting calendars or job fair schedules, and the inclusion of a "frequently asked questions" page. A combined analysis of the hiring web site scores and GPP survey data revealed two interesting correlations. We found a positive correlation between a state's usability score and the average number of applications received per job. We also determined that there is an inverse correlation between a state's content score and the percentage of new hires that are fired during their probationary period (i.e., better content on the hiring web site results in a higher quality employee being hired).

The states that were rated the highest overall were Vermont, Indiana, Washington, and Virginia. Vermont had the highest overall score, due to an extremely high score in the content dimension—well above any other state. Indiana had the highest overall usability score, but ranked only sixth in content. Interestingly, there were many states that had high usability scores but obtained only average scores in content. While these states may receive more applications for their open positions, the simple addition of better content would result in higher quality applicants. Innovative practices that were found in the course of this study included the ability to apply to several jobs simultaneously with one application through a "job basket" feature (Arizona, Georgia, Iowa, Minnesota, Tennessee, and Vermont all offered this feature), and "job search agents" that will contact a prospective applicant when jobs that match their qualifications are posted (Arizona, Indiana, Iowa, Minnesota, and New Mexico offer this feature).

## HUMAN RESOURCE WEB PORTALS

Another administrative use of IT systems is the use of HR web portals, single points of access where employees can find HR-related information and tools. Access to the Internet has changed the manner in which people work. This is as true for HR professionals as for anyone else. Vast amounts of HR information that were previously disseminated in physical form can now be made available via a single HR web site. Forms can be downloaded on demand; personnel rules and regulations are made available in a searchable format; and information on benefits, career planning, retirement, employee assistance programs, and much more are all accessible without a visit to the HR department. Managers and HR professionals also have vastly increased access to information on collective bargaining agreements, pay rates, workforce planning, and other information that they need to carry out their duties.

In addition, advancements in web-based technology have made self-service applications a possibility for HR information systems. The ability of web pages to communicate with and modify databases has eliminated the need for an HR service "customer" (whether employee or manager) to interact directly with a human representative. This not only expedites the processing of transactions, but reduces the dependency on HR staff for the competent execution of these transactions (Florkowski and Olivas-Luján, 2006). Users may be allowed different levels of access to services based on the position that they hold in the organization. Moreover, some services may be available from any Internet-connected computer, while others may limit access only to those computers on the state's intranet. The GPP survey asked respondents to summarize the services that are available to employees, managers, and HR professionals through web portals. Table 16.2 summarizes the various services that states reported as being available to these three types of employees.

**TABLE 16.2   Self-Service Applications Through HR Web Portals**

| Employees | Managers | HR Professionals |
|---|---|---|
| • Change contact information | • Access information on direct reports including: | • Update employee pay rates, promotions, and transfers |
| • Review and print check stubs | • Contact information | • Create and post job announcements |
| • Update direct deposit information | • Employment history | • Track applications for open positions |
| • Manage charitable contributions and other payroll deductions | • Training history | • Access eligibility lists |
| • Update tax withholding information | • Attendance information | • View exam results |
| • Request a duplicate W-2 | • Approve time entry and requested leave | • Administer benefits |
| • Enroll in and manage benefits | • Approve employee business expenses | • View reports and workforce data |
| • View total compensation statements | • Assign alternate approvers | • View and update organizational charts |
| • Enter attendance information | • Enter performance appraisal information | • Administer surveys |
| • Request leave | • Create and update performance management plans | |
| • Donate leave | • Certify completed performance reviews | |
| • Check leave balances | • View reports and workforce data | |
| • Plan for business travel | • Submit and retrieve data files to and from data warehouse | |
| • Submit expense reimbursement requests | | |
| • View training history | | |
| • Enroll in training courses (both classroom-based and online courses) | | |
| • Create and update performance management plans | | |
| • Manage career development | | |
| • Nominate employees for recognition | | |
| • Manage union membership | | |

In addition, 52.5 percent of responding states offer various services to retirees through their HR web portals.

There are a few innovative services that are worth noting. Minnesota has a Customer Service Representative feature that allows an HR professional with the proper security clearance to view an employee's information as it would appear to the employee. This is useful when working with employees over the phone or in situations where the employee may not know all of the information that the HR professional needs to answer their questions. The manager self-service portal in Louisiana allows managers to view the data of their direct reports, their secondary reports, or all employees that they supervise at once. More than just an organizational charting tool, Indiana's Organizational Development feature allows an HR professional to identify, create and update positions and their department and agency relationships, and then updates all HRM applications that request this information.

## KNOWLEDGE AND LEARNING MANAGEMENT SYSTEMS

We now explore an area that has both administrative and strategic components: the use of IT systems for knowledge and learning management. One of the greatest challenges confronting state government is how to lessen the impact of impending personnel losses through retirement. When employees retire, a vast amount of knowledge can be lost when that retiree walks out the door for the final time. In addition, the sharing of knowledge, from basic facts and figures to procedures and best practices, can create efficiencies and synergies among employees within and between state agencies. The practice of *knowledge management* includes the creation, storage, sharing, and usage of the information or knowledge assets of an organization. Hence, a *knowledge management system* (KMS) allows for the creation, diffusion or transfer, and the ready availability of knowledge in the organization (Ghosh and Scott, 2007). There is a distinction between three different "types" of knowledge:

- **Explicit knowledge**—This is essentially information with context. Explicit knowledge, such as specifications, rules, regulations, etc. can be easily codified and captured in a database.
- **Implicit knowledge**—Slightly less easily codified, this is more process-oriented knowledge. Implicit knowledge, such as "best practices" or "lessons learned" can either be captured in a structured way (by placing it in document form) or in a less structured way, such as video recordings of procedures from key management presentations or conference addresses.
- **Tacit knowledge**—By definition, tacit knowledge cannot be codified or captured. It is gained through personal experience, and remains with the individual who acquired it. It can only be transferred through formal learning and experience in the context of an individual's work.

The establishment of a KMS can facilitate the storage and sharing of these "knowledge assets." Clearly, IT systems can be of great use here. From simple knowledge repositories and shared information storage areas to virtual collaborative spaces and networking tools, IT has many applications as part of a KMS. The GPP survey investigated this practice for the first time in its 2007 survey.

Of the forty-two states that responded to the GPP survey questions regarding knowledge management, 39 percent reported having some type of KMS in place but only 32 percent indicated that there is technology in place to support the KMS. Many states reported having implemented only the basic level of knowledge management, with IT systems providing repositories for basic information such as rules, regulations, and standard operating procedures. Both Nebraska and Delaware indicated that Lotus Notes software is used as a collaboration tool. Nebraska uses this product to implement "mail-in" databases for teams and special projects. Users are able to add to these central information repositories via e-mail, making it easy for all team members to have access to the same up-to-date information. In addition, the state uses Lotus Notes to create discussion databases, which allow real-time comments and thoughts to be documented and responded to in real time; the session is then archived so that the information can be accessed by team members not present for the virtual meeting and referred to after the meeting is over.

Also within the realm of knowledge sharing is a *learning management system* (LMS), dedicated to organizing, delivering, and tracking training for the employees of an organization. There are different levels to which IT systems can be involved in this type of system. At the most basic level, an IT system can be used to simply automate the registration and billing process for classroom training. At the other end of the spectrum, a LMS allows for the delivery of training content in the form of either static, pre-recorded content or live, interactive classes. These systems can also track completed training at the individual, agency, and statewide level. As part of the section concerning training and development on the People portion of the 2007 GPP survey, the GPP asked states to indicate the percentage of courses that are available online. Only eighteen states responded to this question, though it should be noted that many states' training efforts are decentralized, occurring mainly at the agency level. The states reporting the highest percentage of online courses were Iowa (62 percent), Alabama (54 percent), Arizona (54 percent), and Virginia (45 percent).

Iowa provides online training or "eLearning" courses from two different providers. They have a library of almost fifty business skills courses provided by Skillsoft, which includes such courses as *Basics of Effective Communication*, *Developing a Strategic Plan*, and *Recognizing Employee Performance*. In addition, they provide over 350 computer skills courses through the Element K Office Productivity Library. Provided over the Internet, these courses are available twenty-four hours a day, seven days a week from any Internet-connected computer.

Massachusetts is in the process of implementing a Performance and Career Enhancement (PACE) system. This system will consolidate the over thirty stand-alone training databases that are currently in use, provide reporting capabilities to help identify training needs, enhance tracking capabilities to ensure compliance with regulatory and licensing agencies, and provide standard registration and training processes across the executive branch. Agencies will be able to share training content with one another, and employees' training records will be easily accessible when transferring to other agencies.

The system that Virginia uses is especially noteworthy. It combines a learning management system with tools that also make it a true knowledge management system. The Commonwealth of Virginia Knowledge Center (CoVKC) is the state government's learning management system. Implemented for less than $100,000, the system is based on a product provided by Meridian KSI that has been adapted to suit the needs of the Virginia Department of Human Resources and the agencies it serves. One advantage of this system is that it can be customized at the agency level. Over forty agencies have web portals to the Knowledge Center that have been customized to suit their specific needs. Agencies are able to pick and choose among the services that are available from the system. For example, the Information Technologies Agency has implemented online classes and licensed external content, while the Department of Corrections implemented a mix of classroom-based and online courses, and was able to import legacy information into the system as a reference library. This feature provides maximum flexibility for agencies, in conjunction with central oversight and the ability to collect information at the state level.

Agencies maintain their own "content banks," but can also share content with other agencies or the entire statewide system. Online instructional content is delivered based on one of several computer-based training (CBT) standards, including the Sharable Content Object Reference Model (SCORM) and the Aviation Industry CBT Committee (AICC) standards. This facilitates the use of externally acquired content as well as easy sharing of content between agencies.

The system features course management capabilities for both online and classroom-based learning, allowing users to sign up for open classes, be added to a waitlist if necessary, and request authorization for those courses that require it. Instructors may also create curricula for multicourse programs. An example is the new Managing Virginia Program (MVP), a seventeen-course series that will standardize leadership training across all agencies. The system also features several individual development and career planning tools. State employees can create a custom training program for individual development, and can add external training events to their transcript, such as licenses and certifications that they have earned. This allows employees to take responsibility for their own training. The career tools include links to the state's career development web site, information about the on-site career center in Richmond, and the ability for employees looking for transfer opportunities within state government to post their resume and search for job opportunities. The Library feature provides a common location for explicit knowledge and resources such as references, research materials, and links to learning and information resources. This feature includes:

- A compilation of common industry issues in a "frequently asked questions" format
- A section dedicated to regulations and policies
- A reference library, capable of storing information in a variety of formats, which can be linked to from online courses
- An online periodicals section, including summaries and links to the web sites
- Shortcuts to other online resources

One feature of the CoVKC that facilitates the sharing of implicit knowledge is the PeerNet. This is a searchable repository of users who have made their expertise available to other users. The listings highlight the skills and expertise of the employees who have chosen to share their knowledge, and contain contact information. Users can search for other individuals using a general keyword search, or a more advanced expanded search. The CoVKC also provides various collaboration opportunities, including online forums, chat rooms, and a Team Center where team members can share documents, communicate via a bulletin board system or chat, and schedule group events. These features encourage both the sharing of implicit knowledge and the creation of new knowledge in a collaborative setting.

## COMPREHENSIVENESS AND AVAILABILITY OF WORKFORCE DATA

Next, we look at the strategic HRMIT function of providing workforce data to use as part of the HR decision-making process. One of the main criteria that the GPP focuses on in its analysis is strategic workforce planning. Organizations conduct this formalized strategic planning of the workforce in order to ensure that their workforce, or "human capital," is optimized to fully achieve the strategic goals of the organization. At the federal level, human capital planning is a key part of the President's Management Agenda (PMA) (United States General Accounting Office, 2004). State governments such as Georgia have also formalized the workforce planning process through legislation (Johnson and Brown, 2004). Central to this process is an analysis of the current state of the workforce. The best workforce plans start with a current snapshot of the workforce that can be viewed from many different perspectives. To be truly useful this data must be readily available to those who are responsible for making decisions regarding the human capital of the organization. It is helpful to understand the following terms when discussing the collection of workforce data:

- A *data warehouse* is defined as a "subject-oriented, integrated, non-volatile, time-variant collection of data organized to support management needs" (Castelluccio, 1996). This central repository of data draws from various administrative systems, such as payroll, benefits, and performance management systems, and provides an up-to-date pool of data that can be queried and reported on across many dimensions.
- *Workforce analytics* are a set of software tools that allow an organization to look for correlations between standard HR metrics (e.g., turnover rates and length of service) and other statistics (e.g., sales and customer satisfaction rates). This helps the organization to clarify how its workforce affects their strategic goals ("IOMA's HR Congress: High-level HR functions now dominate HR tech," 2004).
- A *workforce scorecard* is a tool that allows an organization to measure its success against the performance metrics that it has established as part of its workforce planning efforts. Optimally, this information is then used to strategically manage the success of their workforce (Huselid, Becker, and Beatty, 2005).

The following five states were rated highly by the GPP on the comprehensiveness and availability of their workforce data. Our analysis drew from both survey responses and the examination of documents such as workforce profiles supplied by the states.

## Arizona

Arizona maintains a data warehouse, and has implemented a manager self-service function as part of every manager's employee web portal page. This allows middle managers and agency leaders to access demographic, pay, position, and performance management information without having to use the central HR office as an intermediary. Their HRMIT system has sixteen different job roles for HR professionals with varying degrees of access, which helps to ensure the security of employee data. Arizona's *Workforce Report* for the 2007 fiscal year is quite comprehensive, and includes trending in many areas as well as several useful dimensions of analysis, including:

- Estimated cost of turnover by agency
- Separation rates by ethnicity, occupation, age distribution, and length of service
- Difference in age distribution between new hires and separations
- Ten-year trends in separations (retirements, resignations, terminations, and "other")
- Employee satisfaction survey results (including multiyear trends)

In addition, the results of a yearly compensation survey that collects statewide market data from 102 Arizona employers for 186 job descriptions are available to managers in a variety of reporting formats.

## Georgia

Georgia has implemented a full data warehouse, and is currently in the process of implementing a suite of human capital management tools from PeopleSoft. These tools will upgrade their workforce analytics, data warehouse, and workforce score-card systems. The data provided in the 2007 statewide workforce planning report, as well as the agency-level workforce plans that were submitted is quite robust, and often includes trending across past years, or projections into the future. Examples of the data contained in these reports include:

- Employees by tenure category (also distributed among pay groupings)
- Employees by age group (also distributed among pay groupings)
- Job targeting data
- Job classes most impacted by impending retirement
- Estimated cost of turnover by job code
- Voluntary turnover as a function of tenure category
- Demographic trends of populous job classes
- Vacancy rates

The workforce planning report is easily accessible on the workforce planning web site of the State Personnel Administration.

## Michigan

Michigan prepares workforce reports on a quarterly basis, making them available (along with a rollup for the entire fiscal year) on the Civil Service Commission workforce planning web site. These reports include a snapshot of each department at the end of the quarter, including changes in the number of both full-time equivalent and classified employees, along with other data such as:

- Department-level age/ethnic group/disability/longevity analysis
- Statewide separations

- Department-level new hires, returns, and separations
- Insurance plan enrollment by department
- Five-year employment trend of job categories
- Characteristics by bargaining unit

The annual rollup is even more comprehensive, and includes additional historical data and analysis of data such as annual and sick leave usage at the department level, employee distribution by salary, and total turnover data since 1943. Statistical information is also posted biweekly (per payroll period) by department, bargaining unit, and county.

## North Carolina

North Carolina has just implemented an Enterprise Resource Planning (ERP) system called *BEACON*. This system is designed to integrate all HR processes into a single technology platform supported by a data warehouse called *NC WORKS*. This data warehouse pulls information from a variety of sources, and provides agencies with reporting and workforce analytics to support workforce planning decisions. This data is also used to track progress against a wide range of performance goals set forth in the Office of State Personnel strategic plan as a workforce scorecard. The state's annual HR report includes data on many dimensions of the workforce, including:

- Employment by education level
- Comparison of turnover rate between the 18–25 age group and the total workforce
- Five-year trend of turnover by performance level
- Distribution of performance ratings (overall, by race/sex, and by length of service)
- Career banding information
- Benefits information, including growth of flexible benefits program
- Health and safety information

## Virginia

Virginia has a data warehouse that draws information for a wide variety of sources, including payroll systems, the Virginia retirement system, and the Personnel Management Information System. Reports can be run by anyone with an Internet connection on the Department of Human Resource Management workforce planning web site. Only statewide rollups can be run by the public, but agency-specific reports are available through the state intranet. Also available on the workforce planning site is "Commonwealth Human Resources At-A-Glance," a statewide rollup with a wealth of data, and five-year trends across a wide variety of dimensions, including:

- Average age of new hires
- Personnel expense as a percentage of budget
- Training as a percentage of payroll
- Change in average salary

- Leave usage
- Average employer health claim cost per employee
- Community service program participation

Agency-level "at-a-glance" profiles are provided to agency managers as well. Virginia's state workforce planning report includes additional data on dimensions such as top "at risk" job roles in terms of retirement eligibility percentages, job roles with the highest hiring rates, training metrics, and reasons for all types of separations. Another robust set of tools is available to agencies through *HuRMan*, a HR management file repository. Information about applicant flow, an EEO compliance calculator, training metrics, market salary data, and much more are easily accessible to agency managers and HR professionals.

## COMPARING THE STATES WITH ALL PUBLIC AND PRIVATE SECTOR ORGANIZATIONS

We now compare some of our findings with information regarding the HRMIT systems of organizations in general. The Institute of Management & Administration (IOMA) recently reported the results of the *CedarCrestone 2007–2008 HR Systems Survey*. This survey looks at how HR technologies are being used in organizations of all sizes, including higher education and public administration organizations. Table 16.3 shows the percentages of organizations that have implemented some of the HR activities as part of the HRMIT systems, comparing the results reported by IOMA with the results of the GPP survey.

Note that the respondents to the GPP survey are on par with or well ahead of the overall set of organizations reported by IOMA in the majority of these areas, including strategic activities such as career planning and competency management. In particular, the GPP respondents are significantly ahead of the overall field in adopting data warehouses and implementing workforce analytics. This is consistent with the results of the CedarCrestone survey, which found that both higher education and public administration organizations are above average in this area.

TABLE 16.3  Comparison of HRMIT Services

| HR Activity | IOMA (percentage) | GPP (percentage) |
|---|---|---|
| Payroll | 96.0 | 90.5 |
| Benefits administration | 78.0 | 85.7 |
| Employee self-service | 55.0 | 66.7 |
| Manager self-service | 34.0 | 42.9 |
| Career planning | 16.0 | 14.3 |
| Competency management | 19.0 | 19.0 |
| HR data warehouse | 32.0 | 68.3 |
| Workforce analytics | 11.0 | 22.5 |

*Source: HRIT 'Report Card': Trends for 2008 Plans. (2007).*

## OTHER GPP RESULTS

Rounding out the GPP's inquiry into the state of HR information systems in the state governments are the following three questions (including the percentage of "yes" responses):

- Is the state CIO directly involved in decision making about your HRMIT system? (97.6 percent)
- Is a HRMIT kiosk system available to employees who are not situated at desks? (48.8 percent)
- If your HRMIT system is a combination of applications from different vendors, do you have internal personnel who integrate the different HRM applications? (80.0 percent)

The involvement of the chief information officer (CIO) in the planning and implementation process is almost universal (only one state reported that the CIO is not involved). Support from all top management, including the CIO, is crucial in the successful implementation of an IT system. Less than half of the responding states reported the use of a kiosk system to support employees that do not have a desk (and hence a computer) to access the HR systems. There is evidence that the availability of these self-service functions has a positive impact on the level of employee satisfaction (Paetsch, 2002). Those states that do not have a kiosk system should consider either implementing one, and/or making HR services available through a web portal, in order to make it easier for these employees to access these services, and to increase the efficiencies that an HRMIT system brings. Finally, four out of five responding states that have HR applications from different vendors employ internal personnel to bridge the gap between the systems. Doing so allows these individual applications to communicate with one another when necessary, and facilitates the feeding of HR data into a data warehouse for reporting and analysis purposes.

## THE ROAD AHEAD

When asking about the components of states' HRMIT systems, the GPP also asked states to indicate whether they planned to implement these components in the next two fiscal years. The results showed that there are great plans afoot for automating additional HR activities among the states. Most notably, if all components are implemented as planned, the percentage of responding states with implemented career planning will jump from 14.3 percent to 52.4 percent, and the percentage with implemented competency management will climb from 19.0 percent to 52.4 percent.

As the states proceed with these implementations, they should be aware of certain factors that may inhibit their success. IOMA reports that the following roadblocks can hold organizations back (*HRIT 'Report Card': Trends for 2008 Plans*, 2007):

- Manager resistance which can slow the move to manager self-service.
- Lack of senior-level support.

- No mandate to move to self-service.
- Processes for service delivery are augmented with automation that is not being redesigned, which can also affect data accuracy.
- Difficulty in obtaining access to systems and applications by field workers and small locations.
- If vendor solutions are used, implementation and support costs can increase when programs are integrated with other solutions or when solutions aren't user friendly.

If states remain aware of these potential pitfalls as they enhance their HR information systems, they can succeed in shifting the HR function of state government from a purely administrative capacity into a more strategic role.

## CONCLUSION

Given the substantial proportion of their employees that will soon be eligible to retire, it is crucial that state governments prepare now to attract new employees more effectively, provide current employees with more efficient service, share and retain essential organizational knowledge, and engage in workforce planning that looks beyond simply filling positions as they become open. Our discussion here makes it clear that IT systems can be of tremendous use in addressing each of these challenges. The 2007 GPP survey found that some states have made significant investments in IT that supports both administrative processes as well as strategic decision making in the management of their human capital. Other states have implemented administrative functions, helping them to realize cost savings and efficiencies, but have limited plans to put functions that have strategic value into service. As we highlighted the topics of hiring web sites, HR web portals, knowledge and learning management systems, and workforce planning, some states emerged as clear leaders. It is these states, and the ones that follow their lead, that will be best equipped to handle the impending wave of retirements that looms just over the horizon.

## APPENDIX A: GPP SURVEY QUESTIONS

Which of the following components are implemented as part of your HRMIT system?

*Response choices were "Currently implemented," "Plan to implement in the next two fiscal years," and "Not implemented, no plans to implement."*

- Attendance management
- Benefits management
- Career planning
- Compensation management
- Competency management

- Data mining
- Employee demographics information
- Employee self-service
- Forms (e.g., W-4, W-2, I-9)
- Health and safety information
- Job classification
- Knowledge management
- Labor relation management
- Manager self-service
- Organizational charts
- Payroll
- Performance management
- Recruitment
- Regulatory requirements
- Retirement planning
- Salary planning
- Skills database
- Succession planning
- Workforce planning
- Other (please specify)

Please answer the following questions about your HRMIT system: (yes/no)

- Does your state maintain a data warehouse, incorporating current HRM and non-HRM data?
- Is the state CIO directly involved in decision making about your HRMIT system?
- Is a HRMIT kiosk system available to employees who are not situated at desks?
- If your HRMIT system is a combination of applications from different vendors, do you have internal personnel who integrate the different HRM applications?

Does your state utilize a human resources web portal? (yes/no)
If your state utilizes a human resources web portal, are retiree services of any kind offered through the web portal? (yes/no)
If the state utilizes a human resources web portal, please explain the services that are available to the following types of personnel: (employees, managers, and HR professionals)

## APPENDIX B: RUBRIC FOR HIRING WEB SITE STUDY

Developed by Joseph Orenstein, Government Performance Project

- Components labeled with a "C" address the *content* of the hiring web site
- Components labeled with a "U" address the *usability* of the hiring web site
- Components labeled with an "E" add *extra credit* points to the overall score

## Homepage and/or FAQ Page

| Component | Question | Check Box or Indicate Number |
| --- | --- | --- |
| $Cb_2$ | Is the **privacy policy** *linked from the homepage or FAQ page?* | |
| $Cb_5$ | Is there pertinent information on **internship** opportunities *linked from the homepage or FAQ page?* | |
| $Cb_6$ | Is there a state **news** or current trends feature prominently displayed *on the homepage?* | |
| $Cb_8$ | Is there information *on the homepage or FAQ page* regarding **organizational diversity** in the workplace available on the web site directed toward recruitment efforts? (does not include EEOC statements or diversity statistics) | |
| $Cb_9$ | Is there information or a link presented *on the homepage* regarding **"hot jobs"** or spotlighted jobs that would be hard to fill for the organization? | |
| $Cb_{10}$ | Is there information regarding **veterans' services or preference** featured *on the homepage or FAQ page?* | |
| $Cc_1$ | Does the web site feature a vivid color scheme that is **visually appealing**? (more than two prevalent colors *on the homepage*) | |
| $Cc_2$ | Are there **images** *on the homepage?* (beyond those found on an uppermost web site banner) | |
| $Cc_4$ | Is there **visual balance** on the web site (information presented on both sides *of the homepage*)? | |
| $Cc_5$ | Is the **text readable**? (large enough to read, headers and sub-headers distinctive, and body text organized *on the homepage*) | |
| $Ua_3$ | Are there **language selection options** for non-English speaking applicants *on the homepage or FAQ page?* | |
| $Ua_4$ | Is a **site map** available *on the homepage or FAQ page?* | |
| $Ua_5$ | Is the **navigation bar** (*left side of the page only*) consistent on all pages linked to from the homepage? | |

## Job Listings

| Component | Question | Check Box or Indicate Number |
|---|---|---|
| $Ua_1$ | Note the number of **Job Search features** available:<br>• type-in text search<br>• search by location or region<br>• search by agency<br>• search by income level or pay band<br>• search by job type or category | (0–5) |
| $Ca_1$ | Is pertinent **salary information** displayed *in job listings*? | |
| $Cb_4$ | Is there **recruiter contact information** available *within the job listings*? (name and e-mail/telephone where the applicant can direct questions) | |
| $Ua_2$ | Are there **links to corresponding agency pages** *within the job listings*? | |

## Online Application Process

| Component | Question | Check Box or Indicate Number |
|---|---|---|
| $Ub_2$ | Is there the opportunity to create a **personal profile** that stores information unique to the user for future use? | |
| $Ub_4$ | Do users have the option of **applying online**? | |
| $E_1$ | Does the web site allow the user to **track the progress** of their application review? | |
| $E_2$ | Does the web site **notify the applicant** of relevant job opportunities based on competencies or qualifications of the applicant? | |
| $E_4$ | Does the web site allow the user to create **one job application** and use it to apply for several jobs? | |
| $E_5$ | Does the web site provide a **Job Basket** feature in which the user can store multiple job listings and apply simultaneously for several listings in the basket? | |

## Anywhere on the Site

| Component | Question | Check Box or Indicate Number |
|---|---|---|
| $Ca_2$ | Is there prominently displayed information provided on job **benefit** packages with the job listings *or* otherwise? | |
| $Ca_3$ | Is there prominently displayed information provided regarding **career development** opportunities available to employees? (does not include training calendar or development course offering list) | |
| $Ca_4$ | Is there prominently displayed information provided regarding **cultural values** of the organization that might aid the seeker in determining the workplace environment? (mission statement, employee testimonials) | |
| $Cb_1$ | Is there a **frequently asked questions** section on the site to aid applicants? | |
| $Cb_3$ | Is there a **downloadable version** of job applications on the web site *or* within the job listing? | |
| $Cb_7$ | Are recruiting **calendars**, job fair schedules, or applicant exam schedules available on the web site? | |
| $Cc_3$ | Is there **animation** or video on the web site? | |
| $Ub_1$ | Does the web site encourage and allow the opportunity for users to provide **feedback** as to the effectiveness and usability of the hiring web site as a manner of facilitating improvements to the e-recruitment process? (e.g., feedback forms, direct e-mail links, and user surveys) | |
| $Ub_3$ | Are there **community interfaces** on the web site that encourage communication between an organization and a potential employee? (job message boards, organizational chat rooms, recruiter blogs, e-mail subscription services) | |
| $E_3$ | Does the web site provide tools or counseling in the creation and revision of a **job resume**/application? (does not include online application processes) | |
| $Ua_6$ | Is there an absence of **broken links** or under construction pages on the web site? (link checker) | |
| $E_6$ | How many **clicks from the State homepage** to the Hiring homepage? | |

**Final Subjective Grade:**

## NOTES

1. The 2007 question set was revised through a review of academic and industry journals, such as *Personnel Review*, *Human Resource Management*, and *Expert Systems*; investigation into the features offered by commercial HRMIT software packages; a review of the elements of other HR technology surveys; and consultation with individuals with public sector HR experience. See Appendix A for the full text of the questions dealing with HR information systems from the People portion of the 2007 GPP survey.
2. The basis for these indexes is theoretical, based on a review of both academic and industry literature, and was subsequently confirmed empirically. The groupings were determined by performing a *factor*

*analysis.* One of the applications of factor analysis is to uncover groups of interrelated variables, that is, to classify variables. Each factor is described by those items that are more highly correlated with one another than with the other items (Carmines and Zeller, 1979). In this case, the factor analysis determined that the HR functions grouped here as "strategic" were more highly correlated with each other than with the functions grouped as "administrative," and vice versa.

3. *Cronbach's alpha* is a measure of reliability that is based on internal consistency; it ranges in value from zero to one. The value of alpha depends partially on the average correlation between items in a group; as the average inter-item correlation increases, so does alpha (Carmines and Zeller, 1979). In this case, the values of alpha obtained for the "strategic" factor ($[\alpha]$ = 0.89) and the "administrative" factor ($[\alpha]$ = 0.88) show that the items in these two groupings are very highly correlated with one another, hence the indexes are valid.

# REFERENCES

Beckers, A. M., and M. Z. Bsat. 2002. A DSS Classification Model for Research in Human Resource Information Systems. *Information Systems Management* 19 (3):41–50.

Carmines, E., and R. Zeller. 1979. *Reliability and Validity Assessment.* (Sage University Paper Series on Quantitative Applications in the Social Sciences, Series No. 07-017). Newbury Park, CA: Sage.

Castelluccio, M. 1996. Data Warehouses, Marts, Metadata, OLAP/ROLAP, and Data Mining—A Glossary. *Management Accounting* (USA) 78 (4):59–61.

Changing Strategies in HR Technology and Outsourcing – 2007 HR Technology Trends Survey. 2007. Retrieved on August 26, 2008, from <http://www.watsonwyatt.com/research/resrender.asp?id=2007-US-0151&page=1>.

Eucker, T. 2007. Understanding the Impact of Tacit Knowledge Loss. *Knowledge Management Review* 10 (1):10–13.

Florkowski, G., and M. Olivas-Luján. 2006. Diffusion of Human-Resource Information-Technology Innovations in US and Non-US Firms. *Personnel Review* 35 (6):684–710.

Ghosh, B., and J. Scott. 2007. Effective Knowledge Management Systems for a Clinical Nursing Setting. *Information Systems Management* 24 (1):73–84.

Goldberg, B. 2007. The Costs of Short-Term Thinking. The Century Foundation. Retrieved on February 4, 2008, from <http://www.tcf.org/list.asp?type=NC&pubid=1619>.

Horrigan, J., and A. Smith. 2007. Data Memo: Home Broadband Adoption 2007. The Pew Internet & American Life Project. Retrieved on February 4, 2008, from <http://www.pewinternet.org/pdfs/PIP_Broadband%202007.pdf>.

HRIT 'Report Card': Trends for 2008 Plans. 2007. *HR Focus* 84 (12):1–15.

Huselid, M., B. Becker, and R. Beatty. 2005. *The Workforce Scorecard.* Boston, MA: Harvard Business School Press.

IOMA's HR Congress: High-Level HR Functions Now Dominate HR Tech. 2004. *Human Resources Department Management Report* 4 (6):5–6.

Johnson, G., and J. Brown. 2004. Workforce Planning Not a Common Practice, IPMA-HR Study Finds. *Public Personnel Management* 33:379–388.

Kazan, H. 2005. A Study of Factors Affecting Effective Production and Workforce Planning. *Journal of American Academy of Business, Cambridge* 7 (1):288–296.

Kumar, S. 2003. Managing Human Capital Supply Chain in the Internet Era. *Industrial Management & Data Systems* 103 (4):227–237.

Mistry, J. 2006. Differential Impacts of Information Technology on Cost and Revenue Driver Relationships in Banking. *Industrial Management & Data Systems* 106 (3):327–344.

Ngai, E. W. T., and F. K. T. Wat. 2006. Human Resource Information Systems: A Review and Empirical Analysis. *Personnel Review* 35 (3):297–314.

Paetsch, L. 2002. Employee Self-Service Option Increases Employee Satisfaction, Decreases Company's Cost. *Employee Benefit Plan Review* 56 (7):18–19.

Robb, D. 2004. Marking Time. *HR Magazine* 49 (7):111–115.

SAP Announces 2007 Preliminary Results. 2008. Retrieved on February 3, 2008, from <http://www.sap.com/about/investor/financialnews/adhoc/q4_2007-pre-announcement.epx>.

United States General Accounting Office. 2004. *Human Capital: Observations on Agencies' Implementation of the Chief Human Capital Officers Act.* Statement of J. Christopher Mihm, Managing Director, Strategic Issues. Washington, DC: U.S. General Accounting Office.

# Ethics and Human Resource Management

JONATHAN P. WEST
University of Miami

## INTRODUCTION

The institutionalization of ethics is a major challenge for public institutions. HR managers can help address this challenge by assuming a leadership role in identifying the need for ethics programs and implementing them. They are well positioned to positively influence practices shaping workplace environments, to reduce fiscal risks and liabilities, to apply ethical standards more consistently, and to enhance the reputation of government among its stakeholders. A recent survey jointly conducted by the Society for Human Resource Management (SHRM) and the Ethics Resource Center (ERC) found that nearly seven in ten of the 2,100 SHRM members surveyed said the HR department is a primary resource for ethics policies in their organizations, and about the same percentage said the HR department is involved in formulating ethics policies in their organization.[1]

However, findings also reported an "undercurrent of frustration" with four in ten feeling that they are not truly integrated into the ethics infrastructure of their organization, and are nevertheless frequently asked to "clean up the messes" (Joseph and Esen, 2003:4,5). This pattern of frustration is especially evident among respondents from government. Such findings suggest that there is some ambivalence among public HR professionals regarding the extent of their participation in the development of ethics policy; however, it is clear that HR professionals are often required to deal with ethical issues. They are frequently responsible for ensuring that the right programs and policies are in place, so it is important for them to stay abreast of these ethics issues (Vickers, 2005).

Several government organizations have a designated ethics officer appointed to oversee policy implementation. The same is true in the private sector. An examination of ethics programs in Fortune 500 service and industrial firms reports that an HR officer was ultimately responsible for ethics/compliance management in three of ten reporting firms (Weaver, Trevino, and Cochran, 1999; Weaver and Trevino, 2001). A similar proportion of legal positions (e.g., general counsel) were vested with this responsibility. Public sector studies of the Federal Designated Agency Ethics Officials (DAEOs) indicate heavy reliance on those housed in agency legal offices (Gibson, 2007), but other DAEOs have an HR background. Weaver and Trevino (2001) conclude that "an ethics program is more likely to be perceived as fairly administered when HR clearly is associated with it" (p. 11), in contrast to the legal staff that might be seen as favoring employer over employee concerns. The organizational location and orientation of the DAEO can clearly influence the selection of legal, code-based (compliance) strategies or behavioral principle-and-relationship (values) strategies. Best results are likely achieved when there is a balancing of these approaches. In any event, the role of the ethics officer has gained prominence, reflected in the establishment of a professional society, the Ethics Officer Association.

This chapter briefly reviews the responses that organizations are taking to the ethics challenge and some of the strategies that have been employed to build integrity in the public sector. The particular ethical challenges facing the HR manager are reviewed by briefly examining specific components of public HR systems and processes that are vital in building and maintaining an ethical organization. Leverage points for strategic responses to these ethical challenges by the HR professional are considered. Throughout the chapter the problems and prospects for public integrity and HRM are discussed.

## GENERAL ORGANIZATONAL RESPONSES

Responses to the ethics challenge have been multifaceted, but typically they have taken two complementary tracks: legal and behavioral.[2] Legal action seeks to curb wrongdoing: training activities seek to promote ethical behavior by raising the ethical consciousness of employees. Among the ethical concerns addressed by the legal response are prohibitions of unethical activities (e.g., sexual harassment, discrimination) and mandates regarding such matters as financial disclosure and post-service employment (West, Berman, Bonczek, and Kellar, 1998; West and Berman, 2006; Bowman, West, Berman and Van Wart, 2004). Legal responses have their limitations; they are quite narrow in scope, and they may help in defining the black and white areas of permissible and impermissible behaviors, but they provide insufficient guidance in dealing with the gray areas.

The behavioral response, by contrast, emphasizes training and information dissemination to help managers and employees recognize and cope with ethical problems and conflicts. Such guidance seeks to better inform ethical decision making, to minimize ethical missteps by altering attitudes and promoting ethical awareness, and to provide resources for consultation to aid in thinking through tough ethical issues. Mission, vision, values, and pledge statements have been adopted by some jurisdictions; ethics codes and standards of conduct are used as well. These topics are typically reviewed in training sessions. Increasingly, however, training has gone beyond this, using case studies, role plays, scenarios, games, and other techniques to more closely approximate the "real world" conditions confronting managers and employees, and to foster ethical responsibility.

## SPECIFIC ORGANIZATION RESPONSES AND STRATEGIES

### Code-Based Strategies

Organizational strategies can be further examined by distinguishing between code-based strategies and approaches that stress principles and relationships. Code-based strategies can be categorized as aspirational, prohibitive, and hybrid. Aspirational codes go beyond the letter of the law and are characterized by norms of desired behavior, and provisions ranging from general to specific statements (e.g., stressing trust, integrity). Prohibitive codes, by contrast, focus on illegal and unethical conduct, hearings, investigations, and sanctions for violations. Finally, hybrid codes contain a blend of both aspirational and prohibitive provisions.

### Principle and Relationship Strategies

Principled approaches to ethical decision making can be categorized as deductive, inductive, or a combination of the two. Use of the deductive approach entails a top-down process where decision makers are guided by abstract ethical principles (e.g., honesty, justice) when confronting situations involving moral choice. By contrast, use of the inductive approach is a bottom-up process that focuses on the stakeholders who are most affected by the decision and the relationships among them. Obviously, a training session could be designed which would combine both of these approaches.

A jurisdiction's decision to pursue a law-based or behavior-oriented approach to institutionalizing ethics or a code-based or principle-oriented strategy should be preceded by examining the organization's values, visualizing the ethical environment, and surveying the ethical climate.

### Fostering Ethics in the Organization

What else do we know about shaping and maintaining ethical behavior in organizations? While answers to this question are still evolving, some key system components can be identified: First, executive and managerial leaders set the moral tone for the organization; second, codes of ethics capture core values and norms; third, HR managers use traditional administrative mechanisms (e.g., hiring, promotion, training) to implement these values and norms; fourth, line managers sharpen ethical insight by giving priority to ethical dialogue and timely feedback on job-related behavior; finally, managerial actions to convert ethical insight into ethical action by assisting individuals to internalize ethics and hone their ethical reasoning skills.

The interconnectedness of the system requires specific attention. For example, many jurisdictions go beyond merely adopting an ethics code; their leaders provide sterling examples of ethical conduct and stimulate discussion of ethical issues. They might also offer training covering vexing ethical issues, make ethics a criterion in both hiring and promotion, and consider the range of benefit offerings from an ethical perspective. Such actions are most effective when they are tightly integrated and used in combination with other components in an ethics system and when they are balanced between a values and a compliance orientation.

Up to now we have considered strategies available to those operating in the broader organizational environment. Next we shift and narrow the focus to those factors that relate more closely to the responsibilities of the HR manager. These factors are especially important because both explicit and implicit aspects of ethics programs are subject to the influence of HR managers. Explicit factors are specifically created programs designed to promote ethics (e.g., employee orientation and training programs). Implicit aspects are inherent in the culture, systems, and processes of the organization (e.g., incentive systems and performance evaluation). Both factors are vital in creating and maintaining an ethical organization. The analysis that follows considers the HR systems and processes that reinforce this effort.

## HUMAN RESOURCE IMPLEMENTATION STRATEGIES

### Hiring

Ethical considerations are important in the recruitment and selection process. Subtle and not so subtle messages about organizational ethics are communicated in job announcements, screening procedures, and communications with applicants. At each stage of this process the mission, vision, and values of the organizations can be emphasized and reinforced as employers seek to attract and select employees who share their values. For example, job announcements might highlight "ethical sensitivity" or "meeting customer needs" as a crucial qualification. Similarly, the selection interview presents an opportunity for employers to discuss organizational values and clearly communicate the importance of ethics to job prospects, including examples of acceptable and unacceptable conduct. Interview questions could include situation-specific questions (e.g., "What would you do if your spouse and children had colds and would be alone at home if you left for work?") with responses scored high ("I'd go to work, a cold is not serious") or low ("I'd remain home") (cited in Brumback, 1998). Hirt (2003) poses the hypothetical of an assistant town manager who is told by the city council that they intend to fire the existing town manager shortly. The job candidate is asked to assume the role of the assistant and asked: "[Are] you interested in being considered for the manager's position? What is your response? Do you warn the manager that s/he is about to be fired?" Svara (2007) and Kellar (2004) provide additional scenarios in this vein. Obviously, there are questions to be avoided in interviews as well (e.g., "Do you plan to have more children?" "Would child care issues keep you from getting to work?") (Pomeroy, 2006).

Interviewees can further probe the employers' ethical stance by raising questions about things mentioned in the organizations' Values Creed or Code of Conduct book. More general questions might give clues as well: "What is the profile of a successful person in your jurisdiction?" "Are there any unusual demands in this job that I should be aware of?" Some jurisdictions require a signed pledge from new hires to adhere to ethical principles. Steiner and Gilliland (1996) report that applicants are more positive about the organization and the selection procedures in situations where screening tests are perceived to be fair and to have face validity. Integrity tests, prohibited in certain states and legal in others, are used to assess applicant attitudes on wrongdoing in the workplace or to identify the propensity for irresponsible behavior. For example, Valmores (2005, cited in Menzel, 2007:154) mentions that the Philippines Civil Service Commission is developing an Ethics-Based Personality Test believing it will aid in "recruitment of the right people in all aspects and dimensions." However, caution should be used in employing such screening devices due to increasing legal complexities and litigious job applicants. Integrity tests can raise validity issues and possible decision errors due, in part, to faking (applicants misrepresenting their past history or beliefs), coaching and test retaking (see Karren and Zacharias, 2007). They also raise fairness and privacy concerns.

Employers can demonstrate their commitment to values like fairness and respect in their courteous acknowledgment of receipt of job applications, frequent updates on the status of the search, and tactful letters of rejection (Gibelman, 1996). Privacy concerns can be addressed by safeguarding personal information, exercising discretion in conducting background investigations, and the prudent use of potentially invasive techniques. In general, prospects for ethical hiring are improved when procedures allow for meaningful two-way communication, transparency wherever appropriate, absence of bias, and consistent screening across applicants (Alder and Gilbert, 2006).

## Orientation

New employee orientation sessions afford an opportunity to increase ethical awareness by explicit discussion of the goals and values of the organization as well as the policies and procedures managers and employees are expected to use as guides for behavior and decision making. Among the topics that might be included in new employee orientation are clear statements by top officials of expectations regarding ethical behavior of all employees, and review of relevant laws, ethics codes, rules/regulations, and procedures and the penalties for noncompliance. Other key topics could involve discussion of management's philosophy regarding the organization's mission, values, rules, and the processes for enforcement, safeguards against unfairness, and channels for appeal. More specific orientation subjects might include discussion of behaviors promoting organizational values (e.g., promise keeping, honest dealings) and unethical practices (e.g., conflict of interest, use of public resources for private gain). Also, consideration of frequently encountered dilemmas (e.g., outside employment, gifts) and resources available to aid ethical decision making (e.g., ombudspersons, ethics officers and committees, ethics hotlines, ethics newsletters) is useful. Further, private sector research has found that providing an overview of the organization's ethics code in orientation is linked to "an individual's perception of the importance of incorruptibility [in the hiring decision]" (Valentine and Johnson, 2005:49).

## Compensation

"Equal pay for equal work" was a reform theme in the late 1800s and has been a core value espoused by merit system advocates since that time. However, implementing this principle has proven difficult, and complaints about pay inequities continue to this day. Monetary incentives to do things right and to do the right thing are absent if organizations are rewarding unproductive and unethical behavior or failing to reward productive and ethical behavior. When pay is not linked to performance, but based more on the personal views and prejudices of managers, the potential increases for misuse of discretion and unfairness to employees. Failing to reward top performers and moral exemplars for their efforts sends a powerful message. Often the reward system communicates to employees the "real story" regarding the employer's commitment to ethical behavior. Actions by HR managers can help to ensure employee perceptions of equitable treatment, fair reward systems, compliance with legal mandates for pay fairness, and minimization of wage compression.

## Training

HR managers who decide to deliver ethics training have various tools and resources available. Numerous books or manuals serve as useful instructional and training materials (e.g., West and Berman, 2006; Frederickson and Ghere, 2005; Menzel, 2007; Svara, 2007; Lewis and Gilman, 2005; Richter and Burke, 2007; Huberts, Maesschalck and Jurkiewicz, 2008; Kazman and Bonczek, 1999; Bell, 1997; Kellar, 2004). Also *Public Integrity* is the journal of the American Society for Public Administration Ethics Section and a valuable resource on public service ethics. It is co-sponsored by the International City/County Management Association (ICMA), the Council of State Governments, the ERC and the Council on Governmental Ethics Laws and published by M.E. Sharpe. These resource materials contain case studies, commentaries, scenarios, exercises, "brainteasers," role plays, "ethics moments," self-assessment instruments, problem-solving guides, field reports, individual and group projects, profiles of moral exemplars, analytic frameworks, sample ethics codes, and essays that help reinforce public service values like fairness, honesty, integrity, and belief in democratic processes.

The objectives of ethics training are multiple as well as varied. Training may be designed to: increase ethical awareness; insure familiarity with key legal, code, and policy requirements; explain and discuss ethical standards and expectations; foster insight from situation-specific examples; provide tools and frameworks for resolving ethical conflicts; stimulate ethical reflection; and support practical ways to approach ethical decision making. Such training is needed not just for newly hired employees, but for all employees who periodically need a "booster shot" to inoculate against wrongdoing (West et al., 1998; West and Berman, 2004).

Ethics training takes many forms. Ponemon and Felo (1996) offer a concise summary of twelve key features or ingredients of successful ethics training programs: live instruction, small class sizes, a decision-based focus, the use of a professional trainer, a powerful message from the manager, realistic case materials, significant group interaction, a minimum of four hours of training, comprehensive involvement of employees, separate courses for compliance areas, follow-up communications, and new-employee programs. The potential benefits resulting from ethics training include increased legal protection, improved ethical climate, and enhanced trust linked to more open communication channels. It also helps to assess multiple ethical perspectives, clarify values, and guide ethical action. While two of every three cities currently offer ethics training, the depth of such training is modest at best (West and Berman, 2004). Larger jurisdictions such as Chicago, Tampa, King County in Washington, and Salt Lake County in Utah offer ethics training as merely one part of their ethics management program (see Menzel, 2006).

West and Berman's (2004) empirical study of ethics training in U.S. cities finds a link between ethics training, other ethics activities, leadership, and important organizational outcomes. Specifically, "moral leadership of senior managers affects the use of ethics training, as well as the monitoring of employee adherence to the code of ethics, and using ethics as a criterion in hiring and promotion" (p. 202). Targeted training is also related to positive labor–management relations and a positive organizational culture which is linked to heightened employee productivity, which in turn is related to citizen trust. This research highlights the important role of ethics in improving organizational performance.

## Performance Appraisal

Merit is the stated basis for appraising employee performance in public personnel systems. When questionable appraisal practices occur, it undermines established principles and systems and promotes cynicism (Bowman, 1999). Issues of justice can arise when subordinates are subject to electronic performance monitoring. The gap between theory and practice can be reduced, according to Bowman, when top officials model appropriate behavior; sound policies and procedures are supported by managers and employees; appropriate tools are selected; raters are trained; and continuous, positive, or corrective feedback is provided. Performance appraisal can be viewed as an "accountability episode" that more explicitly includes ethics as a dimension of evaluation. For example, Brumback (1998) suggests that administrators' performance be evaluated on the general conduct and ethics factor together with the more customary managerial or professional/technical factors. Menzel (2007:80) suggests inserting a check box on the appraisal form next to the statement: "Employee treats others with respect and dignity." Building an ethically sound government requires that managers and employees recognize that ethical concerns are inherent in their job responsibilities.

Using ethics as a criterion in evaluations, addressing ethical violations consistently and fairly, and publicly acknowledging examples of positive ethical conduct can demonstrate a unit's commitment to ethical behavior. Relevant questions to consider are: Is the employee performing in compliance with relevant laws, rules, and regulations? Does he/she set a positive example in circumstances where discretion is exercised? Does he/she demonstrate commitment to the organization's mission, goals and values? Are self-appraisals truthful? Considering answers to these questions brings ethics into the performance appraisal process. However, a caution should be noted: The existing appraisal process itself might inadequately address ethical issues. For example, does the system provide a clear avenue of recourse for an employee who doesn't concur with a job evaluation and fails to resolve the issue with their manager?

Managers can use an ethics code, as appropriate, when providing performance-related feedback to subordinates. For example, Berman and West (2003b:36) report interview data where one manager observes:

> We had an incident whereby a manager hung some of her colleagues out to dry by blaming them for a problem and thereby deflecting her responsibility for a mistake. In counseling with her, I used the GFOA Code of Ethics to explain why her conduct violated a provision of the professional code. She recognized the problem, and there has been no recurrence of unethical behavior.

## Employee Assistance Programs

Employee Assistance Programs (EAPs) seek to help people resolve problems that impede workplace performance including difficulties stemming from health or work and family conflict.[3] Problems addressed might include substance abuse, personal debt, domestic violence, or other issues. EAPs provide educational, treatment, and referral services to help employees cope with such matters. Mines, Anderson and Von Stroh (1991) have considered some ethical issues associated with EAPs linked to work with impaired professionals (e.g., Should the clients of impaired professionals be warned, or is there an obligation to respect the impaired professional's confidentiality? What is the EAP's obligation regarding the treatment of the impaired professional? Is treatment considered voluntary or compulsory? What if treatment is refused? What is the obligation to oversee the professional performance?) Those involved in EAPs need to carefully consider these obligations.

Service quality issues also arise, especially given the trends toward outsourcing EAP services. Sharer and White (2002, n.d.) discuss compromised service quality from EAP venders resulting from under-pricing ("low balling"), over-promising, and under-resourcing of services. They express concern about the knowledge, experience, and technical skills of national subcontractors who may lack a contextual understanding of local conditions. They also cite instances of deceptive marketing practices by vendors and outsourced services that in some cases are EAPs in name only. If EAPs are to promote both utilitarian and altruistic objectives, those providing services need to be prepared to deal with ethical issues as well as fiscal concerns and, given widespread outsourcing, to carefully monitor services in order to assure individual well-being and organizational productivity.

## Adverse Actions

Fairness and due process considerations are crucial in discipline or employee discharge cases. Non-probationary public sector employees have traditionally enjoyed job protection and appeals procedures designed to shield workers from arbitrary or capricious punishment and/or wrongful discharge. While there has been some movement in the direction of employment-at-will (e.g., Georgia and Florida; See Bowman and West, 2007; Kellough and Nigro, 2006), civil service procedures typically create a "property interest" or expectation of continued employment assuming satisfactory performance for such employees. Where these protections exist, employees may be terminated only for cause (Kellough, 1999). Managers must be aware of legal strictures and use the ethical principles of fairness, rights, and proportionality as guidance in taking adverse actions against employees.

Are people who violate ethical norms appropriately disciplined? If not, it sends an implied message that misbehavior is tolerated. Also, HR managers must employ sensitivity when implementing downsizing actions, more prevalent in recent years, which can be perceived as violating the psychological contract (Berman and West, 2003a) existing between individual and organization. Giacalone, Jurkiewicz, and Knouse (2003) suggest the use of an Ethics Exit Survey at the time of termination as a way to diagnose ethical problems in work environments and a tool to improve managerial efficiency, responsiveness, and accountability.

## Diversity

Public sector ethics codes often have equal opportunity or nondiscrimination clauses. For example, the ICMA code stresses merit-based personnel actions based on fairness and impartiality. ICMA's implementing guidelines go further to support equal employment opportunities for all persons, prohibit discrimination against those in protected categories and promote diversity. Similarly, the American Society for Public Administration's code, in the section on Serve the Public Interest, states, "Oppose all forms of discrimination, and harassment, and promote affirmative action." The International Personnel Management Association's Statement of Principles and Values contains similar language. As "keepers of the policies," HR managers clearly need to be vigilant in ensuring a workplace free of discrimination, where personnel actions are merit based, fair, and impartial. While reasonable people can disagree on the contentious issue of affirmative action (e.g., Wardlaw, 2000), it continues to be supported in ethics codes of visible national and international professional associations. Cultural diversity is a core value that with proper supporting initiatives can become integral to the cultural fabric of the organization (Buckley, et al., 2001).

## Union-Management Relations

Historically, union-management relations in the United States have been characterized as adversarial. This adversarial approach, when taken to an extreme, can lead to instances of unethical behavior. Wooten (2001:170) has identified five examples of unethical behavior in labor-management relations, including: (1) when one side deliberately misrepresents the organizational position of the other in an effort to win an agreement, (2) when facts are distorted in a grievance case to garner bargaining power, (3) when one side uses bargaining tactics that force the other side to compromise on known needs, (4) when due to technical ineptness one side resists a settlement because of inadequate understanding or unwillingness to solve problems, and (5) when ambiguous demands are made with the intent of polarizing the other party's position.

Increasing fiscal pressures have led many government and union leaders to change the way they look at union-management relations. Competing models emphasizing partnership and cooperation have been proposed and tried in various jurisdictions (see Berman, et al., 2006:Chapter 10). The adversarial model of union-management relations is based on conflicting interests and is not likely to change in the near term. Nonetheless, public sector efforts to create labor-management partnerships based on common interests are promising, and one way to emphasize the value to be derived from fair play and trust between parties is to insert an ethics standards clause into the labor-management contract.

## Health Insurance

Health care coverage is a crucial benefit for most people. However employees can no longer be confident that employers will absorb the full cost of individual health insurance and family health premiums. Costs are increasingly transferred to employees through higher premiums, co-pays and deductibles (Hacker, 2006:139). Further load shedding occurs with the increased use of part-time and temporary employees as organizations economize and downsize (Thompson and Mastracci, 2005; Klingner and Lynn, 2005) with benefits primarily available in the first tier (Clark, 1997). These trends have led Richardson (1998:14) to ask: "Ethically, which carries more weight? Holding down costs or keeping your employees satisfied and healthy?" She further asks: "Is it legitimate for employers to require employees to assume an increasing burden of economic risk 'simply because it is advantageous,' " or "Should organizations, frequently large and well-resourced, accept responsibility for the promotion of employee well being?" As organizations evaluate their responsibilities regarding health insurance, key principles come into play, as noted by West and Bowman (2008: 36: "rights (individual, property), justice (distributive, procedural), utilitarianism (ratio of benefits to costs) and beneficence (serving the good)" in an effort to promote the greatest good and avoid the greatest harm. In doing so, HR managers must carefully weigh both ethical and economic concerns in their search for best practices.

## Human Resource Information Systems

Human resource information systems (HRIS) contain personal data about each employee. The creation and use of such data should be guided by both legal and ethical considerations. Privacy-related issues such as the types of information placed on the system (e.g., pay and health information) and determinations of who has access to such data will confront HR managers. Under the Fifth and Fourteenth Amendments to the U.S. Constitution, an individual's rights to life, liberty, and property cannot be denied without due process of law. Applying these statements to HRIS raises issues of property and liberty interest in HR records management. Those controlling personnel records need to be aware of privacy concerns, and to determine what is and what is not confidential, what may or may not stigmatize an employee, and what information deserves restricted access (Hubbard, Forcht, and Thomas, 1998). Along with legal concerns, moral rights of employees—to fair treatment, respect, and privacy—should be respected (Velasquez, 2001). These legal and moral issues should be kept in mind when employers are responding to requests for job references.

## Health, Safety, and Accessibility Issues

Government agencies face ethical challenges in keeping the workplace healthy, safe, and accessible. Fiscal constraints have prompted cost cutting which, in some cases, has resulted in compromised health and safety conditions at work (e.g., accidents, contaminated food, fires resulting from outdated electrical wiring). Deregulation and privatization may increase the potential risks to health and safety where proper safeguards, monitoring mechanisms, information disclosure, and sanctions are lacking. Health and safety issues can be partially addressed through orientation and training programs, well-conceived contingency plans, and emergency response capabilities. Accessibility issues have emerged in response to the Americans with Disabilities Act and its requirements for reasonable accommodations. Richter and Richter's (1999) analysis of health, safety, and accessibility in international travel demonstrates that providing access to transportation, accommodations, and attractions to the handicapped raises several ". . . ethical questions of fairness and distributive justice, of utilitarian or Rawlsian notions of decision making" (p. 605). These authors admonish public administrators, and we might add HR managers, to acknowledge and confront the ethical issues surrounding health, safety, and accessibility, many of which are neglected in academic training programs.

## Pension Plans

As we noted with health care, individuals are assuming greater responsibility as organizations, facing economic pressures, shift retirement investment risks to workers (Hacker, 2006). The trend is away from defined benefit plans in favor of defined contribution plans. Furthermore, pension deficits at the state and local government levels are increasing; several states have overall pension deficits larger than their total yearly budget (Greenblat, 2007). A pension scandal in San Diego led to the resignation of the mayor and other officials who were charged with conspiracy and fraud for using pension funds to pay expenses and using unfunded pension liability to hide municipal debt (Greenblat, 2007). Prudent pension decision making requires efforts to both preserve security and contain costs. Problems of risk-shifting, underfunding and wrongdoing have led to increased insecurity for many workers. Public officials need to balance both the ethical and economic sides of this problem as they seek to achieve best practice.

## Family/Work Relations

Work/family initiatives are attractive benefits provided by many public and private employers. These might include (but not be restricted to) child care, elder care, flextime and telecommuting, leave sharing and pooling, domestic partner benefits, and adoption assistance (see Berman, et al. 2006: Chapter 7). From an ethical perspective, caring for the needs of members of the "organizational family" is fundamental to insuring a high quality work environment.

## Productivity and Quality

The dueling pressures to improve government performance while simultaneously cutting costs have intensified in the past decade. Calls for diffusing the quality paradigm and businesslike approaches to the public sector have continued along with admonitions to reengineer, reinvent, partner, reorganize, and employ market models to improve government service delivery (Kamarck, 2007). Francis Burke (1999) refers to the "three Es" of efficiency, effectiveness, and economy as vital and enduring values with deep historical roots and contemporary applications in our culture. Paul Light's (1998) analysis of reform tides highlights the importance of these values to the heritage of the public service. Burke outlines a new "three E" paradigm—empathy, evaluation, and ethics—that builds upon the earlier values and provides management tools for the future. She sees benefits in stronger networking (empathy), enhanced accountability (evaluation), and strengthened leadership (ethics). Both sets of "three E" values serve as powerful guides to behavior. Empirical research findings in recent years have confirmed a link between ethics and organizational performance (Menzel and Carson, 1999; Menzel, 2007; Berman and West, 1997; West and Berman 2004). HR managers are encouraged to follow Burke's advice to employ the tools of efficiency, effectiveness, and economy together with those of empathy, evaluation, and ethics. Such leadership by HR managers can help to enhance the integrity as well as the productivity of the organization, enabling managers to make "right good" decisions (Bowman, 1995). Cohen and Eimicke (2002:233–235) offer five useful guidelines to public servants in this regard: seek justice under the law, serve the public interest, ensure thorough analysis, act with compassion and empathy, and take personal responsibility for decisions (see also, Kolthoff, Huberts, and Van Den Heuvel, 2007).

### Privatization

Ethical issues surrounding the move to privatization have been addressed repeatedly in the public administration literature (e.g., Timmons, 1990; Frederickson, 1999; Kettl, 1993; Kolbrack, 1998; Lawther, 2004). Timmons notes five adverse impacts that privatization can have on career employees: "career disruption and dislocation; morale and productivity; relocation and reciprocity; erosion of civil service and merit systems; and undermining trust and credibility." (p. 106). He suggests that employers have an ethical obligation to provide workers with retraining, reciprocity provisions, and advance notice. The other four authors cited earlier, though writing separately, point to additional adverse consequences of privatization and contracting out for services: kickbacks, skimming, fraud, cozy politics (contractors winning or keeping a contract via politics), conflicts of interest, and monitoring problems. Coggburn (2007) and Crowell and Guy (forthcoming) have examined the outsourcing of all HR activities in the state governments of Texas and Florida, respectively; however, preliminary assessments are mixed at best. HR managers may support or oppose efforts to privatize, but two crucial parts of their role are to serve as advocates for the public sector employee and for the public interest. As advocates, they should exercise due diligence, insisting that the pros and cons of privatization initiatives are carefully considered and that harm done to public employees and/or the public interest is avoided or minimized.

### SUMMARY AND CONCLUSIONS

Building public organizations of integrity is the business of all public servants. Top-level officials have a wide range of explicit or implicit strategies to choose from in "managing ethics." HR managers have special opportunities and obligations to ensure that priority is given to ethics. Those with HR responsibilities must recognize the relative importance of government ethics as a precondition for good government. Ethical leadership is required to signal that adherence to ethics standards is expected and that even avoiding the appearance of impropriety is also important. The personnel system contains numerous leverage points where ethical leadership can be exercised.

The prospects for achieving and maintaining organizational integrity are enhanced when the top officials model exemplary moral leadership, adopt an organizational credo that promotes aspirational values, conduct an ethics audit, and develop and enforce an ethics code. Using ethics as a criterion in hiring and promotion, factoring ethics into performance appraisal, and including ethics in management and employee training programs further increase the prospects of institutionalizing ethical behavior. In addition, orientation programs highlighting ethical concerns, pay policies that reward productive and ethical behavior, and fairness in handling discipline and adverse actions enhance the ethical climate.

Prospects for institutionalizing integrity also increase as HR professionals seek ethical resolutions to employee grievances and problems; keep the workplace healthy, safe, and accessible; and act as strong advocates for employee and the public interest in privatization initiatives. A willingness to engage in risk sharing with employees via economically sound and ethically defensible health insurance and pension plans demonstrates appropriate attention to both taxpayer and employee interests. Continuing efforts to ensure a diverse workforce, protect the legitimate privacy interest of employee records, enable employees and managers to balance work and family responsibilities, and improve quality service delivery helps to create the ethical environment. In short, building organizational integrity and advancing a strong sense of public service ethics is one of the major HR challenges in the twenty-first century. Leadership by those with HR responsibility is critical to meeting this challenge.

## NOTES

1. The sample was randomly selected from SHRM's membership data base, which includes approximately 170,000 members (Joseph and Esen, 2003).
2. The two subsections are adapted from West and Berman (2006).
3. The material in the subsections on EAPs, health coverage, pensions, and work/family policies are adapted from a forthcoming chapter by West and Bowman, in Riddick and Coggburn, eds. (2008, Chapter 3.

## REFERENCES

Alder, Stoney G., and Joseph Gilbert. 2006. Achieving Ethics and Fairness in Hiring: Going Beyond the Law. *Journal of Business Ethics* 68:449–464.
Bell, Fleming A. 1997. *Ethics, Conflicts, and Offices: A Guide for Local Officials*. Chapel Hill, NC: Institute of Government.
Berman, Evan M., and Jonathan P. West. 1997. Managing Ethics to Improve Performance and Build Trust. *Public Integrity Annual* 2:23–32.
———. 2003a. Psychological Contracts in Local Government: A Preliminary Survey. *Review of Public Personnel Administration* 23 (4):30–52.
———. 2003b. Solutions to the Problem of Managerial Mediocrity. *Public Performance & Management Review* 27 (December):30–52.
Berman, Evan M., James S. Bowman, Jonathan P. West, and Montgomery Van Wart. 2006. *Human Resource Management in Public Service*. Thousand Oaks, CA: Sage.
Bowman, James S. 1995. Ethics and Quality: A "Right-Good" Combination: In *Quality Management Today: What Local Governments Need to Know*, J. P. West, ed. Washington, D.C.: ICMA, pp. 64–69.
———. 1999. Performance Appraisal: Verisimilitude Trumps Veracity. *Public Personnel Management* 28 (4):557–576.
Bowman, James S., and Jonathan P. West. 2007. *American Public Service: Radical Reform and the Merit System*. NY: Taylor & Francis Group.
Bowman, James S., Jonathan P. West, Evan M. Berman, and Montgomery Van Wart. 2004. *The Professional Edge*. Armonk, NY: M. E. Sharpe.

Brumback, Gary B. 1998. Institutionalizing Ethics in Government. In *The Ethics Edge*. E. Berman, J. West, and S. Bonczek, eds. Washington, D.C.: ICMA, pp. 61–71.

Buckley, M. Ronald, Danielle S. Beu, Dwight D. Frink, Jack L. Howard, Howard Berkson, Tommie A. Mobbs, and Gerald R. Ferris. 2001. Ethical Issues in Human Resource Management. *Human Resource Management Review* 11:11–29.

Burke, Francis. 1999. Ethical Decision-Making: Global Concerns, Frameworks and Approaches. *Public Personnel Management* 28 (4):529–540.

Clark, Charles S. 1997. Contingent Work Force. *CQ Researcher* 7 (40):937–960.

Coggburn, Jerrell. 2007. Outsourcing Human Resources: The Case of the Texas Health and Human Services Commission. *Review of Public Personnel Administration.* 27 (4): 315–335.

Cohen, Stephen, and William Eimicke. 2002. *The Effective Public Manager: Achieving Success in a Changing Government.* San Francisco, CA: Jossey-Bass.

Crowell, E., and Mary Ellen Guy Y. Forthcoming. Florida's HR Reforms: Service First, Service Worst, and Something in Between. *Public Personnel Management.*

Frederickson, H. George. 1999. Public Ethics and the New Managerialism. *Public Integrity* 1 (3):265–278.

Frederickson, H. George, and Richard K. Ghere, eds. 2005. *Ethics in Public Management.* Armonk, NY: M. E. Sharpe.

Giacalone, Robert A., Carole L. Jurkiewicz, and Stephen B. Knouse. 2003. Exit Surveys as Assessments of Organizational Ethicality. *Public Personnel Management* 32 (3):397–410.

Gibelman, Margaret. 1996. Managerial Manners—Notably Lacking in Personal Recruiting. *Administration in Social Work* 20 (1):59–72.

Gibson, Pamela S. 2007. *Examining the Moral Reasoning of the Ethics Advisor and Counselor: The Case of the Federal Designated Agency Ethics Official.* Unpublished paper presented at the Transatlantic Ethics Conference in College Park, MD. March 21, 22.

Greenblat, A. 2007. Pension Crisis. In *Issues for Debate in American Public Policy*, CQ Researcher, ed. Washington, D.C.: CQ Press, pp. 261–283.

Hacker, Jacob. 2006. *The Great Risk Shift.* New York: Oxford University Press.

Hirt, M. J. July 2003. Assessing the Ethical Judgment of a Potential Employee. *Public Administration Times.*

Hubbard, Joan C., Karen A. Forcht, and Daphyne S. Thomas. 1998. Human Resource Information Systems: An Overview of Current Ethical and Legal Issues. *Journal of Business Ethics* 17 (12):1319–1323.

Huberts, Leo, Maeschalck, Jeroen, and Carole Jurkiewicz, eds. 2008. *Ethics and Integrity of governance.* Northampton, MA: Edward Elgar.

Joseph, Joshua, and Evren Esen. 2003. *2003 Business Ethics Survey.* Alexandria, VA: SHRM/ERC.

Kamarck, Elaine C. 2007. *The End of Government as We Know It: Making Public Policy Work.* Boulder, CO: Lynne Reiner.

Karren, Ronald J., and Larry Zacharias. 2007. Integrity Tests: Critical Issues. *Human Resource Management Review* 17:221–234.

Kazman, Jane, and Stephen J. Bonczek, 1999. *Ethics in Action.* Washington, D.C.: ICMA.

Kellar, Elizabeth. 2004. Helping Employees Make Sound Ethical Decisions. *Public Management* 86 (8):4–6.

Kellough, Edward J.. 1999. Reinventing Public Personnel Management: Ethical Implications for Managers and Public Personnel Systems. *Public Personnel Management* (Special Issue—Labor–Management Cooperation) 27 (1).

Kellough, Edward J., and Lloyd G. Nigro. 2006. *Civil Service Reform in the States.* Albany, NY: SUNY Press.

Kettl, Donald. 1993. *Sharing Power: Public Governance and Private Markets.* Washington, D.C.: Brookings.

Klingner, Donald, and D. Lynn. 2005. Beyond Civil Service: The Politics of the Emergent Paradigms. In *Handbook of Human Resource Management in Government*, S. Condrey, ed. San Francisco, CA: Jossey-Bass, pp. 37–57.

Kolbrack, Peter. 1998. Privatization and Cozy Politics. In *The Ethics Edge*, E. Berman, J. West, and S. Bonczek, eds. Washington, D.C.: ICMA, pp. 178–193.

Kolthoff, E., L. Huberts, and H. Van Den Heuvel, 2007. The Ethics of New Public Management: Is Integrity at Stake? *Public Administration Quarterly* 30 (4):399–439.

Lawther, Wendell C. 2004. Ethical Challenges in Privatizing Government Services. *Public Integrity* 6 (2):141–153.

Lewis, Carol W., and Stuart C. Gilman. 2005. *The Ethics Challenge in Public Service.* San Francisco, CA: John Wiley & Sons.

Light, Paul. 1998. *The Tides of Reform.* Washington, D.C.: Brookings.

Menzel, Donald C., and Kathleen J. Carson. 1999. A Review and Assessment of Empirical Research on Public Administration Ethics: Implications for Scholars and Managers. *Public Integrity* 1 (3):239–264.

Menzel, Donald C. 2006. Ethics Management in Cities and Counties. In *The Ethics Edge*, 2nd ed., J. West and E. Berman, eds. Washington, D.C.: ICMA, pp. 108–115.

———. 2007. *Ethics Management for Public Administrators: Building Organizations of Integrity.* Armonk, NY: M. E. Sharpe.

Mines, Robert A., Sharon Anderson, and Patrice Von Stroh. 1991. EAP Ethics and the Professions. *EAPA Exchange:* December.

Pomeroy, Ann. 2006. The Ethics Squeeze. *HR Magazine:* March, pp. 48–54.

Ponemon, Larry, and Andrew J. Felo. 1996. Key Features of an Effective Ethics Training Program. *Management Accounting* (October):66–67.

Richardson, Catherine M. 1998. Ethics and Employee Benefits. *Benefits Quarterly* 14 (1):9–16.

Richter, Linda K., and William L. Richter. 1999. Ethics Challenges: Health, Safety and Accessibility in International Travel and Tourism. *Public Personnel Management* 28 (4):505–515.

Richter, William L., and Frances Burke, eds. 2007. *Combating Corruption, Encouraging Ethics*, 2nd ed. Lanham, MD: Roman & Littlefield.

Riddick, Christopher G., and Jerrell D. Coggburn, eds. (2008). *Handbook of Employee Benefits and Administration.* NY: Auerbach.

Sharer, David A., and William White. 2001. EAP Ethics and Quality: Does National vs. Local Service Delivery Make a Difference. Performance Resource Press (Fall). Retrieved on September 5, 2008, from <http://www.prponline.net/Work/EAP/Articles/eap_ethics_and_quality.htm>.

———. n.d. The Pricing of EAPs. Retrieved on September 5, 2008, from <http://www.eapage.com/The%20Pricing%20of%20EAPs.doc>.

Steiner, D. D., and S. W. Gilliland. 1996. Fairness Reactions to Personnel Selection Techniques in France and the United States. *Journal of Applied Psychology* 81(2):134–141.

Svara, James. 2007. *The Ethics Primer for Public Administrators in Government and Nonprofit Organizations.* Sudbury, MA: Jones and Bartlett Publishers.

Thompson, James, and Susan Mastracci. 2005. Toward a More Flexible Public Workforce: Issues and Applications. In *Handbook of Human Resource Management in Government*, S. Condrey, ed. San Francisco, CA: Jossey-Bass, pp. 125–142.

Timmons, William M. 1990. *A Casebook of Public Ethics and Issues.* Pacific Grove, CA: Brooks Cole.

Valentine, Sean, and Anthony Johnson. 2005. Codes of Ethics, Orientation Programs, and the Perceived Importance of Employee Corruptibility. *Journal of Business Ethics* 61:45–53.

Valmores, D. J. 2005. Commissioner, Civil Service Commission. "Presentation on Fighting and Preventing Corruption." ASEAN+3 Senior Officials Consultative Meeting on Creative Management for Government, September 30–October 1, Bangkok, Thailand.

Velasquez, Manuel G. 2001. *Business Ethics: Concepts and Cases.* Upper Saddle River, NJ: Pearson Prentice Hall.

Vickers, Mark R. 2005. Business Ethics and the RH Role: Past, Present, and Future. *Human Resource Planning* 28 (1):26–33.

Wardlaw, J. Lew. 2000. Strong Disagreement with ASPA Code of Ethics. *PA Times* 23 (5):10.

Weaver, Gary R., and Linda K. Trevino. 2001. The Role of Human Resources in Ethics/Compliance Management: A Fairness Perspective. *Human Resource Management Review* 11 (1–2):113–134.

Weaver, Gary R., Linda K. Trevino, and P. L. Cochran. 1999. Corporate Ethics Programs as Control Systems: Management and Environmental Influences. *Academy of Management Journal* 42:41–57.

West, Jonathan P., and James S. Bowman. (2008). Employee Benefits: Weighing Ethical Principles and Economic Imperatives. In *Handbook of Employee Benefits and Administration*, C. Riddick and J. Coggburn, eds. New York: Auerbach: 29–53.

West, Jonathan P., and Evan M. Berman. 2004. Ethics Training in U.S. Cities. *Public Integrity* 6 (3):189–206.

West, Jonathan P., Evan M. Berman, Stephen Bonczek, and Elizabeth Kellar. 1998. Frontiers of Ethics Training. *Public Management* 80 (6):4–9.

West, Jonathan P. and Evan M. Berman, eds. 2006. *The Ethics Edge*. Washington, D. C.: International City/County Management Association.

Wooten, K. 2001. Ethical Dilemmas in Human Resource Management: An Application of a Multidimensional Framework, a Unifying Taxonomy, and Applicable Codes. *Human Resource Management Review* 11:159–175.

# 18

# Current Developments in Public Sector Labor Relations

PATRICE M. MARESCHAL
Rutgers University at Camden

## INTRODUCTION

In 1956, union density in the American private sector was 34.7 percent, more than three times as great as the public sector rate of 11.1 percent (Labor Research Association, n.d.). By 2006, both sectors underwent a dramatic turnaround with public sector density at 36.2 percent and private sector density at 7.4 percent. Among public sector employees, those employed in local government had the highest union density rate of 41.9 percent. This group consisted of several highly organized professions, including teachers, police officers, and firefighters (Bureau of Labor Statistics, 2007a). The massive shift toward the public sector means that the labor movement will be greatly influenced by issues concerning public employees. This makes the study of current developments in public sector labor relations more important than ever.

In this chapter, I review recent developments in public sector labor relations at the federal and state levels. I begin with a brief discussion of unions' role in the workplace and society. Then I provide overviews of the legal and political/economic environments of public sector labor relations. Next I discuss developments in the post-Clinton era, since 2001. At the federal level, the news for supporters of unions is not positive. At the state level, the results are much more mixed and perhaps even provide grounds for optimism.

## UNIONS AND SOCIETY

Few institutions in America offer mechanisms for working people to express their concerns. Labor unions were established precisely for the purpose of giving workers a voice at their places of employment. As Freeman and Medoff (1979, 1984) demonstrate, the voice function of unions may positively impact productivity, efficiency, and social welfare. For instance, voice at work can boost morale, improve loyalty and commitment, and decrease turnover. Recent studies demonstrate that management responds to union voice by establishing formal procedures that promote efficiency and improve organization effectiveness (Verma, 2005).

Gunderson (2005) contends that the voice function of unions is more significant in the public sector than in the private sector. Many public sector employees entered public service out of a sense of commitment to their clientele and civic responsibility. These characteristics foster loyalty and increase public sector workers' use of voice. Public sector workers tend to be well-educated. For example, 70 percent of the federal workforce is composed of knowledge workers (Tobias, 2004). Thus they are likely to want to have greater involvement in shaping the terms and conditions of their employment.

In addition, unions have a long history of civic education and political participation, so much so that they have been described as "schools of democracy" (Sinyai, 2006:231). In the public sector, union members are disproportionately drawn from the professional ranks. Their professional status enhances their credibility when they advocate for issues that serve the public interest (Gunderson, 2005). Faced with declining union density, the erosion of federal labor protections in the United States, and little prospect of American labor law reform, unions are increasingly focusing their efforts on legislative and regulatory politics (Benz, 2005).

## THE LEGAL ENVIRONMENT

Employees in the private sector gained collective bargaining rights with the passage of the National Labor Relations Act (NLRA) of 1935. The NLRA was amended in 1947 with the Labor Management Relations Act (LMRA) and again in 1959 with the Labor Management Reporting and Disclosure Act of 1959. However, the NLRA as amended excluded federal and state governments from coverage.

Collective bargaining rights in the public sector were established somewhat later and differ across sectors of the government. At the federal level, President Kennedy issued Executive Order (E.O.) 10988 in 1962, granting federal employees the right to form and join labor unions and to bargain collectively. The scope of negotiable subjects for federal employees is narrower than it is for employees at other levels of government, for non-profits, and for the private sector. For instance, federal employees may not negotiate over wages, benefits, or restricted political activities. Strikes by federal employees are prohibited. In addition, federal employees represented by unions may not be compelled to join the union. This creates a tremendous free-rider problem for federal sector unions and has led some researchers to label the federal government as "the nation's largest open shop employer" (Bennett and Masters, 2003:538).

In 1969 President Nixon issued E.O. 11491 to bolster the organizational structure of labor relations in the federal sector. E.O. 11491 set up the Federal Labor
Relations Council to manage the labor relations program and instituted the Federal
Services Impasse Panel to adjudicate bargaining disputes (Masters, 2004). Although
E.O. 11491 strengthened federal sector labor protections, it could easily be rescinded
by a new administration. As a result, federal sector unions advocated for statutory
protections (Bennett and Masters, 2003).

With passage of the 1978 Civil Service Reform Act, collective bargaining
rights for federal employees were codified into law. Title VII, commonly referred to
as the *Federal Service Labor Management Relations Statute (FSLMRS)* regulates
labor relations in the federal sector. The FSLMRS provides coverage to most
employees in the federal sector except employees in the following agencies: the
Government Accounting Office (GAO), Federal Bureau of Investigation (FBI),
National Security Agency (NSA), Central Intelligence Agency (CIA), Federal Labor
Relations Authority, Federal Services Impasses Panel, Tennessee Valley Authority
(TVA), Foreign Service of the United States, Department of State, United States
Information Agency and Agency for International Development, the United States
Postal Service, and employees engaged in carrying out labor-management relations
laws. TVA employees have collective bargaining rights under the Employment
Relationship Policy Act of 1935. Postal Service Employees are covered by the Postal
Reorganization Act of 1970. However, employees of the GAO, FBI, NSA, and CIA
lack legal rights to engage in collective negotiations (Pynes, 2004).

At the state and local levels the legal environment is more complex. To illustrate, prior to 1967, public employees' attempts to form and join unions were often
thwarted by the legal precedent set in 1892 by the Massachusetts Supreme Court in
*McAuliffe v. New Bedford*. In that case, Justice Holmes argued that public employers
could require employees to forfeit their right to organize as a condition of accepting
public employment. Holmes' arguments were utilized as recently as 1963 by the
Michigan Supreme Court in the case of *AFSCME Local 201 v. City of Muskegon* to
prevent police officers from forming a union (Kearney and Carnevale, 2001).

The federal system allows each state the right to craft its own policies regulating
labor-management relations for public employees. The legal system governing collective bargaining for state and local government employees varies across the fifty states
and within states. Of the fifty states, twenty-three states and the District of Columbia
have laws granting all public employees the right to bargain collectively (Bennett and
Masters, 2003). However, twenty-seven states lack a general law protecting public
employees' rights to engage in collective bargaining. On a more positive note, a portion
of the public employees in those states practice collective bargaining under local ordinances, Executive Orders, and limited state laws (Kreisberg, 2004). The end result is a
patchwork system of collective bargaining.

## THE POLITICAL/ECONOMIC ENVIRONMENT

In the private sector, organized labor has been in decline for a number of years so that
there are now almost as many public sector union members as private sector union
members (see Table 18.1). Competitive pressures of globalization and employers'
strategic responses to competitive pressures have undermined the power of unions.

**TABLE 18.1   Union Membership in the Public and Private Sectors, 2000–2006**

| Year | Union Membership, Private Sector (in thousands) | Union Membership, Public Sector (in thousands) |
|------|------|------|
| 2000 | 9219 | 7115 |
| 2001 | 9148 | 7157 |
| 2002 | 8800 | 7346 |
| 2003 | 8452 | 7324 |
| 2004 | 8205 | 7267 |
| 2005 | 8255 | 7430 |
| 2006 | 7981 | 7378 |

*Source:* Bureau of Labor Statistics (2007b).

Although Table 18.1 shows that public sector unions have fared better, they are not immune to the political and economic forces buffeting the private sector. Public sector unions are facing pressures from privatization, reinventing government, and antigovernment advocates at the federal, state, and local levels (Hurd and Pinnock, 2004).

Public sector unions face a number of challenges. First, the influence of right wing conservatives on the Republican Party has made it more difficult than ever to pass collective bargaining legislation at the state level. In this conservative environment, more unorganized public employers are conducting aggressive antiunion campaigns (Kreisberg, 2004).

Governments at all levels are contending with budget deficits and shrinking revenues. At the same time, the public sector faces taxpayers' demands to improve performance and reduce waste, fraud, and abuse. Together, budgetary and performance issues lead to demands to reduce the size of the workforce, limit compensation, and contract out or privatize public services (Masters and Bennett, 2003). In brief, the current political-economic environment is likely to strain existing labor-management relationships and lead to increased conflict over the appropriate role of government in a democratic society.

In the background of the public sector's fiscal and performance crises, the labor movement has confronted a political crisis of its own. Faced with continuing decline in union density, labor unions argued amongst themselves about the best way to revitalize the labor movement. The key elements in the internal struggle were demands for restructuring, increasing the authority of the American Federation of Labor and Congress of Industrial Organizations (AFL-CIO) over its affiliates, and devoting more resources to organizing. In 2005 the Change to Win (CTW) coalition—consisting of the Service Employees International Union (SEIU), UNITE-HERE (formed in 2004 from the former Union of Needletrades, Industrial and Textile Employees [UNITE] and the Hotel Employees and Restaurant Employees International Union [HERE]), the United Brotherhood of Carpenters and Joiners (UBC), the International Brotherhood of Teamsters (IBT), the United Food and Commercial Workers (UFCW), and the United Farm Workers (UFW)—broke away from the AFL-CIO. The split rocked the house of labor and generated resentment among the unions that remained loyal to the AFL-CIO (Hurd, 2007).

## RECENT DEVELOPMENTS IN THE FEDERAL SECTOR

At the federal level both President Clinton and President Bush evaluated the success of their administrations' labor management relations on the extent to which federal agencies effectively carried out the administration's directives (Tobias, 2004). However the similarities end there. In 1993 Vice President Gore noted in the National Performance Review that adversarial labor-management relationships in the federal sector reduced productivity. Shortly thereafter President Clinton issued E.O. 12871. This created a National Partnership Council and a comprehensive program to promote labor-management partnerships in all federal government agencies (Albright, 2004). As of 1998, 67 percent of the federal workforce represented by labor unions was covered by a partnership agreement or council (Masters, 2004).

The record of President George W. Bush with respect to federal sector labor relations stands in stark contrast. Unlike Clinton, Bush did not deem it necessary to work with federal employees through their unions. Almost immediately after taking office, President Bush issued E.O. 13202, dissolving the National Partnership Council and rescinding a Clinton-era directive ordering that federal agencies engage in partnerships with their unions (Thompson, 2007).

In the summer of 2001 President Bush issued his Management Agenda, focused on reforming government. The Management Agenda promoted managerial flexibility and increased managerial authority. In addition, the Agenda called for opening the government to the discipline of competition (Office of Management and Budget, 2001). More precisely, President Bush established the objective of allowing private contractors to compete for the work performed by federal employees or directly converting to the private sector the work performed in 50 percent of the jobs (roughly 425,000 federal employee positions) classified as not inherently governmental (Tobias, 2004).

President Bush further weakened the collective bargaining rights of federal employees after September 11, 2001. For example, he exempted 17,000 employees in the fledgling Transportation Security Administration from collective bargaining rights (Tobias, 2004). After this initial success, Bush repeated this strategy by insisting as a condition of creating the Department of Homeland Security with over 170,000 employees that it be exempted from federal-sector labor relations statutes (Naff and Newman, 2004).

On January 7, 2002, President Bush issued E.O. 13252, exempting the following divisions of the Department of Justice from coverage under the FSLMRS: United States Attorneys' Offices, Criminal Division, INTERPOL—U.S. National Bureau, National Drug Intelligence Center, and the Office of Intelligence Policy and Review (Pynes, 2004). In all, Bush's initiatives stripped 500 Justice Department employees of existing union representation and prevented another 500 Justice Department employees from seeking union representation (Tobias, 2004).

In response to the hostile labor relations climate set by President Bush, a growing number of federal agencies are seeking and obtaining similar exemptions. For instance, in 2003 Congress passed a bill restricting the collective bargaining rights of 700,000 civilian employees in the Department of Defense (DOD). Specifically, the legislation allows the Secretary of Defense to limit his conversations with union representatives advocating for DOD employees. The legislation also substitutes an internal grievance appeal system for employees' rights to appeal adverse actions to the Merit Systems Protection Board (Naff and Newman, 2004).

President Bush struck yet another blow to organized labor following Hurricane Katrina. In September 2005, Bush suspended the provisions of the Davis-Bacon Act of 1931 for cleanup and reconstruction of storm-ravaged areas of Alabama, Florida, Mississippi, and Louisiana. The Davis-Bacon Act requires employers to pay workers prevailing wages for work performed on federal contracts. In issuing the suspension, Bush argued that Davis-Bacon drives up construction costs, and suspending the federal legislation would create more jobs (Edsall, 2005).

It appears that President Bush viewed federal sector labor unions as a threat to organizational effectiveness, which cannot be tolerated when national security is at stake (Wasserman, 2006). The logical flaw in this argument is that if any union poses no potential harm to the national interest it is a federal sector labor union. Federal sector labor unions cannot strike, and the range of issues over which they can bargain is extremely limited. If the Department of Homeland Security's mission would be fatally compromised by the presence of a federal sector labor union, how is it that companies with private sector unions manage to thrive and survive? If unions are so inherently inimical to organizational success, one would expect the enhanced bargaining rights of private sector unions to swiftly lead to the bankruptcy of all of their employers. In the absence of a logical reason for the Bush administration to fear labor unions, labor relations developments in the federal sector appear to display a president who is undertaking "a venture in political opportunism" (Ferris and Hyde, 2004:220).

While President Bush deserves to be criticized by supporters of the labor movement, another noteworthy theme appears in recent research on labor relations in the federal sector—the reinvention of President Clinton as a great friend to American unions. For example, he is described as introducing "a new era in labor management relations" (Ferris and Hyde, 2004:223). Yet, the National Performance Review report issued under his administration established a goal of eliminating 252,000 federal positions (Gore, 1993). Political appointees who did not see the value of labor-management collaboration emphasized downsizing instead of forming partnerships (Tobias, 2004). In the end, the Clinton administration reduced the federal workforce by 384,000 employees (Masters, 2004).

## RECENT DEVELOPMENTS IN THE STATE SECTOR

The fortunes of unions at the state level have been much more variegated than at the federal level. The Bush era witnessed some stunning victories and some crushing defeats for unions at the state level. In the first part of this section, I review previously published research on labor relations developments at the state level. This yields some illuminative results but ultimately cannot determine whether labor is "winning" more battles than it is "losing." This is a nontrivial question to supporters of the labor movement, because the spectacular decline in union density can only be reversed if the political tide turns in labor's favor. To that end, the second part of this section reviews newspaper articles about labor unions in all fifty states from 2001 through June 2007. This yields a somewhat encouraging estimate of union success rates at the state level during the Bush era.

## Case Studies

As at the federal level, there are some grim realities within the states. Specifically activist governors in Kentucky and Indiana abolished collective bargaining rights for public employees. The governors of Colorado and Rhode Island also engaged in punitive measures against state labor unions (Hays and Sowa, 2006). Ironically, a previous article praises Kentucky for providing collective bargaining rights in 2001 (Kreisberg, 2004), but this experiment appears to have been quite short-lived. An executive order issued by Governor Patton in 2002 to create the Governor's Employee Advisory Council, an official body that could bargain with state employees' unions, was rescinded by Governor Fletcher in 2003 (Berg 2004).

Battaglio and Condrey (2006) compare state systems of human resource management, and two of the states in their sample are contrasted with respect to their labor relations policies: Florida and New York. While Florida's governor unilaterally stripped unionized state employees of their collective bargaining rights as part of a systematic reform of the state's public administration, New York's governor collaborated with its unions on reforms that ultimately proved to be more effective (Battaglio and Condrey 2006). Wisconsin is listed in a survey of best practices in state human resource management because of its use of interest-based bargaining (Hays 2004).

Public employees in several states gained collective bargaining rights through a variety of methods including legislation, voter referenda, executive orders and judicial decisions. In 2003, New Mexico granted collective bargaining rights to its state employees (Wasserman 2006). Specifically, the Public Employee Bargaining Act provides public employees in New Mexico the right to "form, join, or assist" labor organizations for collective negotiations. In 2007 Delaware passed legislation granting state employees full collective bargaining rights. Perhaps the most noteworthy successes at the state level during this period occurred in Oregon and Washington, as tens of thousands of home care aides were granted collective bargaining rights through public referenda and achieved substantial improvements in compensation (Mareschal 2006).

In November 2007 Governor Ritter of Colorado issued Executive Order D 028 07 authorizing partnership agreements with state employees. Although Governor Ritter characterized the E.O. as a partnership arrangement as opposed to collective bargaining (Barge and Kelley 2007), the E.O. recognizes labor unions as public employees' representative and allows them to negotiate with the state over issues of mutual concern. Further the E.O. requires the state and the employee organizations to reach agreement though good faith discussions and provides for impasse and dispute resolution. At the same time the E.O. prohibits strikes, the collection of agency fees, and the use of binding arbitration.

The history of public employee collective bargaining rights in Missouri has been more convoluted. In 1945 the Missouri Constitution's bill of rights provided collective bargaining rights. However, in *City of Springfield v. Clouse* (1947) the Missouri Supreme Court ruled that the constitution did not cover public employees. In 1965, most public employees were granted the right to "meet and confer" under state law. Adding another twist in the collective bargaining relationship, in *Sumpter v. City of Moberly* (1982 ) the state supreme court ruled that the meet and confer process was not binding on public employers. As a result public employers were free to terminate collective bargaining agreements at any time.

In 2001 Governor Bob Holden issued an executive order granting public sector employees the right to form and join unions and negotiate contracts with the state. Governor Matt Blunt rescinded the executive order immediately after taking office in 2005. In the latest turn of events, in 2007 the Missouri Supreme Court ruled that the right to organize and engage in collective negotiations guaranteed in Missouri's constitution applies to public employees as well as private employees. The decision in *Independence NEA v. Independence School District* (2007) overturned a 60-year legal standard.

Beyond establishing the right to engage in collective bargaining, public sector unions have attempted to change policies for determining representation. The most commonly used method of establishing union representation is the secret ballot election. If the majority of employees cast a vote in favor of the union, the union becomes the employees' exclusive representative for purposes of collective bargaining. Secret ballot elections are intended to provide a democratic means for resolving representation questions. However, in recent years representation elections administered by government agencies have come under increasing criticism for being too costly, formal, and time-consuming. During the election process, employees are frequently intimidated and fired for supporting the union. The penalties for parties who violate standards for a fair election are weak. As a result, the promise of democracy is rarely fulfilled (Budd 2008).

Not surprisingly, labor advocates are increasingly trying to avoid the secret ballot election as a method of determining representation. In 2005 New Jersey passed card check legislation covering public sector employees and private sector employees not covered by the NLRA. The legislation requires the New Jersey Public Employment Relations Commission to recognize a labor union as the representative of the bargaining unit if the majority of employees have signed authorization cards designating the union as their representative. Since passage of the legislation employees of the state's Housing Mortgage and Finance Authority, food service workers employed by the Camden County Board of Education, employees of the prosecutors' office in Mercer and Atlantic Counties, and professional administrators at Rutgers University have used the card check method to join unions (Friedman 2007; Union of Rutgers Administrators 2007). Similarly, in 2007 Oregon and New Hampshire passed card check legislation for public employees.

There have been some acrimonious struggles within the labor movement over organizing campaigns. The SEIU and the American Federation of State, County, and Municipal Employees (AFSCME) have battled over representation of publicly-funded home care aides and child care workers in California, Illinois, Iowa, Maryland, New Jersey, and Pennsylvania. These same unions have fought turf wars over municipal employees in Texas. In June 2006, the two unions finally reached an agreement resolving twenty-seven jurisdictional disputes (Hurd, 2007).

In an effort to avoid such struggles in the future, the AFL-CIO has created Industry Coordinating Committees (ICC) to manage negotiations and organizing efforts within industries. In August 2006 ten unions representing state and local government employees formed an ICC. One of the primary goals of the public sector ICC is to expand collective bargaining rights for public employees in states that lack comprehensive labor protections (Hurd, 2007).

So the record at the state level is decidedly mixed. But these case studies provide insufficient information on the overall success rate of American labor unions at achieving their state-level political goals. Given the current context of labor-management relations in the United States, political action is more important than ever to the viability of the labor movement. First, as noted earlier, the current situation at the federal level is so gloomy that President Clinton is remembered fondly despite labor's many unsuccessful political battles with him over issues such as North American Free Trade Agreement (NAFTA). Therefore, any cause for optimism must come at the state level. Second, the apparent stability in public-sector union density actually reflects parallel and simultaneous processes of unionization and deunionization (Hurd and Pinnock, 2004). Simply put, labor is "winning" as much as it is "losing" in the public sector, and it must improve its success rates in order to begin rebuilding its numbers and strength.

## EVALUATING THE POLITICAL SCORECARD IN THE STATE SECTOR

I searched the LexisNexis database of U.S. newspapers, which is organized by state, for articles published from 2001 through June 2007 in which the words "labor union" appeared in the title. A subset of these articles was retrieved, in which unions expressed support for a state-level policy or politician. For each article, the database was searched again to determine how the policy issue was resolved. Thus, a "success" occurred if a union supported a politician who was then elected or if the union supported a policy that was then enacted. A "failure" occurred if the union supported a politician who lost an election or if the union opposed a policy that was then enacted. This allows an estimate of organized labor's success rates at the state level in the Bush era, because the newspaper articles represent a sample of all state-level union political activity. It also yields a trove of less well-known but illuminative cases, discussed next. The results are summarized in Tables 2 and 3.

### Failures

The most unusual policy failure for the labor movement may have occurred in Nebraska. The state's AFL-CIO chapter endorsed the election of a state senator who was under indictment for prescription drug fraud ("Labor Union Backs Senator Charged with Felony Drug Fraud," 2004). The following month, he dropped out of the race and entered a rehabilitation facility (Dejka and Reed, 2004). Two years earlier, Pennsylvania's largest union of public employees endorsed a Republican candidate for governor because they were still angry with the actions of the Democratic candidate when he was the mayor of Philadelphia a decade earlier (O'Toole, 2002a). The election resulted in a landslide victory for the Democratic candidate (O'Toole, 2002b), which probably eroded some of the union's political capital at the statehouse. The California Labor Federation spent $5 million in an unsuccessful effort to oppose the recall of its governor (Perkins, 2003).

Alaska's labor leaders mobilized to try to talk the state legislature out of modifying its state pension system for new employees (Cockerham, 2005), but two months later this law was enacted (Inklebarger, 2005). Idaho's teachers' and firefighters' unions protested a law that hampered organized labor's ability to make political donations (Taule, 2003a). As the teachers held a rally a few weeks later, the bill was approved by the state legislature (Taule, 2003b). Colorado's state AFL-CIO was dismayed that their governor vetoed a bill aimed at making it easier for unions to organize (Couch and Brown, 2007).

New Jersey's state AFL-CIO supported paid family leave legislation (Parello, 2001) but this has failed to become law despite its support from the current governor (Morley, 2007). In California, the SEIU spent $9 million in a failed attempt to pass a ballot initiative that would have made it easier for state budgets to be passed (Chorneau, 2004). California unions also lost a close race on a ballot initiative aimed at mandating employer health insurance (Jablon, 2004).

In coalition with a seniors' group, Iowa's state AFL-CIO opposed a law deregulating power plants (Lynch, 2001). This bill was signed four months later by the governor (Boshart, 2001). As part of a coalition, South Dakota's state AFL-CIO opposed a ballot resolution that was designed to make it harder for the state to allow same-sex marriages ("Labor Union against Ballot Measure," 2006). Among eleven ballot initiatives year, that was one of only three which were approved by voters ("Eight South Dakota Ballot Measures Fail," 2006).

## Successes

In Oregon, a union of agricultural employees protested a bill that would ostensibly grant them collective bargaining rights but that was carefully crafted by farmers to be ineffective because it required the certification election campaign to be longer than the harvest season (Prengaman, 2003). This bill continues to be introduced each year but the union is able to prevent its enactment ("Oregon's Largest Dairy Expected to Begin Negotiations," 2006). In Kentucky, labor's supporters continue to block the governor's efforts to establish right-to-work legislation and to repeal prevailing wage legislation (Brammer, 2006). In Maryland, employees of state colleges and universities were permitted to unionize. Within one year, three quarters of the campuses were organized (Manning, 2002). In Colorado, the governor allowed union dues to be deducted from employee paychecks ("Solid Start for Ritter on His Initial Agenda," 2007).

One of New York's most powerful unions held a rally in opposition to budget cuts that would have led to the termination of health insurance for its members (Kriss, 2003). Two months later, the state legislature found the money to allow this program to continue (Precious, 2003). One of California's largest unions also staved off budget cuts that would have erased its members' pay gains through collective bargaining (Chorneau, 2004). Two large public-sector unions in Minnesota negotiated same-sex partner benefits which created a risk that the contracts would not be approved by the state Legislature (Whereatt, 2002). When the legislature never approved the contracts, the union and the state found a way to implement those contracts ("Unions, State to Re-Sign Contracts If House Doesn't Ratify," 2002).

Ohio's state AFL-CIO chapter campaigned vigorously for the Democratic gubernatorial candidate (Hershey, 2006). His landslide victory ended sixteen years of Republican control of the governor's office (Milicia, 2006). New Mexico's state AFL-CIO chapter endorsed the Democratic gubernatorial candidate ("Labor Union Endorses Democrats," 2002), who went on to win by the largest margin in over thirty years (Massey, 2002). In Illinois, the SEIU was an early and enthusiastic supporter of the man who become governor and who has signed legislation allowing tens of thousands of child and home care workers to unionize (Franklin and Rose, 2005).

Oklahoma's state AFL-CIO chapter opposed a ballot initiative that would raise the gasoline tax (Francis-Smith, 2005). This initiative garnered only 13 percent of the popular vote (Price, 2005). California's unions opposed three ballot measures relating to teacher tenure, union political activities, and budget reform. All were defeated (Wildermuth, 2005). Wisconsin's state legislature refused to ratify a union contract that provided free health insurance (Pommer, 2003). When the contract was eventually resolved, the free health insurance was preserved ("Legislature to Play Bigger Role in Contracts," 2003). Rhode Island's governor pleaded with the state workers' union to start paying for health insurance (Gregg, 2003), yet the state legislature prevented this from becoming law during its next session (MacKay and Anderson, 2003).

New Jersey's AFL-CIO sought passage of a bill mandating "project labor agreements" designed to help unionized employers win state contracts (Tedeschi, 2002). This was signed into law by the governor six months later (Jackson, 2002). Minnesota's unions demanded an increase in the state's minimum wage (Smith, 2001). This took place four years later (Condon, 2005). The AFL-CIO of Michigan threatened to introduce a ballot initiative in favor of a two-dollar increase in the state's minimum wage ("Will Voters Decide Minimum Wage? Labor Unions May Push Ballot Measure for Increases If Lawmakers Fail", 2005), and the governor approved a slightly larger increase the following year (Martin, 2006). The Massachusetts AFL-CIO fought to block a one-dollar increase in the state's minimum wage on the grounds that a larger raise was needed (Arvidson, 2006). Less than two months later, legislators had agreed to a minimum wage increase of $1.25 (Donald, 2006). California's governor raised the state's minimum wage by seventy-five cents ("State Minimum Wage Increases to $7.50," 2006), in a move that was perceived as appeasing labor unions (Gledhill and Martin, 2005).

## Did Successes Outnumber Failures?

Nineteen success stories are recounted, along with only eleven failures (see Table 18.2). Success stories are related for sixteen states, while failures are recounted for only nine states. There were three states counted in both groups because both success stories and failures were observed. Interestingly, there were the same number of successes and failures within each of these three states. The net result is that the outcomes of union political activities in the states can be classified into four categories. It should be noted that the most prevalent category is "no reported political activity," occurring in twenty-eight states.

The second most common category is "success," comprised of the following thirteen states: Illinois, Kentucky, Massachusetts, Maryland, Michigan, Minnesota, New Mexico, New York, Ohio, Oklahoma, Oregon, Rhode Island, and Wisconsin. The third most common category is "failure," which includes the following six states: Alaska, Idaho, Iowa, Nebraska, Pennsylvania, and South Dakota. Least common is "neutral," with only California, Colorado, and New Jersey in this group of states showing an equal number of union political successes and failures in the Bush era.

## DISCUSSION

The data in this study do not claim to represent the universe of union political activity at the state level. Nor is the classification scheme entirely accurate. Kentucky, for example, is listed as a success because the legislature blocked some of the governor's

**TABLE 18.2   Union Political Activity Outcomes, by State**

| No Activity | Success | Failure | Neutral |
|---|---|---|---|
| Alabama | Illinois | Alaska | California |
| Arizona | Kentucky | Idaho | Colorado |
| Arkansas | Massachusetts | Iowa | New Jersey |
| Connecticut | Maryland | Nebraska | |
| Delaware | Michigan | Pennsylvania | |
| Florida | Minnesota | South Dakota | |
| Georgia | New Mexico | | |
| Hawaii | New York | | |
| Indiana | Ohio | | |
| Kansas | Oklahoma | | |
| Louisiana | Oregon | | |
| Maine | Rhode Island | | |
| Mississippi | Wisconsin | | |
| Missouri | | | |
| Montana | | | |
| Nevada | | | |
| New Hampshire | | | |
| North Carolina | | | |
| North Dakota | | | |
| South Carolina | | | |
| Tennessee | | | |
| Texas | | | |
| Utah | | | |
| Vermont | | | |
| Virginia | | | |
| Washington | | | |
| West Virginia | | | |
| Wyoming | | | |

antiunion measures. It is also listed among the case studies for having abolished all state unions and their contracts. The data provide a random sample of union political activity because the editors of the various newspapers and wire services did not share a common political agenda. They also offer a fresh perspective, as none of the events described earlier in the case studies were found among the newspaper articles, and very few of the newspaper articles have been previously analyzed in the academic literature.

There are wide variations in union political activity across the states. California leads the way with six instances in the past six years, but only half of these were successful, which is why California heads the list of "neutral" states. The twenty-two states in which the unions have a recent record of political activity correspond pretty closely to Wasserman's (2006) list of twenty-five states that offer comprehensive bargaining rights to a majority of their employees. Three states (Idaho, Kentucky, and Oklahoma) do not offer bargaining rights to most employees, yet the survey of newspaper articles found evidence of union political activity. Eight states offer bargaining rights to most employees, yet the survey indicated no union political activity. These are Connecticut, Delaware, Florida, Hawaii, Indiana, Maine, Montana, New Hampshire, and Vermont.

The most straightforward interpretation of the results is that there have been both successes and failures at the state level, which is consistent with the findings of case study research but which adds little to our estimation of organized labor's success rates. To go a little further out on a limb, it appears that there are more successes than failures. In fact, over twice as many states are in the "success" category than in the "failure" category. (To add some needed perspective, there are over twice as many states in the "no reported political activity" category as in the "success" category.) A success rate greater than 50 percent would seem to be a prerequisite for union growth, and this is being comfortably exceeded in today's state sector.

Some interesting comparisons can be made of the political successes and failures (see Table 18.3). First of all, union support for a candidate for statewide political office appears to average a neutral effect on the candidate's chances of winning an election. In three instances labor's preferred candidate won and on three other occasions the result was an electoral defeat. Second, labor's most effective issue was the minimum wage, accounting for four successes and no failures. Third, unions achieved few political victories when they supported causes that ranged far from the traditional domain of labor-management relations, such as support for same-sex marriage. For example, both attempts to mandate benefits for nonunionized employers were defeated. Conversely, unions did quite well at holding on to their pay and benefits, suffering one political failure but achieving five successes. State labor law reform was also a generally positive area, providing six victories against three defeats. In contrast

**TABLE 18.3    Union Political Activity Outcomes, by Type of Issue**

| Type of Issue | Success | Failure |
|---|---|---|
| Candidate support | Illinois<br>New Mexico<br>Ohio | California<br>Nebraska<br>Pennsylvania |
| Labor law reform | California<br>Colorado<br>Kentucky<br>Maryland<br>New Jersey<br>Oregon | Colorado<br>Idaho |
| Union compensation and benefits | California<br>Minnesota<br>New York<br>Rhode Island<br>Wisconsin | Alaska |
| Minimum wage increases | California<br>Massachusetts<br>Michigan<br>Minnesota | |
| Other social issues | Oklahoma | California<br>Iowa<br>New Jersey<br>South Dakota |

to the situation at the federal level, state-level developments may provide some grounds for optimism to the American labor movement and its supporters.

## CONCLUSIONS

To those who strive for an increase in American union density, developments in public sector labor relations have never been more important than now. For federal employees it quickly becomes apparent that the labor relations system, which was never a totally effective guarantor of workers' rights, is in great peril. President Bush has used national security as an excuse to exempt a growing proportion of the federal workforce from union protection, even though Ferris and Hyde (2004:220) note that "not one post-9/11 analysis has identified the federal personnel system as contributing to either the cause of that disaster or the failure to prevent it."

Public sector union density will plummet unless balance and integrity are restored to labor relations in the federal sector. This will not occur through a process of waxing nostalgically for the days of the Clinton administration. President Clinton can be credited with vetoing the TEAM Act, which was opposed by the labor movement as a thinly veiled attempt to create company unions. Most of the other changes to labor law that occurred during the Clinton era, such as ergonomics regulation, are no longer in force (Moberly, 2006). Also, Clinton battled with federal unions over proposals to modernize public administration which included a speeded-up procedure to terminate employees (Naff and Newman, 2004).

The appropriate comparison to be made of federal labor relations in the George W. Bush and Clinton eras is not how much more labor-friendly Clinton was than Bush. Rather, it is how much more effective Bush was than Clinton at modifying the federal labor relations landscape. Was Bush serendipitously able to take advantage of the 9/11 crisis to further his antiunion aims, an opportunity that history did not present to Clinton? Or did Clinton simply not care as much as Bush about collective bargaining issues as they applied to the federal sector? It is fruitless to blame Congressional opposition for Clinton's lackluster labor relations record, because Bush seemed undeterred by a similar situation. Answering this puzzle is key to revitalizing unions in the federal sector.

At the state level, two scenarios appear to be playing out. In twenty-eight states, there is no evidence of union political activity. Those correspond fairly closely to the states that do not grant collective bargaining rights to their own employees. This raises an issue of causality. Does a lack of union political activity lead to the denial of collective bargaining rights for state employees, or is it the provision of collective bargaining rights that stimulates union political activity? Wasserman (2006) suggests federal legislation be enacted to craft minimum standards for state labor relations systems. It will be a challenge for unions to drum up public support for this cause in many states where they appear to be politically dormant.

In the remainder of the United States, the labor movement is not only fighting but also usually winning at the state level. Successes are about twice as likely as failures. Furthermore, certain patterns are replicating themselves across the country that may be exploitable for organized labor and its supporters. The minimum wage appears to be an excellent social issue for unions to support because it generally leads to success. More radical changes such as paid family leave and gay marriage appear to be less fruitful because they generally fail. This is sobering news for those who would envision a grand coalition of organized labor and other progressive movements fighting for widespread social change. But it is useful information for American unions, because they have neither the time nor the resources to back losing causes. They need a string of successes starting immediately, because they know that failures will also occur.

The biggest issue at the state level that requires the attention of labor's supporters is the need to support winning candidates at above-chance rates. In three of six elections in this survey, the labor movement's preferred choice lost. Colorado's experience shows that backing a winner does not guarantee favorable treatment, just as the situation in California demonstrates that opposing a winner does not prevent the chance to score political victories. In general, it is much better for unions to have the support of a state's governor. They simply do not have the time or resources to guess wrong in half of the gubernatorial elections.

What is perhaps most noteworthy about public sector labor relations developments since 2001 is that they provide some grounds for optimism. If unions could achieve more political successes than failures in the Bush era, they may be able to perform even better should the pendulum swing back toward a political climate that favors collective bargaining rights. It is no exaggeration to state that the future of the American labor movement may be at stake.

## REFERENCES

Albright, Robert R. 2004. The U.S. Department of Transportation's Partnership Experience: Implications for the Future. *Journal of Labor Research* 25:43–54.

Arvidson, Erik. 2006. After Pressure from Labor Unions Lawmakers Back Off Minimum-Wage Vote. *Lowell Sun:* June 22.

Barge, Chris, and Joanne Kelley 2007. "Guv Backs State Unions: Exec Order Giving Workers Stronger Voice Angers GOP." *Rocky Mountain News,* November 3.

Battaglio, Paul R., and Stephen E. Condrey. 2006. Civil Service Reform: Examining State and Local Government Cases. *Review of Public Personnel Administration* 26:118–138.

Bennett, James T., and Marick F. Masters. 2003. The Future of Public Sector Labor-Management Relations. *Journal of Labor Research* 24:533–544.

Benz, Dorothee. 2005. It Takes a Village to Win a Union: A Case Study of Organizing among Florida's Nursing Home Workers. *Politics & Society* 33:123–152.

Berg, Philip 2004. "State of the Unions: The Impact of Administrative Changes in State-Sector Labor Relations." Division of Personnel Solutions, *Winter*

Boshart, Rod. 2001. Iowa Governor Signs Power Plant Siting Bill. *Cedar Rapids Gazette:* July 4.

Brammer, Jack. 2006. House Snubs Fletcher on Labor: Union, Wage Issues Not in Its Budget. *Lexington Herald-Leader:* February 25.

Budd, John W. 2008. Labor Relations: Strking a Balance (2nd ed.). Boston: McGraw-Hill.

Bureau of Labor Statistics. 2007a. Union Members in 2006. Available at <www.bls.gov/news.release/union2.nr0.htm>.

———. 2007b. Union Affiliation of Employed Wage and Salary Workers by Occupation and Industry. Available at http://www.bls.gov/webapps/legacy/cpslutab3.htm.

Chorneau, Tom. 2004. Nation's Largest Labor Union Steps into California Budget Fight. *Associated Press State & Local Wire:* June 26.

*City of Springfield v. Clouse* (1947). 206 S.W. 2d 539.

Cockerham, Sean.2005. National Labor Unions Urge Alaska to Say No. *Anchorage Daily News:* May 7, p. A1.

Condon, Patrick. 2005. After Eight Years, a Bump in State's Minimum Wage. *Associated Press State & Local Wire:* May 3.

Couch, Mark P., and Jennifer Brown. 2007. Ritter Veto Shocks Labor. *Denver Post:* February 11, p. A1.

Dejka, Joe, and Leslie Reed. 2004. Embattled Mossey Ends Bid. *Omaha World-Herald:* October 16, p. 1A.

Donald, Brooke. 2006. Legislators Raise Minimum Wage. *Associated Press State & Local Wire:* August 1.

Edsall, Thomas B. 2005. Bush Suspends Pay Act in Areas Hit by Storm. *Washington Post:* September 9, p. D3.

Eight South Dakota Ballot Measures Fail. 2006. *Associated Press State & Local Wire:* November 8.

Ferris, Frank, and Albert C. Hyde. 2004. Federal Labor-Management Relations for the Next Century—Or the Last? The Case of the Department of Homeland Security. *Review of Public Personnel Administration* 24:216–233.

Francis-Smith, Janice. 2005. Labor Union Joins Fights Against State Question 723. *Oklahoma City Journal Record:* September 2.

Franklin, Stephen, and Barbara Rose. 2005. Labor Union Pushes for Change in Organizing Workers. *Chicago Tribune:* July 30.

Freeman, Richard, and James Medoff. 1979. The Two Faces of Unionism. *Public Interest,* 57 (Fall): 69–93.

———. 1984. *What Do Unions Do?* New York: Basic Books.

Friedman, Sheldon. 2007. Why the Employee Free Choice Act Deserves Support: Response to Adams. *Labor Studies Journal* 31 (4):15–22.

Gledhill, Lynda, and Mark Martin. 2005. 'New Arnold' to Propose $1 Boost in Minimum Wage. *San Francisco Chronicle:* December 31, p. A1.

Gore, Albert. 1993. From Red Tape to Results; Creating a Government that Works Better and Costs Less. Available at <http://govinfo.library.unt.edu/npr/library/nprrpt/annrpt/redtpe93/index.html>.

Gregg, Katherine. 2003. Carcieri Turns to Labor Unions to Share Costs. *Providence Journal-Bulletin:* February 6, p. A1.

Gunderson, Morley. 2005. Two Faces of Union Voice in the Public Sector. *Journal of Labor Research* 26:393–413.

Hays, Steven W. 2004. Trends and Best Practices in State and Local Human Resource Management. *Review of Public Personnel Administration* 24:256–275.

Hays, Steven W., and Jessica E. Sowa. 2006. A Broader Look at the 'Accountability' Movement: Some Grim Realities in State Civil Service Systems. *Review of Public Personnel Administration* 26:102–117.

Hershey, William. 2006. Labor Unions Favor Strickland's Stand, Fear Blackwell's Intent. *Dayton Daily News:* September 4, p. A4.

Hurd, Richard W. 2007. U.S. Labor 2006: Strategic Developments Across the Divide. *Journal of Labor Research* 28:313–325.

Hurd, Richard W., and Sharon Pinnock. 2004. Public Sector Unions: Will They Thrive or Struggle to Survive? *Journal of Labor Research* 25:211–221.

*Independence National Education Association v. Independence School District* (2007). 223 S.W. 3d 131.

Inklebarger, Timothy. 2005. Murkowski Signs Pension Changes into Law. *Associated Press State & Local Wire:* July 27.

Jablon, Robert. 2004. Officials Look for Fixes After Health Care Measure Fails. *Associated Press State & Local Wire:* November 5.

Jackson, Herb. 2002. Passing Laws on the Sly. *Bergen County Record:* August 5, p. A3.

Kearney, Richard C., and David G. Carnevale. 2001. *Labor Relations in the Public Sector,* 3rd ed. New York: Marcel Dekker.

Kreisberg, Steven. 2004. The Future of Public Sector Unionism in the United States. *Journal of Labor Research* 25:223–232.

Kriss, Erik. 2003. Labor Union Protests Pataki's Proposed Health Care Cuts. *Syracuse Post-Standard:* March 16, p. A19.

Labor Research Association. n.d. Statistics and Data—Working Life. Available at <www.workinglife.org/wiki/index.php?page=Statistics+and+Data>.

Labor Union Against Ballot Measure. 2006. *Associated Press State & Local Wire:* October 10.

Labor Union Backs Senator Charged with Felony Drug Fraud. 2004. *Associated Press State & Local Wire:* September 21.

Labor Union Endorses Democrats. 2002. *Associated Press State & Local Wire:* July 3.

Legislature to Play Bigger Role in Contracts. 2003. *Wisconsin State Journal:* May 12, p. C8.

Lynch, James Q. 2001. Labor Unions, Seniors Oppose Iowa Power-Plant Bill. *Cedar Rapids Gazette:* March 28.

MacKay, Scott, and Liz Anderson. 2003. Labor Unions Join Forces to Bolster Public Image. *Providence Journal-Bulletin:* October 5, p. A1.

Manning, Stephen, 2002. Labor Unions Work to Organize University Employees. *Associated Press State & Local Wire:* September 19.

Mareschal, Patrice M. 2006. Innovation and Adaptation: Contrasting Efforts to Organize Home Care Workers in Four States. *Labor Studies Journal* 31:25–49.

Martin, Tim. 2006. Granholm Signs Bill to Boost Minimum Wage. *Associated Press State & Local Wire:* March 28.

Massey, Barry. 2002. Richardson Wins Big in Race for Governor. *Associated Press State & Local Wire:* November 6.

Masters, Marick. 2004. Federal-Sector Unions: Current Status and Future Directions. *Journal of Labor Research* 25:55–82.

Milicia, Joe, 2006. Democrats Score Big in Ohio Election with Strickland, Brown. *Associated Press State & Local Wire:* November 8.

Moberly, Robert B. 2006. Labor-Management Relations During the Clinton Administration. *Hofstra Labor and Employment Law Journal* 24:31–61.

Morley, Hugh R. 2007. Corzine's Hopes Dashed on Family Leave Bill. *Bergen County Record:* June 20, p. B1.

Naff, Katherine C., and Meredith A. Newman. 2004. Federal Civil Service Reform: Another Legacy of 9/11? *Review of Public Personnel Adminitration* 24:191–201.

Office of Management and Budget. 2001. The President's Management Agenda, Fiscal Year 2002. Available at <www.whitehouse.gov/omb/budget/fy2002/mgmt.pdf>.

Oregon's Largest Dairy Expected to Begin Negotiations. 2006. *Associated Press State & Local Wire:* December 2.

O'Toole, James. 2002a. Labor Union Endorses Republican Candidate for Pennsylvania Governor. *Pittsburgh Post-Gazette:* September 13.

———. 2002b. Rendell Wins Easily: Ex-Mayor First Philadelphian Elected Governor in 88 Years. *Pittsburgh Post-Gazette:* November 6, p. A1.

Parello, Nancy. 2001. Labor Unions Pushing NJ for Paid Family Leave. *Bergen County Record:* January 30, p. A3.

Perkins, Joseph. 2003. Holding Labor Unions Accountable. *San Diego Union-Tribune:* October 17, p. B7.

Pommer, Matt. 2003. GOP Gets Itself in Pickle with State's Labor Unions. *Madison Capital Times:* February 17, p. 3A.

Precious, Tom. 2003. Legislators Restore $1 Billion for Health Care. *Buffalo News:* May 2, p. B1.

Prengaman, Peter. 2003. Farm Labor Union Dismayed by Collective Bargaining Bill. *Associated Press State & Local Wire:* April 13.

Price, Marie. 2005. Voters Swamp Gasoline Tax Hike Question. *Tulsa World:* September 14, p. A1.

Pynes, Joan E. 2004. *Human Resources Management for Public and Nonprofit Organizations*, 2nd ed. San Francisco: Jossey-Bass.

Sinyai, Clayton. 2006. *Schools of Democracy: A Political History of the American Labor Movement.* Ithaca, NY: Cornell University Press.

Smith, Dane. 2001. Panel OK's Minimum-Wage Increase; Measure Mainly Pits Business Groups Against DFLers and Labor Unions. *Minneapolis Star Tribune,* March 8, p. 5B.

Solid Start for Ritter on His Initial Agenda. 2007. *Denver Post:* May 9, p. B6.

State Minimum Wage Increases to $7.50. 2006. *Eureka Times Standard:* December 31.

*Sumpter v. City of Moberly* (1982). 645 S.W. 2d 359.

Taule, Corey. 2003a. GOP Leaders Raise Ire of Labor Unions. *Idaho Falls Post Register:* March 4, p. A1.

———. 2003b. Unions Stewing Over Bill's Passage. *Idaho Falls Post Register:* March 14, C1.

Tedeschi, Bruno. 2002. New Jersey Bill Would Help Labor Unions on Public Works Projects. *Bergen County Record:* February 15.

Thompson, James R. 2007. Federal Labor-Management Relations Reforms Under Bush: Enlightened Management or Quest for Control? *Review of Public Personnel Administration* 27:105–124.

Tobias, Robert M. 2004. The Future of Federal Government Labor Relations and the Mutual Interests of Congress, the Administration, and Unions. *Journal of Labor Research* 25:19–41.

Union of Rutgers Administrators. 2007. Background Information. Available at <www.ura-aft.org/releases/042507background.pdf>.

Unions, State to Re-Sign Contracts if House Doesn't Ratify. 2002. *Associated Press State & Local Wire:* May 17.

Verma, Anil. 2005. What Do Unions Do to the Workplace? Union Effects on Management and HRM Policies. *Journal of Labor Research* 26:415–449.

Wasserman, Donald S. 2006. Collective Bargaining Rights in the Public Sector: Promises and Reality. In *Justice on the Job: Perspectives on the Erosion of Collective Bargaining in the United States*, Richard N. Block, Sheldon Friedman, Michelle Kaminski, and Andy Levin eds. Kalamazoo, MI: W. E. Upjohn Institute, pp. 57–83.

Whereatt, Robert. 2002. Domestic Partner Benefits: Pacts that Ended Strike May Be in the Balance. *Minneapolis Star Tribune:* January 27, p. 14A.

Wildermuth, John. 2005. Republican Strongholds Left Schwarzenegger in the Cold. *San Francisco Chronicle:* November 13, p. A6.

Will Voters Decide Minimum Wage? Labor Unions May Push Ballot Measure for Increases if Lawmakers Fail. 2005. *Grand Rapids Press:* January 25, p. C1.

# Outsourcing Human Resources
## Problems and Prospects for the Public Sector

JERRELL D. COGGBURN
North Carolina State University

## INTRODUCTION

Human resource (HR) professionals have been vying for a seat at the management table for some time. Instead of clinging to traditional administrative (e.g., regulatory compliance, record maintenance) and operational (day-to-day HR management) roles, the emergent model calls for HR professionals to be strategic partners, experts in the organization and execution of work, champions for employees, and agents of continuous transformation (Ulrich, 1998). The general argument is that focusing on administrative and operational roles, which are often routine and transactional in nature, has detracted from HR's ability to produce strategic, value-adding service to organizations.

In attempting to reconcile what HR has been with what it could or should be, organizations have undertaken a variety of HR transformation strategies, including human resources outsourcing (HRO). *HRO*, as used here, refers to a client organization (government) contracting with an outside vendor (contractor) for the delivery of one or more HR services.[1] As will be discussed, shifting certain HR functions and services to a third-party vendor holds potential for freeing an organization's HR professionals to focus on more strategically significant roles.

Both public and private organizations have engaged in HRO for some time, though this has typically been for individual HR services. Governments, for example, have long used outsourcing for specialized, short-term projects like wage and salary surveys, job analysis, and job evaluation, and for functional areas like payroll, benefits administration, and employee assistance programs (Lawther, 2003; General Accounting Office (GAO), 2004). What is new in HRO is the bundling of services being outsourced, or "full spectrum outsourcing" (Leinfuss, 2005).

Under this approach, organizations contract with a single vendor that provides an array of HR services, normally through a web-based system. The resulting automation creates a self-service HR environment where employees access and update personal information and complete basic HR transactions (e.g., enrolling for training, requesting leave), and managers access and track information on their direct-report employees and process HR transactions (e.g., submitting job requisitions, requesting job audits, preparing performance evaluations, approving leave requests). The HR professionals in the client agency shift focus from transactional work to providing HR consulting services to management, developing and interpreting HR policy, and managing the HRO relationship. The HRO vendor, in turn, is responsible for routine transactional and administrative tasks (e.g., benefits enrollment, payroll processing, posting and screening applications, maintaining records).

Full spectrum HRO first occurred in the private sector. Most observers trace the phenomenon to British Petroleum's (BP) decision to contract out its HR services to Exult in 1999 (O'Brien, 2005; Lawler et al., 2004). Since then, HRO activity has increased steadily, leading to the conclusion that it is now a pervasive and embedded feature of organizations' HR strategy (Dell, 2004; McClendon, Klass, and Gainey, 2002; Greer, Youngblood, and Gray, 1999; Gilley, Greer, and Rasheed, 2004).

Similarly, interest in HRO is increasing at all levels of government (Fernandez, Rainey, and Lowman, 2006). The Conference Board, for example, reports widespread interest in full spectrum HRO as evidenced by recent activity at the federal (U.S. Transportation Security Administration), state (Florida and Texas), and local (Detroit Public Schools) levels (see Koch, Dell, and Johnson, 2004). The same report indicates similar activity internationally, with HRO occurring in Copenhagen, Denmark, and Victoria, Australia. Such evidence lends credence to the view that HRO is on an upward trend in the public sector (Siegel, 2000; Wilson, 2003; Lavigna, 2005; Rafter, 2005).

Given the emergence of HRO and its radical departure from traditional modes of public HR management, it is important for students of public administration to appreciate the opportunities and challenges associated with it: that is the purpose of this chapter.[2] First, the chapter discusses the reasons why public organizations might wish to pursue HRO. Second, it identifies a number of potential problems with HRO. How these various problems are addressed will go a long way in determining HRO's success. Third, it considers the prospects for HRO, arguing that such activity is likely to increase in coming years. Finally, the conclusion emphasizes the need for additional research on HRO in order to better understand its true effects. The chapter's main focus is on full-spectrum HRO, meaning that the discussion assumes that HRO entails bundled HR functions provided by a single vendor through a web-based platform. Throughout the chapter, reference will be made to two recent high-profile HRO initiatives of this variety: the state of Florida's "People First" initiative and the state of Texas Health and Human Services Commission's (HHSC) "accessHR" (see Exhibit 19.1).

---

**Exhibit 19.1**

## Human Resource Outsourcing in Florida and Texas

In 2004, the Conference Board dubbed the Texas Health and Human Services Commission (HHSC) and Florida Department of Management Services (DMS) "trailblazers" for being among the first governmental entities in the United States to adopt full-spectrum HRO. In both states, the vendor chosen for delivering HR services was Convergys Corporation, of Cincinnati, Ohio. For both Florida's "People First" and Texas' "accessHR," Convergys developed web-based, self-service HR systems with the stated goals of reducing the states' overall HR costs and improving their HR services.

**People First** represented the culmination of efforts, dating to 1997, to replace Florida's aging HR information system, Cooperative Personnel Employment Subsystem (COPES). Early replacement efforts failed, largely due to budget constraints. In 2000, Governor Jeb Bush, who made privatization a priority, directed DMS to determine the feasibility of HRO. DMS, in turn, contracted with MEVATEC to develop a business case for HRO. Their analysis suggested the state could save $80 million in COPES replacement costs and several million more annually by outsourcing. In August 2002, DMS signed a seven-year, $278.6 million contract with Convergys. The contract was extended two years in 2004 (through 2011), bringing the contract total to $350 million. The initiative, which was pressed by an ambitious nine-month implementation schedule, has experienced significant delays and operational problems and the original contract has been amended ten times. Recent customer service survey data and a Commission on Efficient Government report suggest that the system, which is now fully operational, is improving. As of April 2008, DMS reports that People First serves 232,000 individuals spread across 59 customer groups (e.g., state agencies, universities, retirees) and that Convergys' People First service center handles, on average, 51,000 calls per month.

**accessHR** grew out of Texas's response to a $10 billion budgetary shortfall in 2003. Legislators looked to the health and human services (HHS) system, its 46,000 person workforce, and its $20 billion budget as a target for potential savings. With the passage of HB 2292, HHSC was directed to radically redesign the structure and administrative operation of the HHS system. Specifically, HHSC was charged with consolidating the system's administrative functions, including HR, with the mandate that as much work as practicable be outsourced. HHSC moved quickly to consolidate the HHS system's HR staff, management, budget, and functions, then turned its attention to analyzing how its HR program could be optimized, including (per HB 2292) evaluating HR for outsourcing. HHSC developed a business case evaluating the cost effectiveness of providing the optimized HR model in-house or through an external vendor. Shortly thereafter, HHSC

*(continued)*

Exhibit 19.1 *(continued)*

solicited proposals and, on June 3, 2004, announced the tentative award of a contract to Convergys. According to initial HHSC estimates, the five-year contract, valued at $85 million, was estimated to save HHSC approximately $21.7 million over the costs of developing the optimized model in-house. Like People First, accessHR faced a number of delays and operational problems. Also, the initial cost savings estimates, which were faulted by state auditors for errors and omissions, were revised downward to $11 million. The state's Council for Competitive Government is monitoring HHSC to determine if HRO should be extended to other state agencies.

## WHY OUTSOURCE HR?

Researchers have identified a variety of reasons why organizations adopt HRO (Greer et al., 1999; Dell, 2004; General Accounting Office (GAO), 2004), ranging from the relatively mundane (e.g., cost savings and access to specialized expertise and services) to the elegant (e.g., allowing HR to focus on core purposes and strategic roles) (Rainey, 2005).

From a cost perspective, there are several reasons why organizations might pursue HRO. First, HRO may offer operational savings through economies of scale provided by large external providers specializing in HR services. Economies of scale are produced since vendors can provide services to multiple clients with similar needs (Abraham and Taylor, 1996, as cited in Klaas, McClendon, and Gainey, 2001). Second, HRO offers the opportunity to turn the fixed costs of HR services provided by permanent HR staff into variable costs, where HR services are purchased at desired (and fluctuating) levels (Koch et al., 2004; Lawther, 2003; Fernandez et al., 2006). Finally, organizations may be seeking to avoid substantial capital outlays for HR technology upgrades. Many governments' HR capacity and transformation are limited by antiquated HR information systems (EquaTerra, 2006), yet the resources needed to replace these legacy systems are often scarce. Florida provides a good example of an HRO decision justified—at least partially—on cost avoidance grounds: the state was facing an estimated $80 million price tag for replacing its legacy HR information system, Cooperative Personnel Employment Subsystem (COPES). By outsourcing to a firm (Convergys) that had already made investments in state-of-the-art enterprise software, the state avoided making investments in technology upgrades.

On the service side, HRO may allow organizations to buy skills or upgrade to "best-in-class" services, thus offering employees more convenience through self-service applications (Koch et al., 2004; Wilson, 2003; Fernandez et al., 2006). Touting such benefits, Tom Heijmen, a senior HRO advisor to the Conference Board, argues:

> Outsourcing part of the HR function can offer many advantages, not in the least to the government employees themselves. Improved communications, faster feedback, rapid problem-solving, computerized training, do-it-yourself HR programs are just a few of the benefits outsourcing can provide. These elements can help improve employee morale and service level (in Koch et al., 2004:5).

More elegant rationales for HRO have also been identified (Rainey, 2005; Greer et al., 1999). The leading examples here include creating stronger internal focus on core HR functions and delivering more strategic value for the organization. As Greer et al. (1999:89) note, "HR departments often lack a clear strategic focus because they are preoccupied with operational activities. Outsourcing nonstrategic activities permits HR departments to move away from routine administration toward a more strategic role." This often occurs through the creation of web-based, self-service applications for routine transactions, thereby setting the stage for HR's shift to a strategic orientation (e.g., CedarCrestone, 2005). By freeing HR from "the endless communication with employees about pay, benefits, training and education, travel, and so on" (Hyde, 2004:58). outsourcing allows HR to focus on developing human capital, performance management, succession planning, and organizational transformation—just the types of activity envisioned for transformed, strategic HR.

## PROBLEMS TO CONSIDER

Despite compelling reasons for pursuing HRO, there remain a number of potential problems that must be addressed if an initiative is to be successful. Consider the following quote from Brian Friel (2003) describing the U.S. Federal Energy Regulatory Commission's recent HRO effort:

> Here's how not to outsource a human resources computer system: Hire a contractor with no experience to install an untested system; pay more than double the expected amount for setup; establish a contract without performance measures that would determine whether the job got done; spend months upgrading to a software version that will never be used, then upgrade hastily to a version that causes major problems and let the contractor operate the system for two years without a contract.

As this suggests, the HRO process is fraught with challenges. This section explores several of the more salient issues related to HRO.

### What Should (and Should Not) Be Outsourced?

The most fundamental issue for governments contemplating HRO is to determine what is and is not appropriate for outsourcing (Coggburn, 2007; Fernandez et al., 2006; Lawther, 2003; Brown, 2004). Some scholars have addressed this question by looking at what organizations have actually outsourced, concluding that public sector organizations tend to outsource routine and transactional services like health and benefits administration, employee assistance programs, and payroll (Siegel, 2000; Rainey, 2005). Other scholars have focused on developing conceptual frameworks for identifying which HR activities are appropriate for outsourcing (Lawler et al., 2004; Lepak and Snell, 1998; Baron and Kreps, 1999; A. Speaker, in Greer, 2001; Lilly, Gray, and Virick, 2005; Stroh and Treehuboff, 2003). Lepak and Snell (1998), for example, use two dimensions—the (1) value and (2) uniqueness of the HR activity—to generate a four-cell typology of the "architecture" of virtual HR. Their typology suggests that high value-high uniqueness activities represent core HR activities to be retained in-house, while activities in the other three quadrants might be suitable for outsourcing. Similarly, Alan Speaker has developed a four-cell framework using the strategic value of the activity (high or low) and the nature of the activity (transactional or relationship-oriented): activities falling into the relationship–high strategic value quadrant should receive the most internal attention while transactional–low value activities should be outsourced (in Greer, 2001:137; see also Gilley et al., 2004).

Drawing on this work and the general privatization literature (Donahue, 1989; Savas, 1987), Coggburn (2007) proposes eight dimensions for public officials to consider when considering specific functions for HRO, including:

- **Contribution to Public Value** (high↔low): HR activities that contribute to developing core organizational competencies, accomplishing mission, and satisfying stakeholder (both client and citizen) needs—that is, activities that create "public value" (Moore, 1995)—are activities that should be retained in-house.

- **Relation to Public Interest** (inherently governmental↔commercial): Decision making on matters concerning HR, HR policy determination, setting performance standards, and contract management and oversight are inherently governmental activities that should not be outsourced (see National Academy of Public Administration (NAPA), 1997).

- **Standing of Public HR values** (vulnerable↔secure): Certain unique public HR activities exist because society, as expressed through public law, administrative regulation, and/or court order, endorses values promoting the fair and equitable treatment of public employees. If outsourcing a given activity would threaten the fairness of HR decisions, then it is a bad idea.

- **Cost Effectiveness** (low↔high): HRO is often touted for achieving cost savings. If sound costing methodologies demonstrate significant savings, or if better (best in class) services can be gained for the same or lower price as those provided in-house, then it may be cost effective to outsource.

- **Uniqueness of the Activity** (unique↔generic): Generic activities are routine and easily standardized, increasing the chances that there will be a pool of competitive external vendors who can perform them (Lepak and Snell, 1998). Unique activities are specific to the organization or based upon tacit knowledge (i.e., knowledge accumulated through experience); hence they are not as readily available in the market. Such firm-specific and idiosyncratic activities are more likely than generic ones to be retained in-house (McClendon et al., 2002).

- **Type of Activity** (relational↔transactional): Relationship-oriented activities (e.g., employee relations, performance management, and internal consulting) are less appropriate for outsourcing than transactional activities (e.g., payroll, benefits, administration; see Greer, 2001; Gilley, Greer, and Rasheed, 2004).

- **Specificity** (ambiguous↔explicit): Organizations must clearly specify which HR services a vendor will be responsible for providing and how they will be provided (e.g., when, in what quantity and quality, etc.). This gets to the importance of being able to identify specific performance measures so that quality and performance can be effectively monitored.

- **Availability of Vendors** (scarce↔abundant): An ample pool of qualified vendors[3] is important for HRO success. Otherwise, concerns remain about the competitiveness of proposals submitted for government HR contracts and about the availability of replacement vendors should the vendor originally selected go out of business or prove unsatisfactory. Without an adequate supply of vendors, organizations increase their risk of being "held hostage" by a vendor.

Taking things in a more prescriptive direction, some effort has been made to delineate specific HR services that are and are not suitable for outsourcing. The National Academy for Public Administration (NAPA) (1997) has identified a lengthy list of HR services—arranged into 59 major functional areas and over 200 subareas—public organizations should consider for outsourcing. Among these, NAPA identifies transaction-based applications (e.g., benefits administration, payroll, records management) and employee self-service systems (e.g., payroll deductions, benefit changes) as prime targets for HRO. On the other hand, some researchers have identified HR services that should not be outsourced. For instance, Lawther (2003) indicates that labor relations and performance appraisal should not be outsourced. Johnson and Seebode (2006) expand upon this, providing a list of services they deem less appropriate for HRO, including: Equal Employment Opportunity/Affirmative Action (EEO/AA) and diversity programs, HR planning, staffing (recruitment, examination, and selection), training and development, labor-management relations, and grievance resolution. In each of these cases, the list reflects concern for one or more of the issues described earlier.

In sum, public organizations considering HRO must pay careful attention to what is and is not appropriate for HRO. Such attention must go beyond a simplistic examination of cost savings to include salient factors like HR values, the nature of the activity, and the public interest.

## The Business Case for HRO: Who Makes It and How?

One of the main justifications for HRO is that it is cost effective, thus demonstrating that it is becomes important. Indeed, credible and accurate cost data are imperative if governments are to be able to determine if HRO makes economic sense. There are at least two aspects of this that deserve consideration: who conducts the cost analyses, and, what is the costing methodology?

**Who conducts the cost analyses?**   In developing the business case for HRO, a key question involves who develops the cost analyses (Chi, Arnold, and Perkins, 2003). Organizations can pursue one of several strategies when conducting the study: in-house with existing staff, through another governmental entity (e.g., a central procurement office), or through an external consultant. In Texas, in-house HHSC staff developed the cost estimates for accessHR; in Florida, the Department of Management Services (DMS) contracted with MEVATEC (2001), a third-party consultant, to develop the estimates. On the one hand, developing estimates in-house capitalizes on the HR knowledge and expertise of staff, suggesting that the estimates might be more likely to include all relevant HR costs. On the other hand, using an external consultant might be preferable from an objectivity standpoint and, perhaps, from an expertise perspective, since a consultant may be more experienced with developing cost analyses. It is interesting to point out that in both Texas and Florida, the cost estimates were later deemed to be flawed (see next paragraph), suggesting that the methodology employed may be more important than who utilizes it. As for the third option, developing cost analyses through a separate government agency, both Texas and Florida have now created such entities: Texas's State Council on Competitive Government (SCCG) and Florida's Council on Efficient Government (CEG). Both agencies are tasked with developing standardized costing methodologies and ensuring that decisions to outsource governmental activities in their respective states are based upon accurate and complete analyses.

**What is the costing methodology?**    Paralleling the issue of who performs cost estimates is how such estimates are developed. In other words, there is a need for comprehensive and accurate costing methodology. Problems with costing plagued both People First and accessHR. In both instances, government's HR costs—aside from technology costs—were treated as synonymous with the costs of full-time equivalent (FTE) HR employees. HR-related activities that were performed by persons holding "non-HR" titles within both states' classification systems were either not included or were underestimated. This resulted in an inability to determine whether HRO was cost-effective.

In Texas, the State Auditor's Office (SAO) concluded:

> The Commission's decision to outsource its human resources and payroll services management function was not based on accurate cost data. . . . because of significant errors and omissions in the Commission's cost data for both the outsourced optimized in-house models, auditors were not able to determine whether the Commission's decision to outsource was cost-effective (SAO, 2005:i).

Similarly, Florida's Auditor General (AG) concluded:

> [A]bsent complete and objective cost-benefit and risk analysis during the planning phase of the project, the Department [of Management Services] did not demonstrate that viable alternatives, potential hazards, and costs of outsourcing had been fully considered prior to launching the procurement process. . . . Also, not establishing a mechanism for capturing and tracking all Statewide costs incurred in the implementation of People First prevents the measurements of any actual cost savings (AG, 2004:3).

The Texas and Florida experiences underscore the importance of identifying all relevant costs, including direct costs, indirect costs, contract management costs, and equipment and materials (see Wisniewski, 1992).

## Transitioning from In-House to Outsourced HR

Transferring HR services to a vendor does not occur overnight, so it is important not to underestimate the time and effort the transition will take, especially when the new system is web based (Lawler et al., 2004). A typical scenario might entail the vendor gradually assuming its HR roles, and rolling out various HR components over weeks or months while the client agency gradually scales back and ceases its internal HR operations. Given the technical issues involved with merging data sources, developing and customizing applications, and testing systems, problems and delays are not at all uncommon. Similarly, the vendor has to ensure that it has the right number of people with the right mix of knowledge, skills, and abilities to handle the acquired HR workload lest the quality of services suffers. To deal with these issues, organizations need to plan for a successful transition.

To see how delays can occur, consider Florida. People First had several "go-live dates" on which the vendor, Convergys, was to assume responsibilities for various

HR functions. Most of these target dates were missed: the staffing function went live May 5, 2003 (scheduled go-live date, May 1, 2003); HR administration and payroll functions went live in phases, between May 21, 2004 and October 29, 2004 (scheduled go-live date, June 1, 2003); training administration went live July 1, 2006 (scheduled go-live date, September 1, 2003); and benefits administration went live January 1, 2005 (scheduled go-live date, January 1, 2004; CEG, 2008). Often, these delays were created by the complexities of the various system components: instead of using a standard off-the-shelf system to accommodate a standardized HR function, People First had to be customized—to the tune of over 200 unique software interfaces—to meet the requirements of six separate HR systems used by various state agencies (CEG, 2008).

During the transition, it is important to have back-up systems or redundancy in the event that a new system fails to perform or be available as expected. Florida continued to operate its outmoded HR system, COPES, for several years; in fact, the final COPES component, for archival HR data, remained active until November 2007. In Texas, technical glitches with accessHR's recruitment and selection functions forced a brief shut down of those web-based services in August 2005, and coding problems occurred when the system processed its first payroll (October 2005), resulting in about eighty employees receiving paper warrants instead of direct deposits, others receiving incorrect payments, and HHSC temporarily taking payroll back in-house until the problems were remedied. As might be expected, affected state employees were not pleased.

On the staffing front, both the vendor and the contracting agency have issues to contend with. For the contracting agency, HRO invariably means the loss of HR staff positions since cost savings are normally tied to staff reductions. In Texas, HHSC's HR workforce was reduced from 522 FTEs to 51 and its payroll staff was reduced from 48 to 26. In Florida, the CEG (2008) reports nearly a 70 percent reduction in the state's HR workforce, with 862 positions eliminated under People First.

Given the phased-in nature of HRO and the inevitable glitches that occur during transition, these reductions do not—and, indeed, should not—occur all at once. Instead, efforts must be made to retain sufficient HR capacity to implement the change. This should entail devising strategies and incentives to retain some reduced level of in-house HR staff during transitional phases, even though those positions have been targeted for elimination. This can be challenging: organizations can expect morale problems when soon-to-be displaced HR staff are placed in the awkward position of participating in the transition (Bates, 2004; GAO, 2004). At HHSC, one strategy employed was to offer retention pay to the affected employees as the final end date approached. While such a strategy may serve as an incentive for some, it is important to note that other employees—perhaps the most valuable and marketable ones—may opt to transfer to other positions inside or outside government or, if they are eligible, retire.

For the vendor, ramping up for HR service delivery means hiring a properly equipped workforce. This is not always easy. In fact, one of the main problems with People First cited by Florida auditors was the lack of knowledge on the part of Convergys' customer service representatives, a situation that was exacerbated by high employee turnover in Convergys customer service centers (OPPAGA, 2006; CEG, 2008). A strategy for dealing with this problem is for the contract to include provisions requiring the vendor to hire, give preference to, or, minimally, interview those government HR employees displaced by the outsourcing. The benefits of this can be twofold: it can help ease the effects of HRO on government employees whose positions have been targeted for elimination; and, it can provide the vendor with employees who are knowledgeable about government's HR processes (Lawther, 2003). On the other hand, these same employees, though knowledgeable, may feel some sense of resentment toward their former public employer since their new jobs with the vendor may be lesser in terms of pay, benefits, and status.

## Assuming New HR-Related Roles

As a government transitions to an HRO model, HR professionals (i.e., those who remain employed), line managers, and front-line employees all will assume new HR-related roles. Ensuring that each group is aware of and ready for these new roles is an important HRO consideration.

**HR Professionals.**  For in-house HR professionals whose jobs are not eliminated by outsourcing—the so-called "stay back staff" in Texas and "residual organization" in Florida—there will be both transitional and new roles to play. From a transitional perspective, HR staff can be expected to do much of the troubleshooting that occurs as the vendor's HR systems go live and mangers and employees experience problems with new self-service applications. HR staff are also likely to gain an appreciation for the adage "old habits die hard." Dialing into an HR service center or calling up a self-service web site is different than visiting with someone down the hall in HR, so some employees and managers may continue to rely upon in-house HR to provide services in the fashion they had grown accustomed (Cooke, Shen, and McBride, 2005; Lawler et al., 2004). The HR professionals are likely to do so because the old transactional work was part of their pre-HRO comfort zone (Dell, 2004).

As for new roles, outsourcing shifts the responsibilities of HR professionals to contract monitoring, vendor relationship management, and strategic partnership. Oshima, Kao, and Tower (2005) suggest that this requires HR professionals to possess business savvy and relationship management skills (e.g., being a persuasive communicator, serving as an internal and external networker) as opposed to traditional HR competencies (e.g., deep knowledge of HR programs and technology, employee advocacy). On the strategy side, HR professionals are called upon "to perform the more consultative and strategic role of designing and implementing programs aimed at retaining the workforce and enhancing its performance" (Cooke, Shen, and McBride, 2005:417). This means that HR professionals need more generalist (as opposed to specialty) HR knowledge, an understanding of the mission and goals of the organization, and the ability to lead organizational transformation.

As this suggests, both the nature of the HR professional's work and the skill set required for performing it change under HRO. Since HR professionals will be adapting to these new roles at the same time they are being called upon by some in the organization to play their former HR roles, there is a danger for work intensification (Cooke, Shen, and McBride, 2005).

**Line Managers.**  As the transition to an outsourced HR model unfolds, line managers may face a startling reality: HRO creates for them new HR-related work. As mentioned earlier, under traditional arrangements, line managers relied upon HR staff to perform most HR-related services. Instead of this, HRO's web-based, self-service environments place the onus on managers for many HR-related tasks. Managers are likely to face learning curves as they assume responsibility for these HR tasks and transactions. They may also be unhappy about having to assume these new roles since it creates a new inconvenience for them and work intensification (Cooke, Shen, and McBride, 2005).

These issues surfaced in Texas, where the HHS system managers exhibited some initial push back as they began to fully understand their new HR-related roles. The emergence of the new roles that led to this resistance is highlighted in HHSC's 2005–2009 agency workforce plan:

> One outcome of this consolidation of support services will be the shift of administrative responsibilities and expectations from HHS administrative staff to program managers and supervisors, and an increase in the complexity of jobs and the levels of responsibility of program supervisors at the regional and direct service levels. For example, the new HHS HR Manual requires managers and supervisors to assume many of the responsibilities that were previously assigned to HR staff (HHSC, 2005:42).

**Employees.** For front-line employees, HRO creates the expectation for them to access and use a variety of self-service HR applications. This might include submitting timesheets, requesting leave, updating personal information, and managing their benefits. To assume these responsibilities, all employees will need access to computers and training in how the various HR systems work.

In Texas and Florida, accessHR and People First assumed that all employees could access a personal computer and successfully navigate the new HR systems. Experience showed these to be poor assumptions. In both states, there are certain employees whose jobs do not require that a personal computer be assigned. A report by Florida's Office of Program Policy Analysis and Government Accountability (OPPAGA, 2006:5) offers several such examples:

> [T]he Department of Corrections has approximately 16,000 employees, such as prison guards, who do not have routine computer access. Many other agencies have field-based employees who rarely report to an office site with an assigned computer to access People First, including law enforcement officers with the Florida Fish and Wildlife Conservation Commission, and field personnel employed by the Departments of Agriculture and Consumer Services and Highway Safety and Motor Vehicles.

Moreover, Crowell and Guy (forthcoming) found that training on how to use the new technology was not initially provided in Florida, leaving many end users frustrated.

Whether one is an HR professional, line manager, or rank-in-file employee, HRO creates new roles and responsibilities. To ensure a smooth transition, organizations must provide sufficient training and technical support as automated self-service systems go live. To do this, the HRO contract must clearly specify who—the vendor or the client agency—is responsible for providing that support (Rainey, 2005). It is important, too, to realize that it takes time to learn these new roles and to become comfortable with new systems (see Lawler et al., 2004; Hyde, 2004; West and Berman, 2001). Failure to recognize these things can set the stage for a bumpy transition.

## Developing Contracting Capacity

HRO requires strong contract negotiation and management. To be successful, "contracting out requires that a public agency retain sufficient in-house knowledge and resources to effectively monitor the performance of human resources contractors, and to ensure that the contract be designed with performance measures and incentives that encourage the contractor to behave in the best interest of the agency" (Fernandez et al., 2006:220; see also Gormely, 1994; Lawther, 2003). Absent this, contracts can be written that are too favorable to the vendor, lack clear performance standards and expectations, or do not provide flexibility to address technological changes or other contingencies (Lawler et al., 2004).

One aspect of a strong contract is the inclusion of clear performance measures, or HR metrics (see Chapter 11 in this volume). HR metrics are measures of results or outputs focusing on such things as service levels and/or quality, vendor management, and cost effectiveness (Sullivan, 2004). Including HR metrics is crucial to the client organization's ability to measure the vendor's service levels and quality. Lavigna (2005:12) underscores the importance of HR metrics by suggesting that, "If it is not possible to develop performance measures for a function, maybe that activity shouldn't be outsourced."

Texas and Florida's HRO initiatives encountered difficulties with performance measurement. In its 2005 audit, the Texas State Auditor Office (SAO, 2005) found fault with HHSC for not clearly specifying the information technology training and support to be provided by the vendor, a critical problem given accessHR's web-based, self-service format. The audit stated: "the Commission has not developed performance measures to monitor and evaluate the contractor's performance in the area of IT support services. The lack of definitive performance measures makes it difficult for the Commission to hold its contractor accountable for failing to perform to expectations" (SAO, 2005:iii). Similarly, Florida's 2004 audit (AG, 2004) found that the state was not receiving monthly performance metrics reports for People First's Staffing Administration component even though the component had been operational for over one year: The contract specified that monthly performance reports would be provided for system components as soon as they went live.

Effective HRO contract monitoring and management normally require a dedicated contract manager and a project management team. Here, again, both Texas and Florida stumbled. In Texas, a contract manager for accessHR was not hired until eleven months after the contract was executed. The state auditor's 2006 report (SAO, 2006) concluded that hiring the contract manager beforehand would have helped avoid the contract planning and monitoring shortcomings (e.g., not establishing contract monitoring policies and procedures like on-site visits of the contractor's service center) cited in the audit. In Florida, it was several years before the state assembled a full-time People First project team. On this, the CEG (2008:19) found that "Some of the early problems associated with the initiative may potentially be attributed to the lack of a dedicated team to ensure success."

The salience of performance measurement and contract management reiterates the importance of the changing roles of HR professionals under an outsourcing arrangement. The Conference Board puts it this way: "The client's job is to monitor the vendor's performance and manage the relationship to objective standards of service quality. . . . HR professionals must transition from managing a function to managing a vendor" (Koch et al., 2004:16–17).

## Planning for What's Next

Finally, an organization needs to consider what it will do when its HRO contract expires. Will they renew the contract? Will there be another invitation for bids or request for proposals? Will all or some HR services be brought back in house? Similarly, what will be done if the contract is canceled for a vendor's inadequate performance? What if the vendor goes out of business or is acquired by another firm? These are important questions that need to be asked at the beginning of an HRO initiative, not at the end. Failing to create an exit strategy can create a situation where government is held hostage by a vendor. Organizations can become overly dependent on the supplier, losing their internal HR capacity to the point of being unable to monitor their existing vendor or to choose and migrate to a new one (Lawler et al., 2004). The terms of the exit strategy should be included in the original HRO contract. Florida is instructive on this point.

As originally drafted, Florida's contract with Convergys was vague about the state's proprietary interest in the software applications developed for People First. Since the software platform, SAP, has been significantly modified to meet Florida's unique HR requirements and since the state's legacy system, COPES, is no longer available, the state has faced considerable uncertainty about what to do when Convergys' contract expires in 2011. Under a May 2008 contract amendment (the tenth amendment to the original contract), however, the state gained permanent, nontransferable, internal use license to People First systems and the related intellectual property. In plain English, this means Florida gets to keep and build upon the People First system at the conclusion of the contract as opposed to building a new system from scratch (Cotterell, 2008). The state might opt to renew Convergys' contract beyond 2011, contract with another firm, or bring its HR services back in house, but the point is that this late-in-coming development has reduced the risk to the state and clarified an exit strategy that should have been established from the beginning.

## PROSPECTS

At the risk of understating the obvious, the "supply or buy" decision for HR services is not as straightforward as one might initially assume. The road leading from an initial decision to outsource HR to successfully implementing an HRO initiative is difficult to navigate. Despite this, most observers agree that the practice is likely to expand in coming years (Lavigna, 2005; Lawther, 2003; Rainey, 2005; Rafter, 2005; Koch et al., 2004; Siegel, 2000; Chi et al., 2003). There are several reasons why this is likely to be the case.

First, from a political standpoint, there is little reason to believe that government's fiscal pressures and the public's antitax sentiments will subside, so government reforms touted as cost effective will continue to garner interest. What is not known, however, is whether government HRO actually achieves purported cost savings.

Second, outsourcing in general is being viewed in less ideological terms. Historically, outsourcing has been associated with political conservatism and its anti- or smaller-government themes, but several observers suggest that it is shedding some of its ideological baggage (Clark, Heilman, and Johnson, 1995/1996; Brudney et al., 2005; Greenblatt, 2004; Chi et al., 2003). The result is that outsourcing is now being viewed more pragmatically (Gormely, 1994; Auger, 1999; for a contrary view see Walters, 2004), as one of the many tools in the public management tool kit.

Third, on a more theoretical level, arguments about the need for HR to assume a more strategic role continue to be influential. This can be seen in NAPA's assertion that public sector "HR is becoming a partner in the development of human capital rather than a regulator or paper processor" (NAPA, 1997:xi). If HR is to develop and sharpen its focus on core functions like developing human capital and adding strategic value to the organization, then it is necessary that operational and administrative loads be shed. There are a number of alternative service delivery modes available to facilitate this transition (see Note 1), including outsourcing.

Finally, from a practical level, public sector HRO is likely to increase because private sector firms are awakening to the potential market for public sector applications (Friel, 2003; Davidson, 2004; Coggburn, 2007). In fact, some in the HRO industry view the shift to the public sector as HRO's "coup d'état " (Davidson, 2004:86). With this growing recognition, potential vendors have become more aggressive in their marketing to government clients. Armed with their cost-savings arguments—and absent any empirical findings to the contrary—it is likely that there will be at least some eager governmental buyers. But, as the previous section illustrates, such decisions should not be entered into lightly: caveat emptor.

## CONCLUSION

Outsourcing is gaining in popularity as a means for transforming HR and reducing costs, yet the practice remains in a nascent state in the public sector (Koch et al., 2004). Though high-profile HRO initiatives in Florida and Texas have garnered attention, empirical evidence on the reasons why governments pursue HRO and its effects on organizational performance remain scarce. This makes it difficult to evaluate the claims of HRO proponents and, likewise, the concerns of its opponents. However, as public sector HRO matures—that is, as more vendors become available to promote competition, as costing methodologies and HR metrics improve, and as more governments adopt HRO—researchers will be able to draw more definitive conclusions. As this chapter has demonstrated, the prospects for successful public sector HRO are intertwined with a number of challenging problems. Given this, it is easy to understand why governments have been cautioned against viewing outsourcing as a panacea for public sector HR (Fernandez et al., 2006; NAPA, 1997; Siegel, 2000; Chi et al., 2003).

## NOTES

1. Outsourcing is one of many alternative service delivery (ASD) mechanisms available to governments. The National Academy of Public Administration (NAPA, 1997), for example, identifies several forms of ASD, including: agency interservice agreements, competitive contracts with private and public providers, cooperative administrative support units formed with other agencies, franchise organizations, and privatization (see also, Fernandez et al., 2006).
2. Selected portions of this chapter are adapted from Coggburn (2007).
3. There are a number of HR vendors, including Accenture, IBM, Hewitt, Convergys, Aon, and Mercer's SynHRgy (see Hodges and Block, 2005).

## REFERENCES

Abraham, K. G., and Taylor, S. K. 1996. Firms' Use of Outside Contractors: Theory and Evidence. *Journal of Labor Economics* 14:394–424.

Auditor General (AG), State of Florida. 2004. *Department of Management Services People First: Operational Audit.* Report No. 2005-047. Tallahassee, FL: AG.

Auger, D. A. 1999. Privatization, Contracting, and the States: Lessons from State Government Experience. *Public Productivity & Management Review* 22 (4):435–454.

Baron, J. N., and Kreps, D. M. 1999. *Strategic Human Resource Management: Frameworks for General Managers.* New York: John Wiley and Sons.

Bates, S. 2004. Lessons Learned from Federal HR Outsourcing. *HR Magazine* 49 (9):26.

Brown, J. 2004. Business Process Outsourcing: A Cost Saver and Strategic Tool for the Public Sector. *IPMA-HR News.* Alexandria, VA: IPMA-HR. Retrieved on April 18, 2005, from <http://www.ipma-hr.org/index.cfm?navid=222&id=3423&tcode=nws3>.

Brudney, J. L., S. Fernandez, J. E. Ryu, and D. S. Wright. 2005. Exploring and Explaining Contracting Out: Patterns Among the American States. *Journal of Public Administration Research and Theory* 15 (3):393–419.

CedarCrestone. 2005. CedarCrestone 2005 HCM Survey: Workforce Technologies and Service Delivery Approaches, 8th ed. Alpharetta, GA: CedarCrestone, Inc.

Chi, K. S., K. A. Arnold, and H. M.. Perkins. 2003. Privatization in State Government: Trends and Issues. *Spectrum: The Journal of State Government* 76 (4):12–21.

Clark, C., J. G. Heilman, G. W. Johnson. 1995/1996. Privatization: Moving Beyond Laissez Faire. *Policy Studies Review* 14 (3/4):395–406.

Coggburn, J. D. 2007. Outsourcing Human Resources: The Case of the Texas Health and Human Services Commission. *Review of Public Personnel Administration* 27 (4):315–335.

Cooke, F. L., Shen, J. and McBride, A. 2005. Outsourcing HR as a Competitive Strategy? A Literature Review and an Assessment of Implications. *Human Resource Management* 44 (4):413–432.

Cotterell, B. 2008. Convergys, People First See Better Days Ahead. *Tallahassee Democrat:* June 2, 2008.

Council on Efficient Government (CEG), State of Florida. 2008. *Report to the Governor on MyFloridaMarketPlace, People First, and Project Aspire.* Report No. R08-002. Tallahassee, FL: CEG.

Crowell, E. B., and M. E. Guy. Forthcoming. Florida's HR Reforms: Service First, Service Worst, or Something in Between? *Public Personnel Management.*

Davidson, G. 2004. Next Stop, Government: HRO's Coup d'Etat: Shifting Focus to the Public Sector. *HRO Today* 3 (2):84.

Dell, D. J. 2004. *HR Outsourcing: Benefits, Challenges, and Trends.* Research Report R-1347-04-RR. New York: The Conference Board.

Donahue, J. D. 1989. *The Privatization Decision: Public Ends, Private Means.* New York: Basic Books.

EquaTerra. 2006. *Human Resources Transformation in Public Sector Organizations.* Alexandria, VA: International Public Management Association for Human Resources (IPMA-HR).

Fernandez, S., H. G. Rainey, and C. E. Lowman. 2006. Privatization and Its Implications for Human Resources Management. In *Public Personnel Management: Current Concerns, Future Challenges,* 4th ed., N. M. Riccucci, ed. New York: Longman, pp. 204–224.

Friel, B. 2003. Human Resources: Outsource with Care. *Government Executive* 35 (4):69–70.

General Accounting Office (GAO). 2004. *Human Capital: Selected Agencies' Use of Alternative Service Delivery Options for Human Capital Activities* (GAO-04-679). Washington, DC: GAO.

Gilley, K. M., C. R. Greer, and A. A. Rasheed. 2004. Human Resource Outsourcing and Organizational Performance in Manufacturing Firms. *Journal of Business Research* 57:232–240.

Gormely, W. T., Jr. 1994. Privatization Revisited. *Policy Studies Review* 13 (3/4):215–234.

Greenblatt, A. 2004. Sweetheart Deals.*Governing*18 (3):20–25.

Greer, C. R. 2001. *Strategy and Human Resources: A General Managerial Approach,* 2nd ed. Upper Saddle River, NJ: Prentice Hall.

Greer, C. R., S. A. Youngblood, and D. A. Gray. 1999. Human Resource Management Outsourcing: The Make or Buy Decision. *The Academy of Management Executive* 13 (3):85–96.

Health and Human Services Commission, State of Texas (HHSC). 2005. Health and Human Services Enterprise Workforce Plan for Fiscal Years 2005–2009. Austin, TX: HHSC. Retrieved on March 14, 2006, from <http://www.hr.state.tx.us/Workforce/Plans/2004/529-plan-2004.pdf>.

Hodges, M., and D. Block. 2005. Business Process Outsourcing: Current Trends and Best Practices. *Contract Management* 45 (January):8–17.

Hyde, A. C. 2004. The End of HRM. *The Public Manager* 33 (2):56–59.

Johnson, Kevin T., and Thomas F. Seebode. 2006. We vs. They: Are All HR Functions 'In-House' Equally Privatized to the 'Out-House'? *PA Times* 29 (11):3.

Klaas, B. S., J. A. McClendon, and T. W. Gainey. 2001. Outsourcing HR: The Impacts of Organizational Characteristics. *Human Resource Management* 40 (2):125–138.

Koch, J., with D. J. Dell, and Johnson, L. K. 2004. *HR Outsourcing in Government Organizations: Emerging Trends, Early Lessons.* Research Report E-0007-04-RR. New York: The Conference Board.

Lavigna, B. 2005. Successful Outsourcing—A Delicate Balance. *PA Times* 28 (11):9, 12.

Lawler, E. E., III, D. Ulrich, J. Fitz-enz, and J. C. Madden. V. 2004. *Human Resources Business Process Outsourcing: Transforming How HR Gets Its Work Done.* San Francisco, CA; Jossey-Bass.

Lawther, W. C. 2003. Privatizing Personnel: Outsourcing Public Sector Functions. In *Public Personnel Administration: Problems and Prospects,* 4th ed., S. W. Hays and R. C. Kearney, eds. Upper Saddle River, NJ: Prentice Hall, pp. 196–208.

Leinfuss, Emily. 2005. Human Resource BPO Deals Are Getting Bigger. *Outsourcing Essentials* 3 (1): Available at <http://www.outsourcing.com/content.asp?page=01b/other/oe/q105/hr.html&nonav=false>.

Lepak, D. P., and S. A. Snell. 1998. Virtual HR: Strategic Human Resource Management in the 21st Century. *Human Resource Management Review* 8 (3):215–234.

Lilly, J. D., D. A. Gray, and M. Virick. 2005. Outsourcing the Human Resource Function: Environmental and Organizational Characteristics that Affect HR Performance. *Journal of Business Strategies* 22 (1):55–73.

McClendon, J., B. S. Klaas, and T. W. Gainey. 2002. HR Outsourcing and the Virtual Organization. In *Human Resource Management in Virtual Organizations,* R. L. Heneman and D. B. Greenberger, eds. Greenwich, CT: Information Age Publishing, pp. 57–79.

MEVATEC. 2001. Business Plan: Human Resources Outsourcing Initiative. Huntsville, AL: MEVATEC.

Moore, M. H. 1995. *Creating Public Value: Strategic Management in Government.* Cambridge, MA: Harvard University Press.

National Academy of Public Administration (NAPA). 1997. *Alternative Service Delivery: A Viable Strategy for Federal Government Human Resources Management.* Implementing Real Change in Human Resources Management, Phase III: Practical Tools. Washington, DC: NAPA.

Office of Program Policy Analysis and Government Accountability, State of Florida (OPPAGA). 2006. *While Improving, People First Still Lacks Intended Functionality, Limitations Increase State Agency Workload and Costs.* Report No. 06-39. Tallahassee, FL: OPPAGA.

O'Brien, P. 2005. The Rise of Human Resources Outsourcing. *Computer Business Review Online.* Retrieved from <http://www.cbronline.com/article_cbr.asp?guid=3ED008C4-E811-4ABA-8333-C234E774D20F>.

Oshima, M., T. Kao, and J. Tower. 2005. Achieving Post-Outsourcing Success. *HR. Human Resource Planning* 28 (2):7–11.

Rafter, Michelle V. 2005. BPO Bandwagon. *Workforce Management* 84 (12):33–43.

Rainey, G. W., Jr. 2005. Human Resource Consultants and Outsourcing: Focusing on Local Government. In *Handbook of Human Resource Management in Government,* 2nd ed., S. E. Condrey, ed. San Francisco, CA: Jossey-Bass, pp. 701–734.

Savas, E. S. 1987. *Privatization: The Key to Better Government.* Chatham, NJ: Chatham House.

Siegel, G. B. 2000. Outsourcing Personnel Functions. *Public Personnel Management* 29 (2):225–236.

State Auditor's Office, State of Texas (SAO). 2005. *An Audit Report on the Health and Human Services Commission's Consolidation of Administrative Support Functions.* Report No. 06-009. Austin, TX: SCO.

————. 2006. *An Audit Report on the Health and Human Services Commission's Consolidation of Administrative Support Services.* Report No. 06-018. Austin, TX: SCO.

Stroh, L. K., and D. Treehuboff. 2003. Outsourcing HR functions: When—and When Not—to Go Outside. *Journal of Leadership and Organizational Studies* 10 (1):19–28.

Sullivan, J. 2004. Metrics for Measuring Outsourcing Effectiveness. In *Out of Site: An inside Look at HR Outsourcing,* K. V. Beaman, ed. Austin, TX: International Association for Human Resource Information Management, pp. 287–294.

Ulrich, David. 1998. A New Mandate for Human Resources. *Harvard Business Review* 76 (1):124–134.

Walters, J. 2004. Going Outside. *Governing* 17 (8):22–29.

West, J. P., and E. M. Berman. 2001. From Traditional to Virtual HR: Is the Transition Occurring in Local Government? *Review of Public Personnel Administration* 21 (1):38–64.

Wilson, C. 2003. There's More to Outsourcing HT Than Trimming Costs. *IPMA-HR News.* Alexandria, VA: IPMA-HR. Retrieved on December 22, 2004, from <http://www.careerjournal.com/hrcenter/ipma/20030905-ipma.html>.

Wisniewski, S. C. 1992. A Framework for Considering the Contracting Out of Government Services. *Public Personnel Management* 21 (1):101–117.

# ~~~~~~ **Section Four** ~~~~~~

# Conclusion

The preceding nineteen chapters demonstrate some persistent problems and issues in public sector HRM. Many of them have been addressed in the previous four editions of this book, but their enduring nature is not static. Indeed, change—or at least the perceived need for change—is a constant feature of public HRM. Privatization of HRM functions has been experimented with for decades, for instance, but the scope and power of privatization has grown to new proportions, creating new and often unanticipated problems for HR managers. Similarly, Equal Employment Opportunity (EEO) has morphed into Affirmative Action (AA) which mutated into diversity. What is the next stage? HR professionals have at various times been called upon to be specialized technical experts, employee advocates, HR generalists, and, more recently, strategic partners to management in developing human capital. Each of these phenomena (and there are countless others), reflects the dynamic nature of the public HRM field. Importantly, the forces creating such dynamism range from the pragmatic (e.g., devising effective HR recruitment strategies to meet looming baby boom retirements) to the political (e.g., radically reforming the civil service in response to dubious claims about bureaucratic bloat and private sector superiority). Distinguishing the need for real and constructive change from concocted and ill-conceived change remains an enduring problem.

In Chapter 20, James Bowman confronts the turbulence in HRM head on by asking, "Whither the Public Service Ethos?" In building on the foregoing chapters, Bowman discusses the HRM reform phenomenon from its origins to date, and raises provocative questions such as, "Why did reform get deformed?" As the author shows, HRM change risks undermining the critical values and competencies of the public service. He offers a number of interesting examples in support of his thesis, and leaves the reader with a great deal to ponder.

# Conclusion

# 20

# Turbulence in the Civil Service
## Whither the Public Service Ethos?

JAMES S. BOWMAN
Florida State University

As this book demonstrates, the public service is in a time of turbulent change. Indeed, human capital management is a high-risk issue confronting government, one affecting the ability of agencies to accomplish their missions (United States Government Accountability Office, 2007). Decentralization, downsizing, defunding, politicization, privatization, patronage, reorganization, and entirely new personnel systems have called into question the traditional merit system. Until recently, in fact, the distinguishing feature of modern government employment had been neutral competence in administration. This guardian administrative doctrine—a merit-based, impartial career bureaucracy derived from civic culture norms—was the foundation of government. Arguing there was no merit in the merit system, however, the contemporary civil service reform movement introduced commercial values into public service, increased the number of political appointees, relaxed employee protections from partisan influence, and hollowed out agencies by privatizing their management functions. This political administrative doctrine—a patronage-based, partisan, non-career bureaucracy premised on political exchange norms—has profoundly affected American public service.[1]

Building on the preceding chapters, this capstone discussion assesses civil service reform and its effect on the public service ethos—that is, professionals obligated to be apolitical, provide independent advice without fear or favor, and embrace anonymity in service dedicated to the greater good. It begins by briefly describing historical and contemporary reforms and then examines the current status of recent initiatives, including two dominant reform components. Next the extent to which these innovations were based on evidence is considered. The analysis closes with conclusions about the future of public service.

## HISTORICAL AND CONTEMPORARY REFORMS

Modern civil service systems around the nation sprang from the good-government movement of the 1870s and 1880s and the Progressive Era that followed. Degradation of government by the spoils system was a leading issue of the time. The goal of ethical and efficient public service sparked reform to replace political manipulation with merit qualifications in personnel decisions. Competence would be the basis of public management. To protect public servants from unscrupulous politicians, responsible and effective government would be "run like a business" organized by administrative principle and staffed with nonpartisan employees.

Although the merit system was created to rid government of the graft and fraud, it has long been a subject of scrutiny. Indeed, reform increasingly has been on the policy agendas of federal and state government since the latter part of the twentieth century. Advocates have voiced complaints about the "uncivil" service, a system burdened by archaic rules, Byzantine procedures, and outdated policies that impede action, nurture incompetence, and protect those who should be terminated (e.g., Howard, 1994; Osborne and Gaebler, 1992). Republicans and Democrats, elected officials and their appointees, job applicants and incumbents, citizens, and journalists echoed such concerns.

While it is doubtful that public employees behaved differently during the first and second half of the last century, what changed was the propensity of chief executives to use the bureaucracy to implement ideologically driven agendas (Anonymous, 2007). Bolstered by years of "bash-the-bureaucrat" politics and corporate reengineering, reformers—rather than modernizing the system of career professionals—sought a pre-meritocratic system in the name of performance and responsiveness.

Partisans successfully reframed the image of political influence in administration from hindering efficiency to improving it. "[T]he merit system went from being vital to protecting the public interest . . . to having almost no role protecting the public" from the abuse of power (Anonymous, 2007). In the process, some of the same groups that in an earlier era had demanded that a corrupt, patronage-style spoils system be replaced by an efficient, competency-based civil service, now aimed to reduce employee safeguards from political interference.

The contemporary reform movement (Condrey and Maranto, 2001) gained exceptions from merit systems across the nation by expanding management prerogatives and restricting employee rights. Major examples include: Texas nullified its merit system in 1985, making all state employees at will; a 1996 Georgia law mandated that all new civil servants be hired outside of the civil service system; and in 2001 Florida eliminated job tenure for middle managers. South Carolina and Arkansas recently abolished their merit systems; less dramatically, many states (e.g., Indiana, Delaware, Kansas) reclassified career service positions to unclassified ones as a consequence of reductions-in-force, attrition, and/or reorganization (Hays and Sowa, 2006; Kellough and Nigro, 2006). At the national level, before the turn of the century a variety of departments [e.g., Federal Aviation Administration (FAA), Internal Revenue Service (IRS), Government Accountability Office (GAO), National Aeronautics and Space Administration (NASA)] received full or partial waivers from the merit system. The effect of these state and national changes is that the employment status of many public workers is not too different than that found in the business sphere (except for the right to strike and market pay).

As a result of the September 11, 2001 catastrophe, perceptions of reform as policy issues were transformed from a micropolitical to a macropolitical environment, where rhetoric can be particularly influential (Brook and King, 2007; also see Terry, 2005). Like the assassination of a president that led to civil service change in 1883, the crisis emboldened reformists particularly at the federal level (although ongoing state changes benefited from the new environment as well; Hays and Sowa, 2006). The terrorist attacks offered an opportunity to use national security as a justification to achieve political aims in reforming the civil service. The emphasis was placed on agency mission, not management of the bureaucracy (Perry, 2008:5). Thus, the Transportation Security Agency established at-will employment for its personnel, and the departments of Homeland Security and Defense were authorized to create new HRM systems which were seen as blueprints for dismantling the government-wide merit system. The essence was to give department secretaries the same managerial flexibility exercised by corporate officers. The programs were enacted in a response to national security arguments—not the need to reform personnel management (Brook and King, 2008).

These developments represent a shift in three doctrines—representativeness, neutral competence, and executive leadership—that historically have characterized the public service (Kaufman, 1956). Representativeness was the dominant tenet during much of the 1800s as embodied in the spoils system. After the passage of the 1883 Pendleton Act, neutral competence, the principle value of the merit system, grew "upward, outward, and downward" throughout American government for much of the next century. In recent years, however, executive leadership, which had been the emerging doctrine for some time (e.g., under initiatives by Presidents Carter, Reagan, and Clinton), became an increasingly central in public employment. Geared to making the civil service more business-like, more responsive to political leadership and more accountable for performance, changes were made with minimal discussion of their impact on public service ideals and standards.

## CURRENT STATUS OF REFORMS

What has been the fate of recent innovations? Since earlier chapters have investigated selected policies, only a summary of the impact of change is reported immediately below. This is followed, however, by an analysis of two primary features of reform: contracting out and performance pay programs. While the discussion focuses on the federal government, the literature (e.g., Bowman and West, 2007; Kellough and Nigro, 2006) suggests that comparable concerns exist at the subnational level. Cross-agency and cross-jurisdictional generalizations on multiple issues are inevitably both complex and hazardous. The observations given in this chapter, therefore, highlight cardinal aspects of reform and question conventional wisdom about their desirability and feasibility. Based on available data, the outcomes of change to date are not reassuring.

### Overall Impact of Reform

Although a comprehensive assessment of reform does not exist, a careful look at the federal experience by two former senior government executives (Underhill and Oman, 2007) finds that there is little relationship between the difficulties that the civil service faces and the goals of reform (Table 20.1). Most of the common criticisms of the bureaucracy are either not addressed or the changes have, at best, marginal significance. As shown in the Table 20.1, for example, (a) the growing number of political appointees as well as the impending wave of retirements are largely overlooked and (b) new classification, pay, and disciplinary policies, if even well-executed, are unlikely to effect genuine change and could make present problems worse.

### TABLE 20.1   Some Perceived Problems with the Federal Service

| Problem | Assessment of Problem and Possible Impact of Changes |
| --- | --- |
| Difficulty of attracting highly qualified federal employees. | Not fully supported by research. Given problems of many merit pay systems, they may not solve the problem, if it exists. |
| Potential retirement of top civil servants in the next five years. | Even successful merit pay systems had little impact on retention. |
| Too many personnel rules and regulations make hiring difficult. | Depending on details of system, exemptions could make hiring quicker. |
| Firing and disciplining poorly performing civil servants too difficult. | Proposed changes could speed up disciplining and firing of poor employees. Most federal employees and managers believe that firing is too cumbersome. |
| Compensation lags in federal pay. | May be true for critical occupations. Pay-banding may address problem for attracting certain skills. |
| Outdated classification system. | Restructuring under pay-banding could address problem but create others. It could be improved without throwing out the whole General Schedule system. |
| Inadequate training of federal employees. | Studies support thesis of inadequate training funds. The reforms do not directly address this issue. |
| "Stove piping" and lack of cooperation between agencies. | This is a real problem, as shown in 9/11 response. Unclear how reforms would solve problem. |
| Too many and low quality of political appointees. | Supported by Volcker Commission. The reforms would not address this problem. |
| Political hostility to civil service. | If Congress believes that merit pay will improve performance, this could help reduce its hostility. However, problem is much deeper. |
| Poor management skills. | The reforms would not directly address this problem; however, training to administer new system might help. |
| Difficulty of controlling "shadow government" of contracting. | The reforms do not directly deal with this problem. |

*Source:* Underhill and Oman (2007:413). Used with permission.

This may not be surprising because the underlying purpose of reform, as noted earlier, was not better management (Moffit, 2001; Perry, 2008). This is not to suggest that the Administration had no management agenda, but only that it was apart from civil service initiatives (Moynihan and Roberts, 2008). Thus Congress and the courts repeatedly delayed and changed attempts to implement new personnel systems at the departments of Homeland Security (DHS) and Defense (DOD). In 2008, lawmakers stripped DHS of the power to install the once-heralded MaxHR initiative (later renamed Human Capital Operational Plan) for its 110,000 employees. They also rolled back the Pentagon's National Security Personnel System provisions curtailing collective bargaining and appeal rights for 700,000 unionized workers. DOD must now negotiate pay plans and personnel rules which could radically alter the system. Legislators of both parties charged that the departments abused their authority; they believed the programs damaged the ability of the agencies to accomplish their objectives, as well as to recruit and retain personnel. In addition, the Transportation Security Administration is now required to submit detailed reports on its controversial pay and HR system, the results of which will no doubt provoke further debate (Ballenstedt, 2007).

## Key Reform Components

To better understand the consequences of change, two critical dimensions of civil service reform are examined: contracting out and performance pay. Each of these innovations has encountered serious, and predictable, difficulties.

**Contracting Initiatives.**    By one recent estimate there exists a "shadow government," as the number of personnel on federal contracts and grants is 10.5 million compared to 1.9 million federal civil servants. For instance, fifteen of twenty-one Defense Department program offices are staffed primarily by contract workers. In Iraq, the DOD estimates that there are 196,000 contract employees, more than the number of troops deployed. Even the government's online data base, the Federal Procurement Data System, is contracted out.

Paul Light, an author of many works on the federal bureaucracy, points out that "We have no data to show that contractors are actually more efficient than the government" (Shane and Nixon, 2007:1). Every contract, in fact, must pass through the corporate filter of impressive executive salaries, campaign contributions, marketing expenses, and profit margins—costs not incurred in public administration—before services and products are provided. Indeed, privatization is often used as a way to outsource problems (e.g., Hurricane Katrina recovery, tax collection, and prison management) to organizations whose actions are frequently unchecked and therefore unaccountable. Simultaneously, the federal government's contract monitoring workforce, now handling a record number of contracts, is experiencing high turnover due to low pay, retirement, and legislative demands for more reports, restrictions, and inspections.

In Iraq, allegations of war profiteering, work stoppages, and human rights violations by contracting corporations are so widespread that a nonprofit watchdog group maintains an extensive contractor misconduct database. At home, the head of the federal government's top contracting agency (the General Services Administration) was forced to resign in mid-2008 due to partisan misuse of power and embarrassing exposés. A controversial oversight bill tracking legal proceedings against all contracts, domestic and foreign, passed the U.S. House of Representatives and at the time of this writing is being debated in the Senate.

At a strategic level of analysis, the use of contractors has constituted a change in war-fighting capacity without an open discussion of its potential long-term ramifications. Because contractor injuries and deaths are not counted in casualty reports, for example, the public does not know the full human cost of the war. Contracting also has the effect of blunting calls for a military draft. As well, reductions in troop levels may not change the overall American presence in war zones. And with billions of dollars in contracts, companies have become a powerful lobbying group whose pursuit of profit may not coincide with the national interest. To the extent that contracting is based on a rigid antigovernment ideology instead of cost-benefit analysis, it is simply assumed that government should be run like, and increasingly by, business no matter what the cost.

Yet employing contract workers can be effective provided that the overuse and abuse of contracting authority does not damage the legitimacy and accountability of public institutions. The Acquisition Advisory Panel (appointed by the White House and Congress) concluded, however, that the contracting trend "poses a threat to the government's long term ability to perform its mission and could undermine the integrity of the government's decision making" (Shane and Nixon, 2007:24). The advantages of contracting, then, are often overstated while disadvantages are understated. Indeed, the Pentagon was recently authorized to *in-source* because so many contracts were lent without competition and/or resulted in cost overruns, extended delays, poor quality, or outright corruption. A 2008 law authorizing creation of a commission to investigate wartime contracting, modeled after a similar body during World War II, will not be implemented because, the White House stated, it would interfere with executive branch operations.

**Pay-for-Performance Programs.** Incentive compensation is so widely accepted that most organizations say they use it and most employees believe that pay should be tied to productivity. An analysis of economic, social psychological, and management research by two Harvard University faculty members (Bohnet and Eaton, 2003), however, demonstrates that what is supposed to happen in theory seldom occurs in reality.

Thus, pay-for-performance works well if employees have to complete one well-defined task, the output is clearly measurable, and the result can be attributed to one person's efforts. Yet, most white-collar employees are faced with multitasking duties, hard-to-measure deliverables, and team-oriented work environments—none of which fit well with individual incentives. Assumptions about human nature and motivation are also key to pay-for-performance. These programs may be effective if personnel work primarily for cash and if they care about absolute pay levels. People, however, are interested not only in money but also in job satisfaction and challenge, something not subject to performance pay. Most research suggests that humans do not want to believe that they work solely for money, a finding that is especially true for public servants.

Institutional factors affect performance pay programs as well. They operate best when employees know what to do and whom to serve. Clear comprehension of organizational objectives, though, is not given as a result of multiple and/or changing leaders with different goals. This "multi-agency" problem is especially evident when staff serve many masters: chief executives, political appointees, legislators, judges, and senior career managers. It is not claimed that incentives are ineffective under the right circumstances, but simply that ideal conditions are seldom met in real organizations (see, e.g., Jenkins et al., 1998). "There is," write Lane, Wolf, and Woodward (2003:138; also see Bohnet and Eaton, 2003), "an utter lack of empirical evidence in the private and public sectors that pay for performance has any positive effect on either morale or productivity."

In addition to problematic economic, psychological, and institutional factors, federal performance pay programs in the 1970s, 1980s, 1990s, and the first decade of this century have consistently malfunctioned (Berman et al., 2009: Chapter 7).[2] The Department of Homeland Security's program, for instance, produced so many complaints and that it had to be abandoned in 2008. In a triumph of hope over experience, pay-for-performance nonetheless remains as popular as ever. Thus, the sixteen agencies comprising the intelligence community recently began implementing performance pay, a program that officials said is causing anxiety among employees (Ballenstedt, 2008). Yet even Howard Risher (2004), in an enthusiastic endorsement of incentive pay, believes that the technique "may well prove to be the most difficult change any organization has ever attempted" (p. 46). As if to make the point, he offers no less than twenty-nine recommendations to try to make it work.

To summarize this section, an analysis of the current status and impact of recent changes suggests that reform may be good politics, but bad administration. There was no objective record to support the need for civil service reform (Ferris and Hyde, 2004). Under the pretense of good government, cost saving, and productivity, the checkered history of contracting out and performance pay was ignored as the public service was marginalized and politicized. The "success of failure," however, can never be discounted in policymaking: while the changes often did not succeed, they did alter the political environment as the "new normal" became reform initiatives. In this context, it is not an oversight that relevant legislation seldom includes provisions for evaluating the effectiveness of new policies.[3]

## WHY REFORM GOT DEFORMED

How did so much of civil service reform go so wrong? Reform movements tend to exaggerate the problems they seek to correct, with the consequence that misguided innovations frequently exacerbate existing conditions. In the process of promoting change, new programs often were derived from undocumented tantalizing anecdotes and raw political power, not systematically collected evidence, past experience with similar programs, and reasoned debate.[4] If so, why were reforms enacted into law?

Many Americans have long been susceptible to cultural myths such as the unquestioned superiority of the private sector. Relatedly, reform reflects a deeply held belief that government is little more than a necessary evil. Consider, too, the symbolic importance of selected initiatives and how difficult it is, for instance, to question performance pay in a political environment. Policies were also often passed when one party controlled both the executive and legislative branches, and therefore it had the capacity to act. In addition, term limits in many states reduced the number of experienced legislators who might have rejected reform proposals.

Finally, because of the boldness of ideological innovation, reform often developed a momentum of its own that neither rational argument nor political opposition could stop. Thus, whether through ignorance or arrogance, seldom were ramifications of legislation seriously considered. Advocates, *sans souci*, seemed blind to objections, greeting them with contempt or incredulity before they were dismissed as inconsequential.

The new personnel policies, in short, fostered management fictions (such as the impossibility of employee dismissal) and imposed heavy-handed solutions (including contracting out and performance pay). What seemed more important was that oversimplified nostrums were politically attractive and that citizen attention could be distracted from difficult substantive issues. Not only did reform enjoy popularity, but also it had the support of many stakeholders in the public administration community (e.g., the National Academy of Public Administration (NAPA), the National Commission on Public Service, the *Federal Times*, the U.S. GAO) who either backed change and or were simply indifferent to it. Advocates saw administration as an instrument of the chief executive, thereby limiting the constitutional role of Congress, abetting presidential aggrandizement, and putting a premium on the instrumental role of the bureaucracy at the expense of its constitutive role (Thompson, 2001). This state of affairs lead Murray and Wamsley (2007) to write, "If there has ever been time since the end of the 19th century for scholarly concern, and even outrage, . . . this is it" (p. 223).

In summary, while there are problems with the merit system, systematic data does not sustain the claim that there is a severe crisis requiring drastic reform (Rainey and Kellough, 2000; Underhill and Oman, 2007); not surprisingly, ersatz solutions to perceived problems are rarely effective. What is especially striking about most of the changes is their inconsistency with contemporary best practices on how exemplary organizations manage people (Goodsell, 2004; Moynihan and Roberts, 2008; Rainey and Kellough, 2000; West and Bowman, 2003–2004. Although radical change, led by political appointees, has yet to provoke a counter-reform movement, it has yielded headline incompetent leadership and ignoble conduct (e.g., reconstruction of New Orleans and Iraq as well as controversies at the General Services Administration, the Department of Housing and Urban Development and the Department of Justice, among others). Such issues, in fact, are usually blamed on "the government," a phenomenon that scars the career service and erodes support for the public service ethos.

## CONCLUSION

The civil service reform debate is over how government can best respond to the challenges of the new century. The management of HR, as a result, is undergoing a significant transition. While improving bureaucracy is not a new idea in contemporary history, what is new is that today's advocates—while using the symbols of good administration to legitimate change—question the *need* for a merit-based public service. Reformers hold that government today should not be encumbered by dated civil service systems (Report of the National Commission on the Public Service, 2003). Critics fear that changing the merit system reinvents the spoils system of the nineteenth century (Kellough and Nigro, 2006). The recent shift from the guardian model to the politico model affects the fundamental underpinnings of the merit system: selection based on competence, retention premised on performance, and impartial administration of the law.

The reform movement was prompted by the belief in the inherent superiority of private sector employment practices. Attacking the civil service was seen as key to making government more business-like, a peculiar goal in light of reckless accounting and banking dealings of the Enron Era, and today's subprime mortgage/ credit crisis. The difficulty was, and is, there is little objective evidence to support the need for reform. Using powerful illusions about how things work in business, and that its techniques can be easily used in government, reformers "changed the subject" from public policy to management. In so doing, it not only turned attention away from substantive issues but also contributed to the erosion of the public service ideal.

Civil service reform became a diversion from, and substitute for, real policy concerns such as campaign finance, energy, education, health care, and taxes. In a classic example of the "wrong problem" problem, reformers claim that problems facing government are managerial in character. Yet the root causes of issues beset-ting the nation are substantive not functional, political not administrative, and the will necessary to address them. An aggressively ahistorical, "see-no-evil," approach, radical reform is ill-informed reform, one that deeply corrupts the time-honored notion of public service through the use of arbitrary employee cuts, highly paid and unqualified political appointees, relentless pressures to hire unqualified workers, and low pay and diminishing benefits for career employees. Particularly troubling is the enduring lure of the executive leadership doctrine—at the expense of merit-based neutral competence—in a time of few admirable leaders. An apt reform strategy, instead, would be one that strengthens rather than disrupts govern-ment, so it has the normative, regulatory, and cognitive capacity (Terry, 2005) to respond to critical needs.

Public service is more than simply the application of business economics; it is imbued with an obligation of public duty. The Constitution, Article II, Section 2, refers to officers—not employees—of government. Career officials carry a heavy normative burden, one requiring special methods of selection, utilization, and pro-tection, that permits them to pursue their craft skillfully and honorably. As the events of September 11, 2001 so poignantly demonstrated, "(P)ublic service is not . . . essentially an economic transaction; it requires a principled culture of professional responsibility and specialized expertise that merits trusted exercise of the awesome authority of constitutional democracy" (Newland, 2002:645; also see Strivers and Hummel, 2007). The public service ethos, then, is fundamental to democratic gov-ernment as its ideals are ends, not means devoid of purpose. When its raison d'être is denigrated, however, government employment becomes just another job, no longer a career—to say nothing of a calling.

As institutional knowledge and ethical norms decay as a result of radical reform, the politicalization of the civil service is likely to accelerate as the baby boom generation retires and their replacements are not expected to stay in govern-ment for long periods. Together, the corporatization of the public sector and the dete-rioration of a higher purpose embodied in public service help ensure that the society will serve the economy instead of the other way around.

The integrity of civil service systems is a matter of utmost importance for citi-zens; if these systems do not work, then neither does government. Given the parade of self-serving leaders and the political scandals they have produced, it is understandable, if regrettable, that the citizenry is slow to raise questions about a more mundane—but essential—concern: contemporary civil service reforms and their impact on the greater good. There is nothing automatic about the public service ethos, that personnel policies will be free of political interference and that the commonweal will prevail over predatory partisan influences. Devaluing civil servants through extreme reform is an odd way to improve government and to address the genuine problems that it confronts. As Hugh Helco observed,

> the founders thought they knew what had wrecked Athenian democracy and the Roman republic. It wasn't foreign enemies that had defeated them. It was the internal demagoguery and a loss of touch with reality. That is why all the Founders, Federalist and non-Federalists alike, were so adamant about the need for both educated citizens and public-spirited officials (Pfiffner, 2007:422).

The American public service has changed from what Ben Franklin called "posts of honor" to a new, multi-sector public arena that, according the Paul Light (2008) is no longer interested in government. The challenge today is to eschew reckless reform by revitalizing the public service ethos, the ideal of stewardship, and the fiduciary responsibility in the spirit of public administration.

## NOTES

1. Selected portions of this chapter are adapted from the author's recent work, including: Berman et al. (2009); Bowman (2002); Bowman et al. (2003); Bowman, West, and Gertz (2006); Bowman and West (2006); Bowman and West (2008); Bowman and West (2009); West and Bowman (2003–2004); and Williams and Bowman (2007).
2. Gage and Kelly (2003) point out that the traditional federal general schedule is, in fact, a performance-based system that has never been correctly implemented. Supervisors do not take advantage of available incentives—cash awards, within grade increases, quality-step increases—because there are insufficient funds to do so. Thus it is managers, not the system, that fail to reward employees; that will not change with a different system. It should be noted that the Defense Department incentive pay program yielded higher-than-expected raises in 2008. Whether that can be sustained in the years ahead remains to be seen.
3. However, the U.S. Office of Personnel Management (2007) attempted to appraise the new DHS and DOD personnel systems.
4. As Thompson (2008) delicately put it, ". . . the determination as to whether an innovation becomes . . . general policy is less a function of project outcomes . . . than of the visibility (it) acquired . . ." (p. 18).

## REFERENCES

Anonymous. 2007. Merit, Morality, and Administration: The Forgotten Legacy of Civil Service Reform (unpublished manuscript submitted to *Administration and Society*).

———. 2008. Reforming Public Management: Analyzing the Impact of Public Service Reform on Organizational and Managerial Trust (unpublished manuscript submitted to *Journal of Public Administration and Theory*).

Ballenstedt, B. (2008, May 15). Intelligence Community to Launch Pay for Performance System. Available at <www.GovernmentExecutive.com>.

———. (2007, December 18). Catch-All Funding Bill Includes Pay Parity, Personnel Provisions. Available at <www.GovernmentExecutive.com>.

Berman, E., J. Bowman, J. West, and M. Van Wart. 2009. *Human resource Management: Paradoxes, Processes, and Problems,* 3rd ed. Thousand Oaks, CA: Sage.

Bohnet, I., and S. Eaton. 2003. Does Performance Pay Perform? Conditions for Success in the Public Sector. In *For the People: Can We Fix the Public Service,* J. Donahue and J. Nye, Jr., eds. Washington, DC: Brookings Institution Press, pp. 238–254.

Bowman, J. 2002. At-Will Employment in Florida Government: A Naked Formula to Corrupt Public Service." *WorkingUSA: The Journal of Labor and Society* 6 (Fall, 2002):90–102.

Bowman, J., and J. West. 2006. Ending Civil Service Protection in Florida: State Agency Experiences. *Review of Public Personnel Administration* 26 (June):139–157.

———. 2007. *American Public Service: Radical Reform and the Merit System.* NY: Taylor & Francis.

———. 2008. Removing Employee Protections: A "See No Evil" Approach to Civil Service Reform. In *Ethics and Integrity in Governance: Perspectives Across Frontiers.* L. Huberts, J. Maesschalck, and C. Jurkiewicz, eds. Northampton, MA: Edward Elgar, pp. 181–196.

———. 2009. To "Re-Hatch" Public Employees or Not? An Ethical Analysis of the Relaxation of Restrictions on Political Activities in Civil Service. *Public Administration Review.*

Bowman, J., J. West, and S. Gertz. 2006. Florida's "Service First": Radical Reform in the Sunshine State. In *Civil Service Reform in the States,* L. Nigro and J. Kellough, eds. Albany, New York: SUNY Press, pp. 145–170.

Bowman, J., S. Gertz, M. Gertz, and R. Williams. 2003. Civil Service Reform in Florida State Government: Employee Attitudes One Year Later. *Review of Public Personnel Administration* 23 (December):286–304.

Brook, D., and C. King. 2007. Civil Service Reform as National Security: The Homeland Security Act of 2002. *Public Administration Review* 67:399–407.

———. 2008. Federal Personnel Reform: From Civil Service Reform Act to National Security Concerns. *Review of Public Personnel Administration* 28: 205–221

Condrey, S., and R. Maranto. 2001. *Radical Reform of the Civil Service.* New York, NY: Lexington Books.

Ferris, F., and A. Hyde. 2004. Federal Labor-Management Relations for the Next Century—or the Last? *Review of Public Personnel Administration* 24 (3):216–233.

Gage, J., and C. Kelly. 2003. Unions Support Smart Performance Pay for Homeland Security. *Federal Times:* November 10, p. 21.

Goodsell, C. 2004. *The Case for Bureaucracy.* Washington, DC: CQ Press.

Hays, S., and J. Sowa. 2006. Changes in State Civil Service Systems: A National Survey. *Review of Public Personnel Administration* 26 (2):102–117.

Howard, P. K. 1994. *The Death of Common Sense.* NY: Random House.

Jenkins, C., Jr., A. Mitra, N. Gupta, and J. Shaw. 1998. Are Financial Incentives Related to Performance? A Meta-Analytical Review of Empirical Research. *Journal of Applied Psychology* 83:777–787.

Kaufman, H. 1956. Emerging Conflicts in the Doctrines of Public Administration. *American Political Science Review* 50 (4):1057–1073.

Kellough, J., and L. Nigro, eds. 2006. *Civil Service Reform in the States.* Albany, NY: SUNY Press.

Lane, L., J. Wolf, and C. Woodard. 2003. Reassessing the Human Resource Crisis in the Public Service. *American Review of Public Administration* 33 (2):123–145.

Light, P. 2008. *A Government Ill Executed: The Decline of the Federal Service and How to Reverse It.* Cambridge, MA: Harvard University Press.

Moffit, R. 2001. *Taking Charge of Federal Personnel.* Background Paper No. 1404. Washington, DC: Heritage Foundation.

Moynihan, D., and A. Roberts. 2008. *Blinkered by Formalism? Reviewing the Management Failure of the Bush Years.* Paper delivered at the Midwestern Political Science Association Meeting. Chicago, April 3–6.

Murray, W., and G. Wamsley. 2007. A Modest Proposal Regarding Political Appointees. In *Strategic Public Personnel Administration,* Ali Farazmand, ed. Westport, CT: Praeger, pp. 199–126.

Newland, C. 2002. Fanatical Terrorism Versus Disciplines of Constitutional Democracy. *Public Administration Review* 61 (6): 643–650.

Osborne, D., and T. Gaebler. 1992. *Reinventing Government: How the Entrepreneurial Spirit is Transforming the Public Sector.* Reading, MA: Addison-Wesley.

Perry, J. 2008. Symposium Introduction. *Review of Public Personnel Administration* 28 (September):200-204.

Pfiffner, J. 2007. The Institutionalist: A Conversation with Hugh Helco. *Public Administration Review* 67 (May/June):418–423.

Rainey, H., and J. Kellough. 2000. Civil Service Reform and Incentives in Public Service. *In the Future of Merit,* J. Pfiffner and D. Brook, eds. Washington, DC: Woodrow Wilson Center Press, pp. 127–145.

Report of the National Commission on the Public Service. 2003. *Urgent Business of America: Revitalizing the Federal Government for the 21st Century.* Washington, DC: The Commission.

Risher, H. 2004. *Pay for Performance: A Guide for Federal Managers.* Washington, DC: IBM Center for the Business of Government.

Shane, S., and R. Nixon. 2007. Washington, Contractors Take on Biggest Role Ever. *New York Times:* February, 4, pp. 1, 24.

Strivers, C., and R. Hummel. 2007. Personnel Management: Politics, Administration, and a Passion for Anonymity. *Public Administration Review* 67 (November/December):1010–1117.

Terry, L. 2005. The Thinning of Administrative Institutions in the Hollow State. *Administration and Society* 37 (4):426–444.

Thompson, J. 2001. The Civil Service Under Clinton: The Institutional Consequences of Disaggregation. *Review of Public Personnel Administration* 21 (2):87–112.

———. 2008. Personnel Demonstration Projects and Human Resource Management Innovation. *Review of Public Personnel Administration* 28 (3): 240–262.

Underhill, J., and R. Oman. 2007. A Critical Review of the Sweeping Federal Civil Service Changes. *Review of Public Personnel Administration* 27 (4):401–420.

United States Government Accountability Office. 2007. *Human Resource Series: An Update.* Washington, DC: GAO.

United States Office of Personnel Management. 2007. Creating a Foundation for the 21st Century Federal Workforce: An Assessment of the Implementation of the Department of Defense National Security Personnel System. Washington, DC: OPM.

West, J., and J. Bowman. 2003–2004. Stakeholder Analysis of Civil Service Reform in Florida: A Descriptive, Instrumental, Normative Human Resource Perspective. *State and Local Government Review* 36 (Winter):20–34.

Williams, R., and J. Bowman. 2007. Civil Service Reform, At-Will Employment, and George Santayana: Are We Condemned to Repeat the Past? *Public Personnel Management* 37 (March):65–77.

# Index